ECONOMIC PROBLEMS
OF THE CHURCH

FROM ARCHBISHOP WHITGIFT
TO THE LONG PARLIAMENT

BY

CHRISTOPHER HILL

FELLOW OF BALLIOL COLLEGE, OXFORD

OXFORD

AT THE CLARENDON PRESS

Lay not up for yourselves treasures upon earth, where moth and rust doth corrupt, and where thieves break through and steal. . . .

For where your treasure is, there will your heart be also.

MATTHEW vi. 19-21

ECONOMIC PROBLEMS
OF THE CHURCH

FROM ARCHBISHOP WHITGIFT
TO THE LONG PARLIAMENT

Oxford University Press, Amen House, London E.C.4

GLASGOW NEW YORK TORONTO MELBOURNE WELLINGTON
BOMBAY CALCUTTA MADRAS KARACHI LAHORE DACCA
CAPE TOWN SALISBURY NAIROBI IBADAN ACCRA
KUALA LUMPUR HONG KONG

FIRST PUBLISHED 1956
REPRINTED LITHOGRAPHICALLY IN GREAT BRITAIN
AT THE UNIVERSITY PRESS, OXFORD
FROM CORRECTED SHEETS OF THE FIRST EDITION
1963

PREFACE

I WISH to thank the Master and Fellows of Balliol College for making it possible for me to have a sabbatical term, during which the greater part of this book was drafted. I also thank the Leverhulme Trustees for a grant towards my expenses during this sabbatical term.

I am deeply indebted to Miss D. M. Barratt for allowing me to read, and to quote from, her admirable Oxford D.Phil. Thesis, 'The condition of the Parochial Clergy from the Reformation to 1660, with special reference to the Dioceses of Oxford, Worcester and Gloucester', and for much helpful advice. Chapter V draws heavily on Dr. Barratt's work, which I hope will be published in the near future. Mr. M. E. James of Durham University and Mr. V. G. Kiernan of Edinburgh University read the typescript and made many valuable suggestions. I am also grateful for help in various forms to Dr. G. E. Aylmer, Mr. J. E. Bowle, Professor V. H. Galbraith, Mrs. D. M. Garman, Dr. R. H. Hilton, Mr. A. Jenkin, Professor Sir John Neale, Miss Eirwen Owen, Dr. Valerie Pearl, Mr. J. Safford, Mrs. Joan Simon, Miss Doreen Slatter, Mr. L. Stone, Mr. P. Styles, Miss Dona Torr and Miss Anne Whiteman; and to Mr. John Keegan, who generously helped with the proofs. Greatest of all is my debt to my wife. I alone however am responsible for the errors which remain. In a book which covers a good deal of ground, and uses the research of others as well as my own, I have tried to acknowledge debts where I am conscious of them. But there must be many places where I have benefited from discussions with friends and pupils and have failed to say so: I hope they will forgive me.

In all quotations, though not in titles of books, spelling, capitalization, and punctuation have been modernized.

C. H.

June 1955

CONTENTS

ABBREVIATIONS

The following abbreviations have been used

C.S.P.D.	*Calendar of State Papers, Domestic.*
D.N.B.	*Dictionary of National Biography.*
Econ. Hist. Rev.	*Economic History Review.*
English Hist. Rev.	*English Historical Review.*
S.P.	*State Papers.*
Trans. Royal Hist. Soc.	*Transactions of the Royal Historical Society.*
V.C.H.	*Victoria County History.*

INTRODUCTION

What are all our histories and other traditions of actions in
former times but God manifesting Himself that He hath shaken
and tumbled down and trampled upon everything that He hath
not planted? ... Let men take heed and be twice advised, how
they call His revolutions, the things of God and His working of
things from one period to another, how, I say, they call them
necessities of men's creations.

OLIVER CROMWELL, *Speech to Parliament*, 22 January 1655
(W. C. ABBOTT, *Writings and Speeches of Oliver Cromwell*, 1937–47,
iii. 590–1)

THIS book deals with the English church in the two generations which separate the elevation of Whitgift to the see of
Canterbury in 1583 from the meeting of the Long Parliament in November 1640.[1] They were the decades in which Puritanism became a force in England, and in which the opposition
to royal absolutism was building up that strength which was
ultimately to overthrow the old régime in the civil war. They were
also decades of rapid economic change, and of government
attempts to apply on a national scale medieval policies of regulation and control.

The conflicts over religion and church organization, over the
constitution and over mastery of the economic destinies of the
country, were interlocking: and all helped to divide England into
the two camps which fought the civil war. The object of this
book is to try to throw fresh light on the part played by religion
in preparing for the seventeenth-century revolution, and by implication on the relations between Puritanism and capitalism.
The point, originally made by Bodin,[2] and often repeated by historians, that the driving forces which brought about the Reformation were economic and political rather than religious, also
applies to the English Revolution. But the exact nature of the
connexions between religion and economics in these centuries is
still not clear. We no longer speak of the events of 1640–60 as
'the Puritan Revolution' with the same assurance as did Gardiner. This view has been exploded by the researches of the past

[1] In the succeeding pages the phrase 'our period' refers to these decades.
[2] J. Bodin, *Les Six livres de la République* (1576), p. 551.

generation of economic historians, and by studies of the connexions between 'the spirit of capitalism' and the protestant ethic which we associate especially with the names of Weber, Troeltsch, and Tawney, and which ultimately go back to Marx. Most historians would now accept the existence of some links between Puritanism and capitalism, however much they would disagree about the causal nature of those links.

But there are difficulties in replacing the phrase, 'the Puritan Revolution'. The Weber–Tawney analysis still puts the *ideas* of the Puritans in the forefront of any explanation of the great social changes which took place in England, though it hints discreetly that those ideas were not 'really' what they seemed to be. A cruder use of the same analysis suggests that these ideas were just rationalizations, which can therefore be disregarded: and that material conflicts are the only ones deserving serious analysis.

I do not accept the view that ideas can be disregarded merely because they can be shown not to have been quite as disinterested as the people who held them may have believed. And in some recent explanations of the English Revolution the material conflicts seem to me to have been presented too simply, in terms of outs versus ins, country versus court gentry, the bourgeoisie versus a 'social justice' state. Contemporaries knew better. The opposition saw bishops as the main enemy. And this was not merely because they were swayed by Puritan ideas which were rationalizations of their class interests. For the church was far more than a religious institution: it was a political and economic institution of the greatest power and importance. There might be many reasons, over and above the purely religious, why men should wish to overthrow the ecclesiastical hierarchy in 1640. I hope in this book to show some of those reasons.

A full analysis of the non-doctrinal reasons for disliking the established church would need more than one volume. It would have to consider the church as a political, judicial, and educational organization. Bishops formed a solid governmental phalanx in the House of Lords. They had nearly a majority of the votes there under Elizabeth, never less than a quarter under James. They were civil servants and administrators, and under Laud they came to hold key posts in the government. Many bishops ('raised from the dust', as indignant gentlemen noted) used their privileged and influential position to defend Charles I's claim to a right of arbitrary taxation. Church courts interfered in countless petty ways in the daily life of every citizen: and the High Commission collected over £100,000 towards the repair of St. Paul's by means of heavy fines falling largely on the gentry.[1]

The church controlled the universities and most schools. The pulpit was the main source of information and ideas on political subjects, of instruction on economic conduct. Ecclesiastics exercised an effective censorship of books. There was no other opinion-forming organ—no press, no wireless, no political parties, not even rival religious sects functioning legally. The church had a monopoly. And the government controlled this monopoly, 'tuning pulpits' very nearly as it wished. 'Under such a government', Adam Smith observed of the reformed Church of England, 'the clergy naturally endeavour to recommend themselves to the sovereign, to the court, and to the nobility and gentry, by whose influence they chiefly hope to obtain preferment. . . . Such a clergy, however, while they pay their court in this manner to the higher ranks of life, are very apt to neglect altogether the means of maintaining their influence and authority with the lower.'[2]

All these subjects would have to be discussed before we could grasp the hatred which not only a Puritan but also a non-Puritan layman might feel for the Laudian church. This book is concerned only with the church as an economic institution, and with the effects on it of economic developments in the sixteenth and seventeenth centuries. These developments created a number of new problems for the church. The attempts to solve those problems helped to align the two sides for the civil war. For the hierarchy's solutions all involved asserting for the church powers which it had lost and which would have had a cramping effect on the economic no less than on the political advance of the country. It was the retrogressiveness of the hierarchy's solutions, their unacceptability to the social groups which the House of Commons represented, that forced the bishops into that close co-operation with the government which reached its height under Laud, and brought church and state down together.

In so wide a survey as that attempted in this book, any selection of subjects for treatment is necessarily somewhat arbitrary. Church courts are economic as well as judicial institutions, and

[1] R. Newcourt, *Repertorium Ecclesiasticum Parochiale Londoniense* (1708–10), i. 4.
[2] A. Smith, *The Wealth of Nations* (World's Classics), i. 450.

their activities certainly had economic effects: they should have been
discussed, if space had permitted. Parochial fees have been considered but not the poor relief which the parishes administered,
nor the discipline which some Puritans wanted parishes to administer. The governmental activities of bishops have been largely
ignored, and I have not discussed the problems (partly economic) which arose from the appointment of lecturers by town
corporations.

Some of the subjects treated, I believe, are discussed for the
first time in this context. My object was to establish the existence
of problems: for this purpose literary evidence, evidence of
opinion, has been used, though I hope with caution, and not
where it conflicts with other evidence. For the same reason I have
relied mainly on printed sources, since my object was to cover as
wide a field as possible. But there is room for far more thorough
investigation here—using the State Papers rather than the Calendar,
and drawing on the valuable material that lies buried in the
judicial archives of the church.

I have already had to use the word 'Puritan', that dragon in the
path of every student of this period: so I had better say what I
mean by it. Confining myself to the period before 1640, I use the
word to cover that body of opinion which was opposed to the
general religious policy of the hierarchy, but which did not carry
its opposition to the point of raising separatism to a principle.
That is to say, I adopt contemporary usage: I call Puritans those
who would have been called so by contemporaries. Many of the
distinctions which later historians have imposed upon the early
history of religious sects would have been difficult for contemporaries to understand. So I shall not dwell upon the niceties
which differentiate between separating and non-separating con-
gregationalists. There seems to me sometimes to be as much
fiction and unwarranted assumption—and sheer waste of time—
in tracing the genealogy of sects as of individuals. In the history
of ideas, at least, environment is more important than heredity.
Independency took one path in exile in the Netherlands, another
in revolutionary England, a third as the ruling power in New
England, and yet another in adversity in post-Restoration England. In eighteenth-century New England presbyterianism was
a liberating force, as it had not been in old England in the sixteen-
forties.

So one of the objects of this book is to look at the environment by which English Puritan ideas were moulded. The interaction between those ideas and the society which gave birth to them is a complicated and two-way process.

I have confined myself to the economic problems of what contemporaries called 'the state-ecclesiastical'. The conflicts to which these problems gave rise are not more important than the disputes about theology and church government, which receive greater attention in most accounts of this period. But these problems have been unduly neglected, especially in the thirty years' gap between the periods treated in R. G. Usher's *Reconstruction of the English Church* and W. A. Shaw's *History of the English Church during the Civil Wars and under the Commonwealth*. I have suggested at various points connexions between the economic conflicts and disputes about doctrine and discipline. But the economic problems of the church were only a special form of general problems affecting whole groups of property-owners. So if we are to establish links between economics and theology, they must be between the economic life of society as a whole and the thought of that society. The church is merely a convenient object of analysis: Laud was a great landowner and virtual prime minister as well as a theologian with strong views on church government.

But no philosophy of history should be read into my selection of subjects for treatment or omission. *Lycidas* is easier to appreciate if we know enough about the church of Milton's day to understand the reference to

> such as for their bellies' sake
> Creep and intrude and climb into the fold.
> Of other care they little reckoning make
> Than how to scramble at the shearer's feast,
> And shove away the worthy bidden guest;
> Blind mouths!

But *Lycidas* is not an economic treatise. This book bears the same relation to Puritanism as a footnote on ecclesiastical careerism in the sixteen-thirties would to *Lycidas*. There is much more to be said, and I say it now in order to avoid wearisome repetitions later. Puritanism would not have been the historical force it was if it had been a mere economic reflex. The courage which enabled Prynne, Lilburne, and George Fox to endure their several martyrdoms was dedicated to very diverse ends, but none of them can be described simply in economic terms.

All I would suggest is that revolutions are made, not only by the great symbolic figures whom posterity recollects, but also by nameless masses of men and women. The higher flights of theory may have passed them by. They expected, however, that political ideas or platforms of church government should be rooted in experience. So the more we know about the facts of everyday life for the average man and woman, the better placed we are to understand the appeal of the programmes worked out by the leaders, the heroes, and the saints.

PART I

The State of the Clergy

The state of the clergy is not altogether so bare as may perhaps be conjectured by the smallness of their revenue, for that they never raise nor rack their rents as the noblemen and gentlemen do to the uttermost penny; but do let their lands as they were let 100 years since, reserving to themselves and their successors some commodities besides the bare rent, as corn, muttons, beef, poultry or such like; but to say the truth, their wings are well clipped of late by courtiers and noblemen, and some quite cut away, both feather, flesh and bone.

SIR THOMAS WILSON
The State of England, Camden Miscellany, xvi. 22–23

I

THE MITRE AND THE CROWN

I do protest, I see not that condition
Of man, that hath a fortune in fruition,
That is not perilous. . . .
The king complains·of want: his servants say
They stand engag'd in more than they can pay. . . .
There's new occasion every day of spending,
And much more borrowing than good means of lending.
'Tis said, some royal rents to sale were proffer'd:
That jewels of the crown to pawn were offer'd:
That church revenues, for the present need,
Sequester'd are (to stand a while in stead
Of temporalties). And some themselves persuade
That they shall now be lay possessions made.

GEORGE WITHER, *Brittans Remembrancer* (1628), pp. 437–8, ed. of 1879–80

It will likewise be fit that the flourishing of the church should
hold proportion with the flourishing of the commonwealth
wherein it is. If we dwell in houses of cedar, why should they
dwell in skins?

SIR BENJAMIN RUDYERD, in the House of Commons, May 1641
(J. A. MANNING, *Memoirs of Sir Benjamin Rudyerd*, 1851, p. 186)

I

THE Henrician Reformation impoverished the church and weakened it politically. At the dissolution of the monasteries landed property bringing in a net annual income of over £136,000, and bullion, plate, and other valuables worth possibly £1–1½ million, were taken away from the church.[1] First-fruits and tenths, over £40,000 per annum, were transferred from Rome to the crown. To convey the significance of these figures we may recall that royal revenue from land never exceeded £40,000 a year

---

[1] A. N. Savine, *English Monasteries on the Eve of the Dissolution* (1909), p. 100. The valuation of 1535 probably understates the value of the lands.

before 1542.[1] With monastic property the church lost the right
to present to some two-fifths of the benefices of the kingdom. It
also lost a great deal of that vast apparatus of patronage—lucrative
posts for laymen no less than for ecclesiastics—which Sir Edwin
Sandys noted as one of the main sources of the church's strength
in Roman Catholic countries at the end of the sixteenth century.[2]
The removal of abbots from the House of Lords meant that the
clerical vote there changed from an absolute majority to a minority; and bishops, cut off from the international church, became
more directly and obviously dependent on the crown.

The theological changes of the Reformation may have increased
men's respect for religion: they did less to increase their respect
for the church. They were accompanied by destruction of altars,
windows, miracle-working statues, &c., all of which reduced
popular regard for the traditional sacramental religion which had
so largely occasioned and justified the church's outward show of
pomp and wealth. Men learnt that church property was not sacrosanct, that traditional ecclesiastical institutions could disappear
without the world coming to an end; that laymen could remodel
not only the political and economic structure of the church but
also its doctrine—if they possessed political power. Protestant
theology undermined the uniquely sacred character of the priest,
and made the members of his congregation think more highly of
themselves. This helped men to question clerical claims to divine
right, including their divine right to tithes. Preaching became
more important than sacraments; and so men came to wonder
what right non-preaching ministers, or absentees, had to be paid
by their congregations. It took a long time to follow these new
lines of thought to their logical conclusions: but ultimately they
led men very far indeed.

From the reign of Elizabeth onwards many men wished to press
the Reformation further.. Those whom we call Puritans wanted
changes in doctrine and discipline; they and others wished to see
the political and judicial powers of the hierarchy diminished;
many cast greedy eyes on the remaining church property. For all
opponents of the church 'popery' became a convenient technical
term of abuse, which had more than doctrinal content. It was a

---

[1] F. C. Dietz, *English Government Finance, 1485–1558*, University of Illinois Studies
in the Social Sciences, ix, no. 3 (1932), pp. 80–82, 138, 221.

[2] Sir E. Sandys, *Europae Speculum* (The Hague, 1629), pp. 53–55.

widely extensible term. For Bishop Jewell pluralism was popish; Thomas Lever and William Crashawe thought the same of impropriations. Tobacco was 'a rag of popery' for a Puritan weaver in Chapman's *Monsieur D'Olive* (1606); so was sale of livings for Robert Burton.[1] At the end of Elizabeth's reign the mayor and citizens of Salisbury accused their bishop of seeking 'to tyrannize over them by his popish charters'.[2] Londoners in the sixteen-thirties referred to the produce of the soap monopolists as 'popish soap', and by 1640 had come to regard the office and jurisdiction of bishops and deans as popish.[3] More radical critics looked upon tithes and a national church as popish and anti-christian too.

We shall often come across the term employed against Laud's attempts to preserve or revive medieval institutions and practices. Because of the close associations of protestantism and English patriotism the word 'popery' acquired emotional overtones. It was a convenient phrase under which opposition stemming from the most divergent causes could be united. 'We charge the prelatical clergy with popery to make them odious', said Selden with disarming frankness, 'though we know they are guilty of no such thing.'[4]

All sorts of men, then, for divers reasons, wished the Reformation to be carried further. They tended to denounce as popish the persons, institutions, and ideas which had been handed down from the Middle Ages and now stood in their way.

II

Archbishops, bishops, and deans and chapters were great landowners. They shared the problems of other landowners in an age of rising prices, of expanding production for the market (wool and food), and of improved estate management. Insufficient research has yet been done for historians to agree about the effects of this critical period upon the landowning class, or about the

[1] J. Jewell, *Works* (Parker Soc., 1845-50), i. 999; T. Lever, *Sermons* (ed. E. Arber, 1901), p. 125; W. Crashawe, *Epistle to Sir John Saville*, prefixed to W. Perkins's 'The Calling of the Ministerie' in his *Works* (1609), iii; R. Burton, *Anatomy of Melancholy* (Everyman ed.), i. 321; G. Chapman, *Dramatic Works* (1873), i. 214-15.

[2] F. Street, 'The Relations of the Bishops and Citizens of Salisbury, 1225-1612', *Wilts. Magazine*, xxxix. 360-1.

[3] The Root and Branch Petition, in S. R. Gardiner, *Constitutional Documents of the Puritan Revolution* (3rd ed., 1906), p. 140.

[4] J. Selden, *Table Talk* (1847), pp. 158-9.

methods by which some survived and prospered whilst others
got into difficulties. But there would be general agreement that
there was a crisis, and that some landowners were able to meet
it more successfully than others. Those whose incomes remained
fixed were obviously at a disadvantage in an inflationary age.

It is even less easy to speak with confidence about the landlord
policy of bishops and deans and chapters. Much more work needs
to be done upon their estates and estate management. But two
points seem clear, both of which were made by Sir Thomas Wilson
in the passage quoted as epigraph to Part I of this book. First, the
Tudor monarchs freely granted, to courtiers and others, long
leases of church lands on favourable terms. The ecclesiastical
dignitaries had to accept this because of their post-Reformation
political dependence on the crown: indeed placing some of his
patronage at the royal disposal was a way for a bishop to win
favours for himself.[1] The effect was to put most of the profits from
lands so leased into the pockets of the lessees. Secondly, there is
general agreement among contemporary observers that bishops
and deans and chapters were easy-going landlords, at least towards
tenants from the aristocracy and gentry of their dioceses, with
whom they, like the monasteries before them, had every reason
to wish to maintain a relationship of friendly patronage.

Bishops and ecclesiastical corporations, alone among great landowners, did not hand their property on to their heirs. So they
were not personally interested in long-term improvements which
would demand heavy capital investment. The monks had at least
had time to devote to the management of their estates, though it
does not always seem to have been well employed. But prelates
had many other responsibilities. They were used by the government in administrative offices, both central and local; and so they
were often absentees. Martin Marprelate accused the bishops of his
day of wrongful extortion from their tenants.[2] But he is a very
prejudiced witness, and there is little contemporary support for
the accusation. No doubt many bishops agreed with the saintly
Lancelot Andrewes that 'good husbandry was good divinity',[3]
and were as likely as other landlords to look after their own
interests. We know all too little about the relations of ecclesiastical

[1] See Chapter II below.
[2] M. Marprelate, *The Epistle* (1588), *passim.*
[3] D. Lloyd, *Memoires of the Lives, Actions, Sufferings and Deaths* ... (1668), p. 317.

landlords with their humbler tenants. But there is much evidence to confirm contemporary accounts of their conservative leasing policy.

Bishops and deans and chapters frequently leased out whole manors, with all their profits, often for long periods. Substantial incomes might be made by lessees who merely sub-let. Ecclesiastical landowners did not enclose even where 'by all theories of self-interest, of competition and economic advantage, there should have been a rapid and decisive enclosure movement,' where 'the difference in value between open and enclosed lands makes it clear that enclosure was economically advantageous'.[1] Rents in kind were not uncommon. Ecclesiastical landlords failed to take economic rents. Heavy entry fines were more to their liking, which enriched them personally at the expense of their successors, who got lower rents. So the future was sold. Thus, for instance, the rectory of Bywell St. Peter was farmed by the Dean and Chapter of Durham for £28 a year in 1635; yet Peter Smart accused his chapter of asking a fine of £2,000 for renewal of the lease, a sum almost as great as their total rental.[2]

Bishop Goodman of Gloucester was a propagandist for the old order, so we need not take his idyllic account of the leasing policy of the Dean and Canons of Windsor too literally. 'When we came to visit our tenants,' wrote the bishop long after the event, '. . . we took all at their own relation, yet we knew they did undervalue things, but we did desire to use them as church tenants.'[3] The parliamentary survey of church lands in Wiltshire enables us to check this statement, even if only very inadequately. It covers a number of properties leased by the Dean and Canons of Windsor, among other ecclesiastical landlords in that county. It seems to confirm the easy-going attitude of such landlords in general, and to suggest that the Dean and Canons of Windsor had no exceptionally benevolent approach to the gentry. Forty rectories leased by bishops, deans, and chapters before 1642 for a total of £1,193. 4s. 5d. were held to be worth £8,967. 18s. 3d. in 1649–50:

[1] T. S. Willan, 'The Parliamentary Surveys for the North Riding of Yorkshire', *Yorkshire Archaeological Journal*, xxxi. 281; E. Kerridge, 'The Movement of Rent, 1540–1640', *Econ. Hist. Rev.* 2nd series, vi, no. 1, 33–34.

[2] Ed. G. Ornsby, *The Correspondence of John Cosin* (Surtees Soc., 1868–72), i. 167.

[3] G. Goodman, *The Court of King James* (1839), i. 342 Cf. T. Powell, *The Art of Thriving*, in *Somers Tracts* (1809–15), vii. 204–5. Goodman draws a rather different picture of the landlord policy of Trinity College, Cambridge, in *The Two Great Mysteries of Christian Religion* (1653), sig. a. 3.

a divergence of over 750 per cent. Eight of these properties, leased by the Dean and Canons of Windsor for £264. 14s. 8d., were valued by the parliamentary surveyors at £1,639. 18s. 4d., a divergence of only 621 per cent.[1]

There are other pointers in the same direction. Sir Thomas Wilson estimated in 1600–1 that the twenty-six bishoprics were worth altogether £22,500 a year, a figure that is very close to Leighton's £23,217 (excluding *commendams*) of a generation later.[2] But when bishops' lands were sold after 1646, at not less than ten years' purchase, they brought in at least £676,387, which suggests that the surveyed value of the lands was over three times the old rents. Wilson estimated dean and chapter lands at £4,500 a year, and they were sold after 1649 for at least £1,170,000. This is 260 years' purchase on Wilson's figures. Either he had seriously under-estimated, as is suggested by Peard's estimate of £28,000 old rent per annum, presented to Parliament in 1641; or dean and chapter lands were let at even greater undervalues than bishops': this is suggested by the fact that dean and chapter lands were first offered for sale, on a glutted market, at twelve years' purchase, though this was soon reduced to ten.[3] Both may well be true. Until more research has been done on ecclesiastical landholding in this period, we have to be content with such inadequate indications. Meanwhile we can only speculate about the extent to which the gap between 'old' and 'improved' rents was bridged by entry fines.

Many bishops, prebendaries, and rectors were lord of manors, on which they held courts leet and baron, and shared the privileges and problems of lay lords.[4] Thus the Bishop of Rochester, as lord of the manor of Bromley, had return of writs within the manor, assize of bread and ale, view of frank-pledge, &c.[5] The Bishop of Chester, as rector of the rich living of Wigan, had a long struggle

---

[1] E. J. Bodington, 'The Church Survey in Wilts., 1649–50', in *Wilts. Magazine*, xl. 253–72; xli. 1–39, 105–24. See pp. 35–38 below.

[2] Wilson, op. cit., pp. 22–23; A. Leighton, *An Appeal to the Parliament, or Sions Plea against the Prelacie* (1628), p. 264. For *commendams*—a large omission—see pp. 233–5, 316–17 below.

[3] W. A. Shaw, *A History of the English Church . . . 1640–1660* (1900), i. 59, ii. 515; H. J. Habakkuk, 'Interregnum Finance', *Econ. Hist. Rev.*, 2nd Series, xv.

[4] For examples, see Newcourt, op. cit. i. 115–230, ii. 413; D. Lysons, *The Environs of London* (1792–6), ii. 190, 311, iii. 345, 612–15; H. Smith, *Ecclesiastical History of Essex* (n.d.), p. 271; R. G. H. Whitty, *The Court of Taunton in the 16th and 17th centuries* (1934), pp. 84, 96–97, 120; W. McB. and F. Marcham, *Court Rolls of the Bishop of London's Manor of Hornsey, 1603–1701* (1929), *passim*.

[5] Lysons, op. cit. iv. 308–9.

with the inhabitants of that town arising from his attempts to make them continue to grind their corn at his mill: attempts which were abandoned by his successors after the Interregnum.[1]

Their property and jurisdictional rights involved many other clerics in disputes. At Exeter quarrels between Bishop and civic authorities were perennial. Under James I the government supported the Bishop, his Majesty understanding 'that the citizens were Puritans'.[2] There were few cathedral cities in which there was not a standing conflict between the dean and chapter and the municipal powers. A long struggle between the Bishop and city of Salisbury was finally settled in 1612, when the latter wrung a charter from the crown. This put an end to the Bishop's jurisdiction over the town and confined it to the cathedral close: only there did he retain his courts leet and baron, his separate commission of the peace. In 1615 he had the satisfaction of erecting his own whipping-post in the close.[3] At Taunton, until the citizens won a charter in 1628, the Bishop of Winchester exercised rights of imprisonment which the common lawyers regarded as illegal for a court leet. Bishop Neile thought this charter 'very prejudicial to the inheritance of the Bishopric', and urged Laud to warn the king against similar attempts by other corporations.[4] At Winchester itself the Bishop enjoyed a 'temporal jurisdiction which is exercised weekly in his court', with constables and tithing men who collected taxes, including Ship Money. His liberties, challenged by the town, were confirmed by the Star Chamber in 1637: cancelled, on appeal to Parliament, in June 1641.[5] In the same year an alderman of Gloucester spoke in the House of Commons of the 'infinite pressures' which 'many cities near unto deans and chapters have endured by them and their procurement', as an argument for the abolition of deans and chapters.[6]

The Archbishop of York, the Bishop of Ely, the Dean of Westminster, the Universities of Oxford and Cambridge, and

[1] G. T. O. Bridgeman, *The History of the Church and Manor of Wigan* (Chetham Soc., 1888–90), pp. 330, 486–93.

[2] *City of Exeter MSS.* (Hist. MSS. Commission), pp. 118, 131, and *passim*.

[3] F. Street, op. cit., esp. pp. 336–61; D. H. Robertson, *Sarum Close* (1938), p. 161.

[4] Whitty, op. cit., pp. 115–16; *MSS. of the Earl Cowper* (Hist. MSS. Commission), i. 466–7; cf. F. Blomefield, *History of the County of Norfolk* (1805–10), iii. 377–8.

[5] Ed. W. R. Stephens and F. T. Madge, *Documents relating to the history of the cathedral church of Winchester in the 17th century* (Hants Record Soc.), pp. 7–12.

[6] J. Nalson, *An Impartial Collection* (1682), ii. 290; cf. J. Hacket, *Secrinia Reserata* (1693), ii. 173.

many other ecclesiastical bodies had rights of secular jurisdiction. The palatine Bishop of Durham approximated closely to the royal power in his right to wardship, marriage, and other feudal dues. In 1634 he was vying with the king in extracting fines for distraint of knighthood.[1] The lords spiritual and some of the wealthier clergy had to provide men, horses, and arms for military service when the king called upon them. The Bishop and clergy of the diocese of Bangor provided armour for 100 men.[2] Wigan and two other Lancashire rectories had to equip a light horseman apiece: so had the Dean and Chapter of Chester.[3] Two prebendaries of York were supposed to supply a light horseman between them, but (so one of them was assured by his agent in 1625) 'for armour, though in extremity, you need not show any'.[4] The higher clergy shared so many privileges and burdens with conservative lay landlords that they naturally tended to share their outlook too.

III

Only in one respect did the position of ecclesiastical landowners differ sharply from that of lay landowners other than the king. Lay magnates could get into debt, could mortgage their estates, and in the last resort could sell. Land thus passed from one landlord to a purchaser who, whatever his social origins, then joined the landed class. A succession of such sales and purchases might bring into that class men with a new economic outlook: but it did not affect the structure of the social hierarchy. Church and crown, however, were differently placed. Their economic position and problems were similar to those of other landowners: not so their political and social situation. They had been endowed with lands to maintain them for the performance of specific functions. It was a matter of public concern if their revenues declined so that they could not carry out those functions satisfactorily. A private landowner could in the last resort be bought out and disappear from

---

[1] Ed. W. Knowler, *The Earl of Strafforde's Letters and Dispatches* (1739), i. 267.
[2] *C.S.P.D., 1629–31*, p. 230.
[3] R. Halley, *Lancashire, its Puritanism and Nonconformity* (1869), i. 177–8; R. V. H. Burne, 'The History of Chester Cathedral in the Reigns of James I and Charles I', *Chester Archaeological Soc.'s Journal*, xxxix. 30.
[4] Ornsby, op. cit. i. 82. Summonses to clerical tenants-in-chief to present themselves for military service against the Scots in 1640 are to be found in J. Rushworth, *Historical Collections* (1721), iii. 1227–8, 1253.

the landlord class without the social order as a whole being a penny the worse. But church and crown could not be left to the automatic adjustments of the market. Their bankruptcy would cause a political crisis.

So the church and the king faced a special economic problem. Like all great landowners they found estate management and supervision difficult, and revenue became increasingly inadequate to meet expenditure. Things went from bad to worse as capital was destroyed by, for instance, reckless sale of timber; or as the crown sold estates and as both church and crown anticipated income by selling or granting long leases. Crown and bishops had slipped into the position of inactive rentiers. Their estates were managed, and profits were taken, by lessees.

In a sense the absentee landownership of ecclesiastical landed proprietors paved the way for its own downfall by depersonalizing relations between landlord and tenant. All great landowners were by our period ceasing to be peripatetic patriarchal figures, and most had become absentee rentiers, known to their tenants only through the intermediacy of a steward or bailiff. Still more often manor courts were held, and rents and fines collected, by a farmer. Their non-functional capacity was argued against deans and chapters in 1641. 'They come indeed once a year to receive the rents and profits of the said lands', Alderman Pury told the House of Commons, but they do not relieve the poor, keep hospitality, or repair highways and bridges. Their lands could and should be put to better uses.[1]

During the Interregnum, the sequestration committees replaced crown, bishops, and royalist landlords as rent-collectors, with the minimum of friction. It made little or no difference to tenants that the careful and elaborate system of warrants, authorizations to pay, and so on, now ran in the name of a county committee, and not in the name of a king, a bishop, or a peer. So we may say that the beginning of the conversion of the king into a figurehead, a rubber stamp, his transformation from great landowner to head of the civil service, dates from the Interregnum, but had been prepared by his gradual removal from any personal connexion with the management of his estates in the course of genera tions. The effective figure in the countryside was the man who

[1] Nalson, op. cit. ii. 290. So far from preaching, Pury added, they 'have been the chief instruments to hinder the same in others'.

directly supervised the processes of production—the yeoman, the
lessee, the clothier. The revolutionary events of the seventeenth
century merely gave political and institutional form to what had
already become economic and social fact—the dominance of these
new classes. The end of an epoch is symbolized in the familiar
formulae of the country sequestration committees: 'to X or his
assigns, this shall be your warrant'—formerly the personal note
of king, bishop, or great lord, now taken over, with the minimum
of administrative dislocation, by an impersonal collective entity.

IV

So the church hierarchy was closely associated with the landed
class. It was only in the seventeenth century, in the interests of
protecting church property among other things, that efforts were
made to regain independence for the church. Then it was the
Laudians, those fanatical devotees of the monarchy, who criticized
Archbishop Abbott for his excessive anxiety to please the gentry
of Kent, and Bishop Williams for his close relations with the
county families in his great diocese. (Predestinarian theology
perhaps predisposed these bishops to accommodate themselves to
the slowly changing social order: it was the Arminians, the
believers in free will, who set themselves against the stream.) The
Laudian attempt to end this amicable bargain, by which bishops
and deans enjoyed status and port and respect, whilst their lands
passed into the effective economic control of lessees, outraged the
gentry no less than did James's and Charles's attempt to increase
revenue from wardships and the other feudal perquisites of the
crown.[1] A closer parallel is perhaps to be drawn between the
Laudian attempt to make church lands a paying proposition *for
the church* and the royal policy of controlling industrial production
through monopolies to the profit of the crown. Both ran up
against the interests of the gentry and of the small and middling
business men in town and country.

The Laudian policy brought to a head the antagonism between
the new and the old forces in society. But there had long been an
ambivalent attitude towards the property of church and crown
among the gentry and others of the taxpaying community. On the
one hand, individuals of this group profited by the situation—to

[1] See Part III below.

buy or lease crown lands, to lease church lands and tithes. The poverty of the crown gave the House of Commons its chance of exercising political control: the poverty of the church gave a section of the moneyed men the possibility of buying their way into positions of patronage and profit. Under Henry VIII and his children plunder of the church helped to keep rates of taxation low. On the other hand, the inability of the king to live of his own, the failure of parsons' stipends to attract able men into the church, set very serious problems. Government and preaching must be carried on. We shall see later a real contradiction in the position of those members of Parliament and others who wanted both to retain impropriations in lay hands and to have a better-paid, resident preaching ministry.[1] They were forced to cast covetous eyes upon the revenues of bishops, deans, and chapters as the only source from which the reorganization of the church could be financed, if they were not to dip their hands into their own pockets.

The financial problem was ultimately to be solved by a system of national taxation and the payment of salaries to public servants, including the king; and by partial state augmentation of ministers' stipends. But this is looking forward to the late seventeenth century, and beyond. In the meantime, pending such a drastic reorganization, the House of Commons was hostile to alienation of the royal demesne, and wished to have ecclesiastical property efficiently devoted to preaching: for the financial reorganization necessary would raise the whole question of confidence, of political power. If it was to take place, and if taxation was to be increased, then those who paid the taxes were going to demand control of the state machine.

This is the background against which we must set the financial clashes of the reigns of James and Charles. It explains why the Great Contract failed in 1610, though in 1660 Charles II could be given a fixed annual income in return for the abolition of feudal tenures: for in between the transfer of political power had taken place. It explains also the conflict between Laud and the Puritan Feoffees over the buying in of impropriations.[2] It helps to explain why the status and property of the hierarchy were at the centre of all the religious and political disputes of the early seventeenth century.

[1] See Chapter VI below.   [2] See Chapter XI below.

II

THE PLUNDER OF THE CHURCH

> That which Moses spake unto givers, we must now inculcate
> unto takers away from the church, Let there be some stay, some
> stint in spoiling. . . . It hath fared with the wealth of the church
> as with a tower, which being built at the first with the highest,
> overthroweth itself after by its own greatness; neither doth
> the ruin thereof cease with the only fall of that which hath
> exceeded mediocrity, but one part beareth down another, till
> the whole be laid prostrate. For although the state-ecclesiastical,
> both others and even bishops themselves, be now fallen to so
> low an ebb, as all the world at this day doth see; yet because there
> remaineth still somewhat which unsatiable minds can thirst for,
> therefore we seem not to have been sufficiently wronged.
>
> HOOKER, *The Laws of Ecclesiastical Polity* (*Works*, 1836, iii. 404)

I

THE plunder of the church developed apace under Edward
VI. Half-heartedly checked under Mary, it was resumed in
Elizabeth's reign, but more decorously: the golden stream
flowed through the court, where the fortunate few grabbed at the
lands of bishops, and of deans and chapters, either by means of
long leases, of exchanges, of outright seizures, or by the traditional method of inserting themselves into administrative positions
in the church. Thus the Earl of Leicester, Elizabeth's favourite,
was steward to four bishops, and held official positions or reversions in two other bishoprics.[1] Impropriated tithes, sold freely
by Henry VIII, continued to be disposed of to speculative con-
tractors by Elizabeth and James I. Gloriana disposed, by sale or
grant, of tithes in 2,216 parishes, her successor in 1,453.[2]

An act of 1559 (1 Eliz., c. 19) centralized the plunder of the
church in the hands of the crown, by forbidding archbishops and

---

[1] L. Stone, 'The Anatomy of the Elizabethan Aristocracy', in *Econ. Hist. Rev.*
xviii, nos. 1 and 2, p. 31.

[2] H. Grove, *Alienated Tithes* (1896), part iii, *passim*.

bishops to lease the lands of their sees for longer than three lives or twenty-one years, or at less than the usual rent, *unless to the queen*. This meant that beneficial leases granted to courtiers were in the first instance made over to the queen. So pressure on the church had to be exercised through the court. It was so exercised by the Earl of Leicester, who continued his father's spoliation of the church through rather different means but no less effectively: and by Sir Christopher Hatton, who received 105 leases of tithes.[1]

1 Eliz., c. 19 also defined the queen's rights to the temporalities of a see during vacancy, and allowed for exchanges of land between the crown and any vacant see. Under this act, which Strype called an act for the plunder of the church, Elizabeth could seize, during vacancy, any episcopal estates which she (or her courtiers) wished, and exchange them for impropriations or other former monastic property annexed to the crown.[2] Many sees were kept vacant for a very long time—Oxford for forty-one years, Ely for nineteen. Bristol was vacant for fourteen years of the reign, and held *in commendam* with Gloucester for twenty-seven. Courtiers did not miss these opportunities.

> Scarce can a bishopric forepass them by,
> But that it must be gelt in privity.

wrote Spenser. The Earl of Oxford had £1,000 a year from the bishopric of Ely; and the émigré king of Portugal was familiarly known as the Bishop of Ely because of the large share of the revenues of that see which he received.[3]

Before the act of 1559 leases of church property were often granted for periods of up to eighty or ninety-nine years. This was disastrous in an age of rising prices. The successors of the bishop (or of the dean and chapter) who made the lease not only lost their chance of raising rents to meet the general rise in the cost of living, but they forfeited for a very long time even the opportunity of extracting heavy fines for renewal of leases. The cheapest and most popular way for the crown to reward a courtier or a civil servant was to get him a long lease of ecclesiastical property.

---

[1] H. Lansdell, *The Sacred Tenth* (1906), p. 308.

[2] J. Strype, *Annals of the Reformation . . . during Queen Elizabeth's happy reign* (1824), I, part i. 142–3; II, part i. 443; J. Stevens, *An Historical Account of Taxes* (2nd ed., 1733), pp. 193–6, 221–4.

[3] E. Spenser, *Works* (Globe ed., 1924), p. 517; Sir John Harington, *A Briefe View of the State of the Church* (1653), p. 79.

'I find no other suit so fit for your majesty to grant me as this', wrote Lord Keeper Puckering to Elizabeth in 1595, asking for a lease of lands belonging to the Bishopric of Ely: 'for the exchanges, fee-farms and leases of your majesty's own lands are to be taken from your own self, and from your royal revenues.'[1] An episcopal lease would cost the thrifty queen nothing. Sometimes, in early days, the see might be directly expropriated by such a transaction: Veysey, Bishop of Exeter in Henry VIII's reign, granted lands outright, reserving annuities for himself instead of the usual rents to the see. As he was over eighty-seven years old at the time, the loss to the bishopric was immediate and irreparable.[2]

In 1584 Thomas Godwin obtained the Bishopric of Bath and Wells only after making a ninety-nine years' lease to the queen for Ralegh's benefit; but his position had been weakened by an indiscreet marriage, at the age of sixty-seven, to a rich widow. In 1589 Richard Fletcher was appointed to the long-vacant see of Bristol on terms which almost secularized its property. Six years later he was less complaisant over his translation to London. He had to be imprisoned in his own house for refusing to pass leases and to pay £2,100 in *douceurs* as the price of his promotion. Ultimately he submitted, only to die 'discontented, by immoderate taking of tobacco'.[3] It seems a little hard that he too should have incurred royal disapproval by his marriage, a disapproval expressed with such violence that it hastened his death. The second Mrs. Fletcher, whom he espoused at the age of nearly seventy, may have been a lady of questionable reputation; but there were no doubts about her wealth. And the unhappy Bishop had been promoted so rapidly, and had had to pay so heavily for his moves, that his financial affairs were in sad confusion.

In 1591, and again in 1598, the see of Salisbury was hawked around to the highest bidder. The successful purchasers had to gratify Ralegh and Sir Robert Cecil. In 1595–6 Winchester fell vacant twice within a year. Bishop Day, despite desperate resistance, had to pay £1,000 to Sir Francis Carew for possession; Bishop Bilson had to grant an annuity of £400 to the queen as

---

[1] Strype, *Annals*, iv. 344.

[2] A. L. Rowse, *Tudor Cornwall* (1941), pp. 294–5. For early examples of long leases see Sir George Paule, *The Life of John Whitgift* (1699), pp. 27, 38; J. Collier, *Ecclesiastical History* (1852), ix. 295–8; *C.S.P.D., 1634–5*, pp. 206–7.

[3] A. Wood, *Fasti Oxonienses* (1813–20), i. 191.

well as £1,200 (or its equivalent in leases) to Carew. Again resistance was unavailing. In 1597 Gervase Babbington purchased his translation from Exeter to Worcester by alienating from the former see the manor of Crediton, worth more than all the rest of the temporalities.[1] So high a price was asked for the Bishopric of Ely, even after it had been stripped by Bishop Cox, that it long proved difficult to dispose of. It was ultimately purchased by Martin Heton, who had to grant so many leases that humorists found his signature of Mar. Ely or Mart. Ely highly appropriate. The preacher of Lancelot Andrewes's funeral sermon thought him worthy of special praise because he had refused two bishoprics which he could have had at the price of alienating their lands.[2]

It was not easy for bishops to resist the pressures to which they were subjected. In 1594 Sir Robert Cecil and Sir John Wolley wrote a letter of stern reproof to the Bishop of Durham, who had been so misguided as to apply the word simony to the queen's requirements in the way of leases before she would promote him to the vacant Archbishopric of York. 'We think it very absurd', they wrote with pious indignation, 'to make the person of a prince and a subject anything like . . . These niceties will hardly be admitted where such a prince vouchsafes to entreat.'[3] Most newly appointed bishops were ready to sacrifice part of the revenues of the see in order to win access to the rest. But such an entry was hardly likely to produce pastors in whose economic behaviour the opponents of episcopacy could find nothing to criticize.

Exactly similar pressures were applied to deans and chapters, and to colleges at Oxford and Cambridge. The Dean and Chapter of Norwich, 'being poor', as their Bishop put it, were bribed in 1579 by a Mr. Pooley to agree to lease to the crown some lands

---

[1] Browne Willis, *A Survey of the Cathedrals* (1742), i. 649.

[2] Harington, op. cit., pp. 22–27, 79–80, 88–93; F. O. White, *Lives of the Elizabethan Bishops* (1898), pp. 283, 310–12, 322–4, 351, 360–1, 401; White Kennett, MSS. notes in his copy of *The Case of Impropriations* (1704) (Bodleian Library), p. 191; J. Buckeridge, *A Sermon Preached at the Funeral of . . . Lancelot Andrewes* (1626), p. 19. For the depredations of Bishop Cox at Ely, and his persecution by Lord North and Sir Christopher Hatton, see *Salisbury MSS.* (Historical MSS. Commission), ii. 120–2; Strype, *Annals*, II, part ii. 533–50; Browne Willis, op. cit. ii. 339–41; H. Hall, *Society in the Elizabethan Age* (5th ed., 1902), pp. 115–17; White, op. cit., pp. 90–94; E. St. J. Brooks, *Sir Christopher Hatton* (1946), pp. 146–52. There are proposals for a general post of bishops for fiscal purposes in Strype, *Annals*, II, part i. 575–6; IV. 301, 343–5.

[3] Ed. J. Raine, *The Correspondence of Dr. Matthew Hutton* (Surtees Soc., 1834), pp. 93–94.

which he had long been trying to acquire. Only the intervention of the Bishop (who had apparently not been bribed) prevented the transaction from going through. A few years later Sir Thomas Shirley managed, through Burghley's influence, to get a ninety-nine years' lease from the same Dean and Chapter, notwithstanding the Dean's sad cry to the Lord Treasurer ('the friend of the church'): 'We have no parcel of lands, no not the houses within our cathedral church, but that they have been offered to sale: or else money taken beforehand for long leases hereafter to be granted.' In 1596 the Dean of Windsor had to give Elizabeth several leases of parsonages, including one for fifty years. Towards the end of Elizabeth's reign 'discovery' of 'concealed' church lands, which should have been forfeited to the crown, and the purchase of a grant for them, became a lucrative trade.[1]

II

The higher clergy were not, of course, merely innocent victims in all this. They were appointed for political reasons; unlike their predecessors, they mostly had legitimate families to provide for; they would have been badly thought of if they had not provided for them. Their office was for life only, so it was natural to wish to leave adequate maintenance for widows and children. Elizabeth's dislike of episcopal marriage is believed to have been accentuated by her bishops' habit of raising families out of the revenues of the church: so she seized those revenues for her lay favourites instead. A pamphleteer of 1642 thought that clerical marriage was to blame for the long leases passed by the higher clergy before Parliament stopped them.[2] The lines between family affection and nepotism, between insurance and simony, were narrow: and we must not judge by twentieth-century standards. Nevertheless, even to contemporaries, some bishops seemed a little too anxious to profit by their opportunities.

Bishop Hughes of St. Asaph (1573–1600), who held an archdeaconry and sixteen benefices *in commendam*, is reported to have

[1] Strype, *Annals*, ii, part ii. 266–7; iii, part ii. 62, 576–9; *Life of Whitgift* (1822) i. 196–9; White, op. cit., pp. 412–13. Examples of court pressure on Oxford colleges to grant favourable leases at the end of Elizabeth's reign are given in L. Pearsall Smith, *Life and Letters of Sir Henry Wotton* (1907), i. 32.

[2] Browne Willis, op. cit. i. 525; J. Fountain, *A Letter written to Dr. Samuel Turner concerning the Church and the Revenues thereof* (1642), p. 4.

leased episcopal manors for long periods to his wife, children, sisters, and cousins. His Dean and Chapter did the same, the Dean being a non-resident youth of twenty-two. Hughes paid starvation pittances to his vicars; sold presentations; squeezed the clergy at visitations; neglected hospitality and charity: and left a large fortune at his death. Gilbert Berkeley, Bishop of Bath and Wells (1560–81), found the manor of Wells charged with annuities to the value of £300. Only one of the episcopal residences survived, and the land all round that one was let, so that he could not drive up to his front door without his tenant's leave.[1] Nevertheless, he too died very rich. When Sandys succeeded Grindal as Archbishop of York, he accused his predecessor of corruptly seizing six score leases and patents for his kinsmen and servants before departing for Canterbury. Grindal, meanwhile, was making similar charges against his predecessor at Canterbury. Sandys's own reputation at Worcester (1559–70) left something to be desired. His brother, wife, and servants were given profitable leases; Sandys himself pulled down episcopal houses and chapels for their building materials and lead. His solicitude for his family, at the expense of his church, was still remembered in Worcester in the eighteenth century.[2] Sandys's son found, after his father's death, that the leases which he held of the see of York were 'the chief stay of his living'.[3]

Bishops Parkhurst of Norwich (1560–71), Scambler of Peterborough (1561–84) and Norwich (1584–94), Curtis of Chichester (1570–82), Scory of Hereford (1559–85), Fletcher of Bristol (1589–94) and London (1594–6), and Aylmer of London (1577–94), among many others, were accused of impoverishing their sees. During Parkhurst's sway at Norwich it had commonly been said that everything in the diocese was for sale. Nevertheless, Scambler was believed to have owed his translation to Norwich to his readiness to assist in the further plunder of that see after stripping Peterborough. He alienated manors to his patron, Burghley, and passed long leases for the benefit of Sir Thomas Heneage. He was accused of embezzling clerical subsidies. He too left a large fortune, and a large family to enjoy it. His reputation long survived

---

[1] Strype, *Annals*, III, part ii. 471–5; White, op. cit., pp. 197–8, 136.

[2] Browne Willis, op. cit. i. 631, 646; White, op. cit., pp. 100–1; W. Pierce, *A Historical Introduction to the Marprelate Tracts* (1908), pp. 101–2, 51, 66.

[3] Whitgift to Hutton, 19 Aug. 1595, in *The Correspondence of Dr. Matthew Hutton*, pp. 104, 145.

him: his successor at Norwich in 1638 described him as 'that *fundi nostri calamitas*'.¹ Aylmer and Fletcher were both accused of selling long leases. The sees of Scory and Fletcher both suffered heavily from Elizabeth's depredations. Scory had conformed under Mary for long enough to renounce his wife. But in the following reign he demonstrated his family affection by numerous grants of sinecures and prebends. He also pulled down houses to sell the lead, and got into trouble with the queen for felling timber. He too was a wealthy man when he died.

It is rare indeed to hear of bishops' palaces which were maintained in proper repair, or of their London houses which had not passed into the possession of some courtier. When the Prince-Bishop of Durham came up to take his seat in Parliament, he had to hire Camden's house at Westminster: Durham House belonged to Sir Walter Ralegh. At Peterborough Dean Palmer (1597–1607) sold all the lead from off the cathedral roof.²

It was difficult to stop bishops or deans, who had only a life-interest in their lands, from selling timber so as to make quick profits at the expense of their successors. Aylmer, who bought lands to the value of £16,000 shortly before his death, was alleged to have felled trees worth £6,000, Curtis so much 'as there is scarce sufficient for firewood'. We shall later find Laud and Charles trying vainly to put an end to this practice. It had gone so far that an optimistic projector, Richard Day, himself the son of a former Bishop of Winchester, proposed that he should be allowed £2,000 a year and expenses in order to plant woods in bishops' lands. He was actually permitted to start in the see of Gloucester, to the disgust of Bishop Goodman, who regretted that Day had 'first come to the poorest bishopric'.³

When long leases fell in, bishops treated the fine as their own property, not the see's. It was a particularly valuable form of

---

¹ Lambeth MS. 943, f. 620.

² Strype, *Annals*, III, part i. 481–2; White, op. cit., pp. 15–18, 148–51, 159–61; E. Cardwell, *Documentary Annals of the reformed Church of England* (1839), i. 315; Pierce, op. cit., pp. 102–4; R. G. Usher, *The Reconstruction of the English Church* (1910), i. 115–16, 226–7; Harington, op. cit., pp. 84, 129; Goodman, op. cit. i. 420; Stone, op. cit., p. 29; G. Soden, *Godfrey Goodman* (1953), p. 176. Sir H. Spelman gives a list of episcopal palaces, extant and lost, in *English Works* (1727), ii. 211–14. See also *C.S.P.D., 1634–5*, p. 102 (dilapidated palaces in Norwich diocese), and ibid., *1638–9*, pp. 138, 307 (the Dean of Durham allowing his house to fall into decay).

³ Strype, *Life of Aylmer* (1821), p. 127; *C.S.P.D., 1627–8*, pp. 245–7, 339, 352, 523; *1625–49*, p. 398. We shall meet Day again. See below, p. 319.

property, since fines, unlike rents, were not liable to payment of first-fruits or subsidies. Bishop Davenant of Salisbury in James I's reign used such windfall fines to supply marriage portions for his nieces. He was said to have been given the bishopric as a means of providing for the thirteen children of his predecessor and brother-in-law: it was the only bishopric which Buckingham did not sell. So the government could not have thought there was anything disreputable in his behaviour. It was not so well thought of in Salisbury, Aubrey tells us, since Davenant married all his nieces, with the aid of these portions, to clergymen to whom he then gave preferment in his diocese; and though he had made more out of his bishopric than anyone since the Reformation, he left it no more than £50 in his will.[1] When lead was discovered in the Mendip Hills, it was thought only right and proper that the Bishop of Bath and Wells for the time being should reap the benefit. Bishop Still (1592–1607) 'raised a great estate and laid the foundation of three families' on this leaden basis. Although he was said to have had the harvest, there were gleanings left for his successors.[2] Lancelot Andrewes, again, received rare praise from his biographer for refusing large fines for renewal of leases in a case where he thought it 'might be prejudicial to succession'.[3]

As the example of Davenant shows, the government had no objection to bishops providing for their families. Indeed, in a sense, they were expected to. A bishop was a public servant. He was useful in this capacity not merely because of the political subordination of the church since the Reformation, but also because a bishop had local prestige as a landowner, and yet his land-ownership was non-hereditary. So his family ties did not run counter to his loyalty to the government. If he was to be an effective agent of the central authority, and not become the mere puppet of the gentry in his diocese, he had to surround himself with persons whose loyalty was to *him*, and who were not distracted by local allegiances.

It was thus not merely nepotism when (to take examples from

[1] [Ed. T. Birch], *The Court and Times of James I* (1848), ii. 254–5; J. Aubrey, *Brief Lives* (1898), i. 202; Sir A. Weldon, *The Court and Character of King James* (1651), p. 120. Contrast T. Fuller, *The History of the Worthies of England* (1840), i. 232. For the marriages of Davenant's nieces, see J. E. Bailey, *The Life of Thomas Fuller* (1874), pp. 96–97, 147–8.

[2] Fuller, *Worthies*, ii. 276; iii. 85–89.

[3] Fuller, *Abel Redivivus* (1651), sig. xx, 4ᵛ (unnumbered pages after p. 440).

the diocese of London only) Bishop Aylmer made his second son
Archdeacon of London; when Bishop King made his eldest son
('well provided already with spiritual livings' at the age of twelve)
prebendary of St. Pancras and Archdeacon of Colchester, his
second son prebendary of Kentish Town at the age of twenty-one;
when Laud made his nephew, Edward Layfield, prebendary of
Harleston and Archdeacon of Essex, and Thomas Turner, a
Reading man like himself, a Fellow of Laud's college and his
chaplain, prebendary of Newington, his Licenser and Chancellor.[1]

Unless the bishop could surround himself with loyal dependants, he could neither represent the crown in his diocese nor retain
independence of the local landowners. What this might mean is
best illustrated by the extreme case of the Bishop of Sodor and
Man, whose dependence on the Earls of Derby was as great as
even the latter could wish. The Earls nominated the bishop. 'No
subject that I know hath so great royalty as this', wrote the seventh
Earl, whom Parliament executed in 1651. The Earl usually chose
a man who already held an English benefice. He was then expected
to remember his maker by passing favourable long leases, 'whereby . . . few bishops have at any time enjoyed the full benefit, and
have contented themselves to be called lords'. The only difficulty
was to persuade them to reside in the diocese from which they
got so little profit, a point on which the Earl nevertheless insisted.
However, he reminded his son, the cost of living on the Isle of
Man was low, and in order to humour the bishop 'you may give
way to leasing some petty thing or other of little moment'. The
main point was to preserve the Earl's 'prerogative', and to ensure
that bishops 'have the only obligation to yourself, and have no
dependency of another. For it may displease you if they talk too
much of York, as some ill chosen heretofore have done.'[2]

So the nepotism of bishops has its explanation in a dilemma
which had been familiar since medieval days: the agents of the
central government could win independence of the local powers

---

[1] Birch, op. cit. i. 448; Newcourt, op. cit. i. 63, 92, 172, 115, 189; cf. p. 222. Layfield
and Turner each held two livings in plurality as well: to which Turner added the
Deanery of Rochester in 1641, and that of Canterbury in 1643 (J. Walker, *Sufferings
of the Clergy*, 1714, ii. 6, 48. There is much evidence in this work of members of
bishops' families holding offices and preferments in all dioceses.)

[2] *The History and Antiquities of the Isle of Man*, by James, seventh Earl of Derby,
in Peck, *Desiderata Curiosa* (1779), pp. 432, 436. The see of Sodor and Man was in the
province of York. The Earl's treatise was written between 1643 and 1651.

only by putting their own kinsmen and dependants into administrative offices. This led to nest-feathering: Thomas Gataker's reverend father-in-law, Charles Pinner, said that 'as the times then were a prebend's place and a bishop's chaplaincy were two shrewd snares'.[1] But we should not regard bishops as uniquely reprehensible in thus using and rewarding their own relatives. For centuries administration and politics had been run on the basis of family loyalties. Among the many historical achievements of Puritanism was the fact that it gave men an abstract ideal to be loyal to, in place of the previous personal and local loyalties. Dod and Clever, commenting on Proverbs xiv. 20, observed that 'Vicinity and neighbourhood will fail, and alliance and kindred will fail, but grace and religion will never fail. If we adjoin ourselves unto [godly men] for their virtue and goodness, they will not separate themselves from us for our calamities and trouble.'[2] This new loyalty to an idea marks an important stage in the transition from the household politics of the Middle Ages to the party politics of more modern times. God was a better lord than the Earl of Derby, or even the king: devotion to the cause of God could, ideally, cut across all earthly ties.[3]

III

The total social effects of the spoliation are in dispute. Some historians have light-heartedly seen that ubiquitous class, the rising bourgeoisie, as the main instigator and beneficiary both of the dissolution of the monasteries and of the Elizabethan plunder. Others, more realistically, have observed that the lay landowning class was in the best position to urge and profit by acts of spoliation. The weight of evidence suggests that the bulk of the property passed to peers and gentlemen. Hooker certainly regarded the would-be plunderers of his day as coming from the bankrupt section of the landowning class, 'who having wastefully eaten out their own patrimony would be glad to repair if they might their decayed estates with the ruin they care not of what nor of whom so the spoil were theirs, whereof in some part if they happen to

---

[1] T. Gataker, *A Discours Apologetical* (1654), p. 47.

[2] J. Dod and R. Clever, *A Plaine and Familiar Exposition of the Thirteenth and Fourteenth Chapters of the Proverbs of Salomon* (1609), p. 119.

[3] I owe this point to discussions with Mr. M. E. James of Durham University.

speed, yet commonly they are men born under that constellation which maketh them I know not how as unapt to enrich themselves as they are ready to impoverish others, it is their lot to sustain during life both the misery of beggars and the infamy of robbers'.[1]

This interesting passage suggests that we have by no means fully defined the social effects of the plunder of the church when we say that the spoils went to the gentry. What was their effect on that stratification of this class which takes place during our period? Did they contribute to 'the rise of the gentry' or to 'the decline of the gentry'? Or did they accelerate the double process? Hooker's remarks are an early example of a large literature, of which Spelman's *History of Sacrilege* is the most notorious example, arguing that the recipients of church lands came to no good. As is usual with historical legends, there is no doubt something in it: though I suspect Hooker is nearer the truth than Spelman.

Land-grabbers who were already in economic difficulties would be those least 'apt to enrich themselves' permanently. The loot might bring economic salvation to some; to others it would be an incident in their downward career, a short-term delaying factor. Fuller, combating the legend, wrote effectively: 'Let land be held in never so good a tenure, it will never be held by an unthrift.' 'These abbey lands, though skittish mares to some, have given good milk to others. . . . If they prove unsuccessful to any, it is the user's default, no inheritance of a curse in the things themselves.'[2] The Earl of Oxford squandered his £1,000 a year from the revenues of Ely on current expenditure, and it did not enable him to stave off bankruptcy for long. But more prudent men used the spoil of the church to build up massive fortunes. Thomas Sutton, for instance, leased—either direct or via the Queen—coal-bearing lands from the Bishop of Durham. From this and other sources he made enough money to found Charterhouse.[3] The long-term beneficiaries would be men born under a very different constellation from the bankrupt aristocrats whom Hooker describes.

---

[1] Hooker, *The Laws of Ecclesiastical Polity* (Everyman ed.), ii. 455.

[2] Fuller, *The Historie of the Holy Warre* (1651), p. 240.

[3] When George Wither wished to give examples of great prosperity, he wrote 'Of Spencer's wealth, or our rich Sutton's store'. (1615—in *The Poetry of George Wither*, Muses Library, 1902, i. 194.) The first Lord Spencer of Wormleighton was reputed the richest man in England at James I's accession; his money came from sheep-farming. Or Wither may refer to Sir John Spencer, Lord Mayor 1594–5.

Many Elizabethan bishops were induced, by one means or another, to surrender old episcopal lands and receive royal impropriations in their place. From the church's point of view there were two major objections to this exchange. First, an economic objection: impropriated tithes, like other tithes, might be difficult to 'improve' so as to make revenue keep pace with rising prices. They might involve the owner in much tedious and unpopular litigation. For this reason it was probably sensible to lease them out to lay farmers; but they had to be leased at low rents. The bishops lost in exchange 'good finable lands'. The see of Lincoln suffered most in this way: but Oxford and others were also affected.[1] The second objection related to public opinion. Those bishops or deans and chapters who held impropriated tithes were living off revenues which could have gone to provide decent stipends for parochial clergy. They could hardly support the most obvious method of bettering the lot of poor vicars—a restoration of impropriations. This situation naturally led to anti-episcopal sentiments among the lower clergy, to a questioning of the wealth of the hierarchy in general.[2]

Similar objections applied to the practice whereby bishops were prevailed upon to give up manors and lands in return for being allowed to collect the tenths from ministers in their dioceses, which would otherwise have been due to the crown. This was again disastrous, since tenths were fixed once for all in 1535, and so could not be 'improved' to meet the rise in prices; and their collection from the poorer clergy by rich bishops caused great discontent. The Archbishop of Canterbury, the Bishops of Bath and Wells, Chichester, Ely, Hereford, London, and Worcester collected tenths in this way.[3] Deans and chapters were occasionally relieved of the liability to pay the crown first-fruits or tenths, in exchange for granting away lands; another transaction which worked to the detriment of their successors.[4]

The total effect was that whilst the livings of many ministers kept pace with the rise in prices, those of bishops did not. The assessment of their livings in the *Valor Ecclesiasticus*, on which taxation was based, remained far closer to reality in their case

[1] Sir Thomas Ridley, *A View of the Civile and Ecclesiasticall Law* (2nd ed., 1634), pp. 209–10; Browne Willis, op. cit. ii. 37, 64; iii. 417.
[2] See Chapter VI below.
[3] J. Ecton, *Liber Valorum et Decimarum* (3rd ed., 1728), p. xii.
[4] Ibid., p. xiii.

than in that of the more fortunate of the parochial clergy. Some actually declined below the level of Henry VIII's reign, Winchester, Durham, and Lincoln very sharply. This helped to keep bishops dependent on the court, from which additional sources of revenue were to be secured.

Many bishoprics were seriously impoverished. One of the richest, Durham, was valued at £2,821. 1s. 5d. in 1535, £1,000 less in 1575. In 1649 it was still carrying a rent charge of £1,020 to the crown, which had been the price at which some of the alienated lands of the see had been recovered in Elizabeth's reign.[1] Winchester, another rich see whose nominal value stood at £3,700 in 1559, was reckoned by its holder in 1587 (no doubt with a certain amount of special pleading) to be worth £398. 9s. 2d., after deducting first-fruits, tenths, subsidies (which of course did not fall due every year), and annuities to the queen and her courtiers. A few years later Bishop Bilson (1597–1616) put the nominal value of this see at £2,513, his net income at £500. Lincoln fell from £1,962. 17s. 4d. in 1535 to £894. 18s. 1d. in 1575; York from £2,035. 3s. 7d. to £1,609. 19s. 2d.

At the other end of the scale, Bangor was estimated at £66 per annum in 1559; seventy years later Bishop Bayley complained that he had to keep hospitality above his means, and had expended £600 from his own pocket on repair of the cathedral. St. Asaph was worth £187, which may help to account for the scandalous pluralism of Bishop Hughes, noted above. The archdeaconry which he held *in commendam* was estimated at several times the value of his see. So, as with so many government offices in the sixteenth century, the economic advantage of a bishopric might be not so much the stipend attached to it as the opportunity it gave for by-earnings. In 1583 St. David's was said to be 'not £263 clear', although it had been worth £458 in 1535. Llandaff, where 'a bad *Kitching* did for ever spoil the good meat of the bishops' by long leases, was valued at £154 in the fifteen-nineties, £130 a few decades later. In 1583 Rochester, after deducting tenths, subsidies,

---

[1] Strype, *Annals*, II, part i. 441–2; cf. III, part ii. 468–70. The charge was not restored in 1660. Fuller has an agreeable but improbable story that this charge—ostensibly for the maintenance of the Berwick garrison—arose from Elizabeth's jealousy when courtiers told her that Bishop Pilkington gave as large portions with his daughters as Henry VIII had left for his (*Church History*, 1842, ii. 130, 514; *The Appeal of Injured Innocence*, 1840, pp. 474–6; cf. *C.S.P.D., 1547–80*, p. 273; Browne Willis, op. cit. i. 227–8).

and other expenses, was worth £220, with *commendams* adding another £120. Of this total of £340, the Bishop declared that £250 went on meat and drink, leaving only £90 for all other charges. Chester was worth £420. 1s. 8d. in 1575, but twenty years later the Bishop claimed that only £73 a year was left for his expenses after all necessary payments had been deducted. Sodor and Man was worth 'but £90 in money' in Elizabeth's reign, £140–150 in the sixteen-thirties, but improvable to over £300 when leases fell in. But would the Earl of Derby allow his Bishop to enjoy the improvement?[1]

IV

So far as the bishops were concerned, the great days of hospitality were over. Strype put the blame for this in the first instance on the Marian bishops, who, foreseeing the storm, granted leases, patents, and annuities to their children, relations, and 'house-keepers'.[2] But it is part of a general tendency affecting all landed proprietors: only it was more exclaimed against in bishops. Wilson, indeed, in a well-known passage, suggested that there was deliberate policy in

the keeping low of the clergy from being over rich, for that order of men have most damnified England by their profuse spending on their pleasures, and upon idle serving men and other moth-worms which depended upon them and ate the fat of the land and were no way profitable; for it is not long since you should not ride nor go through country or town but you should meet such troops of these priests' retinue as exceeded 100 or 200 of these caterpillars, neither fit for war nor other service, attending upon this pontifical crew, furnished and appointed in the best manner that might be, but since their wings were clipped shorter they hold opinion that England hath flourished more. . . .[3]

Whitgift had put it more succinctly twenty-five years earlier: 'The temporalty seek to make the clergy beggars, that we may depend upon them.'[4]

---

[1] *C.S.P.D., 1629–31*, p. 230; Strype, *Annals*, III, part ii. 226–8; iv. 18, 315–17; Wilson, op. cit., pp. 22–23; Browne Willis, op. cit., *passim*; White, op. cit., pp. 178, 256, 268, 318; Fuller, *Worthies*, ii. 506; *C.S.P.D., 1633–4*, p. 547; Bridgeman, op. cit., p. 372; A. H. Dodd, *Studies in Stuart Wales* (1952), p. 42. Kitchin of Llandaff (1545–63) had conformed under Mary.

[2] Strype, *Annals*, I, part i. 232–3.   [3] Op. cit., p. 38.

[4] Kennett, op. cit., appendix, p. 23. Whitgift, still only Master of Trinity, to Bishop Cox of Ely in 1575.

The bishops, in short, were being transformed from feudal potentates, powerful in their own right as landowners, to hangers-on of the court, making what they could of their office whilst they held it. Before the Reformation bishops took their place with the nobility. But in Hooker's time 'the mean gentleman that hath but £100 land to live on would not be hasty to change his worldly estate and condition with many of these so over-abounding prelates'.[1] Compared with London citizens, said Goodman sadly, bishops left little to their heirs.[2] The Archbishop of Canterbury was the only churchman who sat in Elizabeth's privy councils, though the Archbishop of York was usually a prominent figure in the Council in the North. The Reformation diminished the social status of bishops (and destroyed that of the other ecclesiastical peers, the abbots) much as the Wars of the Roses had destroyed or diminished the power of many of the old feudal families. Bishops, like other civil servants, tended henceforth to be 'new men', dependent on the crown, with no great family connexion.

On the Elizabethan bench of bishops we find the sons of merchants, weavers, tailors, yeomen, small gentlemen. By the seventeenth century the government depended more and more on lay officials like the merchant Cranfield, or bishops of merchant origin like Abbott, Laud, Neile, Juxon, Goodman, Wren, Pierce, Morton, Wright. Peers were apt to be too interested in what they could get out of government office to buttress their private fortunes: many gentlemen were out of sympathy with government policy. It was the hey-day of middle-class officialdom. Selden observed that bishops were formerly either canonists or civilians, promoted because of their ability, 'or else great noblemen's sons, brothers and nephews, and so born to govern the state; now they are of a low condition'.[3] When an occasional aristocrat like Anthony Grey or George Herbert found his way into the church, he was likely to be far too holy and independent a person to make a satisfactory bishop. As James I was reported to have said, by way of apology for creating careerist bishops, 'No good men would take the office on them'.[4] It was not until

---

[1] Hooker, *Works*, iii. 405. 'A common artisan or tradesman of the City', Hooker continued, could be compared 'with ordinary pastors of the church'. Cf. Rowse, op. cit., pp. 143–4; J. Stoughton, *History of Religion in England* (1881), iv. 187.
[2] Goodman, op. cit. i. 287–8.   [3] Selden, *Table Talk*, p. 20.
[4] Lord Brooke, *A Discourse opening the nature of that episcopacie, which is exercised*

Charles II's reign, when bishops had been divested of most of their political functions, that saints could be appointed to episcopal sees.

Sneers at the low social origins of bishops became a commonplace among the parliamentarians, whether grandees like Lord Brooke, men of middle rank like D'Ewes ('bishops . . . raised from the dust'), or humbler and more virulent gentlemen like Prynne ('lordly prelates raised from the dunghill', 'equal commonly in birth to the meanest peasants').[1] Fuller tried to vindicate the respectable origins of the Caroline bishops, but he could find only three of undoubted landed stock. He rightly claimed, however, that the others came of non-plebeian parentage.[2]

Yet clerical pretensions did not diminish with the social rank of bishops. Martin Marprelate criticized Whitgift, the Grimsby merchant's son, for refusing to admit a parson recommended by the Earl of Warwick, but especially because he had said he would not 'be beholding to never a nobleman in this land', since he was the second person in it.[3] That was the Laudian note. Laud himself, wrote Mrs. Hutchinson, was 'a fellow of mean extraction and arrogant pride'.[4] It was the combination that annoyed the gentry, as in the case of Archbishop Neile, Laud's collaborator in 'pompous innovations' who was the son of a tallow chandler, and of Bishop Wren, son of a London merchant.

Whether, as Wilson thought, 'England' flourished more because of this reduction in the status of bishops depends on the point of view of the observer. Certainly many gentlemen flourished. Bishops' lands were in Elizabeth's reign what monastic lands had been in her father's—the fund from which pensions were paid and favours dispensed. Feckenham, Marian Abbot of Westminster, made it an argument against conforming to the Elizabethan establishment 'that he can see nothing to be sought, but the spoil of the church, and of bishops' houses, and of colleges' lands; which, he saith, maketh many to pretend to be puritans, seeking for the fruits of the church'.[5] The point was often to be made later.

in England (1642), p. 94; in W. Haller, *Tracts on Liberty in the Puritan Revolution* (1933–4), ii. See below, pp. 209–10.

[1] Brooke, op. cit., *passim*; ed. W. H. Coates, *Journal of Sir Simonds D'Ewes* (1942), p. 46; ed. S. R. Gardiner, *Documents relating to the proceedings against William Prynne* (Camden Soc., 1873), p. 52; [W. Prynne], *A Looking-Glass for all Lordly Prelates* (1636), p. 79. [2] Fuller, *Church History*, iii. 428.

[3] M. Marprelate, *The Epistle* (ed. Arber, 1895), p. 25.

[4] Lucy Hutchinson, *Life of Colonel Hutchinson* (1846), p. 88.

[5] Strype, *Annals*, 1, part i. 529.

V

Not all ecclesiastical authorities were altogether happy about this wholesale spoliation. But during Elizabeth's reign their protests, and even legislation aimed at checking the plunder, were not effective. Archbishop Parker remonstrated against the act of 1559 which legitimized long leases to the crown.[1] One of his last acts was to write to Elizabeth 'with some vehemency' against the plunder of the church. This almost-posthumous act of courage came to nothing, however: the letter was never sent, and the compliant Whitgift revealed its contents to Burghley, one of the 'great men' whom Parker had attacked as responsible for the policy. A similar ineffectiveness was shown by Grindal. He was very upset at the plundering of bishops' lands, and wrote a letter to Peter Martyr about it; but it did not stop him accepting his bishopric.[2] In the Convocation of 1563 there was a pious resolution, drafted by Sandys of Worcester: 'Forasmuch as bishops are not born for themselves, but for their successors, and are only possessors for their own time, every bishop, by the subscription of his hand, promiseth that he shall not, either by lease, grant, or any other means, let, set, or alienate any of his manors, or whatsoever heretofore hath not been in lease, except only for his own time, and while he is bishop.'[3] The resolution seems to have come to nothing; and Sandy's own later conduct is an ironical comment on the unimpeachable but impracticable sentiments here expressed.

An act of Parliament of 1571 (13 Eliz., c. 10) sought to provide a remedy for fraudulent conveyances by bishops (or other clergy); and extended to deans and chapters, colleges, hospitals, and all clergy, the limitation of leases to twenty-one years or three lives. This statute, strengthened in 1576 by 18 Eliz., c. 11, did something to discourage the habit of living on capital by granting long leases for a cash sum down: and at least one chapter, that of Ely, agreed in 1588 to impose upon itself a self-denying ordinance abjuring leases for three lives: no lease was henceforth to exceed twenty-one years.[4] But there is plenty of evidence to suggest that these statutes were often simply disregarded.[5] The landlord could always find pretexts

---

[1] Strype, *Annals*, I, part i. 142–3.
[2] Pierce, op. cit., p. 57; Strype, *Life of Grindal* (1821), p. 42.
[3] Strype, *Annals*, I, part i. 506.
[4] Ibid. III, part ii. 72.
[5] See *The Diary of John Young, Dean of Winchester, 1616–45* (ed. F. R. Goodman,

for inserting another life, changing a life, or otherwise levying a fine. In the case of bishops and deans, the future that was thus sold for immediate cash was probably a successor's future. The statutes of 1571 and 1576 did not produce a *regular* income from church lands that bore any relation to the real value of the lands.

Whitgift took a rather firmer stand than any of his predecessors against the dissipation of the church's heritage. Izaak Walton reports a lecture on sacrilege which the Archbishop gave the queen, arising out of a dispute with Leicester over ecclesiastical property. 'Religion', he told the queen, 'is the foundation and cement of human societies: and when they that serve at God's altar shall be exposed to poverty, then religion itself will be exposed to scorn and become contemptible, as you may already observe it to be in too many poor vicarages in this nation.' For the rest of Elizabeth's reign, Walton concluded, 'God seemed still to keep him [Whitgift] in her favour, that he might preserve the remaining church lands and immunities from sacrilegious alienations'.[1] But Whitgift was as angry as anyone when in 1595 a Fellow of an Oxford college allowed zeal so far to outrun discretion as to preach a sermon on the text 'My house shall be called the house of prayer, but ye have made it a den of thieves', and to apply the words to 'the noblemen of this realm especially, and in sort also to the bishops'.[2] And as late as 1601, when the government was in grave financial difficulties, an act was passed for confirmation of grants made to the queen by corporations and by her to individuals (43 & 44 Eliz., c. 1): so the plunderers of the church ensured their gains.

Hooker, as usual, went deeper than most of his contemporaries in his economic analysis. He saw that there was a connexion between the decline in episcopal revenues, rising standards of expenditure in lay society, and the universal accusations of ecclesiastical corruption which he barely attempted to rebut. *Relative* poverty, he observed in his measured prose, is

a stronger inducement . . . than perhaps men are aware of unto evil and corrupt dealings for supply of that defect. For which cause we must

---

1928), pp. 58–59, 139.; ed. J. F. Williams and B. Cozens-Hardy, *Minute Books of the Dean and Chapter of Norwich* (Norfolk Record Soc., 1953), p. 75. Cf. W. Notestein, F. Relf, and H. Simpson, *Commons Debates, 1621* (1935), vii. 46–51.
    [1] I. Walton, *Lives* (World's Classics), pp. 191–5. Note Whitgift's emphasis on the poverty of *vicarages* (see below, pp. 109–13).   [2] Strype, *Whitgift*, ii. 319.

needs think it a thing necessary unto the common good of the church that, great jurisdiction being granted unto bishops over others, a state of wealth proportionable should likewise be provided for them. Where wealth is held in so great admiration, as generally in this golden age it is, that without it angelical perfections are not able to deliver from extreme contempt, surely to make bishops poorer than they are were to make them of less account and estimation than they should be.[1]

Granting the assumptions, that was unanswerable. By the end of Elizabeth's reign there seems to have been general realization that a halt must be called to the plunder. In 1595 Bishop Wickham of Winchester declared in a sermon preached before the queen that if the temporalities of the bishops should suffer during the next thirty years as much as in the thirty years preceding, there would hardly be enough left in any see to keep the cathedral in repair.[2]

Such considerations began to bear fruit in the next reign. James I wanted to preserve the landmarks of the old order. An act of 1604 (1 Jac. I, c. 3) took a decisive step when it forbade archbishops and bishops to alienate the lands of their sees even to the crown. By this means the king 'religiously stopped a leak which did much harm, and would else have done a great deal more'.[3] The parsimonious Elizabeth was supreme plunderer of the church; the extravagant James was defender of its revenues. It may be worth asking why the change came when it did. One obvious answer is that the end of the Spanish and Irish wars seemed to have alleviated the financial situation. But there were indications of new attitudes in the last decade of Elizabeth. There were deeper causes at work than the mere accident of personality, causes which brought about a general shift in the emphasis of government policy about this time. For it is from the last decade of Elizabeth's reign, after the defeat of the Armada, that the rift within the politically effective nation began to make itself felt for the first time. A new economic policy of regimentation and control was initiated in this decade, which looks forward to the social policy of Charles I's personal government. Financial quarrels first reached serious proportions, and led to the outcry in the 1601 Parliament and the government's retreat. At the same time, under Whitgift, a serious campaign of repression against the Puritans

---

[1] Hooker, *Works*, iii. 395–6.
[2] Harington, op. cit., pp. 66–67.
[3] F. Bacon, *Works* (1861), xiii. 32; cf. xii. 352.

was begun: and at Cambridge the first stirrings of opposition to the dominant Calvinist theology were heard, foreboding the rise of Arminianism under the Calvinist James, and its triumph under Charles.

In the early years of Elizabeth, with the clergy only dubiously protestant, the political subordination of the church had still been a matter of concern to the government: so privy councillors had been content to see church property plundered, and to take their share of the booty. The economic resources of the hierarchy were used to reward courtiers and to keep taxes down. The demand remained under the early Stuarts. But once the political nation ceased to be united, the government's need of the church increased. The latter's political dependence was now so absolute that it could under no circumstances become a threat to the monarchy, under whose protection alone the hierarchy survived.

So the considerations which Whitgift had put before Elizabeth became valid. If the church, through its pulpits and courts, its sermons and discipline, was to help to preserve the social order, then its own dignity and property must be safeguarded. In a famous sermon at Paul's Cross, which is in effect a shrewd and hard-hitting political speech, Bancroft reminded the richer members of his audience that the clergy could preach against the wealth, greed, and exploitation of landlords no less effectively than the laity could attack the wealth, luxury, and pride of prelates. His conclusion was not that landlords should cease to make the poorer sort 'groan under the heavy burdens' laid upon them, to rack their rents, take great fines, and keep them 'in very unchristian slavery and bondage', in order to maintain their own 'pride in apparel, their excess in diet, their unnecessary pleasures': he mentioned these matters only to show what he could do if provoked. His conclusion was rather that the propertied class should respect the riches and prestige of the church because of its usefulness to them, and because they had common enemies.[1] We are dealing here with a fundamental shift in political thought and political alignments. 'No bishop, no king, no nobility': this version of King James's epigram was recorded by a bishop.[2]

Yet the self-denying ordinance of 1604 cut across another essential part of James's policy of conservation, his declared

---

[1] R. Bancroft, *A Sermon Preached at Paules Crosse* (1588), pp. 25–26.
[2] Goodman, op. cit. i. 421.

intention of subsidizing the aristocracy. It was courtiers who forwarded 'importunate suits' to bishops. The act came too late to save Norhamshire, Norham Castle, and Holy Island, alienated by the Bishop of Durham to the king, and immediately granted to George Hume, Earl of Dunbar.[1] It also came after the king had obtained (by act of Parliament) a ninety-nine years' lease of the rectory of Great Bedwin from the Dean and Canons of Windsor for Robert Carr, later Earl of Somerset.[2] And indeed, though Ridley rejoiced that James had now protected the church against 'the too easy facility of many bishops in yielding to such suits'[3] (and also against the facility of the king himself), how else were deserving English and Scottish peers to be subsidized without ruinous cost to the crown, itself in financial difficulties? If the amount of patronage which the crown could dispense was to be drastically cut down, how long could it preserve the loyalty of the aristocracy?

Three years later, in fact, we find the king negotiating with two syndicates of London business men for the sale of impropriate rectories and chantry lands still in his possession: part of the object was to provide pensions for courtiers.[4] If the church was not to be despoiled further, the crown had to sell its own capital. Chances like that which enabled the Bishop of Durham to recover his London palace from the disgraced Sir Walter Ralegh occurred rarely; and Durham House was lost again to the Earl of Pembroke in 1640. Bishop Wren of Ely used the Court of Requests to recapture Ely House from Lady Hatton at the height of the Laudians' power; this short-lived triumph was reversed by the House of Commons in 1641.[5]

There was a real dilemma here, from which the government could never escape. As Ridley, like Whitgift, very rightly emphasized, the church was politically useful in so far as it taught subjects the duty of obedience to the prince. The hierarchy's too facile compliance with economic abuses had, however, brought it into disrespect. A halt must be called to the spoliation of the church, and to the disrepute into which it had fallen, if a church

[1] R. Surtees, *History of Durham* (1816), i. lxxxviii; P. Heylyn, *Examen Historicum* (1659), pp. 176–8.

[2] Bodington, op. cit. xli. 38. The rectory was valued in 1649 at over £200 a year more than the £77 annual rent paid for it.

[3] Ridley, op. cit., p. 211.   [4] Lansdell, op. cit., pp. 306–10.

[5] Nalson, op. cit. ii. 270.

of the traditional type was to continue usefully in existence. James even refounded the Deanery of Ripon, and endowed it from crown lands. The endowment was not very generous, less than £100 a year, 'so that he that shall have it had need of other means to support it', Archbishop Abbott observed, 'if he will live in any fashion'.[1] But it was a gesture. Even Buckingham went very circumspectly to work when he wanted the Archbishop of York to exchange York House for lands in Yorkshire. He got the transaction approved (with some difficulty) by Parliament.[2] This was very different from the way in which Elizabeth's favourites had behaved. The bishops, said Speaker Finch (a government nominee) in 1628, those lights of the church, should be set in golden candlesticks, and should not be made contemptible by parity and poverty.[3]

Yet on the other hand it remained to be seen whether opposition to bishops would not equally be stimulated by their economic immunity: especially as it was inevitable that a revivified episcopacy, enjoying the confidence of the crown, would attempt to recover some of the old economic and political position of the church in society. James was trying to protect both the church and the aristocracy against the new levelling power of money. The church was being protected in part because of its usefulness to the established order of society and its ruling class; but it had to be protected *against* that ruling class. It is noteworthy, indeed, that effective measures for the preservation of church property came neither from the bishops nor from the crown alone, but from Parliament. Yet if the tax-paying classes had at last decided to discontinue the plunder of the church, how was the gap in government finance to be filled?

VI

As I suggested earlier, we know far too little about the management of the lands of the hierarchy. But it seems safe to suggest certain advantages which were enjoyed by their tenants:

1. A courtier had a good opportunity of getting a long lease on nominal or highly favourable terms.

---

[1] Peck, op. cit., p. 291; Knowler, op. cit. i. 25. Fuller put the endowment at £247 per annum (*Church History*, iii. 204–5).

[2] Hacket, op. cit. i. 187–8.

[3] J. Rushworth, *Historical Collections* (1721), i. 482.

2. Even without such influence, bishops and deans and chapters were in the habit of granting long leases until forbidden by statute; and even after 1559 and 1571 a lease for three lives could still be granted. In such cases future rents were sold for a cash fine, to the advantage of the bishop but to the detriment of the see. And tenants who held a long lease tended to be less politically dependent on their landlords than was traditionally thought desirable.

3. The rise in prices then brought the holders of long leases their 'unearned increment'.

One line of argument put forward in 1640–1 against the proposal to confiscate church property stressed the advantages enjoyed by tenants of bishops and deans and chapters. The estates of all tenants of church lands who held for three lives would fall in value by at least 20 per cent. if they were sold, Secretary Nicholas thought in 1640. In May 1641 Hacket argued that tenants enjoyed six parts of seven in pure gain.[1] More than five parts in six, said Laud at his trial.[2] The argument was too good not to become standard. Dean and chapter lands, the University of Oxford pleaded in their defence, afforded 'a competent portion in an ingenious way to many younger brothers of good parentage', and were 'the chief support of many thousand families of the laity who enjoy fair estates under them in a free way'.[3] So ecclesiastics strove to make themselves friends with the Mammon of unrighteousness. Charles I, arguing in 1647 against the alienation of church lands, reminded M.P.s that 'many of his subjects [had] the benefit of renewing leases at much easier rates than if those possessions were in the hands of private men'.[4]

That such arguments were not mere propaganda is shown by Nicholas's belief that he and his father would lose £1,500 a year by the change of landlords.[5] It was generally agreed, even in the eighteenth century, that 'men of letters and bodies corporate cannot so well manage their estates as laymen or a single person may do, if they keep them in their own hands, or let them out at

---

[1] *C.S.P.D., 1640–1*, p. 213; Sir Ralph Verney, *Notes of Proceedings in the Long Parliament* (Camden Soc., 1845), p. 76. 'Tenants may be tenants still', replied Dr. Burgess (ibid., p. 77).

[2] W. Laud, *Works* (1847–60), iv. 192.

[3] J. Nalson, op. cit. ii. 305–6. The monasteries had earlier been defended on the same grounds. See also Spelman, *English Works*, i. xxv–xxvi.

[4] Gardiner, *Constitutional Documents*, p. 329; cf. *Church Lands not to be sold* (1648), attributed to John Warner, Bishop of Rochester, pp. 19–20.

[5] D. Nicholas, *Mr. Secretary Nicholas* (1955), p. 134.

a rack rent (especially when they are distant from them)': rents and fines had scarcely been increased since the Reformation.[1]

Against the undoubted advantages to tenants of church lands so often listed by ecclesiastical spokesmen we must set disadvantages which would be felt especially by entrepreneurial lessees. Professor Nef has made this point with regard to coal-bearing properties, of which ecclesiastical authorities owned many in various parts of the kingdom. Entrepreneurs here certainly made high profits in relation to rents paid. But Professor Nef suggests that the heavy capital investment needed for the development of the coal industry may have been retarded by ecclesiastical ownership. Bishops and deans and chapters would not put up this capital themselves; they could not be forced to lease or sell; and they might impose unfavourable leasing conditions, being out of sympathy with the industrialists' objectives.[2] The first leap forward of the coal industry in England occurred only after coal-bearing lands had passed from the dead hand of the monasteries into lay ownership. The Palatine Bishop of Durham, still retaining an independent feudal jurisdiction, was in a peculiarly strong position *vis-à-vis* all his tenants, being judge in his own cause.[3]

Similar factors may have prevailed in agriculture. Ecclesiastical landlords may have deliberately delayed the adoption of capitalist farming methods on land which they leased out: this appears to be Mr. Willan's explanation of the absence of enclosure on some church lands in the North Riding of Yorkshire.[4] The subject deserves further investigation. Heavy capital investment was always risky on land that was not freehold: that was a seventeenth-century commonplace. It became doubly risky when Laud inaugurated a policy of shortening leases.

The general result was summarized by Sir Thomas Wilson in the passage which appears as epigraph to Part I of this book, and which Mr. Willan's researches in Yorkshire appear to confirm.[5]

[1] *Sir Isaac Newton's Tables for Renewing and Purchasing the Leases of Cathedral-Churches and Colleges* (6th ed., 1742), pp. 89–90.

[2] In 1635 the Dean and Chapter of Wells demanded one-seventh and one-tenth of the lead dug in one of their manors by a prospector to whom they granted a licence (*MSS. of the Dean and Chapter of Wells*, Hist. MSS. Commission, ii. 412). Cf. Bridgeman, op. cit., p. 397.

[3] J. U. Nef, *The Rise of the British Coal Industry* (1932), i. 37–38, 135–9, 143.

[4] Willan, op. cit., pp. 281–2.

[5] Ibid., pp. 276, 288–9. See also Kerridge, op. cit., pp. 33–34, and references there cited.

The church had potential reserves which might one day be drawn on to the advantage of the institution rather than of individuals. Between 1628 and 1631 Bishop Buckeridge of Ely took fines to the total value of £4,300. 'Vast sums' tumbled into the coffers of Bishop Davenant on the expiry of long leases set by an Elizabethan predecessor.[1] If leases could be shortened, fines reduced, and rents racked, a much higher proportion of the surplus produced by improved farming techniques could be won for the church, though at the cost of worsened relations with its tenants. And if the operation were successful, ecclesiastical tenants might be reduced to greater dependence. I shall consider later Laud's attempts in this direction.[2]

[1] *C.S.P.D., 1631–3*, p. 46; Aubrey, op. cit. i. 202, and above, p. 21.
[2] See Chapter XIV.

III

THE CHALLENGE TO THE HIERARCHY

> In the clergy, some are so poor that they *cannot* attend their
> ministry, but are fain to keep schools, nay, ale-houses some of
> them; and some others are so stately, they *will not* attend their
> ministry; and so between them the flock starved. But our evils have
> more especially proceeded from the excessive worldly wealth and
> dignities of one part of the clergy:—I mean such as either are in
> possession or in hopes of bishoprics. . . . To speak plain English,
> these bishops, deans and chapters do little good themselves,
> by preaching or otherwise; and if they were felled, a great deal of
> good timber might be cut out of them for the uses of the church
> and kingdom at this time. . . . The clergy in the maintenance of
> their greatness, which they are neither willing to forgo nor yet
> well able to maintain upon the principles of the reformed
> religion, finding . . . the Popish principles, whereon the Bishop
> of Rome built his greatness, to suit well unto their ends, that
> maketh them to side with that party, and that must needs bring in
> superstition.
>
> NATHANIEL FIENNES
> in the House of Commons, 1 Feb. 1641 (Nalson, op. cit. i. 760–1)

I

THE sixteenth-century spoliation was doubly detrimental to
the hierarchy. Its members were weakened economically,
their social prestige was lowered; and it was manifest that
what remained of their wealth and power depended on government
support. On the other hand, bishops were still rich and powerful
enough to be envied and criticized. Canterbury, Winchester, and
Ely were all worth more than £2,000 a year; York, Durham,
Salisbury, London were all over £1,000. The sixteenth-century
plunder had whetted the appetites of greedy laymen; it had not
sufficiently depressed the hierarchy to satisfy the egalitarian
principles of Puritan ministers. A petition to queen and Parliament in 1584 attacked the feudal state of prelates, and asked that

the bishops, 'being enriched with such lands and livings as now they do possess and do enjoy, be not compelled, either by law or custom, hereafter to keep in their family so great a number of idle gentlemen and serving men as now they use to do'. Instead they should maintain scholars, so that their houses would become more like Christian schools and less like princes' courts, 'as now they are'. Then the goods of the church could be profitably bestowed, 'which are now for the most part unprofitably and prodigally spent, spoiled and wasted'.[1] Or the property of the hierarchy might be used to relieve poverty: a use which Lancelot Andrewes regarded as spoliation and waste, and from which he looked to the crown to protect the church.[2]

The Puritan complaint is illustrated by the £448 a year which Archbishop Parker spent on servants' wages, exclusive of maintenance; by the 100 servants, 40 of them gentlemen wearing chains of gold, who attended Archbishop Whitgift on his first journey into Kent; by the 80 servants of Aylmer, Bishop of London; by the 32 servants of Bishop Parkhurst of Norwich, and the 50 of Bishop Lake of Bath and Wells; by the 40 persons whom in 1568 the Bishop of Chester claimed to maintain regularly, 'besides comers and goers', out of a revenue of some 500 marks a year; by the £250 which the Bishop of Rochester said in 1595 he was spending annually on food and drink, out of a total revenue of £340; by the Bishop of Carlisle's claim in 1578 that his expenses exceeded his income by £600 a year.[3]

The critics' attitude towards the church seems today entirely reasonable, because history has gone that way. We must constantly remind ourselves that a profound revolution was needed before bishops ceased to be, and to be thought of as, primarily territorial magnates and royal officials. Elizabeth heartily approved of Whitgift's army of retainers, his lavish hospitality, his well-furnished stable and armoury. The sixty armed retainers whom the Archbishop threw into action against Essex in 1601, whilst prudently holding 40 horse in reserve, were invaluable to the queen. When James I made Abbott archbishop he solemnly charged him to 'carry his house nobly', and to live like an arch-

---

[1] Strype, *Annals*, III, part ii. 298–9; I, part ii. 266. Cf. *An Admonition to Parliament*, in W. H. Frere and C. E. Douglas, *Puritan Manifestoes* (1907), pp. 13, 30–31.

[2] L. Andrewes, *XCVI Sermons* (1629), pp. 293–4.

[3] T. H. Buckle, *Miscellaneous and Posthumous Works* (1885), i. 429–30; Paule, *Life of Whitgift*, pp. 97–98, 103–7; Fuller, *Worthies*, ii. 12.

bishop.[1] Maintenance of port was part of his function, of the function of all royal officials. Lord Deputy Wentworth defended himself indignantly to Archbishop Laud against the suggestion that he 'lived meanly, below that which I owe to the honour of His Majesty and dignity of the place I exercise'.[2]

The Puritan theorists objected on principle to inequalities between ministers, to prelates who were also barons. What is interesting, and to the student with modern prepossessions perplexing and even repellent, is the apparent cynicism with which the godliest reformers were prepared to offer bribes to potential aristocratic allies in plundering the church. There was, of course, a good deal of history behind this. The radical reformers had supported the Duke of Northumberland only with some heart-searchings. 'Papistry is not banished out of England by pure religion', admitted Lever in a sermon preached at Paul's Cross just after Northumberland's rise to power, 'but overcome, suppressed and kept under within this realm by covetous ambition.' The king's godly proceedings were perverted by the covetousness of his ministers, the preacher declared frankly: 'Ye know in whose hands this rich spoil remaineth. . . . If ye will have a godly reformation effectuously to proceed, trust not the servants of Mammon.'[3]

Yet it was not so easy to dispense with Mammon's servants. The experience of Scotland, France, the Netherlands, and indeed of the dissolution of the monasteries in England, had taught men the importance of establishing vested interests in opinions: an anti-episcopal vested interest was one of the easiest to establish. Nevertheless, the case against the hierarchy rested largely on its economic defects—bishops squandered on lordly living and ostentatious ceremonies sums which should have been devoted to painful preachers and education. It is therefore at first sight a little surprising to find how readily Puritans appealed to lay self-interest. Their enemies noted the fact with some pleasure. It was 'the spoil of the church', Whitgift suggested, which the Puritans sought 'under pretence of zeal'.[4] Bancroft thus summarized what he held to be Cartwright's opinion of his lay supporters: 'Whilst they hear us speak against bishops and cathedral churches . . . it

---

[1] J. Collier, op. cit. vii. 311; Rushworth, op. cit. i. 450.
[2] Knowler, op. cit. ii. 106.   [3] Lever, op. cit., p. 95; cf. p. 113.
[4] J. Whitgift, *Works* (1851–3), i. 11; cf. ii. 389, and Strype, *Whitgift*, i. 126.

tickleth their ears, looking for the like prey they had before of the monasteries. . . . They care not for religion, so they may get the spoil.'[1] Hooker assumed that 'the sacrilegious intention of church robbers . . . lurketh under this plausible name of reformation'.[2] The lay pamphleteers who wrote against Martin Marprelate made the same point as the clerical controversialists: it was indeed obvious enough. Even so relatively impartial a figure as Francis Bacon wrote of 'certain mercenary bands which impugn bishops and other ecclesiastical dignitaries, to have the spoil of their endowments and livings'.[3]

These allegations were unfair but not outrageous. For even so sincere a man as John Penry was ready to offer church lands as a bribe. Of his honesty of purpose there can be no doubt. In 1593 he was hanged, drawn, and quartered. He could almost certainly have saved his life by a judicious recantation. Burghley seems to have been anxious to spare him. If ever a man died for refusing to compromise on what he held to be right, it was Penry. Yet this man, two months before his execution, wrote a letter from prison to the Earl of Essex, in which with naïve cynicism he offered the favourite the plunder of the church if he would help to abolish episcopacy. 'An infinite mass of wealth, even the very greenness of the land, which these locusts now unprofitably devour', was there to be 'spoiled'. 'We desire that we may have your aid in it, and we doubt not but you shall be sufficiently rewarded. I offer your lordship of her spoil.' The second Earl of Essex should play the same part as his predecessor Thomas Cromwell. Such service would advance 'the glory of God, the good of his church, the wealth of her majesty's state and your own particular'. 'You shall not have the like favour in court always', added Penry, with imprudently accurate directness. 'Use your opportunity then.'[4]

These men, in fact, thought the episcopal hierarchy so evil in itself, that almost any price was worth paying to get rid of it. Episcopacy burdened the consciences of men; but purses were burdened as well. On another occasion Penry had written: 'We think that her majesty might greatly glorify God, and bring much peace to her subjects, in taking the lordly revenues of the prelates

[1] Bancroft, op. cit., p. 27; cf. his *Survey of the Pretended Holy Discipline* (1593), pp. 244–6.
[2] Hooker, *Works*, iii. 350; cf. p. 377.
[3] Bacon, *Works*, viii. 90.
[4] *The Notebook of John Penry, 1593* (ed. A. Peel, Camden Soc., 1944), pp. 85–93.

and priests into her own hands, to employ them otherwise as her majesty shall think good to her highness's own use, and the benefit of the land.'[1] A Barrowist petition of 1603 also asked for the confiscation of church lands and their conversion to better uses.[2] The Baptist Helwys, some nine years later, offered the king the following inducements to take over bishops' lands and tithes: (1) it would overthrow that high pride and cruelty of the image of the Beast; (2) it would advance the kingdom of Jesus Christ; (3) it would enrich the crown; (4) it would 'enrich the whole land above measure, and that in disburdening the land of all those courts with all the suits and services that belong unto them, the taxations, fees and penalties whereof are without number. And the king would stand [in] no need of taxes and subsidies. . . . Oh what a full and ready consent would there be in the king's people to these things, how profitable would it be unto them. . . .'[3]

It is a main thesis of this book that behind the Puritan attack on the church there lurked economic considerations, appealing especially to the interests of land-hungry magnates and of business men great and small. To many readers this will seem far-fetched, or at best a logical reconstruction which cannot be substantiated by contemporary evidence. The comments of Whitgift and Bancroft, quoted above, may perhaps be dismissed as partisan. They are discredited by the wilder accusations of Heylyn later, who saw little in clerical presbyterianism but clerical ambition, in lay presbyterianism but a desire for plunder. ('The lay-brethren with unsatiable covetousness gaped after the possessions and lands of the bishops. . . . It was the church's goods which they most gaped after, not the church's good.' Many lay patrons 'would have crucified Christ himself to have had his garments'.)[4]

But the best evidence is not that of enemies of the Puritans, nor even that of a judicious observer like Bacon, but the direct and conscious appeal to lay cupidity made by sincere religious leaders like Penry and Helwys. We have here surely the answer to the problem which has troubled some historians—the fact that great 'Puritan' peers might be far from bourgeois in their ethics and

[1] C. Burrage, *Early English Dissenters* (1912), ii. 73.

[2] R. Barclay, *The Inner Life of the Religious Societies of the Commonwealth* (1876), p. 59.

[3] T. Helwys, *The Mistery of Iniquity* (1935 reprint), pp. 21–22.

[4] P. Heylyn, *Ecclesia Vindicata*, General Preface, sig. B3ᵛ, in *Historical and Miscellaneous Tracts* (1681).

outlook. In the first place, any direct equation of 'Puritan' and 'bourgeois' in the sixteenth century is a vast over-simplification; but secondly the word 'Puritan' describing such politicians should be put in heavy quotation marks. They were Puritans in the same sense that John of Gaunt was a Wyclifite—that is to say in no religious sense at all. To patronize a politically useful group need not involve acceptance of all their standards of value. No doubt few of the big business men who subsidized Sir Oswald Mosley in the nineteen-thirties thereby felt committed to his whole philosophy.

God and Mammon joined hands again in the curious alliance which existed for a short time after the failure of the Spanish marriage project, between John Preston, the great Puritan preacher, and the Duke of Buckingham. The Duke helped Preston to win a popular Cambridge lectureship, in the teeth of opposition from heads of colleges and the Bishop of Ely. He offered him a bishopric. And they discussed together the confiscation of dean and chapter lands, in order to subsidize preaching and pay the king's debts. It is hardly likely that either of them supposed that Buckingham would get nothing out of the transaction: Preston was a highly sophisticated person. Hacket imagines him saying 'If a crumb stick in the throat of any considerable man, that attempts to make a contrary part, it will be easy to wash it down with manors, woods, royalties, tithes, etc.'[1]

For a long time, in fact, there was always the possibility that some great court figure—a Northumberland, a Leicester, an Essex, a Buckingham—might lead the attack on the church. 'The most crafty and clawing piece of all was that the destruction of these sacred foundations would make a booty for a number of gentlemen.'[2] Thus the church could be reformed peacefully. The chances of this solution diminished sharply with the rise of Bancroft and the accession of James I, just because the weakness of the church began to be seen as weakening the state. Buckingham's flirtation with Preston was perhaps an incident in his erratic foreign policy rather than serious business; and from the ascendancy of Laud it was clear that this approach to the problem was closed.

[1] T. Ball, *The Life of the renowned Dr. Preston* (1628), 1885 ed., pp. 98–101; Hacket, op. cit. i. 203–5; W. Haller, *Rise of Puritanism* (1938), pp. 70–74.
[2] Hacket, op. cit. i. 204.

Autres temps, autres hommes: the failure of reform led to revolution. Lay land-grabbing support was still needed, but it was found outside the court circle. When episcopacy was abolished in 1646, the device by which state creditors were induced to reinvest money owed to them by the government in the purchase of bishops' lands—'doubling'—was in the best tradition of Puritan politico-economic thought. 'By this means we got the bishops' lands on our back, without any grudge, and in a way that no skill will get them back again.'[1] At last the vested interest had been created. When Milton in 1660 made his final despairing plea for the establishment of a free commonwealth by means of the dictatorship of a rich oligarchy, he looked gloomily back to the history of protestantism to justify the casting out of devils by Beelzebub. 'To forsake, or rather to betray a just and noble cause for the mixture of bad men who have ill-managed and abused it'—if our fathers had done this, 'what had long ere this become of our gospel, and all protestant reformation, so much intermixed with the avarice and ambition of some reformers?'[2]

II

But though we should never forget 'the avarice and ambition' of some lay reformers, it was from the lesser clergy, and from those among the laity who were genuinely worried by their plight, that the most dangerous critics of the hierarchy came. A wide economic gulf was fixed between bishops and cathedral clergy on the one hand, and the mass of the parochial clergy on the other. This division was not new: but there were many reasons why it was more vigorously challenged after the Reformation.

It had been shown that the property of the church was not sacrosanct. The very disappointment of the reformers with the results of the dissolution, when abbey lands had not been devoted to educational purposes, led them to cry for further confiscations. Men had got into the dangerous habit of asking what useful purpose church property served. The dependence of the higher clergy on the crown was made manifest, and so they shared a common unpopularity as their defence of the *status quo* lost favour in the eyes of the newly-powerful forces in society. Some

---

[1] R. Baillie, *Letters and Journals* (1785), ii. 244 (1 Dec. 1646).
[2] J. Milton, *Prose Works* (Bohn ed., 1853), ii. 114.

of the lesser clergy were absolutely poorer than they had been,
and most were relatively poorer. For some groups in lay society
were getting much richer very quickly, and were demanding a
ministry whose standard of education should equal their own.[1]
The Reformation had called in question the whole hierarchical
principle; bishops had been abolished in some countries, their
powers and wealth drastically curtailed in others. Inevitably there
was widespread discussion of these matters in England. Diverse
motives combined to make men ask whether the riches and political
powers of bishops could be justified from the New Testament.

Many of the higher clergy held impropriated tithes or livings
in plurality: it was easy to see that the wealth of the few came at
the expense of the many. So clerical egalitarianism focused attention on the wealth of the hierarchy. Lay and clerical reformers
saw assets wasted in maintaining the pomp and circumstance
of the hierarchy which could be used for better purposes—either
to increase the regular revenues of the lesser clergy, or for education
and charity. William Ames spoke of 'a pomp that doth not agree
to a minister of the gospel; as the pompous state of a baron or
earl . . . that requireth many idle attendants, for no other use but
only for comportment and lustre of state; that which must have
so much time spent in bridling of the bishop's horses as the ancient
bishops took to preach divers sermons in'.[2]

Recalling Bancroft's comments in his sermon at Paul's Cross,
we may note how easily such criticisms of the *wastefulness* of
lordly pomp could be turned against the profuse expenditure of
lay lords. Had 'barons and earls' really any better justification
for their 'many idle attendants'? 'Comportment and lustre of
state' was hardly sufficient excuse, on the Puritan standard of
values. Hooker noted this point, and drew out the dangers in-
herent in the Puritan position. If the bishops 'abuse the goods of
the church unto pomp and vanity, such faults we do not excuse
in them . . .'. But 'let all states be put to their moderate pensions,
let their livings and lands be taken away from them whosoever
they be, in whom such ample possessions are found to have been
matters of grievous abuse: were this just? Would noble families
think this reasonable? The title which bishops have to their

---

[1] See pp. 204, 224 below.
[2] W. Ames, *A Fresh Suit against Human Ceremonies in Gods Worship* (1633), p. 408;
cf. Prynne, *A Looking-Glasse for all Lordly Prelates*, p. 70.

livings is as good as the title of any sort of man into whatsoever we account to be most justly held by them.'[1] When Oliver Cromwell said in the Long Parliament that he could not understand the necessity of the great revenues of bishops, it was at once retorted that 'if we made a parity in the church we must at last come to a parity in the commonwealth'.[2] The connexion of ideas had become familiar.

There was then a real division of interest within the ranks of ecclesiastics; and many nobler reasons than mere greed could lead laymen to wish to confiscate the revenues of bishops and cathedral clergy. When a committee of the House of Commons reported in March 1641 'touching the grievances in church matters', it listed as the third grievance 'the great revenues of deans and chapters, the little use of them, and the great inconveniences that come by them'. The first two grievances were illustrated by a wealth of argument: but for the third the rapporteur 'brought no reasons, because the matter was plain evident'.[3] D'Ewes disposed of the traditional plea that conversion of church lands to secular purposes was sacrilege with the same trenchant and novel utilitarianism: 'As the deans and chapters are now useless, we may well dispose of their revenues to better uses.'[4]

III

The following consequences of the economic changes so far discussed, then, were revealed in the seventeenth century.

First, a significant decline in the wealth of bishops. They ceased to be feudal magnates in their own right. Consequently the office no longer attracted even the occasional representative of baronial or magnate families. Men of middle-class origin preponderated on the episcopal bench, men who had no great connexions and no economic independence. Their subservience to the crown was a natural consequence.

Secondly, there was a danger that if the plunder of bishoprics and deaneries went much further, all degree and hierarchy in the

---

[1] Hooker, *Works*, iii. 402.

[2] Ed. W. Notestein, *Journal of Sir Simonds D'Ewes* (1923), pp. 339–40. Lancelot Andrewes had made the same point in a sermon preached before James I on 5 Aug. 1607 (*XCVI Sermons*, p. 777).

[3] Notestein, op. cit., pp. 458–9.

[4] Quoted in Shaw, op. cit. i. 55; cf. Nalson, op. cit. ii. 290.

church would be destroyed. The bishops naturally opposed further spoliation; but the king and a section of the landed class came to agree that complete stripping of the hierarchy would render the church unable to perform its function as buttress of the existing social order. Parity in the church would lead to parity in the state.

But thirdly, it was not easy to call a halt. Whenever there was a financial problem to be solved, some men's eyes turned longingly towards the church. In the seventeenth century there were always financial problems, and they increased as governments ceased to use the wealth of the church to supplement its sources of patronage. The idea of the equality of all ranks of the clergy had been stimulated by the theological Reformation. The criterion of utility was becoming popular, especially with the urban middle class whose wealth and scientific knowledge were advancing so spectacularly during our period, and who formed the principal support of protestantism. Was clerical property being utilized to the greatest national advantage? This seemed very questionable to those who were profiting by the new ways of producing wealth, who tended in any case to be out of sympathy with the social traditions which the defenders of the hierarchy wished to preserve, and who resented the standing threat to property rights which they saw in the Laudian régime and its clerical spokesmen.

Fourthly, by exchanges of lands many bishops had become holders of impropriated tithes; others held livings *in commendam*. They therefore connived at, were themselves the greatest examples of, pluralism and non-residence. It was easy for sincere laymen and parochial clergy to criticize them on this score: and the bishops had no adequate reply. The poorer they were, the greater the temptation to simony, corruption, plunder, and nepotism. They could hardly stand forth as the apostles of an economic reform which so many clerics and laymen felt to be needed. On all the issues we shall be considering most bishops tended to be impotently conservative.

So, fifthly, by the seventeenth century a parting of the ways had been reached. The rise in prices and in lay living standards meant that something must be done to augment the poorer ministers' stipends. If this was not to be by restoring impropriations to the church or by taxing the laity, the only resource left was bishops' and deans' and chapters' lands. If lordly and unpopular prelates could be got rid of, their property might be used to increase clerical stipends. On the other hand, if bishops and cathedral clergy were to be maintained, if the church's economic problems were to be solved at the expense of the laity, the economic and political power of the hierarchy would have to be substantially increased. There could be no standing still, as both Bancroft and Laud saw. 'Archbishop Abbott's "Yield, and they will be pleased at last" was a great miscarriage; Archbishop Laud's "Resolve, for there is no end of yielding" was great policy.'[1] Time was on the side of the bishops' enemies. Unless the church could recover much of its pre-Reformation wealth and power, danger threatened even what it still retained. But it was a losing battle, and the leaders of the episcopal reaction knew it. Even Bancroft had grim forebodings. He cancelled the will in which he left his library to Canterbury, because he feared that all cathedrals might be despoiled; and Cambridge benefited by this accurate if insufficiently far-sighted premonition.[2]

[1] D. Lloyd, *Memoires*, p. 265.
[2] D. Lloyd, *State-Worthies* (1766), ii. 51. The decision is an interesting refutation of the usual allegation of the hierarchy's spokesmen, that the opponents of bishops and cathedrals also wished to overthrow the universities. For Laud's fears, see *Hastings MSS*. (Hist. MSS. Commission), iv. 76–78. Cf. Rushworth, op. cit. i. 420 —similar forebodings by Williams in 1626.

IV

BENEFICES AND ADVOWSONS

When ye buy an advowson, or patronage of an ecclesiastical
living, to what end is it? . . . Do you not intend to gain by such
a bargain, either by placing some of your kin, or by selling it in
the vacancy to him that will be your best chapman? Is not this
the general practice?

H. BURTON, *A Censure of Simonie* (1624), pp. 35–37

It is very requisite for a prince to have an eye that the clergy be
elected and come in either by collation from him, or particular
patrons, and not by the people.

F. QUARLES, *Enchyridion* (1641), First Century, No. 54

I

THE economic problems of the church began right down in
the parishes—in the livings of incumbents. These two words,
so universally used, reveal some interesting attitudes. For
the parson his cure of souls was first and foremost a source of
livelihood: it was his benefice, something that did him good
(though originally *beneficium* is any land granted on condition of
doing military service, later merely an estate for life).[1] From the
standpoint of the appropriator, the impropriator, or anyone else
who might have drawn even larger profits from the parsonage if
it had not been necessary to pay a vicar, the clergyman was an
'incumbent'. He lay upon the property, reducing its value.[2] (The
word in this sense, of being in possession, occurs only in the
English language.) In neither point of view did the spiritual welfare of the parishioners take the first place. A benefice was a piece
of property in which a properly inducted minister had rights at
common law. Its legal definition was correlated to the receipt of

[1] Spelman, *The Original, Growth, Propagation and Condition of Feuds and Tenures by
Knight-Service in England*, in *English Works*, ii. 9.
[2] Sir E. Coke's definition contains a little special pleading: '*Incumbent*, cometh of
the verb incumbo, that is, to be diligently resident . . . and therefore the law doth
intend him to be resident on his benefice.' (*First Part of the Institutes*, 1670, p. 119ᵛ.)

tithes rather than to the performance of duties. 'The profits will come in', a future bishop noted, 'whether the duties be conscientiously performed or no.'[1]

It was also a *freehold* property. In 1573 Cartwright complained that this gave security of tenure to any reading minister, however incompetent: and Whitgift in reply defended the minister's rights. 'If the minister were but tenant at will, or of courtesy (as you would seem to have him) his state should be most slavish and miserable, and he and his family ready to go a-begging whensoever he displeaseth his parish.'[2] Robert Harrison attacked 'freehold parsonages and vicarages' since they 'hinder the free election and deposing of the minister'.[3] This was an extreme sectarian position. But in the Parliament of 1621 Coke pointed out that there was no means of getting rid of an habitually drunken minister; and a bill was prepared to amend the law as it affected 'scandalous ministers'. There was a similar bill in 1626.[4]

But in other respects the common lawyers and the parliamentary opposition came to favour security of tenure for ministers, since they were more likely to be ejected by their ecclesiastical superiors for nonconformity than by their parishioners for scandalous behaviour. As more Puritan patrons appointed more Puritan ministers, so the common lawyers began to claim to protect any man, even a nonconforming minister, in his freehold, against all attempts to extrude him. Induction, the common lawyers thought, was an act of a temporal nature.[5] About the time of the Marprelate controversy Beale—a government official but sympathetic to the Puritans—quoted Magna Carta: ministers ought not to lose their benefices, their freeholds, for offences 'mere temporal, for speeches or making of books'.[6] Bancroft in 1604 recognized that a distinction must be drawn between 'men beneficed' on the one hand, and curates or lecturers on the other. The latter had no freehold interest in their places and were 'no

[1] W. Watson, *The Clergyman's Law: or, the Complete Incumbent* (1720), pp. 1–4; R. Sanderson, *XXXV Sermons* (1681), i. 210.   [2] Whitgift, *Works*, ii. 459–60.

[3] Ed. A. Peel and L. H. Carlson, *The Writings of Robert Harrison and Robert Browne* (1953), p. 119.

[4] Notestein, Relf, and Simpson, op. cit. ii. 439–40; ed. H. Ellis, *Original Letters* (1825), iii. 222–3.

[5] E. Gibson, *Codex Juris Ecclesiastici Anglicani* (1713), p. 860.

[6] Quoted by Faith Thompson, *Magna Carta. Its rôle in the making of the English Constitution, 1300–1629* (Minnesota, 1948), p. 221. Cf. Heylyn, *History of the Presbyterians* (1670), pp. 304–6; Usher, op. cit. i. 406–7.

longer to enjoy them "nisi quamdiu se bene gesserint"'. 'Men beneficed' would have to be formally deprived.[1]

In the Parliament of 1625 Sir Nathaniel Rich moved that silenced ministers be allowed to preach in all points agreeable to the doctrine and discipline of the Church of England. 'They refuse not', he said, 'to subscribe to the articles according to the statute. But another subscription is required by canon [i.e. the canon of 1604]; and no canon can compel a man under a penalty to lose his freehold.'[2] Fourteen years later Bagshawe, Reader at the Middle Temple and ultimately a royalist in the civil war, asked 'whether the fine, imprisonment, deprivation and excommunication of a clerk for enormous offences (and no offence named) be good or void in law'? He thought it void; and he added—with clear reference to the High Commission—'here is a free subject quite destroyed in his goods by his fine; in his land and living by his deprivation; in his body by his imprisonment'. It was contrary to chapters 1 and 29 of Magna Carta.[3] The point was frequently made by parliamentarian pamphleteers.[4] After the Restoration, Bagshawe's position, which was also Coke's, appears to have been accepted.[5]

Typically, John Williams 'disrelished' depriving a minister even for drunkenness or incontinency, because of his freehold rights in his benefice. 'If a gentleman or citizen', he asked, 'had been convicted upon an article of scandal in his life, was it ever heard that he did confiscate a manor or a tenement?'[6] The good Bishop apparently did not believe that membership of the clerical profession called for a higher code of moral conduct than that of lay property-owners.

Other ecclesiastical offices, as well as benefices, were, rather less controversially, regarded as freeholds. This, we are told, was 'a post-Reformation development', although 'steps had already been taken in that direction' earlier.[7] Henry Burton quoted Coke

---

[1] Cardwell, *Documentary Annals*, ii. 75.

[2] Gardiner, *Debates in the House of Commons in 1625*, p. 26.

[3] Thompson, op. cit., p. 368.

[4] See, for example, *Englands Complaint to Jesus Christ against the Bishops Canons* (1640), sig. B.2.

[5] Thompson, op. cit., p. 372. Cf. Coke, *The First Part of the Institutes*, pp. 341–4.

[6] Hacket, op. cit. i. 97–98. The same argument was used by Bishop Goodman in his dedication to Cromwell of *The Two Great Mysteries of the Christian Religion* (1653), sig. a.

[7] B. L. Woodcock, *Mediaeval Ecclesiastical Courts in the Diocese of Canterbury* (1952), p. 39.

to show that 'lay-simony in buying and selling all sort of offices, great and small, of public justice and private service' derived from ecclesiastical simony: and later historians have held that the conception of an office as a piece of freehold property was an extension to civil offices of an ecclesiastical notion.[1] In 1582 the Bishop of Coventry declared that 'the office of a chancellorship within the diocese is granted to one for term of life'. It was generally accepted that this office, which comprehended those of Commissary and Vicar-General, was a freehold; though in 1640 it was still necessary to lay down in a canon that such office should not be granted 'for any longer term than the life of the grantee only', and should not be sold.[2] Not only the wardenship of Manchester College, but also the reversion to it, seem to have been purchasable like any lay office.[3] Laud had to take special action to stop the sale of offices and reversions within his own cathedral church of Canterbury. One of the accusations made against him after the Long Parliament met was that he had bilked purchasers of reversions to offices in ecclesiastical courts.[4]

II

Lay patronage had of course been familiar enough in the Middle Ages. Landowners might found or contribute to the founding of a church for the use of their tenants. They then automatically acquired the right of nominating an incumbent and presenting him to the bishop for institution. This right of patronage, the advowson, became appendant to a manor, and descended with it as part of the property.[5] It seemed as natural for the lord of the manor to wish to nominate the parson as it was for the king to want to nominate his bishops; and the parson of the village had even less chance of defying his lord for long than a bishop had of defying the king.

To the judicious Hooker the system seemed eminently right and proper. 'In this realm . . . where the tenure of lands is altogether

[1] H. Burton, op. cit., p. 97; R. W. Swart, *Sale of Offices in the 17th century* (The Hague, 1949), pp. 47, 49, 83.

[2] Strype, *Annals*, III, part i. 133; Gibson, op. cit., pp. 1027–8; Cardwell, *Synodalia* (1842), pp. 409–10. [3] Halley, op. cit. i. 265.

[4] Laud, *Works*, v. 455; *Hist. MSS. Commission, Fourth Report, Appendix*, pp. 69, 103.

[5] J. Doderidge, *A Compleat Parson: or, A Description of Advowsons* (1630), p. 30; Prynne, *Jus Patronatus* (1654), p. 45.

grounded on military laws[1] . . . the building of churches and consequently the assigning of either parishes or benefices was a thing
impossible without consent of such as were principal owners of
land; in which consideration for their more encouragement
hereunto they which did so far benefit the church had by common
consent granted (as great equity and reason was) a right for them
and their heirs till the world's end to nominate in those benefices
men whose quality the bishop allowing might admit them thereunto.' 'The people did not choose [the minister]', said Dr.
Johnson, rather less magniloquently, 'because the people did not
pay him.' But Hooker, determined to have it both ways, argued
that, by a kind of virtual representation, all incumbents were
chosen by the inhabitants, since 'their ancient and original interest
therein hath been by orderly means derived into the patron who
chooseth for them'.[2]

The advowson of a vicarage was normally appendant to the
rectory. So at the dissolution all the lay rectors who succeeded the
monasteries became patrons of vicarages, except in a few cases
where other arrangements had been made when the vicarage was
first endowed.[3] The advowsons of perhaps one-third of the livings
in the country thus passed from ecclesiastics to laymen. This was
not in itself quite such a startling revolution as it sounds, for lay
influence on ecclesiastical appointments had always been considerable: but the Reformation legalized, clarified, and exposed this
lay supremacy, in the parishes no less than at Westminster. The
really significant results of the transformation, however, lay ahead.

The exchanges of episcopal lands in Elizabeth's reign, the sale
of crown manors under her and the first two Stuarts, effected a
further transfer of patronage from bishops and crown, largely to
the advantage of the landed families. The crown, no doubt, tried
to hold on to 'the best sort of ecclesiastical livings', as Bishop
Cooper noted in 1589; but the mass of ordinary livings fell to the
nobility and gentry.[4]

[1] This phrase is worth pondering by those historians who believe that 'the feudal
system' was invented by Sir Henry Spelman.
[2] Hooker, *The Laws of Ecclesiastical Polity* (Everyman ed.), ii. 464–5; *Works*, iii.
287; J. Boswell, *Life of Johnson* (Everyman ed.), i. 474.
[3] Doderidge, op. cit., pp. 32–33. The rector of St. Peter's, Leeds (the Dean and
Chapter of Christ Church, Oxford), was not the patron. See p. 59 below. Nor was
the rector of St. Sepulchre's, London (R. P. Stearns, *The Strenuous Puritan*, 1954,
p. 36).
[4] T. Cooper, *An Admonition to the People of England* (1895), p. 108.

The full social consequences of this only began to be revealed with the slow development of that division among the gentry which takes place in the century before 1640, as a result of economic changes in the countryside. A growing section of the gentry began to engage in the clothing industry or in production for the market on their own estates, or developed trading connexions in the City. By and large, over the country as a whole, religious radicalism was strongest in the economically advanced areas; and in these areas we find an increasing number of landowners supporting the new ideas, often from conviction, sometimes no doubt from mere coincidence of interests.

On the Continent the sixteenth-century religious stalemate was expressed in the formula *cujus regio ejus religio*: each petty princeling determined the worship of his own dominions, arbitrarily and without appeal. This naturally set up a polarizing tendency, which increased rather than diminished the tension. Something very like a *cujus regio* settlement grew up in England after the Reformation, quite unintended by the government, as a result of the combination of lay patronage with a serious cleavage of interests (economic, political, and religious) within the class of lay patrons. So patrons would be likely to favour the religious tendency which suited them: and a seventeenth-century character-writer could take it for granted that for the humble villager 'his religion is a part of his copyhold, which he takes from his landlord and refers it wholly to his discretion'.[1]

The divisions within the landowning class were carried over into (though of course did not create) a war of ideas inside the church itself. 'If the patron be precise', wrote Robert Burton, 'so must his chaplain be: if he be papistical, his clerk must be so, or else be turned out.'[2] The bishop was legally bound to accept the patron's nominee unless he was manifestly scandalous in morals or knowledge. A bishop who objected was faced with a common-law writ of *Quare impedit*. The common-law courts were beginning to assert their jurisdiction over these matters, and the law 'admitteth of a very mean tolerable sufficiency in any clerk',

---

[1] J. Earle, *Microcosmographie* (1628), in J. Morley, *Character Writings of the 17th Century* (1891), p. 182. John Bruen of Bruen Stapelford used literally to *take* his tenants and neighbours, as well as all his servants, to church each Sunday. (W. Hinde, 'Life ... of John Bruen', quoted in *The Journal of Nicholas Assheton* (ed. F. R. Raines, Chetham Soc., 1848), p. 3.

[2] R. Burton, op. cit. i. 322; cf. Strype, *Whitgift*, ii. 12.

so a bishop had to be on very firm ground indeed before challenging a patron's nominee.[1] His role was becoming as formal as that of a dean and chapter faced with a royal *congé d'élire*.

The exact significance of lay patronage for the development of Puritanism has never been thoroughly studied: but certain facts are familiar enough. Richard Rich, founder of the great Rich dynasty, had been Chancellor of the Court of Augmentations in Henry VIII's reign, and he used his position to accumulate more church livings than are likely to have been held by any other single family. At his death in 1567 he held no fewer than thirty advowsons, mostly in Essex. They formed the basis of the great Warwick patronage, which in the seventeenth century helped to keep Essex firmly Puritan and parliamentarian, and spread over into Suffolk, Warwickshire, Leicestershire, and Northamptonshire.[2] Sir Nathaniel Bacon in Norfolk, in James I's reign, made it his business to get ministers who shared his Puritan sympathies for parishes round his estate.[3] In the following reign Sir Nathaniel Barnardiston, grandson of the Sir Richard Knightley who protected Martin Marprelate, used the family patronage to promote Puritans.[4]

Usher listed the names of some of these great families—Rich, Bacon, Grey, Knightley, Montagu, Hastings, Coke—who used their extensive patronage rights in this way.[5] To these we might add the Russell, Fiennes, Greville, Cope, Petre, Barrington, and Barnardiston families as obvious examples calling for further investigation. The local influences which kept Buckinghamshire so steadily radical in religion would also be worth studying.[6] One effect of this concentration of patronage was to increase the

[1] Strype, *Whitgift*, iii. 146; Cardwell, *History of Conferences* (1840), p. 191; ed. Cardwell, *Reformation of the Ecclesiastical Laws* (1850), pp. 59–61, 66; Doderidge, op. cit., pp. 2–3; W. Hughes, *The Parsons Law* (1641), ii. 55–64; Watson, op. cit., pp. 250–306. Cf. Coke's views, Notestein, Relf, and Simpson, op. cit. ii. 440.

[2] Newcourt, op. cit. ii, *passim*; P. Morant, *The History and Antiquities of the County of Essex* (1768), *passim*; C. Fell-Smith, *Mary Rich, Countess of Warwick (1625–1678)* (1901), pp. 198–213; H. Smith, *Ecclesiastical History of Essex under the Long Parliament and the Commonwealth* (n.d.), *passim*.

[3] Ed. H. W. Saunders, *Stiffkey Papers, 1580–1620*, Camden Miscellany, XVI. xvi. 194–7.

[4] S. Clarke, *The Lives of Sundry Eminent Persons in this Later Age* (1683), ii. 113.

[5] Usher, op. cit. i. 270.

[6] Fuller, *Church History*, ii. 5; cf. W. H. Summers, 'Some Documents in the State Papers relating to Beaconsfield, etc.', in *Records of Buckinghamshire* (Bucks. Architectural and Archaeological Soc.), vii. 97–114.

number of absentee patrons, to weaken the links between patron and congregation, and so to increase the tendency towards congregational independence. This tendency was deliberately fostered by patrons like Lord Brooke who encouraged congregations to suggest nominees for vacant livings.[1]

Also worthy of examination is the exercise of patronage by corporations. Usher gave Boston, Ipswich, Lincoln, Northampton, and Coventry as examples; Warwick, Bedford, St. Albans, Leeds, Gloucester, Newcastle, Norwich, King's Lynn, Yarmouth, Shrewsbury, and Plymouth might be added: there are no doubt many others. In addition there were the nine or ten livings to which the Lord Mayor and aldermen presented in the City, as well as four in Essex.[2] Corporations tended to be Puritan, or at least anti-Laudian: and in the sixteen-thirties battles royal raged over the right of presentation in Yarmouth, Shrewsbury, and Plymouth.[3] Apparently the ownership of advowsons by corporations was not nearly as extensive as their practice of appointing lecturers; but where such patronage existed it was of great political significance once the ruling urban groups had lost confidence in the government's conduct of affairs. In 1634, when Archbishop Neile consecrated St. John's chapel, Leeds, built at the expense of a local layman, he expressed anxiety at the arrangement whereby patronage was vested jointly in the corporation and the vicar of Leeds. He would have preferred the choice of minister to be left to himself; failing that, the vicar should have an absolute veto. The Archbishop was right to be worried: the first sermon preached

---

[1] S. Palmer, *Nonconformists' Memorial* (1775), i. 90; T. Powell, op. cit., p. 196.

[2] Usher, op. cit. i. 270–1; *C.S.P.D.,1637*, p. 393. Warwick corporation owned four advowsons (*V.C.H., Warwickshire*, iii. 68; Sir W. Dugdale, *Antiquities of Warwickshire*, 1730, i. 465). For Bedford, see J. Brown, *John Bunyan* (1928), p. 83; for St. Albans, see Newcourt, op. cit. i. 785; for Leeds, *V.C.H., Yorkshire*, iii. 58; for Gloucester, Soden, op. cit., pp. 237, 258; for Newcastle, Ornsby, op. cit. ii. 207–8; for Norwich, Blomefield, op. cit. iv. 381, 390–4; for King's Lynn, M. Keeler, *The Long Parliament* (1954), p. 361. For London, see Cambridge University Library MS. Mm. 6/61 (I owe this reference to the kindness of Mr. Lawrence Stone); Newcourt, op. cit. i. 236–566, *passim*; ii. 187–8; D. A. Williams, 'Puritanism in the City Government, 1610–40', in *The Guildhall Miscellany*, no. 4, p. 10.

[3] For Yarmouth, see J. Browne, *History of Congregationalism . . . in Norfolk and Suffolk* (1877), pp. 122–32; *Hist. MSS. Commission, Fourth Report*, p. 72. For Shrewsbury, *C.S.P.D., 1637–8*, pp. 58–59; *1638–9*, p. 209. For Plymouth, H. F. Whitfeld, *Plymouth and Devonport in Times of War and Peace* (1900), pp. 91–93.

by the curate whom the corporation chose was so unsatisfactory that the ecclesiastical authorities deprived him.[1]

But patronage by corporations offered some possibility of at least the more well-to-do members of congregations having a say in choosing their ministers. Edward Reyner, who was appointed rector of St. Peter's, Lincoln, in 1627, believed that he was called thither 'by the general vote of all the godly' in the city.[2] William Strode saw that patronage gave a chance to wealthy merchants to present Puritans. His Livebyhope spoke of

> The patronage of churches in sea-towns,
> Where popular choice maintains a faction
> Brought in with merchandise from foreign parts.[3]

III

A benefice was unlike other forms of freehold property in that it could not lawfully be sold by the incumbent. His estate was for his life only. At most he could lease the right to collect the emoluments of his living. The ultimate rights in the benefice, the advowson, belonged to the patron. The patron had his title by civil inheritance. He might sell or devise the right to present. 'Being their own, they may do with them as they list.'[4] Patronage was bought and sold like any other property right. There was a market in livings, even if not an entirely free market. Thomas Adams speaks of four to five years' purchase as the price of an advowson, though he had heard of as much as ten years' purchase being asked.[5] In 1632 two Northamptonshire livings were offered for sale to a college at three years' purchase. This seems to have been a bargain, especially if it was true, as was alleged, that both the incumbents were over fifty years of age.[6]

In some cases the advowson was held by the parish, as with fourteen London livings and St. Thomas à Becket, Chapel-en-le-Frith. At Chapel-en-le-Frith the rights of the inhabitants seem

---

[1] *V.C.H., Yorkshire*, iii. 58.

[2] E. Reyner, *Precepts for Christian Practice: or, the Rule of the New-Creature* (11th ed., 1658), Dedication; A. G. Matthews, *Calamy Revised* (1934), p. 408.

[3] W. Strode, *Poetical Works* (1907), p. 189. Such patronage, the speaker ('a Favourite') continued, 'were better taken to the crown'.

[4] H. Burton, op. cit., p. 31.

[5] T. Adams, *Workes* (1629), p. 1060.

[6] Ed. F. S. Boas, *The Diary of Thomas Crosfield* (1935), p. 60.

normally to have been exercised by the chief landowners; in London trustees often acted for the parish. At St. Mary Alderman-bury and St. Saviour's, Southwark, the advowson belonged to the select vestry; at St. Peter's, Leeds, to a group of trustees for the parish. Here was yet another influence making for congregational independence. Many City companies owned advowsons, in London and elsewhere, and they too were likely to be amenable to the wishes of congregations, or of their richer members. The Salters' Company were patrons of St. Swithin's, London Stone, and under them the parish claimed the privilege of electing its own minister.[1] But under Laud pressure was brought to bear on the companies. In 1635 the Grocers' Company were compelled to accept a royal nominee for St. Stephen's, Walbrook, after a minister recently appointed by them had been forced to resign. Three years later the Mercers were commanded by the crown to dismiss a lecturer whom they had appointed. They complied under protest, but presented him forthwith to a vicarage in their patronage.[2]

So, through lay patronage, divisions within the propertied class came to be reflected among the rank and file clergy. One section of the patron class, Professor Haller has shown, was 'growing into something like a party, conscious of interests it had to protect and extend'; it was also conscious of the importance of parsons in 'the work of guiding and forming the public opinion of a new day'.[3] Under Laud the hierarchy was beginning a serious counter-attack.

In the seventeenth century, when the Earl of Warwick presented an Edmund Calamy, a Hugh Peter, or a John Owen to his livings, and when Plymouth corporation had to be prohibited from appointing Edmund Ford, recently sent down from Oxford for seditious preaching, the political use of patronage is clear.[4] In the

[1] Cambridge University MS. Mm 6/61; W. B. Bunting, *The Parish Church of St. Thomas à Becket, Chapel-en-le-Frith* (1925), pp. 62–75; S. and B. Webb, *The Parish and the County* (1906), p. 34; R. Thoresby, *Vicaria Leodiensis* (1724), pp. 51–53, 60–63, 210–13; Matthews, *Calamy Revised*, p. 97; *Walker Revised* (1948), p. 55; J. G. Whitebrook, 'The Two John Sheffields', in *Transactions of the Congregational History Soc.* xi, no. 5, 218.

[2] *Calendar of Court Minutes of the Grocers' Company, 1616–40*, pp. 883–4; Repositories of the Acts of the Court of the Mercers' Company, 1637–41, f. 43. I owe these references to the kindness of Dr. Valerie Pearl. Cf. also *C.S.P.D., 1633–4*, p. 444.

[3] Haller, *The Rise of Puritanism* (1938), pp. 39–40.

[4] Palmer, op. cit. i. 74, 153; Stearns, op. cit., pp. 29–30; Prynne, *Canterburies Doome* (1646), pp. 174–6. Not only was Plymouth forbidden to elect Ford, but the Bishop of Exeter was also forbidden by the government to admit him as vicar or

sixteenth century the extension of patronage to Puritan ministers was probably often merely a defensive measure by protestant patrons: for at the beginning of Elizabeth's reign it seems clear that a majority of the greater landowners was hostile to the new religion. Only 'men meaner in substance' than in Mary's reign could, it was thought, be trusted as J.P.s.[1] But slowly, under steady pressure from parliament, the balance began to tip. An act of 1606 (3 Jac. I, c. 5) deprived papist patrons of their rights of presentation, and transferred them to Oxford and Cambridge. Many recusants, it is true, continued to present after this date.[2] Henry Burton took it for granted that they sold their rights of presentation, in order to obtain money for the maintenance of their own priests.[3] Certainly they could hardly be expected to take great pains to nominate the best available candidate. The government, reluctant to enforce the laws against recusants, turned a blind eye to such practices. It was consistently trying to preserve a balance. But the trend of development was against it.

Nevertheless, although the number of Puritan patrons and ministers slowly grew, they long remained a small minority. In London, where lay Puritanism was strongest, 60 out of 107 livings were in the gift of bishops, deans and chapters, and colleges. The crown exercised patronage rights in another sixteen parishes, and peers in five. Thus a bare quarter of the City livings, at most, were in the gift of laymen likely to be sympathetic to Puritanism, which helps to explain the paucity of Puritan ministers before 1640.[4] Outside London there is evidence that, on occasion at least, the patronage of deans and chapters might in fact be exercised by or at the nomination of the crown.[5] A prelate like the Bishop of Lincoln, with 150 livings at his disposal, even though some of them were of small value, enjoyed a position of influence which

---

lecturer even if he was elected; and ultimately the town was forced to surrender its patronage rights to the crown. Cf. *MSS. of the Earl of Westmorland and others* (Hist. MSS. Commission), p. 558. The corporation recovered its rights in 1641 (*Hist. MSS. Commission, Ninth Report, Appendix*, i. 281). For Ford's later career, see W. G. Hoskins and H. P. R. Finberg, *Devonshire Studies* (1952), pp. 359–72.

[1] G. Burnet, *History of the Reformation* (1825), iv. 393; C. Read, *Mr. Secretary Cecil and Queen Elizabeth* (1955), pp. 321, 489.

[2] Sir C. E. Mallet, *History of the University of Oxford* (1924–7), i. 238; G. H. Ryan and L. J. Redstone, *Timperley of Hintlesham* (1931), p. 133.

[3] H. Burton, op. cit., pp. 113–14.

[4] Newcourt, op. cit. i. 236–566, *passim*; D. A. Williams, op. cit., p. 10.

[5] *V.C.H., Worcestershire*, ii. 58–59.

it is difficult to measure.[1] The Bishop and Dean and Chapter of Hereford between them had patronage rights in a hundred churches and chapels in the county of Hereford. They did not use these rights to promote preaching, if we are to believe a correspondent who wrote to Sir Robert Harley in August 1641. For he estimated that there were only 'twenty constant preachers' in the shire, and 'never a one of the twenty' had been presented by the Bishop or the Dean and Chapter. If the kingdom were surveyed, he continued, similar information would probably come in from some if not all other counties. For 'the fault is not personal but official, and to redress [it] the government must be set upon a new base'.[2]

Even if not in the interests of preaching, advowsons were eagerly sought after by some ecclesiastical corporations. Colleges like Emmanuel at Cambridge and Queen's at Oxford were trying in the sixteen-twenties to increase the number of their livings. The seventeenth-century biographer of John Preston, Master of Emmanuel, is brutally frank in his account of the motives which actuated the Fellows of Cambridge's most Puritan college. They wanted rich livings for the same reason as they wanted 'opportunities to live in noblemen's houses' and lectureships in which they could 'make themselves known unto such as had it in their power to prefer them'.[3] Most historians would shrink from such naïvely economic explanations of a ministerial calling.

All over the country, then, the patronage system produced a majority of ministers whose political outlook, if they had one of their own, we should expect to be conservative. Even where the patron was a radical, he was still a propertied radical. 'Gentlemen', Selden observed, 'have ever been more temperate in their religion than the common people, as having more reason, the others running in a hurry.'[4] So the ecclesiastical battle was fought within a confined space: virtually no ministers with really democratic views won possession of a pulpit from which they could exert wide influence before 1640. One of the few who did was the Rev. Peter Simon of the Forest of Dean, who in 1631 was accused of preaching the equality of all mankind. He owed

---

[1] Browne Willis, op. cit. ii. 39.
[2] *MSS. of the Duke of Portland* (Hist. MSS. Commission), iii. 79.
[3] Ball, op. cit., pp. 81–84, 162–4; Boas, op. cit., p. xix.
[4] Selden, *Table Talk*, p. 77. See pp. 71–72 below.

his presentation not to a local gentleman, but to the Haber-dashers' Company of London.[1]

No doubt many ministers and rank and file Puritans agreed with Udall in thinking that patronage was a work of antichrist:[2] but if Satan was to be cast out of the English church at all, the aid of Beelzebub was clearly necessary. For what, after all, were the alternatives to presentation by laymen? They were episcopal nomination or popular election. The bishops could never tolerate the latter: the opposition would never allow the former. The gentry would cling on to their inheritance, their advowsons and impropriations. For both sides acceptance of the patronage system was the lesser evil: like the Tudor monarchy itself, and like the royal supremacy, the continuance of lay patronage was the product of tensions between contending forces. When Laud began to challenge the compromise, there followed at once a united onslaught on the hierarchy. Only after the overthrow of bishops were the divisions between the two wings of Parliament's supporters revealed; and then the struggle was waged, among other things, over the demand for the abolition of lay patronage and its replacement by congregational election of ministers.

'What the nobles are to politics, that are the priests to religion', declared Buckle.[3] Any established priesthood tends to be con-servative, to defend the established order. From the end of the sixteenth century nobility and clergy were on the defensive and rallied to each other's support. The monarchy interested itself in maintaining the prestige of both. A proclamation of June 1626 was directed against all who should write or speak anything against temporal peers or spiritual men.[4] But until Laud's advent the parson continued to be very much the junior partner, and he got short shrift if he forgot it.[5]

---

[1] See pp. 268–9 below.

[2] J. Udall, *A Demonstration of Discipline* (ed. Arber, 1880), pp. 29–30. Bancroft (if it is he) quoted the two *Admonitions to Parliament* to illustrate the point that presbyterianism threatened the rights of patrons (*Tracts ascribed to Richard Bancroft*, ed. A. Peel, 1953, p. 44).

[3] T. H. Buckle, *History of Civilization in England* (World's Classics), ii. 109. The whole passage, pp. 108–16, is interesting.

[4] Boas, op. cit., p. 4. This proclamation is not recorded in R. Steele, *A Bibliography of Royal Proclamations, . . . 1485–1714,* 2 vols. (1910), unless the diarist has given a garbled account of No. 1473, 'A Proclamation for the establishing of the Peace and Quiet of the Church of England,' which is to be found at length in Rushworth, op. cit. i. 412.

[5] See below, pp. 215–16, 219–23.

IV

In such a society it was inevitable that the minister should dance
to the tune called by the patron, and that other considerations than
purely religious should enter into relations between them. Hall,
before he was a bishop, described feelingly how

> They may feed with words, and live by air,
> That climb to honour by the pulpit's stair;
> Sit seven years pining in an anchore's chair
> To win some patched shreds of minivere;
> And seven more plod at a patron's tail
> To get a gelded chapel's cheaper sale.[1]

Evidence for bad financial treatment of ministers by corrupt or
capricious patrons is quoted in Chapter IX. The most outrageous
practice was that of patrons who, 'wanting for the present a good
chapman', put a minister in to serve the cure until a better bargain
could be driven with someone else. The minister was compelled
to give a bond that he would resign at three or six months' notice,
like a servant. 'By this device the patron holds the incumbent in
miserable servitude, as being his tenant at will. . . . The incumbent
is bound not to reprove anything his good master doth or saith,
but must say Amen to all, or else farewell all.' But cases in the
reigns of James I and Charles I established the lawfulness of such
bonds; and these precedents were followed by the common-
law courts.[2]

Thomas Adams spoke of the patrons' 'poor servitors (ashamed
I am to call them so) the vicars'.[3] For in countless ways the parson
lay at the mercy of the squire. An example may be given from the
recusant family of Timperley in Suffolk. In 1586 Thomas Timperley (who sympathized with the old religion but never openly
declared his allegiance to it) presented John Pagett to the rectory
of the family manor of Hintlesham. In 1606, as we have seen,
recusants were deprived of the right to present. In 1608 recusancy
proceedings were started against Nicholas Timperley, son of the

---

[1] Joseph Hall, *Satires*, book iv, satire 2, in *Works* (1839), xii. 222. Minivere was
a kind of fur used as lining and trimming, here presumably of an academic hood.
In May 1627 Chief Justice Hyde, it was said, 'will rather quit his minivere than
subscribe' to the forced loan (Knowler, op. cit. i. 38).

[2] H. Burton, op. cit., pp. 42–43; Gibson, op. cit., p. 842; *Harleian Miscellany*
(1808), i. 496; cf. *C.S.P.D.*, *1639*, p. 176.

[3] Adams, op. cit., p. 38.

now deceased Thomas. Nicholas thereupon took Pagett to the Bishop of Norwich, and the rector swore that his patron was no recusant. The Bishop got the recusancy proceedings stayed. It is difficult not to believe that, as was afterwards alleged, the rector and his patron had been in a conspiracy together.[1] 'He had need be a bold man', said the royalist Jeremy Taylor, 'that shall tell his patron he is going to hell.'[2]

More frequent than outright sale of the perpetual inheritance of rights of patronage was *ad hoc* sale of the right of next presentation. The former type of sale was rare 'in these parts', the Bishop of Chester reported in 1639: he knew only of Wigan (one of the wealthiest parsonages in England) which had recently changed hands for £1,010. The Bishop estimated Wigan as worth £570 a year clear, but he was concerned to minimize its value.[3] The price of the right of next presentation—i.e. of the right to select a name for the patron to nominate to the bishop—would naturally vary with the age and expectation of life of the incumbent.

The transaction was perfectly legal at common law, but the church courts disliked it. It inevitably led to simony, since most purchasers of a right of presentation would be making an investment. In 1627, for instance, Tobias Crispe was deprived by the church courts of the rectory of Newington Butts on account of a simoniacal contract. He had been presented only a few months earlier by a group who had leased the presentation from the Bishop of Worcester.[4] A really enterprising patron might sell the next presentation but one as well.[5] The abolition of such practices was often discussed.[6] It became one of the battlegrounds in the war over jurisdiction. In 1638 the High Commission quashed a sale of the right of presentation. It had been transferred ten years earlier by the patron to a Fellow of a Cambridge college, and

---

[1] Ryan and Redstone, op. cit., pp. 53–54.

[2] J. Taylor, *Works* (1836), i. 446; cf. p. 849. How different was the conception of discipline held, in theory at least, by a Calvin or a Knox!

[3] *C.S.P.D., 1638–9*, p. 523; Bridgeman, op. cit., pp. 416–18, 483. There was some wild talk next year of £5,000 being offered for this advowson, five years' purchase on an estimated value of £1,000 a year.

[4] Lysons, op. cit. i. 394.

[5] H. J. Wilkins, *A Copy of the Deed of the Sale of the next Presentation but one to Henbury Vicarage . . . in A.D. 1678* (1909), pp. 3–7.

[6] Cardwell, *Synodalia*, p. 504; Strype, *Whitgift*, ii. 379; Doderidge, op. cit., pp. 2, 64–65; Powell, op. cit., p. 197. Powell had hoped to draw up a list of benefices and their patrons for the use of would-be applicants; but he found that it would be an impossible task without the co-operation of the bishops.

by him sold for £650. The purchaser also bought off a rival for £260.[1]

By purchasing the right of next presentation to a living, a successful business man or yeoman could nominate his son or other relative, 'prove he at all adventure fit or unfit, good or bad, scholar or man'.[2] So the practice opened a door into the church to children of those who had money but no social influence. A minister might thus enable his son to succeed him in his cure. This was done by a Puritan like Walter Hornby no less than by a royalist like William Pelsant.[3] Similarly a parish by leasing the presentation might hope to nominate its own minister. But so long as episcopal approbation was needed, such devices offered only slight opportunity for Puritans to enter the church. With the abolition of the hierarchy, and different conditions of entry into the ministry, the practice of sale of next presentation seems to have lapsed during the Interregnum, though it revived after 1660.[4]

'Patrons nowadays', it was stated in 1584, 'search not the universities for a most fit pastor, but they post up and down the country for a most gainful chapman. He that hath the biggest purse to pay largely, not he that hath the best gift to preach learnedly, is presented.' It was hard, Convocation complained two years later, 'to wring a free presentation from a lay patron.'[5] 'You do well', said a lawyer to a patron in *The Return from Parnassus* (1601 or 1602), 'to bestow your living upon such an one as will be content to share, and on Sunday to say nothing.'[6] The next age, observed Malevole in Marston's *The Malcontent* (1604), could not know the sin of simony only 'because (thanks to some churchmen) our age will leave them nothing to sin with'.[7] Men hunted after the purchase of patronage, Henry Burton noted, as a good investment.[8] When Sir Thomas Temple's younger son went into the church, £1,200 was invested in the purchase of the

---

[1] *C.S.P.D.*, *1637–8*, p. 497.

[2] H. Burton, op. cit., p. 38; Watson, op. cit., pp. 35–37. For a form of grant of next presentation, see Ecton, op. cit., pp. 455–7; for examples, see C. W. Foster, *Lincoln Episcopal Records*, *1571–84* (Canterbury and York Soc., 1913), pp. 241–56.

[3] Palmer, op. cit. ii. 230; *C.S.P.D.*, *1639*, p. 111; Matthews, *Walker Revised*, pp. 9, 241. [4] Z. Cawdrey, *A Discourse of Patronage* (1675), p. 36.

[5] *The Decades of Henry Bullinger* (Parker Soc. 1849), I. i. 7 (Preface by translator).

[6] *The Return from Parnassus, or the Scourge of Simony*, Act·III, scene 2; cf. Act II, scenes 2 and 3.

[7] Ed. H. H. Wood, *The Plays of John Marston* (1934–9), i. 150.

[8] H. Burton, op. cit., p. 31.

advowson of Bourton-on-the-Water.¹ Simony was a likely consequence of such expenditure, especially given the 'conscienceless and wicked patrons, of which sort', Hooker tells us, 'the swarms are too great in the church of England'.²

There might be financial agreements between patron and prospective incumbent which did not amount to direct sale. The Lambeth Articles of 1561 threatened with deprivation any parson who made a secret compact for alienation of the glebe, to forgive the patron's tithes, or other simoniacal agreement. But only the minister could be put on oath in such cases, not the patron, which proved a fatal weakness.³ A minister could clear himself of accusations of simony before the High Commission by the medieval practice of finding compurgators to swear for him.⁴ From 1589 (31 Eliz., c. 6) causes involving simony could be taken before the common-law courts, although the church courts did not lose their right to try them.

'*Omnia erant venalia*', moaned Archbishop Parker of the diocese of Norwich in 1567; 'the best of the county, not under the degree of knights, were infected with this sore, so far that some one knight had four or five, some seven or eight benefices clouted together, fleecing them all.'⁵ 'If there be an insufficient man', wrote Bishop Cooper, 'or a corrupt person within two shires of them, whom they [patrons] think they can draw to any composition for their own benefit, they will by one means or another find him out', and get him into the benefice by some legal shift or other, even if the bishop demurred.⁶ Lay patrons might have replied to Parker and Cooper that they were only following the example of the prelates. Hooker, choosing his words gingerly, could not suspect simoniacal corruption 'to be amongst men of so great place' as the bishops. 'So often they do not, I trust,

¹ E. F. Gay, 'The Temples of Stowe and their debts', in *Huntington Library Quarterly*, ii, no. 4. 405–6. Like so many of Sir Thomas's investments, this one failed to return the expected dividends: we find this son in 1643 as a captain of parliamentary horse.

² Hooker, *Works*, iii. 384.

³ Cardwell, *Documentary Annals*, i. 265; *Synodalia*, pp. 508–9, 270. Cf. *The Reformation of the Ecclesiastical Laws*, pp. 85–87.

⁴ *C.S.P.D.*, *1634–5*, pp. 115–16.

⁵ W. P. M. Kennedy, *Elizabethan Episcopal Administration* (1924), i. cxlvii–cli. Mr. Kennedy gives evidence of simoniacal practices. There were complaints of 'embezzled glebe' and ruined parsonages from Norwich diocese during Sir Nathaniel Brent's visitation in 1635 (Gardiner, *History of England, 1603–42*, 1883–4, viii. 109).

⁶ Cooper, op. cit., p. 110.

offend by sale, as by unadvised gift, . . . a fault nowhere so hurtful as in bestowing places of jurisdiction and in furnishing cathedral churches.'[1]

The Anglican apologist's acquittal of the fathers of his church had been far from absolute. A generation later the Puritan exile, William Ames, was less mincing in his words. 'Many conformable men will . . . swear', he testified, 'that nothing hath hindered them all their days from benefices, and kept them in curateships, but only the general abuse of simony. Every page and lackey at the court, and many scriveners, can tell how much this and that bishop or dean gave to such or such a Buckingham; and how much the said bishop received from his under-officers and others by him promoted. Neither', he added like Hooker, 'is all simony in buying of benefices and bishoprics. Selling of visitations . . . is a usual practice of our prelates. . . .'[2] It was in fact charged against Bishop Wren at his impeachment.[3] In 1633 it was being said (correctly) in the city of Salisbury that their Dean and Chapter were selling livings, though they denied having sold direct to a minister.[4]

Whether or not ecclesiastical patrons were as bad, certainly lay patrons remained unreformed. In 1641 Mr. George Catesby, 'one that will talk zealously for religion', was accused by a pamphleteer of having sold the living of Acton, Northants., to two successive scandalous ministers, and of intending to sell it again, 'the old incumbent being hurt and sickly'. 'When benefices are exposed to sale', our source commented virtuously, 'the choice of a minister can never be good, for chapmen that buy in this kind are commonly obnoxious men, or none of the best sort.'[5]

Thomas Adams and Henry Burton in the sixteen-twenties described precisely such bargains as were forbidden by the Lambeth Articles of 1561 and by 31 Eliz., c. 6. Their allegations are confirmed by a minister's precise account of requests made to

---

[1] Hooker, *Works*, iii. 385.

[2] Ames, op. cit., p. 419. Scriveners were presumably mentioned as money-lenders from whom prospective simoniacal purchasers borrowed the wherewithal. Cf. Ornsby, op. cit. i. 208, where the Bishop of Durham virtually admitted that his Dean had obtained his office by simony. There would seem to be substance in the more general allegations of Sir A. Weldon (op. cit., pp. 119–20).

[3] Rushworth, op. cit. iv. 354.

[4] *C.S.P.D., 1633–4*, p. 505; *Hist. MSS. Commission, Fourth Report*, p. 129; *Wiltshire Notes and Queries*, i. 19.

[5] [Anon.], *A Certificate from Northamptonshire* (1641), pp. 12–13.

him by his patron in 1627. He was asked to sign a promise (i) either to reside himself or to appoint a curate whom his patron should approve; (ii) to allow the clerk to live in a house built upon the glebe; and (iii) to let an estate in reversion of a tenement belonging to the parsonage, to a tenant named by the patron. The minister, according to his own account, rejected such suggestions with virtuous indignation; nevertheless, he was being accused of simony a few years later.[1]

Adams and Burton list a number of evasive devices adopted by ministers and patrons. These included 'matrimonial simony'—obtaining a benefice at the price of marrying a daughter or kinswoman of the patron, where one would have thought the offence brought its own punishment; dealing through a factor or servant, or by ostensible purchase of some other commodity; giving a bond to resign at short notice if the patron can find a better customer; giving a lease, fine, or rent to the patron, or releasing him from tithes. Such practices were, according to Burton, almost universal: they were very difficult to detect or punish, if indeed the bishops' hands had been clean, and if they could have afforded to attack the landowners as a class.[2] Burton wanted the oath against simony to be administered to patrons as well as to ministers.[3]

Sir Benjamin Rudyerd moved in the Commons in 1621 that some course might be taken for bridling covetous, presumptuous patrons, 'who dare sell that to God which was his own before'. Like Burton, he wanted a law against simony in patrons as well as in ministers; and he asked cogently 'How can such a patron ever be edified by such a pastor, whom he knows to have made shipwreck of his conscience by breaking his oath? This will continually non-preach whatsoever he can preach afterward.'[4]

In 1634 the vicar of Shottesbrook, Berks., was accused before the High Commission of simony for having promised before

---

[1] 'Laudian Documents', in *Collectanea II* (Somerset Record Soc., 1928), pp. 206–7.

[2] H. Burton, op. cit., pp. 42–43, 38, 102, 115; Adams, op. cit., p. 79. In the Puritan *Viewe of the State of the Clargie within the Countie of Essex*, which makes every possible allegation against ministers whom its authors dislike, only 6 of 106 clerical bad characters are accused of simony.

[3] H. Burton, op. cit., p. 109. Burton added in his *Conclusion* (1624–?5) that the House of Commons had unanimously voted that this should be done; he expressed his confidence that the Lords would agree (sig. 2ᵛ). I have not found confirmation of this story.

[4] Notestein, Relf, and Simpson, op. cit. iv. 343–4.

presentation to make his patron a lease of tithes below the true value. But he was acquitted, since contract before presentation could not be proved, 'the law being favourable in that case where the incumbent, finding his patron weak in estate, may relieve him in case of necessity'—comfortable law for patrons.[1] There must have been many cases where 'indiscreet covetousness' led clergymen, in Calibute Downing's agreeable phrase, 'to make no distinction betwixt free and friendly compositions with a bountiful patron and sacrilege'.[2] Such distinctions were indeed difficult to draw. The notorious fact that 'he which have money, or the letter of some great man, or favour by other means' could always get himself a benefice, 'and so the guides of our souls are appointed unto us without our advice and counsel', was one of the stock arguments by which separatists demonstrated the extreme corruption of the English church, in which 'other lords besides Christ do rule over us'.[3] And those who bought benefices, it was argued in the Commons in 1621, were those who already had other livings;[4] so the abolition of sale and purchase would also be a blow against pluralism.

V

Suits concerning patronage were decided at common law. In legal disputes about the right to present, it is treated as a purely economic matter; patronage may be compounded for like any other piece of property.[5] This property right interfered very seriously with any project of ecclesiastical reorganization, such as Laud's scheme for enriching bishoprics by the perpetual annexation of livings *in commendam*.[6] The major problem of the church of the old régime, all would have agreed, was that most of the livings were not adequate to maintain a learned clergyman. It was

---

[1] *C.S.P.D., 1634–5*, p. 336. Cf. ibid., *1635–6*, pp. 520–1, where a minister was acquitted on a charge of simony by the same court, which stated its belief that the action had been brought by persons ill-affected to the church.

[2] Calibute Downing, *A Discourse of the State-Ecclesiasticall of this Kingdome, in relation to the Civill* (2nd ed., 1634), p. 102.

[3] Robert Harrison, *A Little Treatise uppon the firste Verse of the 122 Psalm*, in *The Writings of Robert Harrison and Robert Browne*, pp. 86–87. See also ibid., p. 534: this passage was one of those which worried the government.

[4] Notestein, Relf, and Simpson, op. cit. iv. 344. See below, p. 221.

[5] See, for example, *The Diary of Sir Henry Slingsby* (ed. D. Parsons, 1836), pp. 37–38.

[6] See pp. 312, 316–17 below.

difficult to persuade a lay rector to augment a living; the church had no funds available. One solution, recommended by Bacon, was the union of parishes. Bancroft joined a few; but here again the rights of patrons stood in the way. 'The thing is not in the bishop's authority, nor possible for him to do. Every parish hath a sundry patron, which will never be brought to agree to that purpose, and to forgo their patrimony and heritage.' And it would arouse too much opposition for it to be possible to proceed by legislation.[1] So pluralism and dumb dogs remained.

Thus the property rights of lay patrons stood in the way of that reform of the church which the Puritans claimed most to wish to see. Convocation could not touch the title of patrons, Ames assured one of them, since they held it 'by civil inheritance'.[2] But then how was reform to come? Parliament was not likely to tamper with the property of the gentry. Lay patrons could balk the reforming schemes of the hierarchy. It remained to be seen whether they and their Puritan allies could agree on their own plan of reform.

Under Laud's influence some irritating scratching of the surface went on. In 1632 Charles had ordered Abbott and all the bishops to ascertain what presentations had been made since 1588 by other laymen to livings rightfully in crown patronage. Bishops were to be careful henceforth to admit no minister until they had made sure that the living was not in the king's gift.[3] Laud sent visitors into parishes to suspend Puritan ministers, by whomsoever presented. It does not appear that this first attempt was very successful; but the threat to the rights of patrons was too serious to be ignored.[4] Men might suspect that the bishops interfered with patronage rights in order to give livings to men of like sentiments with themselves rather than in the interests of reform. Thus Bishop Pierce of Bath and Wells collated his son to a living of which Sir Francis Popham claimed to be the patron. One of the articles of impeachment against Bishop Wren alleged that 'he hath very much oppressed divers patrons of churches, by admitting, without

---

[1] Bacon, *Works*, x. 121, 124; Usher, op. cit. i. 337–9, ii. 53, 263–6; Cooper, op. cit., p. 87.

[2] Ames, op. cit., p. 418.

[3] Lambeth MS. 943, f. 333; *C.S.P.D., 1631–3*, pp. 376, 383–4. A number of concealed vicarages were discovered, especially in the diocese of Lincoln (ibid., pp. 511, 523).

[4] H. R. Trevor-Roper, *Archbishop Laud* (1940), p. 194.

any colour of title, his own chaplains, and others whom he affected, into livings which became void within his diocese; unjustly enforcing the true and right patrons to long and chargeable suits to evict such incumbents and to recover their own right'.[1]

At Christmas 1635 it was even rumoured in Oxford common rooms that the king would take all ecclesiastical patronage into his own hands (except that of bishops and colleges) because of the many corruptions and abuses committed by lay patrons. But the Fellow of Queen's who noted the story in his diary added sadly, 'This is supposed too good to be true',[2] and he was right. Nevertheless, it was remembered against Laud in the Long Parliament 'that he had injured divers gentlemen in their patronages'.[3] Neither the hierarchy nor Parliament could tackle the abuse of patronage in a root and branch way.

The rights of patrons were defended both by those who wished to nominate Puritan ministers for the benefit of parishioners' souls, and by those who wished to exploit patronage for the benefit of their own pockets. God and Mammon were once again in alliance against the Laudians' attempt to impose their type of uniformity. Their property rights enabled the opposition gentry to frustrate episcopal plans for reorganization; but these same rights prevented their undertaking a drastic reorganization of their own when bishops had been overthrown. Patronage was too deeply embedded in the social and economic life of the time.

VI

So there was much ambivalence in the Puritan attitude towards patronage. The rights of patrons created a dependence of parson on squire of which Puritan disciplinarians could not approve; and they were an obstacle to national ecclesiastical reorganization. Yet the political support of a group of lay patrons was essential before 1640. After the civil war the crown, the hierarchy, and papist and royalist patrons lost their rights, as did the universities until they had been purged. Thus control of patronage was removed from

---

[1] *C.S.P.D., 1637*, p. 263; Rushworth, op. cit. iv. 354. Popham was an opposition member of the Long Parliament. For Wren and Pierce see p. 223 below.

[2] Boas, op. cit., p. 82.

[3] Ed. A. H. A. Hamilton, *Notebook of Sir John Northcote* (1877) p. 111.

the enemies of Parliament, from all defenders of the old order.
Beyond these negative steps agreement proved impossible. The
retention of patronage, or its abolition and replacement by popular
election, remained a burning issue between right and left throughout the revolution. It survived to split the radical wing of the
parliamentarians in the Barebones Parliament.

For the retention of patronage seemed to the conservatives a
social matter of the first importance. Prynne, defending the
patronage system, put it like this. Patrons were

commonly of good quality and better able to judge and make choice of
fitting ministers than the people. . . . The generality of the parishioners
and people of most parishes throughout England are so ignorant,
.vicious, irreligious, injudicious, profane, neglectful of God's public
ordinances and enemies to all soul-searching, soul-saving ministers,
who would seriously reprove and withdraw them from their sins and
evil courses, that we may sooner find a hundred conscientious, religious,
godly patrons, careful to present, protect and encourage such ministers,
than one such parish wherein the generality and swaying part of the
people are so well-affected and qualified as such patrons.[1]

In 1587 Convocation had thought that 'the common sort of
men' were inflamed with great hatred against the ministers of the
church.[2] Fifty-four years later their opening proceedings were
graced by a sermon in which Laud's protégé, Dr. Turner, took as
his text the words: 'Behold, I send you forth as sheep in the midst
of wolves: be ye therefore wise as serpents, and harmless as
doves.'[3] Prynne's outspoken comments suggest that the popular
attitude still had not changed, and help us to understand why, for
the radical sects, the parson remained throughout the revolutionary period public enemy no. 1. For the same reasons there was a
natural alliance between parsons and squires anxious to 'discipline' the lower orders into virtue. There could be no democracy
in England until ministers were dependent on congregations, not
nominated by the gentry or the government; until the propaganda
monopoly of the state church (whether Laudian, presbyterian,
or Cromwellian) had been overthrown. The Leveller and Quaker
onslaught on tithes and hireling priests was motivated by religion
and politics far more than by economics: the ministers' public

---

[1] Prynne, *Jus Patronatus*, p. 28.
[2] Strype, *Whitgift*, i. 500; cf. Cooper, op. cit., pp. 102–3.
[3] Nalson, op. cit. i. 357. The text is from Matthew, x. 16.

maintenance was essential to the continuing power of the gentry. The successive withdrawals of the protectorate government from its announced intention of abolishing tithes are symbolic of its compromise with the landed class, of its acceptance of the fact that the revolution was over.[1] In 1660 bishops were brought back to safeguard a national church, as king and House of Lords were to safeguard the common law. One may suspect that the gentry's appreciation of the economic and political importance of church and law, learned during the revolutionary decades, had at least as much to do with these restorations as abstract royalist or episcopalian sentiment.

[1] Cf. pp. 166–7, 298 below.

PART II

Iscariot's Purse

Of the maintenance of our Saviour and his Apostles, we read only that they had a purse (which was carried by Judas Iscariot).

THOMAS HOBBES, *Leviathan* (Everyman ed.), p. 292

V

TITHES

It is felt to be a great indignity that tithes are rendered each year
to parochial ministers by the poor and labouring peasantry,
whilst wealthy merchants and men abounding in learning
and skill contribute practically nothing to the necessities of the
ministry; especially since the latter stand in no less need of the
services of the clergy than do the peasants.

The Reformation of the Ecclesiastical Laws (1571), pp. 128–9

One man pleads he is to pay nothing to a minister, because the
Pope has given him a dispensation, and made his land tithe-free.
Another man saith he hath a prescription to pay but a penny
(it may be) for the value of a shilling. Another saith he hath
converted his lands into pastures, and hath by his artifice so
ordered it that little is due for tithes. Another saith he dwells
in a city or market town, and hath no land, though it's like
he gains more by trade than ten poor countrymen that pay tithes
do by their lands. Another saith he pays tithe to an impropriator,
and he cannot afford to pay both him and a minister. . . . The rich
generally pay little, and the poor husbandman bears the burden.

ANTHONY PEARSON
The Great Case of Tithes (1657, ed. of 1754), p. 64

I

THE system of appropriating 10 per cent. of the produce of
the community to the maintenance of a priest is of great
antiquity. It existed not only among the Jews, but also in
many pagan tribes. As Selden reminded his readers, there were
tithes in England before the introduction of Christianity.[1] Tithes,
originally paid in kind, presuppose a subsistence economy, and
a conception of the priest as the servant of the community, performing valued functions on its behalf. From the early Middle
Ages both laymen and monasteries had tried to divert tithes to
their own uses. But as production for the market disintegrated the

[1] Selden, *History of Tithes*, in *Works* (1776), iii. 1089 sqq., 1214.

village community, tithe disputes arose which were different in kind from those arising from the traditional reluctance of laymen to pay tithes, or the traditional desire of the rich to appropriate them.

Tithes could be divided in two ways. First, into predial, mixed and personal; secondly into great and small. Predial tithes were due from 'that which doth arise and grow by reason and virtue of the grounds, as fruits [including grain, grass and hay] and increase of beasts, fishes and fowls'. Personal tithes were due from 'lawful and honest commodity obtained and procured by art, science and the manual occupation of some person'. They were to be paid at the rate of one-tenth of clear gains, after expenses had been deducted.[1] Mixed tithes came largely from the produce of livestock—milk, cheese, wool.

Great tithes, those which went to the rector, normally comprehended tithes due from corn, hay, and wood; small tithes, due by endowment or prescription to the vicar where there was one, arose from all other predial tithes, plus mixed and personal tithes. The division between great and small tithes might be varied by local custom—e.g. where a crop that would normally have yielded small tithes became the main crop of the parish, the rector might demand that it pay great tithes; and in one quite exceptional case the great tithes were paid to the vicar.[2] Small tithes were easier for the vicar, the man on the spot, to collect than for an absentee rector or his agents: amicable personal relations meant a great deal. But such relations came under increasing strain during our period.

Production in medieval society was overwhelmingly rural, and the products—the fruits of the earth, the increase of flocks—were visible, measurable, difficult to hide. Men evaded payment of tithes, naturally: but the principle involved was clear and comprehensible. God sent a natural increase: this was divided physically into ten parts, at the lambing season and at harvest; and one of these parts went to the priest. Increase of flocks was a little more difficult to tithe than the fruits of the earth, since ten were not always born at a litter; but custom established simple con-

---

[1] [Anon.], *Tithes and oblations According to the Lawes established in the Church of England* (1595), p. 6; H. Rolle, *Un Abridgment des Plusieurs Cases et Resolutions del Common Ley* (1668), i. 656.

[2] H. Smith, op. cit., p. 259.

ventions, such as that tithe became due at the sixth or seventh animal or bird, and that the minister should give a penny or a halfpenny 'change' for each beast when the number was below ten.[1] At all events the facts about what had been produced were, in an agricultural community, rarely in doubt. Similarly, although it was impossible to be quite sure that an artisan who kept no books was fairly tithed, a certain rough justice was possible in a small community, where everybody knew about everybody else's business. The inhabitants of towns may have been under-assessed to tithe; but their share in the total production of medieval England was so small that an error here was statistically insignificant. (It is, however, worth noting that the lead in opposition to payment of personal tithes, tithes on business profits, came from urban groups like the heretical Waldenses. The early Dominicans and Franciscans also opposed the payment of personal tithes to parochial clergy, no doubt not without hope of securing part for themselves.)[2]

In England we hear complaints of neglect to pay personal tithes in London from the beginning of the fourteenth century. The causes at work include poverty, social unrest, preaching by and confession to friars, anti-clericalism, heresy, the encroachments of the common law.[3] Wyclif thought that tithes should be withheld from non-residents, a view shared by John Knox, and by the English Parliament of 1576.[4] In the fourteen-twenties William Russell of Greyfriars, London, taught that personal tithes should not be compulsorily paid to the parish priest. Instead, an equivalent sum should be spent on the poor, *at the discretion of the payer*. Russell was naturally excommunicated, but his ideas were too attractive to die with him. In Henry VIII's reign the heretic Richard Hunne thought tithes were 'never ordained to be, saving only by the covetousness of priests'.[5]

Nor were such views confined to heretics. In the York Mystery

---

[1] *Tithes and oblations*, p. 31.

[2] G. Carleton, *Tithes Examined and proved to be due to the Clergie by a divine right* (2nd ed., 1611), pp. 1, 22ᵛ; Selden, *Works*, iii. 1163–4.

[3] N. Adams, 'The Judicial Conflict over Tithes', in *English Hist. Rev.* lii. 22.

[4] See pp. 159–60 below.

[5] H. Prideaux, *An Award of King Charles I . . ., shewing that Personal-Tithes are still due by the Law of the Land*, in *Ecclesiastical Tracts* (2nd ed., 1716), p. 302; A. G. Little, 'Personal Tithes', in *English Hist. Rev.* ccxxxvi. 67; A. Ogle, *The Tragedy of the Lollards' Tower* (1949), p. 61. Erasmus also opposed the exaction of tithes, Selden noted (*Works*, iii. 1164).

Plays, performed under the auspices of the city from the fourteenth to the late sixteenth century, there was pointed reference to the 10 per cent. which Judas Iscariot thought his due. The thirty pieces of silver amounted, in his calculation, to 10 per cent. of the value of the box of ointment which ought to have been sold for the benefit of the poor.

> But for the poor nor their part
> Pricked me no pine,
> But me tened for the tenth part.[1]

The sentence of Hobbes's cited at the beginning of Part II, which reads like a very sophisticated piece of intellectual scepticism, in fact echoes the sort of broad anti-clerical jest which had delighted townsfolk for centuries.

But in the sixteenth century wealth produced in new ways suddenly acquired vast significance in the English economy. The possibilities of tithe evasion became proportionately greater, the loss to the clergy more serious. The problem for the church, as the first epigraph to this chapter suggests, was to devise means of tapping the new and rapidly expanding sources of wealth—the profits of merchants, clothiers, miners, graziers, improving farmers, market gardeners, money-lenders, &c.

Tithes were traditionally paid on the produce of the earth, the free gifts of God. In certain areas they were customarily paid also on wealth *extracted* from the ground, as well as on the natural increase of the soil: in other areas the liability of such products to tithe was questioned. One has only to list coal, tin, lead, and other metals, building stone, slates, bricks, tiles, gravel, clay, chalk, marl, lime, salt, alum, to recall how greatly these industries, in which tithe-claims were not clearly and universally agreed, expanded during our period. Infinite possibilities of argument and evasion opened up.

There were also the new industries catering for the urban market in commodities which had previously been manufactured at home—e.g. beer. In 1613 a Bristol parson tried to claim tithes on beer which, he said, had been bought for £500 and sold for £1,000. But he failed to convince the common-law judges of his right to

---

[1] Ed. L. Toulmin Smith, *York Mystery Plays* (1885), pp. 225–32. (The MS. dates from the first half of the fifteenth century.) The whole tone of the plays is strongly anti-hierarchical, Annas and Caiaphas being referred to as 'bishops'—a suggestion elaborated by Prynne in *A Looking-Glass for all Lordly Prelates*, pp. 53–56.

a tithe of such retail profits.[1] In other food industries it was the sudden expansion of production that made the commodities of new interest to ministers—e.g. fish and salt.

The economic changes affected agriculture too, which produced raw materials for industry (wool, hemp, flax, rape, woad, hops), as well as food for the towns. Production for the market transformed the animal husbandry of many peasant households, and led to countless disputes over tithes. In 38 Eliz. the judges decided that tithe must be paid on agistment—the taking in of someone else's cattle to pasture for payment. Agistment was particularly difficult to keep track of, especially when beasts were pastured outside the parish and when the numbers involved were small.[2] Enclosure for pasture created a whole series of problems for tithe-collectors. When cultivators switched over from corn-growing to vegetable-gardening or fruit-growing, as they were doing especially in the area around London, this meant that there was no longer a single easily measurable harvest, but a steady series of cash sales, of which it was very difficult for the minister to keep check: and the commodities might be small, such as parsnips, or parsley, sage, mint, rue, and other garden herbs. How were tithes to be reckoned in such cases? The solution usually reached seems to have been an agreement by the minister to accept a fixed annual sum in lieu of tithes. But such agreements were not always reached peaceably.

Trees were the cause of a great many quarrels. Tithes were due on all fruits, and on the parings, bark, branches, and body of all trees except timber trees of over twenty years' growth; also on underwoods and coppices if cut down and preserved to grow again, but not if they were cut for immediate use. There were innumerable complications and local variations, such as that cherry trees in Buckinghamshire were deemed to be timber, and so were tithe-free.[3] The result was that disputes were endless, not only between minister and parishioners (in 1641 John Pym was being sued for tithe wood)[4] but also between rector and vicar.

There were many marginal problems. Tithes were due on

[1] E. Bulstrode, *Reports* (1657), ii. 141; Gibson, op. cit., p. 699.

[2] Hughes, op. cit. (1st ed., 1641), ii. 73; (3rd ed., 1673), pp. 272–3; T. Bateman, *A Treatise on Agistment Tithe* (2nd ed., 1778), *passim*.

[3] W. Sheppard, *The Parsons Guide: or the Law of Tithes* (2nd ed., 1670), pp. 19–25.

[4] Nalson, op. cit. ii. 393; cf. H. Johnstone, *Churchwardens' Presentments, Archdeaconry of Chichester* (Sussex Record Soc., 1947–8), p. 53.

apples: were they also due on windfalls? Cherries were tithable (outside Buckinghamshire): were wild cherries when they were gathered for sale? Were the profits of greenhouses liable to tithe? The common-law courts ruled in 1630 that they were not, since they grew 'by the labour and industry of man' and were not the free gifts of God.[1] If a nursery gardener sold young trees from his orchard, must he pay tithes on the proceeds? Rather surprisingly it was decided that he must: but this was in 1640, with Laud's influence still in the ascendant. Very few of these problems were new in themselves. They got taken to court in our period because of their new importance in consequence of the rapidly growing food market.

There were also disputes over new crops, such as hops, saffron, potatoes, rape, tobacco. In 38 Eliz. and 1 Car. I the judges declared most of them liable to pay small tithes.[2] Hemp and flax were very difficult to tithe. Woad was another contentious industrial crop whose garden cultivation was expanding. The shift away from corn-growing to pasture or intensive agriculture meant the ultimate replacement of great tithes by small, which were more difficult to collect; as well as the displacement of many tithe-payers.[3] The vicar of Calceby, Lincolnshire, reported in 1638 that his parish was 'decayed by oppression in rents and unoccupied houses', and thought that his own miserable income of £13. 6s. 8d. a year could be improved only if something was done to repopulate the parish.[4]

The change away from corn-growing naturally led to quarrels between rectors and vicars. Thus in 1611 the rector of St. Leonard's, Shoreditch (who had the advantage of also being Archdeacon of London), with the approval of the Bishop of London, persuaded his vicar to agree that the rector should for the future receive tithes from all plots of land over half an acre in area which had recently been turned into gardens; and also all tithes on bricks made in the parish. In Hexton, Hertfordshire, the rector received

---

[1] Gibson, op. cit., p. 709.   [2] Hughes, op. cit. (3rd ed.), p. 265.

[3] Cf. J. A. Venn, *The Foundation of Agricultural Economics* (1923), pp. 98–104, the best brief modern survey known to me. It is marred only by the author's failure to distinguish between the period after 1640, when Coke's authority was generally accepted, and the earlier period when the church courts were still in a position to challenge it.

[4] *C.S.P.D., 1637–8*, p. 181. Mr. Beresford counts Calceby as a 'lost' village (M. Beresford, *The Lost Villages of England*, 1954, p. 57).

tithes from some orchards, giving the vicar an annual pension in
their place. The rector of Packlesham, Essex, got tithes for all
manner of fruits, and for roots, onions, &c. At Cottenham,
Cambridgeshire, tithes on fruit and hay were in dispute in the
sixteen-twenties. At Hockley, Essex, tithes on lambs, wool, and
wood were disputed between rector and vicar in 1610.[1] In 1612
the lay rector made 50 hogsheads of cider from the apple tithes
of two impropriate Monmouthshire parishes.[2] When the vicar
retained the small tithes in fruit-growing or market-gardening
areas, he might sometimes do very well out of them. Thus the
vicarage of Battersea, valued at £13. 15s. 2½d. in the King's Books,
was worth £100 to the vicar in 1658, whilst the rectory was only
£80. The advance came from tithes on gardens, at the expense of
the small producer.[3]

Beasts *ferae naturae* were exempt from tithe. The common-law
courts helped the rich by deciding that deer, even if kept in parks,
were wild animals. When turkeys were introduced it was even
argued, successfully, that they were *ferae naturae*.[4] Fish too were
ferae naturae, but the fishing industry was expanding under government patronage, and ministers were reluctant to abandon their
claims. The act 2 & 3 Ed. VI, c. 13, allowed tithes on fish
to be collected wherever they had been paid by local custom
between 1509 and 1549. It was therefore to the advantage of
ministers to preserve or create such customs, of their parishioners
to forget them. This gave rise to conflicts in most fishing ports.

In 1621 a bill was introduced into Parliament against the exaction of tithes upon fishing voyages, whether off the English coast
or farther away, whether upon the profits of the voyage or the wages
of mariners. It led to long debates. In support of the bill it was
argued that since 'this fish is not taken within any man's parish',
no tithes were properly due. 'By the common law the parson can
claim no tithe out of the parish. The soil of the sea is the king's,
and if any tithe be due it is to the king.' Such tithes, it was alleged,
had been demanded 'but of late years', i.e. presumably *since* the
statute of 1549. (The remark appears to have referred especially to
the Newfoundland fishery.) Up to 10s. a man, it was complained,

[1] Newcourt, op. cit. i. 685, 833; ii. 458, 330; ed. W. W. Cunningham, *Common Rights at Cottenham and Stretham, Camden Miscellany*, xii. 180–1, 246–9.
[2] Ed. J. A. Bradney, *The Diary of Walter Powell* (1907), p. 6.
[3] Lysons, op. cit. i. 35.
[4] Coke, *The Second Part of the Institutes* (1671), p. 651; Gibson, op. cit., p. 714.

might be demanded where the clear profits were no more than £5 a head—i.e. a fair 10 per cent. was regarded as a grievance.[1] In consequence of these 'unjust demands, many poor fishermen have died excommunicate and left the land'. 'The discouraged mariners go rather to the Dutch and French than submit themselves to such unreasonable demands.'

On the other side it was argued that for ministers in fishing ports this tithe was their principal source of maintenance; and Convocation apparently made the large concession of admitting that the *amount* to be paid in tithe might be regulated by Parliament, although the minister's *right* to tithe was divine and could not be abolished.[2] The bill was not passed; tithes remained to increase costs in the fishing industries of England and Ireland, despite the efforts of the common-law courts to seize jurisdiction over cases where customs of tithing fish were in dispute.[3] Everywhere attempts to levy tithe from the new industries and new agricultural processes gave occasion for squabbles and bickering —and for clashes between the church and common-law courts.

II

For the views of common and ecclesiastical lawyers were diametrically opposed on most of the issues in dispute. Coke, for instance, declared that tithes were not payable on anything that was of the substance of the earth and not annual; consequently they were not due on stone, tin, lead, bricks, tiles, lime, marl, coals, chalk, pots of earth. Nor were they due on peat or turf, since this was part of the freehold. He supported these contentions by citing judgments in the King's Bench from the last decade of Elizabeth and from the reign of James I. They flatly contradicted medieval practice.[4] Sir Thomas Ridley, Archbishop

[1] In some parishes there was a custom of paying on the twentieth fish (e.g. Scarborough) or the twelfth fish (e.g. Brixham, Devon). (H. Wood, *A Collection of Decrees by the Court of the Exchequer in Tithe-Causes*, 1798, i. 5–6, 53.)

[2] Notestein, Relf, and Simpson, op. cit. ii. 135–6; iii. 335–6; iv. 42, 104, 385; v. 253, 490.

[3] W. Bohun, *The Law of Tithes* (3rd ed., 1744), p. 360. See discussions about tithes on fish in Ireland between Laud and Strafford in Knowler, op. cit. ii. 138; Laud, *Works*, vii. 399.

[4] Coke, *Second Part of the Institutes*, pp. 651–2; W. Easterby, *The History of the Law of Tithes in England* (1888), pp. 57–58. Salt and tobacco pipe-clay were also held by the common lawyers not to be tithable (W. Bohun, *A Tithing Table*, 1732, pp. 13–14).

Bancroft's Vicar-General and spokesman, regarded tithe as due on stone, turfs, and minerals. Minerals, he declared, renew themselves again when extracted, 'which is a thing so notorious in quarries of stone . . . that the law itself, and other good authors, have set it down for an undoubted experience that being digged up they do renew again'.[1] Such beliefs were more likely to be held by clerical academics than by miners, and they soon became old-fashioned in England, though they survived in less industrially developed countries like France.[2] But, though the common lawyers were on safe ground scientifically, they were undoubtedly changing the law.[3]

By local custom a minister might receive tithes of things which were not tithable of common right, such as coal or metals. Tithes were paid by custom on tin in Devon and Cornwall, for instance, on lead in Derbyshire.[4] But there were struggles over such tithes, even where the clergy liked to regard a custom as firmly established. Disputes in Derbyshire in the early seventeenth century ended in court decisions being given in favour of the recipients of tithes, who included the powerful John Gell of Hopton (later Sir John), owner of tithes formerly belonging to the Dean and Chapter of Lichfield, as well as to ministers. In 1624 the miners introduced into the Commons a bill to abolish tithes on lead ore: the local custom had arisen, they said, only as a result of popish clergy preying on the superstitions of the miners to make them believe that priests' prayers helped to discover lead. The clergy were trying to establish a general right to tithes on lead, and to extend it to districts where tithes had never been paid. The ministers in reply used the argument that lead 'grew and renewed in the veins', and suggested that lead-mining destroyed good agricultural land which would otherwise have been tithable. Only a small group of wealthy miners, they alleged, were unwilling to pay tithes. The House of Commons rejected the miners' bill,

---

[1] Ridley, op. cit., pp. 217–23.

[2] Nef, *War and Human Progress* (1950), p. 282, quoting an Intendant's report of 1709. Linnaeus also believed in the eighteenth century that minerals grow, which is curious in view of the extensive development of mining in Sweden (S. F. Mason, *A History of the Sciences*, 1953, p. 268).

[3] After the Restoration, pamphleteers of all shades of opinion tended to accept Coke's position about such tithes—interesting evidence of the legal revolution which had taken place, and which the Restoration did not reverse.

[4] Fuller, *Worthies*, i. 390; Sir S. Degge, *The Parsons Counsellor with the law of Tithes* (1676), p. 186. Degge's work was mostly written before 1640.

possibly more out of consideration for the property rights of impropriators like Sir John Gell than from mere solicitude for the welfare of parsons.[1] The issues were mixed up.

In England (unlike most countries, and despite much opposition) tithes were paid on wages until day labourers were exempted from personal tithes by 2 & 3 Ed. VI, c. 13. This clause was a victory for employers, on whom the burden would ultimately have fallen. This was pointedly expressed in Ellis *v.* Drake (14 Jac. I), when it was decided that ploughmen should not pay tithes on their wages : there being 'as much reason that the servants of the plough, as that the cattle of the plough, should be exempt from tithes'.[2] It was one of the many respects in which employers and employees had common interests in opposing the church's demands : the common-law courts expressed these interests.

Tithe continued to be required from labourers in some parishes after 1549, possibly from those whose contract was for a long period.[3] In 1640 two examples were quoted from Kent of ministers who refused communion to labourers who would not pay tithe on wages. In one case ten labourers were cited before the church court. They escaped payment of the 12*d.* demanded, but as they had to face costs of 15*s.* or 16*s.* a head, they would think twice before insisting on their rights a second time.[4] As late as 1683 a determined effort to collect ¼*d.* in the shilling on all servants' wages was made by a rector with the backing of the church courts. But by that date church courts had lost much of their power, and local employers told their servants to fight it out, since all the rector 'could do at them was to excommunicate them, which was only their not going to church'. The employees won.[5] There are other examples where customs survived by which servants paid tithes on their clear gains; but in general tithe on wages sank into insignificance after 1549, partly as a result of the statute, partly from the difficulty of collecting it in face of opposition from employers and employees alike.[6]

---

[1] *V.C.H., Derbyshire*, ii. 331–3. In 1652 the miners tried again. In a petition to Parliament they claimed that tithes on lead were not due at common law : they had only been paid by ignorant miners, 'seduced by the covetous clergy, believing their prayers available for the finding of lead'.

[2] Rolle, op. cit. i. 646; Gibson, op. cit., p. 699.

[3] See pp. 83–84 above for tithe on mariners' wages.

[4] Ed. L. B. Larking, *Proceedings, principally in the County of Kent* (Camden Soc., 1862), pp. 105, 230.   [5] Venn, op. cit., p. 107.

[6] Degge, op. cit., p. 245; Sheppard, op. cit., pp. 5, 59–60; J. S. Purvis, *Select*

The economic changes of the sixteenth century gave a new significance to types of earnings which were difficult to assess to tithe. The fruits of the earth, the Laudian Richard Montagu complained, were 'open, apparent, and in the view of all'; the new wealth was 'secret, unknown, reserved, and purposely kept close by traders, whose credit in the opinion of the world abroad is oftentimes much more than their estates'.[1] Quite apart from the natural man's desire to evade taxation, secrecy about his financial position seemed to the nascent capitalist almost a business necessity. So economic change created a real problem, apparently technical (like the need for a reorganization of national taxation), but affecting the pockets and deepest interests of almost all laymen; and so it became an issue of political power.

It could indeed be argued that trading and industrial profits should be altogether exempt from tithe, since they were not the free gifts of God. The ecclesiastics denied this argument, and claimed personal tithes as no less due from profits than from any other earnings.[2] Others, as we saw in the Commons' debates on tithes of fish, claimed that tithes were due only on increase arising within the parish.[3] But the really great accumulations of wealth in the sixteenth century were amassed outside any parish—by plunder, piracy, Newfoundland fishing, or overseas trade—or by the humbler expedient of pasturing sheep in another parish.

Since the propertied classes wished the church to continue in existence, some compromise had to be reached. Statutes were passed declaring which of the new types of wealth were liable to tithe. Statutes normally accepted existing custom, and did not support the full ecclesiastical claims. Timber of great woods of over twenty years' growth was exempted from tithe by 45 Ed. III, c. 3, when such timber was sold either for the profit of the owner or in aid of the king in his wars. This statute acquired a new significance with the sixteenth-century fuel famine and the need to conserve timber for the navy: the price of timber soared, and landowners pocketed all the profits, to the indignation of the clergy. The latter heartily disliked this statute, and made

16th century Causes in Tithe (Yorkshire Archaeological Soc., 1949), pp. 38–39; Little, op. cit., p. 81; ed. A. Peel, *The Seconde Parte of a Register* (1915), ii. 175.

[1] R. Montagu, *Diatribae upon the First Part of the late History of Tithes* (1621), p. 67.

[2] Selden, *Works*, iii. 1071; Little, op. cit., pp. 69, 81–82.

[3] Selden, *Works*, iii. 1156; Sheppard, op. cit., p. 17.

persistent efforts to get it modified.[1] By 2 & 3 Ed. VI, c. 13, new iron mills, fulling mills, lead mills, powder mills, edge mills, copper mills, tin mills, and paper mills were exempted from payment of tithes. To claim that a mill was 'old', the minister had to prove that tithes had been paid for forty years before 1549. In 16 Jac. I the common-law courts asserted their jurisdiction in a case where tithe was demanded from a fulling mill making profits of £4 a week. Unless a custom could be proved, the common lawyers said, tithes were not payable 'of such things whereof the gain comes by the labour of man'.[2] The importance of this far-reaching principle is clear, especially as the common law claimed jurisdiction in all cases where custom was alleged. The statute of 1549 had declared that personal tithes on merchandise, handicrafts, &c., were due at the rate of 10 per cent. on clear profits; but they were to be paid only as they had customarily been paid during the preceding forty years. There was scope for evasion and argument over the definition of 'clear profit' no less than over custom.[3] But the intention of the statute was clearly to relieve all new industries from personal tithes; and the common lawyers so interpreted it.

Even when statutes did aim to preserve ministers from utter destitution, the remedy was itself a new disease, since henceforth it could be argued that the right to collect tithes was based on positive law, and not on the law of God. There seems to have been an element of deliberate policy here. Thomas Cromwell, as Vicar-General, based the obligation squarely on statute; Cranmer apparently left it an open question; Convocation in Mary's reign insisted on the right to tithe by canon law. Elizabeth's Injunctions went back to Cromwell's position. The emphasis on statute as against divine right was accepted by the Elizabethan bishops and was later made much of by Selden; it was Lancelot Andrewes and the Laudians who tried to revive the Marian doctrine.[4] For human laws could be changed, as the divine law could not. The statutes enforcing payment of tithes did not explicitly deny a divine right

---

[1] Cardwell, *Synodalia*, pp. 439, 447, 575; Ridley, op. cit., pp. 229–35; Sheppard, op. cit., pp. 19–25.

[2] Bohun, *The Law of Tithes*, pp. 119–20.

[3] Sheppard, op. cit., pp. 29–31.

[4] Burnet, op. cit. ii. 230, 389–90; iv. 321; Hughes, op. cit. (1st ed.), ii. 73; Cardwell, *Documentary Annals*, i. 185. For his doctorate of divinity Andrewes defended the thesis that tithes were due by divine right.

to tithe in the way that statutes for an economic lent specifically disavowed any superstitious observation of times and seasons; but it was a short step for men to demand Christian liberty in refusing to pay tithes as in refusing to fast on formally established occasions.

Statutes were all very well: but they came up against the same difficulties of enforcement in the towns as the canons of the church had done. Lambs and stooks could be counted, but the new wealth, as Montagu complained, was much less visible than the products of medieval agriculture, and therefore far more difficult to assess. Profits from investments in overseas trade, from money rents and fines, from employment of wage labourers in production for the market, from lending money, from buying wholesale to sell retail, might be known to exist, but the precise sums involved were not manifest and notorious. John Preston, the famous Puritan preacher, evaded taxation on the 'great incomes' from his pupils which he was too frugal to spend, by investing in the East India Company, since estates there were invisible.[1] Many no doubt followed his example in those days of arbitrary taxation and tithe disputes. Even in agriculture, as production for the market increased, so disputes increased: the rival parties sometimes managed to have astonishingly diverse views not only about the cash value of crops, but even about acreage under cultivation.[2]

The very conception of 'profit' contained ambiguities. How should it be defined in relation, say, to a coal-mine, a privateering expedition, or a drainage scheme involving heavy initial capital expenditure? Or in relation to 'unimproved' rents compensated by steep entry fines?[3] Was tithe due on the profits of speculative buying and selling? The courts decided in 11 Jac. I that a man who bought a house for £300 and promptly sold it again for £500 was not liable to pay tithe on his gains.[4] Business expenses might be deducted before calculating the clear gains of which one-tenth was due as personal tithes. Business men's ideas of a legitimate expense account would no doubt vary then no less than now. If balance-sheets were kept, the ecclesiastical authorities had no right of access to them. They had to rely on the statements of the

---

[1] Ball, op. cit., pp. 94–95.

[2] See a case of 1639 in J. M. J. Fletcher, 'A Century of Dorset Documents', in *Proceedings of the Dorset Natural History and Antiquarian Field Club*, xlvii. 49.

[3] Cf. Purvis, op. cit., pp. 101–3; and see pp. 119–21 below.

[4] Rolle, op. cit. i. 657. Cf. the case cited on pp. 80–81 above.

producer, checked only by 'common fame', the testimony of his not unsympathetic neighbours. Income-tax revenue today would fall pretty sharply if there were no Inland Revenue authorities to check up on the honesty and accurate memory of business men.

Before the Reformation, though of course litigation was the normal resort, the confessional might also be used to encourage the payment of such tithes as the priest thought were due. After the abolition of confession, the parson's only remedy was to bring expensive legal action against a man who either was not worth prosecuting or had a purse long enough to fight an interminable legal delaying action. Even the church courts had no means of getting at the truth except by putting a man on oath: that was one of the many reasons for their addiction to this procedure, and for its unpopularity with laymen of the propertied classes. It was abolished, as a means of ascertaining tithes, in 1549.[1]

This really meant the end of personal tithes in the towns. In 1535, as Mr. Little has shown, they were still worth fighting for, amounting to anything from 5 to 20 per cent. of the minister's total income in rural areas, and more in market towns.[2] But the climate of opinion had long been against their payment. They had become so notoriously difficult to assess that before 21 Hen. VIII, c. 6, a mortuary (the second-best living beast) was demanded in lieu of them: so natural was the assumption that they would not have been fully paid in the dead man's lifetime. If he had not paid his predial tithes, the omission would have been deliberate, not accidental, and remedy would have lain at law.[3]

The first cause for the disappearance of personal tithes (with the partial exception of those on fish and 'old mills') is to be sought in long-term economic developments. But abolition of the oath was a main secondary cause. Nor is it without its significance, for that age of Bibliolatrous protestantism, that there is no authority in the Bible for personal as opposed to predial tithes.[4] Whatever the

---

[1] Prideaux, op. cit., pp. 289–300; Degge, op. cit., p. 245. That is what oaths were for in primitive societies: to produce evidence on which disputed cases could be decided. The increasing efficiency of the state, as well as the declining efficacy of supernatural sanctions, explains the simultaneous disappearance of torture and the judicial oath. Leviathan is a *mortal* god. In opposing oaths the Anabaptists and Quakers were in effect making a rational criticism of an outmoded judicial system as well as a religious protest against the searching of consciences.

[2] Little, op. cit., pp. 87–88.　　　　　　　　[3] Fuller, *Church History*, i. 382.

[4] R. Stock, *A Commentary upon the Prophecy of Malachi* (1865), p. 223. For Stock, see p. 256 below.

cause, the fact is clear. A paper drawn up for the Convocation of 1563 speaks of 'the universal subtraction of privy or personal tithes'. In 1585 Whitgift declared that personal tithes 'are in a manner wholly gone, because there is no way to recover them, but by the large conscience of the parishioners'. The law, complained Dr. Burgess forty years later, 'debarreth us of the principal and indeed the only means of finding out what every dishonest man's gains are: namely the oath of the parties that is to pay'.[1] No wonder parsons wanted the oath back.

So 2 & 3 Ed. VI, c. 13, was really disastrous for the church. Passed just after the Norfolk rebellion of 1549, in which the peasants had complained of litigation for increased tithes by parsons and vicars, it limited canon law in several respects. It abolished the oath; it exempted from the obligation to pay personal tithes all those who could not be proved to have been paying during the preceding forty years; it freed day labourers from tithes on wages; it gave land newly brought into cultivation seven years' exemption from tithe payments; it laid no obligation on the owner of corn, hay, &c., to notify the parson of its harvest or cutting, and this was interpreted by the common-law courts as leaving the onus on him: the parishioner had done his duty by setting the minister's tenth part aside.[2]

The full consequences of this statute could hardly have been foreseen by its authors. In the first place, it dates from the period when the rise in prices was just beginning to make itself felt; and so its effects were cumulative. In the second place, it was followed by a gradual usurpation of jurisdiction in tithe cases by the common-law courts, more sympathetic to laymen than the church courts, more alive to the needs of a business society, more interested in written contracts than in ministers' equitable claims. These circumstances combined to make it increasingly difficult for parsons to collect their traditional tenth of the national income.

Quite apart from formal legal changes, there was always the additional possibility of mere evasion by fraud or concealment, which this atmosphere did nothing to discourage. In 1619 James I thought it worth while to grant a commission to certain patentees

[1] Cardwell, *Synodalia*, p. 509; cf. pp. 421, 439, 447, 510; Strype, *Annals*, iii. 174; C. Burgess, *A New Discovery of Personal Tithes* (1625), pp. 64–65.

[2] Coke, *Second Part of the Institutes*, pp. 612–13, 649; Easterby, op. cit., p. 80. See Prof. Sykes's criticisms of this paragraph in *English Hist. Rev.*, lxxiii. 298.

'to enquire . . . what tithes . . . have been concealed from the
king and to compound with any person pretending title to the
tithes concealed'. The patentees were authorized to compound
for tithes not within the precincts of any parish, as well as for
concealed parochial tithes. This commission was severely criticized in the House of Commons of 1621, largely because the commissioners had the right to put men on oath, but also because of
the claim that 'tithes belonging to no spiritual person belong to
the king as supreme spiritual person'. The commission, said Sir
Edward Coke, was against law. It caused parsons to flock around
and play the informer. The commission was condemned as a
general grievance, both in the original and in the execution.[1] This
commission no doubt had a lot to do with the bill 'for the general
quiet of the subject against all pretences of concealments whatsoever', which provided that the king could not lay claim to any
land that had been out of his possession for sixty years—'which',
observed Sir Anthony Weldon, 'was more beneficial to the subject
in respect of their quiets, than all the Parliaments had given
[James I] during his whole reign'.[2]

III

In all these circumstances it was inevitable that profits made by
business men in towns and rural industrial areas, by big producers for the market in country districts and by improving landlords, should be seriously under-assessed to tithe in comparison
with the much more visible wealth of the peasant producer or
artisan. Even if an equitable tenth of trading and industrial *profits*
could have been collected, that was still less than the 10 per cent.
of his *total product* which the countryman was expected to pay:
only half as much, a pamphlet of the Interregnum suggested.
10 per cent. might come close to the husbandman's total profit.[3]

This had, of course, always been true. But it was beginning to
be felt as an anomaly now that so much more of the country's
wealth was made in urban centres. It was felt most acutely,

[1] Notestein, Relf, and Simpson, op. cit. ii. 243; iv. 120; v. 20, 49; vi. 277, 291–2;
vii. 344–5, 562. One of the commissioners, John Smyth added, was a 'decayed
haberdasher'.

[2] Ibid. ii. 316–17; Weldon, op. cit., pp. 171–2.

[3] Heylyn, *Historical and Miscellaneous Tracts*, i. 174; [Anon.], *The Husbandmans
Plea Against Tithes* (1647), *passim*.

perhaps, not by the traditional small cultivator so much as by the business man with capital to invest in agriculture who was accustomed to city conditions. For only the *profits* of merchants and craftsmen were tithed, and they could claim allowance for expenses. Whereas the farmer was liable for tithe on all his produce, including the seed corn which could be regarded as part of his capital, and the grain which he fed to his cattle (on whose increase he again had to pay tithe). Nor did he receive any allowance for investment in new stock or farm equipment.

So the go-ahead type of farmer, the man with capital to invest, regarded tithes, which hit his capital as well as his income, as a crippling grievance. Tithes added to the cost of producing food. It could also be argued that they were a contributory cause of depopulation, since landlords could get more by leasing land to graziers than from a tenant who cultivated the land. And depopulating enclosures in their turn were prejudicial to ministers. So all the main changes in the economic life of the country in our period tended to work to the disadvantage of the clergy.

Tithes, like other rents and taxes originally rendered in kind, had in some cases been commuted for money payments by the sixteenth century.[1] This commutation took the form of an agreement between parson and parishioners (collectively or as individuals) known as a *modus decimandi*. (A *modus* did not necessarily imply commutation: it meant any agreed method of assessing tithes.) This agreement was normally unwritten, and although no doubt often intended to be perpetual, this intention was difficult to prove—or to disprove. Then the cost of living rose, by some 650 per cent. between 1500 and 1640. Wheat prices rose much more sharply—by perhaps 800 per cent. in the same period.[2]

Wherever tithes were commuted, therefore, the recipient lost heavily, and the tithepayers' gained correspondingly. Rates of composition varied considerably, according to their date and the manner in which they had been arrived at. In Essex they ranged from $\frac{1}{2}d.$ to $4d.$ for a calf or a pig, from $2d.$ to $8d.$ for a milch cow. The higher figure, in each case, came from a composition at

---

[1] In the paragraphs that follow I have used R. G. Usher's *Reconstruction of the English Church*, especially vol. i, chapter 10. But he was guilty of a number of facile generalizations for which the evidence is not revealed. In attempting to find my way through the confusion left by Usher I have been greatly helped by Miss D. M. Barratt's thesis.

[2] Sir J. Clapham, *A Concise Economic History of Britain* (1951), pp. 186–8.

Bumstead Helion which had been approved by Bishop Bancroft in 1598.[1]

Here was another fruitful source of conflict. 'Those customs of paying a halfpenny for a lamb or a penny for a calf', said Dr. Cowell in 1607, 'by such as have under seven in one year, how long soever it hath endured, is but very unreasonable in these days when both lambs and calves are grown four times dearer and more than they were when this price was first accepted.'[2] There is much evidence of friction. An undated terrier of Hunsdon rectory, Hertfordshire (? after 1627), was significantly signed by the churchwardens only, not by the rector. For it stated as a parochial custom that if the parson refused 'to take ½d. for every lamb under seven (as hath always heretofore been paid and accepted) and shall think good to drive [i.e. to carry forward], as if he please he may, that then he shall drive but one year'.[3] The church courts supported the practice of not demanding tithe on calves, pigs, or lambs in any year in which they amounted to less than ten, but of carrying the total forward until a total of ten was reached, so that tithe in kind could be claimed. The common-law courts would have backed up the churchwardens. They would indeed have encouraged them to go further, for they were in the habit of issuing prohibitions to stop such practices altogether.[4]

White Kennett believed that 'the perverse *modus decimandi* (which must every age grow into a greater oppression of the vicar)' was 'in great measure a stratagem of the monks, to incline the tenants to pay their full tenth of corn and hay to their [i.e. the monks'] proper uses, and to give but a trifle for their smaller tithes to the vicar'.[5] We may perhaps attribute more to secular price trends than to popish wickedness: but the facts are not in dispute. All those dependent on fixed money payments got into difficulties in this inflationary age.[6]

---

[1] Newcourt, op. cit. ii. 108–9; cf. i. 825, ii. 410, 437, 458, 500, 508. Houses in Nether St., Chingford, Essex, actually paid 9d. a cow; but elsewhere in the parish the rate was 6d. (H. Smith, op. cit., p. 276).

[2] J. Cowell, *The Interpreter* (1607), s.v. 'tithes'; cf. Stock, op. cit., pp. 227–8.

[3] Newcourt, op. cit. i. 839. This meaning of the word 'drive' is not given in the *Oxford English Dictionary*, but it seems clear from the above and other examples—e.g. H. Wood, op. cit. i. 185.

[4] Gibson, op. cit., pp. 707–8. See p. 125 below.

[5] Kennett, op. cit., pp. 58–59.

[6] This point is made in Stephens's Introduction 'To the Reader' to Spelman's *Larger Treatise concerning Tythes* (1647), in *English Works*, i. lxi–lxii. Cf. H. Burton,

Poverty resulting from commutation was a major cause of pluralism, a pamphlet of 1641 implied.[1] Ministers whose tithes had been commuted suffered perhaps more acutely than laymen from the price revolution, because they had usually no reserves of capital, and because they were not themselves producing commodities for the market. Where, on the other hand, tithes had not been commuted and could be collected, and where there was easy access to a market—especially in corn-growing areas—their value might increase considerably, as the steep rise in wheat prices would suggest. But only rectors received corn tithes.

Miss Barratt's researches for the dioceses of Oxford, Worcester, and Gloucester (and there is no reason to suppose that this area was in any way exceptional) show that Usher exaggerated the extent of commutation, and ante-dated it. He was quite mistaken in thinking that by 1600 most tithes had been commuted; though in most parishes there was *some* commutation. A paper of 1588 spoke of customs *de modo decimandi* as prevailing 'in most parishes'; but Selden observed that tithes were more paid in kind in England than in all Italy and France.[2] Miss Barratt distinguishes sharply between great and small tithes. The former, rectorial tithes, were normally still paid in kind down to 1640. Tithes on wheat were never commuted. 'Customary *modi*' existed, in certain parishes or groups of parishes, for some particular commodities on which small tithes, vicarial tithes, were payable. These were usually the most perishable and least marketable commodities. Such *modi* gave rise to the greatest amount of litigation, and so bulk large in the records.

In addition there were 'prescriptive *modi*' affecting *all* the tithes due from a parish or from a single piece of land.[3] Thus the villages of Mixbury and Chibney, Oxfordshire, paid respectively £4 and £6. 13s. 4d. a year in lieu of all tithes due. In the parish of Old Romney ½d. an acre was paid for all meadow and pasture, in lieu of all tithes; gardens in Lambeth paid 4s. per acre.[4] Usher appears

---

op. cit., pp. 100–1, quoting Bishop Jewell; Carleton, op. cit., p. 27; Heylyn, *Historical and Miscellaneous Tracts*, i. 175.

[1] *A Certificate from Northamptonshire*, p. 8.

[2] Cardwell, *Synodalia*, p. 575; Selden, *Table Talk*, p. 208. Cf. Willan, op. cit., pp. 275–6; Rowse, *The England of Elizabeth* (1950), p. 431; *C.S.P.D., 1637*, p. 479.

[3] *Tithes and oblations*, pp. 54–61; W. C., *A Tithing Table* (1633), sig. G–G3, H–Hᵛ; Degge, op. cit., pp. 353–4.

[4] H. Wood, op. cit. i. 57, 91, 3, 98.

to have missed this type of commutation, which was probably the most harmful to the clergy. Prescriptive *modi* were especially frequent on enclosed or imparked land, and such *modi* might remain valid even if a park reverted to cultivation. So land on which new types of farming were being tried out by enterprising farmers, land from which the biggest profits might be made, often paid little or nothing in tithes. If a gentleman erected, for instance, a windmill on land which paid a prescriptive *modus*, no increased tithe was due, however much his income increased. Juries would stretch the law against ministers in such cases.[1]

It was the gentry and richer farmers who profited by 'prescriptive *modi*': not the smaller cultivators. That the volume of litigation about prescriptive *modi* appears to have been less than that about customary *modi* may only witness to parsons' dependence on the big men of the village, and to the advantages enjoyed by the rich at law, especially by appeals from church to common-law courts or Chancery, and vice versa. Only in the sixteen-thirties, under Laud's patronage, do clerical attempts to revise *modi* to their advantage appear to have increased.[2]

These various kinds of *modi*, then, might work to the serious detriment of vicars. Fruit-growers and market-gardeners producing for the London market tended to favour compositions. In other areas, even where tithes had not been commuted for money, agreements were often reached by which they were stabilized at a fixed contribution per acre or per number of animals. In all such cases the minister would fail to share in an increase resulting from improved methods of production. His losses were made statutory by 2 & 3 Ed. VI, c. 13, which laid it down that the custom of the preceding forty years was to be observed in payment of tithes. The Laudian Richard Montagu believed that composition invariably benefited laymen, who would always offer less than a fair 10 per cent. All compositions and prescriptions, Comber thought, originated in the power and policy of the laity, taking advantage of the negligence or corruption of the clergy.[3]

[1] Sheppard, op. cit., p. 77; Rolle, op. cit. i. 651; Hughes, op. cit. (3rd ed.), pp. 282–3.
[2] See pp. 101–3, 119, 327 below.
[3] Montagu, op. cit., p. 334; Comber, op. cit. i. 242.

IV

It was inevitable that there should be many bitter disputes. Law-suits usually turned not so much on a refusal to pay tithes as on disagreement about the customs of the parish. What sort of *modi* were valid? 'By compositions and grants', wrote Selden, 'every man, as well lay as spiritual, by the common law (before the statute of 13 of Elizabeth, made against leases and grants of parsons) might be discharged of tithes'.[1] The legal advisers of the crown in Charles I's reign held that an impropriator's relinquishment of his right to collect tithes from a freeholder extinguished the tithe.[2] Would the same argument apply to tithes not impropriate? The common law tended to obliterate the distinction between tithes paid to clerics and to laymen.

Ecclesiastical lawyers approached matters differently. The only (unsuccessful) attempt to codify the law of the church after the Reformation declared that tithe customs were to be observed only 'if equitable compensation for tithes is rendered'.[3] 'A prescription wherein a layman doth prescribe the manner of tithing', declared Sir Thomas Ridley, '. . . albeit by the common law [it] is counted to be good by paying a thing never so small in lieu thereof, yet neither by the canon law, neither by the law of God itself, could it ever be less than the just tenth.'[4] Such a position necessarily conflicted with the stand which parishioners took on their custo-mary and prescriptive rights, which the common law would pro-tect if they were old enough. But the common-law courts would disallow a 'rank *modus*'—that is, one which was so large that it could hardly have originated before the rise in prices. Such a *modus* had to be proved by evidence of recent agreement: the common law would always enforce contract. So yet again the price revolution turned to the disadvantage of ministers.[5]

Here then was a real conflict of interest, and of two different conceptions of 'right', lurking behind the rivalries over jurisdic-tion in tithe causes. In this conflict divisions between ministers

---

[1] Selden, *Works*, iii. 1279–80; E. Stillingfleet, *Ecclesiastical Cases relating to the Duties and Rights of the Parochial Clergy* (1698), i. 277. The statute to which Selden referred was 13 Eliz., c. 20.
[2] *C.S.P.D., 1634–5*, p. 381; cf. *1637*, p. 254.
[3] *The Reformation of the Ecclesiastical Laws*, p. 128.
[4] Ridley, op. cit., pp. 179–80.
[5] Easterby, op. cit., p. 93.

of differing outlook on theological and disciplinary matters
were less important than the division between tithe-payers and
tithe-recipients. A Puritan like Hakewill could assure the near-
papist Bishop Goodman that he too wished 'customs of tithing
. . . were all overthrown, and the same I think do the greatest
part of parsons and vicars in this kingdom'.[1] The *modus* may
have been even more significant as a cause of friction between
clergy and parishioners than as an explanation of the former's
poverty.[2]

It might sometimes be to the minister's advantage to compound
with tithe-payers, or to lease tithes, where they were disputable, or
where the inconvenience or odium of collecting them personally
was very great, or in a bad year. In Danby Wyske, Yorkshire,
commutation took place *at the instance of the minister* in 1569, when,
the harvest having been destroyed or wasted during the rebellion
of that year, he was 'contented to take in money of everyone
much less than the tithes were worth if such trouble had not been'.
The parish subsequently tried to hold him to this commutation in
perpetuity:[3] so customs were made. Thus when Fuller took the
initiative in about 1635 in an agreement to commute the small
tithes of his parish of Broadwinsor, Dorset,[4] this may be evidence
of his easy-going nature. But we should not make the assumption
too lightly, nor think parsons excessively stupid for agreeing
to commutation even at this late date. It was when a *modus* or
lease became stabilized whilst prices rose that the minister,
or more probably his successor, suffered. Here the precedent of
Nowell *v.* Hicks was of decisive importance. In this case, in
1601, the judges laid it down that a custom once established
became a property which the common-law courts would protect,
even though in this instance the *modus* had not been observed
during the preceding twenty years.[5] Hence the indignation of the
clergy with compliant members of their order who sought present

---

[1] G. Hakewill, *An Apologie or Declaration of the Power and Providence of God* (3rd
ed., 1635), book v, p. 60.

[2] Miss Barratt believes that Usher exaggerated the total loss of income to the
clergy by commutation, because he failed to realize that tithes on corn and livestock
continued to be paid in kind in most parishes (though not perhaps always by the
richest parishioners). She thinks that far less importance should be attached to
commutation in reducing clerical incomes than to impropriation.

[3] Purvis, op. cit., p. 120; cf. pp. 42, 72.

[4] Ed. G. F. Nuttal, *The Letters of John Pinney* (1939), p. 101.

[5] Coke, *Second Part of the Institutes*, pp. 653–4.

peace at their successors' expense. At West Heath, Kent, we are told, 'before the civil war, here was paid to the vicar 12 pence per acre of marshland; but he who then had it, to ingratiate himself with the people, abated 2*d*. an acre', and the custom of 10*d*. per acre was established.[1]

Apart from the fact that many *modi* may not have been intended to be permanent, the long-term trend in prices is far clearer to us than it was to contemporaries. In 1576 even the House of Commons did not realize what the very astute Sir Thomas Smith was up to when he arranged that colleges should be allowed to take one-third of their rents in kind or in money, at their discretion. It was not until the seventeenth century that Fellows began fully to appreciate his wisdom.[2] Sir Henry Spelman seems to have been the first Englishman to give clear theoretical expression to the conception of a secular rise in prices, and his work was not published in his lifetime.[3] Leaving the rise in prices out of account, there is truth in Heylyn's observation that 'the same men who took no thought for parting with their tithes in kinds' were much more reluctant to hand over ready cash.[4]

V

So the *modus* and the price revolution are the first reasons to stress in accounting for the failure of ministers to profit by the increase in the national wealth in the century before 1640. But in the second place the clergy, and especially vicars, suffered from the change which came over English farming in the late fifteenth and sixteenth centuries. Rectorial tithes, so much more important in medieval society, were calculated with nicer accuracy than vicarial. Personal tithes, we have seen, proved more and more difficult to collect as the sixteenth and seventeenth centuries wore on, and especially difficult to collect in kind. Mixed tithes continued to be

[1] Dr. Ducarel, *A Repertory of the Endowments of Vicarages in the Dioceses of Canterbury and Rochester* (1782), p. 119.

[2] Fuller, *History of the University of Cambridge* (1840), pp. 202, 230; Strype, *Life of Sir Thomas Smith* (1820), pp. 144–5. The statute was 18 Eliz., c. 6.

[3] G. N. Clark, *Science and Social Welfare in the Age of Newton* (1937), pp. 152–3; cf. Heylyn, *Mikrokosmos* (1629), p. 795.

[4] Heylyn, *The Undeceiving of the People in the point of Tithes* (1648), in *Historical and Miscellaneous Tracts*, i. 177. In the fifteenth century landlords had found greater difficulty in collecting money rents than they had earlier experienced in enforcing labour services or rents in kind.

collected, but the pressure to commute was strong, in the interest of both parties. Once they were commuted, the price revolution did the rest.

Yet in consequence of the agrarian changes the relative importance of wealth liable to vicarial tithes increased incalculably. Tithe litigation in our period is overwhelmingly concerned with *small* tithes. The whole economy of a village might be switched from arable to pasture farming, or from corn-growing to market-gardening. In one case, enclosure by agreement between lords and freeholders reduced the tithe corn by 90 per cent.[1] At enclosure, moreover, common land allocated to finance the repair of the church might disappear;[2] the parson might lose his common rights, and he was not in a good position to bargain for fair compensation. Even the glebe was apt to be 'eaten away by vermin', as the rector of Widdrington, Essex, expressively worded it in a terrier of 1610.[3] 'It was an easy matter for a greedy lordship to swallow up a little glebe', said a Buckinghamshire terrier of 1625.[4]

'Many a straggling close, wandering out of the way, would long since by sacrilegious guides have been seduced into the possession of false owners' were it not for the glebe terriers which Bancroft had caused to be drawn up in 1610. So John Foord, vicar of Eltham till 1627, noted in his parish register. He was lamenting the surrender by one of his predecessors of 15 acres of woodland to Sir William Roper for ninety-nine years by 'a most ungodly lease', at only 10s. rent a year. In return for this the vicar had been entitled to diet at Sir William's table, but even this privilege had been denied to his successors.[5] At Argam, Yorkshire, the patron held glebe worth £40 a year, paying an incumbent a nominal £1. 6s. 8d. for fulfilling his canonical obligations by saying occasional prayers on the site of the destroyed church.[6]

Such scandalous deals continued into the Laudian period. In

[1] *MSS. of Leeds, Bridgewater, etc.* (Hist. MSS. Commission), p. 257.
[2] F. Trigge, *The Humble Petition of Two Sisters; the Church and Commonwealth* (1604), sig. F2ᵛ, F5.
[3] Newcourt, op. cit. ii. 660. For other examples of lost glebe, see ibid. i. 812, 860 (Herts.); ii. 49, 79, 92, 266, 277, 334, 355–6, 362, 373, 379, 390, 418, 463, 505, 614 (all in Essex).
[4] M. W. Beresford, 'Glebe Terriers and Open-Field Bucks.', in *Records of Bucks.*, xv, part 5, 286–7.
[5] Lysons, op. cit. iv. 408; cf. *C.S.P.D., 1633–4*, p. 548.
[6] Beresford, *The Lost Villages of England*, pp. 100–1.

1633 Bishop Wright of Lichfield and Coventry found that the absentee minister of Stretton Baskerville, Warwickshire, was drawing £13. 6s. 8d. per annum from a parish which had been depopulated 140 years earlier. At Hartley, Northumberland, an encloser continued to pay tithes for some time after he had depopulated the parish, in order to avoid a lawsuit with the lay impropriator.[1] In 1633–4 the parson of Knaptoft, Leicestershire, was said to have received a personal lease 'to stop his mouth' about loss of glebe to his church.[2] In the same county tithes worth £44 a year were, so the vicar of Aby reported, detained from him, principally by the Earl of Lindsey and his servants; small tithes were violently withheld from the vicar of Hemswell by the corporation of Lincoln. Despite frequent promises of augmentation, they left him with a stipend of £11 plus fees amounting to £13. 6s. 8d.[3] At Horton in Northamptonshire, we are told, 'Parsonage house, glebe and tithes' were all engulfed by enclosure for pasture. The rectory in question had lately come into the possession of the Earl of Manchester, Lord Privy Seal, who maintained a stipendiary curate 'at some mean rate', although the church had not been presentative 'of late years'.[4] In 1650 it was alleged that tithes to the value of £300 per annum (four times the value of the rectory) had been filched from the parish of Ramsden Bellows, Essex.[5]

'In many other places', said Fuller, 'where the tithes are not quite impropriated, but yet so gelded by pretended prescriptions and unconscionable, nay unreasonable customs *de modo decimandi*, etc., and they many times confirmed by prohibitions, . . . the poor Levite hath . . . not the tenth, in some not the twentieth part of the tithe.'[6] Evidence for depredations of this kind is necessarily scrappy, since it is usually only in the exceptional case where the victim hit back that any record survives. And only after Laud's advent to power had parsons much hope of assistance. Thus in

---

[1] Ibid., pp. 62–64.

[2] Beresford, 'Glebe Terriers and Open-Field Leicestershire', in *Studies in Leicestershire Agrarian History*, ed. W. G. Hoskins (1949), pp. 82–84. See also L. A. Parker, 'The Agrarian Revolution at Cotesbach, 1501–1612', in ibid., pp. 62–63, for pressure exercised on a rector by the patron to make him agree to enclosure.

[3] *C.S.P.D., 1637–8*, p. 170; *1637*, pp. 392–3.

[4] *A Certificate from Northamptonshire*, p. 5.

[5] H. Smith, op. cit., pp. 242–3.

[6] Ed. J. E. Bailey and W. E. A. Axon, *The Collected Sermons of Thomas Fuller, D.D., 1631–59* (1891), i. 431.

1638 the vicar of Newington, Middlesex, petitioned the king against Sir Francis Popham, who had leased the manor from St. Paul's and paid no tithe on a demesne of 300 acres; the rest of the parish paid 1s. 6d. per acre in lieu of tithes, making a total living of £15. The petition was referred to the Archbishop of Canterbury and the Lord Keeper.[1] In the same year William Cooper, rector of St. Thomas the Apostle, London, implored Laud's help against churchwardens who, Cooper said, refused to bring in a true terrier of the glebe. The rector found Laud 'readier to assist him than he could expect'. He prayed the Archbishop to put in a favourable word with the judges in the ecclesiastical court, before which the case was to be tried; and Laud did so.[2]

But without powerful support from above there was little that a vicar as an individual could do to protect the church's income: and the hierarchy and the government, at least until Laud's ascendancy, failed to come effectively to his assistance. A commission of 1552, headed by Cranmer, proposed that all predial tithes should be paid in kind, and tried to arrange for fair tithing of the new types of wealth—profits of mills, peat- and turf-cutting, coal-mines, stone quarries, grazing—which were most in dispute.[3] But it came to nothing. Whitgift in 1585 was lamenting the evil effect of enclosure on clerical incomes; Bancroft failed to abolish *modi*. Not till Laud came to power did parsons receive real encouragement. In 1635 the Archbishop's Vicar-General was warned to keep a special look-out for 'divers churches ruined by enclosures, etc.'.[4] Such an approach began to produce more examples of enclosure to the church's disadvantage. Thus in 1635 we hear of the recovery of a salt marsh in Lincolnshire, which by conversion from pasture to arable reduced the vicar's incomings from £60 to £8. 10s., since he lost his tithes on sheep.[5] Another complaint of loss of tithe at enclosure came from Romney Marsh four months later. The Earl of Winchilsea, Sir Edward Hales, and other great men there had depopulated the area, the ministers com-

---

[1] *C.S.P.D., 1637–8*, p. 461. Ibid., *1635–6*, pp. 520–1, gives a complaint by the vicar of Staverton, Devon, that he was molested by many suits in Chancery because he would not agree to pretended customs very prejudicial to the church. Cf. Beresford, *Lost Villages*, p. 324.

[2] *C.S.P.D., 1637–8*, p. 426.

[3] Selden, *Works*, iii. 1203; cf. *The Reformation of the Ecclesiastical Laws*, pp. 128–9.

[4] Laud, *Works*, vii. 645.

[5] *C.S.P.D., 1635*, p. 518. Cf. ibid., *1629–31*, p. 452, for 'a particular of the state of the tithes' in six Lincolnshire parishes 'lately improved by draining'.

plained; and Sir Edward had brought pressure to bear on many poor ministers to accept a *modus* of 2*d.* per acre in lieu of tithes of wool and pasturage from land worth 20*s.* to 30*s.* a year.[1] In 1637, again from Lincolnshire, we hear of a vicar who had lost his small tithes by marsh drainage, which benefited only the farmers of the impropriation. Laud urged Sir John Lambe to show the vicar all lawful favour.[2]

In the seventeenth century, as corn-growing became more profitable, enclosure worked increasingly to the detriment of vicars, and added yet another cause of friction between vicar and rector: and the rector was often a layman, who might be the chief tithe-payer in the parish. In October 1638 the vicar of Dorney, Bucks., complained that his parish had lately been converted to arable. Corn now grew where there had been coppice woods. Instead of small tithes for the vicar, the land now produced great tithes for the rector, who was Sir John Parsons, sheriff of Bucks. The land was more productive, but the vicar got less out of it. His petition was referred to the Archbishop, the Lord Keeper, and the Lord Privy Seal, with instructions to send for the impropriator and take action to help the vicar.[3]

Where a minister did resist losses consequent on enclosure, without backing from his ecclesiastical superiors, he might get himself into financial difficulties. Thus Thomas Twisse, parson of Burcot, Berkshire, secured a decision from Chancery in 1634 which gave him £140 a year in rents instead of the £40 he had received before enclosure. But his legal expenses were so great that he had to mortgage the rents for his lifetime, and also the next two presentations. His petition to this effect in 1638 was referred to Laud, Juxon, and the Lord Keeper.[4]

If tithes of lambs and wool continued to be paid in kind, the vicar might gain where the rector lost by conversion from arable to pasture; the rector might gain at the vicar's expense by the reverse process. But enclosure was a suitable moment for establishing a *modus*, as we saw in the Lincolnshire examples of conversion of pasture to arable. At such a moment a vicar was in a weak bargaining position, as against either the rector, the lord of the manor, or the richer parishioners. 'A mighty great rich man',

---

[1] Ibid., *1635–6*, p. 195. Hales was an opposition member of most Parliaments in the reigns of James I and Charles I, including the Long Parliament.

[2] Ibid., *1637*, p. 28.   [3] Ibid., *1638–9*, p. 77.   [4] Ibid., *1637–8*, p. 476.

like Edward Allen, owner of the priory of Hatfield Purnel, could simply withhold tithes from a fifteen-acre field. (A generation later it is hardly surprising to find that Sir Edmond Allen is a baronet. He then paid the miserable vicar £13. 6s. 8d. in lieu of all tithes, and leased the vicarage for £1. 8s. 0d. per annum.)[1] Another 1610 terrier from Reed, Herts., tells us that 'Sir Robert Chester . . . hath paid tithes . . ., as old men say, for his sheep walk, but will pay none now'.[2]

Enclosure of land to form a park might also lead to total disappearance of tithes and glebe, and sometimes to their replacement by a stipend. James I granted £26. 13s. 4d. a year to the vicar of Hampton in lieu of tithes and glebe enclosed in the park at Hampton Court, and an annuity of £56 to the vicar of Cheshunt for lands swallowed up by Theobald's Park.[3] But pensions of this kind did not increase as prices rose, payment was unreliable, and depended entirely on the benevolence of the encloser. There was no remedy at common law if he offered nothing.[4] In any case, such pensions rarely represented more than a fraction of what would have been due in tithes.[5]

Blank refusal of tithe by the very powerful was not unknown. Thus when the eighteenth Earl of Oxford had presented the Rev. Mr. Copinger to the living of Lavenham, Suffolk, he announced that he did not propose to pay tithes on his park. Since this was equal to almost half the parish, Copinger offered to resign. In this instance the Earl paid up; but it afterwards cost Copinger £1,600 (or so he said) to enforce payment by the Earl's successor.[6] 'God's ministers', wrote Francis Trigge, 'may make that complaint of enclosers that Jacob made of Laban: thou hast now changed my wages ten times. . . . But in all their exchanges it hath fallen out as it doth commonly in casting of metals: that which hath come in the second place hath not been so good as was the former. Their

---

[1] Newcourt, op. cit. ii. 73; H. Smith, op. cit., p. 305. For Sir Edmond's gracious augmentation of the vicar's maintenance, see p. 293 below.

[2] Newcourt, op. cit. i. 860. For examples of quarrels over composition for tithes, see ibid. ii. 418, 493, 616. See *Camden Miscellany*, xii. 251–2, for composition at enclosure.

[3] Newcourt, op. cit. i. 622–3, 820; cf. p. 623—£10 paid in lieu of tithe for 60 acres enclosed in Cole-Kennington Park.

[4] Sheppard, op. cit., pp. 47–48. For examples see *C.S.P.D., 1636–7*, pp. 242, 404.

[5] For two examples see H. Smith, op. cit., p. 272.

[6] Fuller, *Church History*, iii. 310–11. The account by the sycophantic David Lloyd (*State Worthies*, ii. 100) is less discreditable to the Earl.

sums of money which they do now allow are not so good in value as were heretofore tithes in kind; and again, the money due is not so easily obtained at their hands'. Owing to depopulating enclosure churches in many places may become chapels.[1]

The parson, like any other smallholder, risked losing his right of common at enclosure. He might also lose his tithes, great or small, and get inadequate compensation for his glebe. Even if he did get a fair share, he had less chance of becoming an improving farmer than a yeoman, since in the first place this was officially frowned on,[2] and in the second place a yeoman would have a greater chance of raising capital, and all his time and energies were devoted to farming.[3] The parson had no more than a life-interest in his estate.

Ecclesiastical opposition to enclosure, then, was based on hard economic realities as well as traditional sentiment. 'Where villages decay, there also do tithes': that fact had been noted in Henry VII's reign.[4] 'One of the best ways to further the minister to become learned', wrote a bishop in 1597, 'is to revise [? revive] the statutes for tillage.'[5] But the church was never able to stop the determined depopulator.[6] 'Decay of tillage' halved the value of a rectory belonging to the Archbishop of Canterbury, a fact which Laud did not fail to emphasize to the culprits as part of the reason why he was 'a great hater of depopulations in any kind, as being one of the greatest mischiefs in this kingdom'. The Rev. George Garrard, indeed, emphasized Laud's 'great care of the church' in describing to Wentworth his general anti-enclosure policy.[7] Blith also gave economic reasons for the observed fact that 'the minister hath seemed to be the opposer of [enclosure] most usually', since depopulation in some parts has overthrown minister and all.[8] Where a village was completely depopulated, and the church fell into disuse, tithes might cease to be paid at all: a not undesirable consummation for the landowner whose God was Mammon.

[1] Trigge, op. cit., sig. E7, F7.
[2] See below, p. 216.
[3] M. James, 'The political importance of the tithes controversy in the English revolution, 1640–60', in *History*, N.S., xxvi. 2.
[4] John Rous, *Historia Regum Angliae*, quoted by Beresford, *Lost Villages*, p. 81.
[5] Usher, op. cit. i. 232.
[6] Beresford, *Lost Villages*, p. 63.
[7] Laud, *Works*, vi. 520; Knowler, op. cit. i. 491.
[8] W. Blith, *The English Improver Improved* (1652), pp. 77–78.

VI

*church loss of revenue —
monastic land exempt from tithes
+ monastic land exempt from tithes*

By 31 Hen. VIII, c. 13, former monastic lands were exempt from tithe even when they had passed into lay hands.[1] In 1896 Mr. Grove tracked down over 86,000 acres still exempt for this reason, and thought the figure could be increased many times over by further research.[2] This exemption was an irrational anomaly, by which it was estimated in 1588 that the church had lost nearly £100,000 a year,[3] and it opened a wide door to further evasion of tithes. For once a monastic estate had been split up and sold, endless disputes were possible about the distinction between land formerly owned and farmed by the monastery, and land merely leased by them. From the latter tithes were due upon increase of cattle, from the former they were not.[4]

Royal demesne and royal forests were tithe-free whilst in the king's ownership: but liable to pay tithe once they had been transferred to anyone else.[5] This too left large loopholes for evasion and dispute. Enclosed commons and reclaimed land were exempt from tithes, by 2 & 3 Ed. VI, c. 13. When such land was 'improved' and converted into arable or meadow, it was tithe-free for seven years—a period which might easily be infinitely extended. Henry Best in Yorkshire does not seen to have expected to have to start paying after the seven years.[6] Marsh and fenland was held not to be within the meaning of the statute, and so not exempt from tithes when brought under cultivation. But the distinction between 'waste and barren land' and marsh was arguable, as was indeed the definition of 'waste and barren land'. Coke laid it down that pasture land should count as 'barren' for the purposes of the statute, even if it had paid tithes of lambs and wool before

[1] Cf. Selden, *Works*, iii. 1202, 1279–80; Stock, op. cit., p. 227; Stillingfleet, op. cit. i. 277. For examples, see H. Smith, op. cit., pp. 281, 304.

[2] Grove, op. cit., pp. 601–5.

[3] Strype, *Whitgift*, i. 535.

[4] For cases involving such disputes, see Purvis, op. cit., pp. 160, 166; Newcourt, op. cit. ii. 82.

[5] Strype, *Annals*, 1, part ii. 425; Earl of Hertford *v*. Leach, 1636, in H. Gwillim, *A Collection of Acts and Records of Parliament, with Reports of Cases . . . respecting Tithes* (1801), ii. 486–501; *Sussex Archaeological Soc. Collections*, xxiii. 267 and *passim*; *Transactions of London and Middlesex Archaeological Soc.* N.S., iv, parts 4 and 5. 443.

[6] Ed. C. B. Robinson, *Farming and Account Books of Henry Best* (Surtees Soc., 1857), pp. 38–40; cf. R. Welford, *Records of the Committee for Compounding with Delinquents in Durham and Northumberland* (Surtees Soc., 1905), p. 243.

conversion to arable.[1] If this question was decided by a jury, the parson would rarely get the benefit of the doubt. Not unnaturally, a clerical spokesman like Sir Thomas Ridley wanted definition of waste and barren land, and cognizance of cases regarding it, to be the exclusive concern of the church courts.[2] *The Husbandmans Plea* argued in 1647 that by the logic of 2 & 3 Ed. VI, c. 13, all land should be tithe-free since all land becomes barren if capital is not invested in its cultivation!'[3]

In the countryside there were bitter quarrels because ministers were still able to enforce their tithe claims. If we hear of fewer disputes in towns and cities it is because personal tithes had virtually ceased to be paid there. Nor was there likely to be much glebe or revenue from great tithes. Whitgift in 1585 thought that the incomes of rectors in cities and towns had declined by 50 per cent. in fifty years.[4] 'Tradesmen', it was noted in 1613, 'do utterly deny to pay anything in the name of a tithe. . . . The citizen doth disdain that the countryman should exceed him or come near him in any kind of expense; he will have a house of greater price than the countryman's, he will have dearer household stuff than the countryman's, he will have richer apparel than the countryman's, he will have costlier victuals than the countryman's, only he will have a minister that costs him less than the countryman's.'[5]

Where there was no glebe or predial tithes—i.e. in the larger cities especially—the end of personal tithes tended to put the minister at the mercy of voluntary contributions from his flock.[6] In fact, by general agreement of contemporaries, towns were seriously under-assessed to tithes by comparison with rural areas. The paper of 1563 previously quoted speaks precisely of 'all cities, market towns, boroughs, thoroughfares, where the greatest multitudes are, and those more ingenious and civil', as containing the parishes devoid of a preaching ministry.[7] Yet ministers' expenses were higher in the cities. Vicars in market towns, Laud noted,

---

[1] Coke, *Second Part of the Institutes*, pp. 655-6.

[2] Ridley, op. cit., pp. 223-9; Degge, op. cit., pp. 221-5; cf. Purvis, op. cit., pp. 98-106.

[3] *The Husbandmans Plea*, p. 102.

[4] Strype, *Whitgift*, iii. 174.

[5] F. Robartes, *The Revenue of the Gospel is Tythes* (1613), pp. 100, 123-4.

[6] See Chapter XIII below.

[7] Strype, *Annals*, I, part i. 481; cf. *The Reformation of the Ecclesiastical Laws*, pp. 128-9.

were worst provided for of all.[1] Hence, among other reasons, the attempts by Puritans and corporations to establish lectureships in market towns, and the endless squabbles that arose therefrom. A few years later Pearson agreed that 'the rich generally pay little, and the poor husbandman bears the burden'.[2]

VII

If we relied upon literary evidence only, it would be almost as easy to argue convincingly that ministers had got richer in the period before 1640 as that they had got poorer. This confusion in contemporary opinion suggests that the question is wrongly posed. To ask whether 'the clergy' prospered or not is like asking whether 'the gentry' rose or declined during this period. The only possible answer is 'both'. Some gentlemen and some ministers throve: others got into financial difficulties. The answers given by contemporaries varied according to the prejudices of the observer; but either case could be supported by factual evidence. It all depended where you looked for it.

I shall argue that the total real income of all parsons at least did not rise in the century before the Long Parliament met. Yet the national income was increasing sharply during that period. So in 1640 most parsons were farther than in 1535 from obtaining that 10 per cent. of the national income to which they felt themselves entitled; and they were farthest of all from it in the richest areas—London, the towns, and the industrial and sheep-farming areas.

The poverty of the clergy, then, of which we hear so much in this century, may or may not have become *absolutely* greater for the profession as a whole, though it did for numerous members of it. But it was becoming greater in proportion to the visibly increasing wealth of the community.

Much of the new national wealth was concentrated in the hands of a relatively small class of merchants, yeomen, and gentlemen, who set new standards of living for professional men. They also set new intellectual standards, and began to demand a learned and preaching clergy—something quite new. Lay Puritanism was the

---

[1] Laud, *Works*, v. 327.
[2] Pearson, op. cit., p. 64. For the special position of London, see Chapter XII below.

expression of an educated middle class, reading and discussing the Bible for itself, and expecting ministers to be able to do so too. It is this simultaneous rise in the demands made upon the rank and file clergy, and relative decrease in the rewards (for the financial plums went to a favoured few) that constitutes the fundamental problem of the church.

The processes so far described suggest that recipients of great tithes (rectors, including impropriators) had a good chance of holding their own in face of the rise in prices: that vicars, receiving small tithes, would have greater difficulty in doing so; and that curates, depending on a stipend or on such residue of tithes as the impropriator thought not worth collecting, fared worst of all. Vicars in unendowed vicarages would for these purposes be as badly off as curates. Most unhappy of all were curates in peculiars, exempt from the jurisdiction of the ordinary, who were at the absolute mercy of impropriators. Such were all livings formerly held by the Priory of St. John of Jerusalem, and very many more.[1]

Thus when Heylyn suggested that benefices 'improved proportionably' to the rise in commodity prices,[2] he was generalizing in a way possible only to one who could assume that the plums of the church were likely to come his way. For if benefices improved, they certainly did not improve equally. And in the divergences lies the key to much clerical discontent. Whitgift stated in 1585 that vicarages, by the decline in offerings and the decay of personal tithes, 'are everywhere by more than a third part decayed' since 1535.[3] Owing to *modi decimandi*, Fuller thought, 'in many places (vicarages especially) a small shiver of bread falls to the share of the minister, not enough for his necessary maintenance'. In some places *modi* have 'almost . . . tithed the tithes'.[4] There is plenty of evidence that vicars suffered, at least in comparison with rectors.

In Leicestershire, for instance, the total value of seventy-eight benefices increased nearly four times between 1535 and 1603: in the same period prices roughly trebled. But this increase fell unevenly, and exaggerated the differentiation within the ranks of the clergy. Whilst the total value of all rectories had risen more than prices, the average vicarage had *diminished* in real value.[5]

---

[1] Ecton, op. cit., p. iv.   [2] Heylyn, *Historical and Miscellaneous Tracts*, i. 175.
[3] Strype, *Whitgift*, iii. 174; cf. i. 407, 500.   [4] Fuller, *Church History*, i. 271, 172.
[5] Hoskins, *Essays in Leicestershire History* (1950), pp. 2, 13, 16–17.

In fourteen Warwickshire rectories listed by Sir Simon Archer in 1623–4, the value had increased some eightfold over that given in the King's Book, from an average of £14. 8s. 4d. to an average of £115. 14s. 5d.[1]

The table on p. 111 gives some further figures. They represent a random sample except for those from Cheshire and Lancashire. In these two counties the vicarages are mostly (though not exclusively) those which the county committees thought required augmentations during the Interregnum; some of the rectories got into the committees' papers because they were very rich. In compiling the figures no case has been included where either the exact nature of the cure or one of the amounts was in any doubt. Such cases are extremely few, and cannot affect the general trends.[2]

At first sight, these figures seem to conflict with the argument that the real income of all but the richest clergy had failed to keep pace with the rise in prices. But closer examination will suggest that this is not so. In the first place, an unknown but certainly large number of ministers leased their livings, and so did not themselves receive the full value.[3] Secondly, the figures are distorted by the existence of a number of very rich livings indeed. These livings, moreover, were frequently held in plurality by bishops, cathedral, or court clergy.[4] It was to the wealthier clergy that Wilson seems to have been referring when he suggested in 1601 that the real value of some livings might be ten times that recorded in the *Valor Ecclesiasticus*.[5] The absolute and percentage increase in value of livings of the poorer clergy was considerably less than the figures in this table suggest.

But there are further defects in the figures as an indication of absolute income. The King's Book in 1535 probably understated the then value of livings, especially of rectories.[6] The parliamentary

---

[1] Archer MSS., Shakespeare's Birthplace, Stratford-on-Avon, of which a transcript was very kindly given to me by Mr. Philip Styles. See also his *Sir Simon Archer*, Dugdale Soc. Occasional Papers, no. 6, p. 31. For other spectacular increases in the real value of rectories, see *Lindsey MSS.* (Hist. MSS. Commission), pp. 177–80; Soden, op. cit., pp. 61, 110.

[2] For the King's Book figures I have used Bacon, *Liber Regis* (2 vols., 1786), checked where necessary by J. Adams, *Index Villaris* (1680), and Ecton, op. cit.

[3] See below, pp. 114–17.   [4] See below, pp. 227–32.

[5] Wilson, op. cit., p. 27.

[6] Thus Bernard Gilpin's rectory of Houghton, Durham, was already worth £400 in the first half of Elizabeth's reign, although in the *Valor Ecclesiasticus* it is set down at £124. (W. Gilpin, *The Life of Bernard Gilpin*, 2nd ed., 1753, pp. 189, 218.) But see p. 190 below for a suggestion that vicarages were over-assessed.

County	Date	Rectories: Number	Rectories: Total (£ s. d.)	Rectories: Average (£ s. d.)	Rectories: % increase	Vicarages: Number	Vicarages: Total (£ s. d.)	Vicarages: Average (£ s. d.)	Vicarages: % increase
Lincolnshire	1535	50	651 9 1	13 0 7		42	348 8 9½	8 5 11	
	1604		1,510 4 2	30 4 1	231		572 0 0	13 12 4	139
Essex	1535	154	2,229 3 9	14 9 6		88	1,147 14 5¼	13 0 10	
	1609*		9,994 2 5	64 17 10	448		3,864 6 8	43 10 11	345
	1650		12,933 4 9	83 19 7	580		4,451 14 10	50 11 9	387
Essex (additional)	1535	75	1,111 2 11	14 16 3		43	577 5 8½	13 8 6	
	1650		6,426 7 8	85 13 8	578		2,278 6 2	52 19 5	394
Hertfordshire	1535	38	650 16 9	17 2 6		25	330 11 6	13 4 5	
	1650		4,426 0 0	116 9 5	679		1,548 10 0	61 18 5	468
Cheshire	1535	5	197 16 3	39 11 3		9	122 9 3	13 12 1	
	1650		953 6 8	190 13 4	481		282 13 4	31 6 2	230
Lancashire	1535	5	167 17 10	33 11 7		18	201 8 7½	11 3 9	
	1650		1,023 19 0	204 15 10	618		897 13 4	49 17 5	446
Nottinghamshire	1535	10	79 7 7	7 18 9		10	63 19 3	6 7 11	
	1650		475 0 0	47 10 0	600		200 6 8	20 0 8	312
Suffolk	1535	17	221 19 7	13 1 2		15	145 10 3½	9 16 0	
	1650		883 0 0	51 18 10	397		547 0 0	36 9 4	381
Wiltshire	1535	32	420 6 6	13 2 8		26	350 13 4½	13 9 11	
	1650		2,752 0 6	86 0 0	655		1,326 0 0	51 0 0	377
Worcestershire	1535	83	1,155 1 0¼	13 18 4		48	592 9 11½	12 6 10½	
	1650		5,386 1 6	64 3 4	466		2,022 11 0	42 2 8	342
Diocese of Worcester	1535	110	1,359 9 8½	12 4 4		80	859 13 6	10 14 11	
	1664		8,782 0 0	79 16 9	646		2,893 0 0	36 3 3	336
Environs of London	1535	24	387 15 6½	16 3 2		23	347 15 0	15 2 4	
	1650		2,333 0 9	97 4 2½	603		1,804 15 0	78 9 4	518
London	1535	82	1,534 5 4	18 14 2½		8	166 8 4	20 16 0½	
	1650		6,890 0 1	84 0 5½	449		1,000 4 8¼	125 0 7	600
Total (excluding Lincs. and diocese of Worcester)	1535	525	£8,155 13 0¾	£15 10 8		313	£4,046 5 8¾	£12 18 6	
	1650		£44,482 0 11	£84 14 6	549		£16,359 15 0¼	£52 5 4	404

* The year 1609 is a guess at the date of the Puritan survey. 1650 is given for all parliamentary surveys, though in fact some were made in 1649 and a few in 1658.

Sources: Ed. C. W. Foster, *The State of the Church in the reigns of Elizabeth and James I* (Lincolnshire Record Soc., 1926), pp. 355–62; *A Viewe of the State of the Clargie within the Countie of Essex* (1895 reprint), pp. 3–17, 38; H. Smith, op. cit., pp. 236–320, *passim*; W. Urwick, *Nonconformity in Herts.* (1884), *passim*; ed. W. A. Shaw, *Minutes of the Committee for the Relief of Plundered Ministers* (Lancashire and Cheshire Record Soc., 1893–7), *passim*; *V.C.H., Nottinghamshire*, ii. 72; *V.C.H., Suffolk*, ii. 45–46; Bodington, op. cit. xl. 253–72; xli. 1–39, 105–24; Urwick, *Nonconformity in Worcestershire* (1897), pp. 163–71; Lysons, op. cit., *passim*; Newcourt, i. 236–566, *passim*. The figures for the diocese of Worcester are from Miss Barratt's D.Phil. thesis.

surveys include the values of ministers' houses, and may in any case have tended to over-estimate: the contrast between the increase in the value of vicarages in the diocese of Worcester between 1535 and 1664, and that recorded for Worcestershire in the parliamentary survey, seems to confirm this. There is therefore almost certainly an exaggeration of the *absolute* increase over the values in the King's Book, especially in the case of vicarages. The figures in the Puritan survey of Essex are suspiciously round, more so even than those of the parliamentary surveyors: and in any case the authors had a case to prove, and it would have suited their book to exaggerate the livings of scandalous ministers. But in fact their general conformity with the main trend is remarkable, and gives one confidence in their relative reliability.

But even if we discount their absolute significance, the figures are of value because of the trends which they indicate. If we exclude London and its environs for the moment, we see that rectories increase by just over 500 per cent., vicarages by only two-thirds as much. The Hertfordshire and Lancashire vicarage figures are in each case upset by one quite exceptional vicarage:[1] if these are omitted the percentage increase is almost exactly 300 per cent. In the environs of London the picture is rather different; and this is what we should expect in an area where vicars had the chance of profiting by market-gardening and fruit-growing for the capital; whilst in the City itself, where there were no great tithes, vicars have actually done better than rectors.[2]

But over the country as a whole, as in lay society, the rich were getting richer, the poor poorer. In 1535 vicarages averaged 83 per cent. of rectories; in 1650, 61 per cent. And these percentage figures conceal the real discrepancies. It would not be much consolation to the vicar of Backford, Lancashire, to think that his rate of increase (£5. 0s. 5d.–£40) was nearly as great as that of the rector of Malpas (£48. 8s. 4d.–£400), and greater than that of the rector of Astbury (£68–300) in the same county. In Oxfordshire, of 11 vicarages, not one had trebled in value between 1535 and 1675; the rectory of Westcott Barton had risen from £7 to £50.[3] There were 18 livings in Essex, 16 in Worcestershire, 6 in

---

[1] Ashwell, Herts., £22. 3s. 6d.–£520; Croston, Lancs., £31. 11s. 10½d.–£379. 13s. 4d.

[2] For London, cf. Chapter XII below.

[3] Miss Barratt's D.Phil. thesis.

Lancashire and Cheshire, 2 in Suffolk, which had not doubled in value between 1535 and 1650: 11, mostly in towns, had actually decreased.

The following table shows the values of Essex livings as given by the parliamentary surveyors. Its significance can be summarized by saying that whilst in 1650 63·75 per cent. of rectories were worth £70 and over, 81·6 per cent. of vicarages were worth less than £70.[1]

Value of living	Number of	
	Rectories	Vicarages
£10–29	6	22
£30–49	31	50
£50–69	46	35
£70–89	50	12
£90–109	48	8
£110–149	31	3
£150–199	8	1
£200–249	8	0
£250–299	0	0
Over £300 . . .	1	0
Total	229	131

Below rectors and vicars was the least fortunate class of all, curates. About their stipends the *Valor Ecclesiasticus* gives us no information. But a few facts can be supplied. Fifty-one curates in Lancashire and Cheshire were paid an average of £8. 17s. 11d. apiece in 1650. They can hardly have prospered greatly during the preceding 115 years. If we leave out the three best paid (£52. 10s., £40, and £25 respectively), the remaining 48 received an average of almost exactly £7 each; 23 of them got £5 or under, down to £1.[2] Agricultural labourers were paid better than that.

To him that had was being given; if nothing was being taken from him that had not, at least very little was being added. The incidence of taxation widened the gulf. For it was based on the value of livings given in the *Valor Ecclesiasticus*, and so fell most heavily on those who had been least successful in raising their revenues above the level of 1535.[3]

---

[1] H. Smith, op. cit., pp. 236–320.
[2] *Minutes of the Committee for Plundered Ministers, passim.*
[3] See below, pp. 189–95.

VIII

But even when the nominal value of rectories or vicarages kept
pace with the rise of prices, we still cannot be sure who got the
increase. An uncertain but large number of incumbents of the
richer livings leased their benefices (or at least the tithes) to
laymen. Cranmer appears positively to have favoured the practice,
making the fact that it was forbidden at canon law an argument
against that law.[1] In 1563 it was stated that 'almost all benefices
of any reasonable value are let out for many years', and all that
Archbishop Parker hoped to be able to do by way of remedy was
to forbid leases for more than three years.[2] In 1585 34 out of 98
ministers in the diocese of Worcester leased the whole or part
of their livings.[3] The bishops were not successful in preventing
the practice, if indeed they ever seriously wished to. 13 Eliz.,
c. 20, perpetuated by 3 Car. I, c. 5, ordered that leases of livings
should be valid only during the residence of the minister, and
that pensions should not be charged on benefices. But that parliamentary reform, so far as it was effective, checked only the
grossest abuse.

There were many temptations. The quickest way for a simoniac
to recover his purchase price was by leasing his living and
absenting himself in pursuit of preferment elsewhere.[4] By
leasing, an incumbent avoided the inconvenience, expense, and
odium of collecting his own tithes. Thomas Gataker gave this
reason for leasing the tithes of Rotherhithe, due mainly from
absentee butchers and graziers.[5] John Donne leased the tithes of
St. Dunstan's to the parish.[6] The minister was subject to all kinds
of pressures from his patron and powerful neighbours, and could
often be persuaded to make favourable terms for himself at the
expense of his successors. In 1575 Whitgift, then Master of
Trinity, asked Bishop Cox of Ely to 'consider how long and in-
jurious leases there be of the most part of ecclesiastical livings,

---

[1] Burnet, op. cit. ii. 324.

[2] Cardwell, *Synodalia*, pp. 507–8; cf. Jewell, *Works*, ii. 984, 999, and Purvis, op.
cit., pp. 47, 133.

[3] I owe this information to Miss Barratt's thesis.

[4] H. Burton, op. cit., p. 105; cf. p. 231 below.

[5] T. Gataker, op. cit., pp. 47–48. He got £100 per annum for the tithe and glebe:
this seems to have been in James I's reign. Cf. p. 211 below.

[6] *Times Literary Supplement*, 16 September 1955.

dignities, prebends and benefices, so that that living which is worth to the farmer 200 marks is not worth to the incumbent £20, as I myself am able to prove in divers and sundry such kinds of livings'.[1]

Ten years later Whitgift, now Archbishop, lamented that the majority of good rectories were held by laymen on long leases, with most unequal conditions to the incumbents, who gained no advantage from the rise in agricultural prices.[2] The shortage of preachers in Northumberland was explained by the Archbishop of York in 1595 by the fact that 'the greatest livings, which were in the Queen's hands, were let to farmers, who would not contribute anything to a preacher'.[3] We see here how all the problems of the church were bound up together. The provision of preaching, so ardently called for by the Puritans, raised far-reaching economic issues. Since the revenue from letting impropriations was essential to royal finance, this particular abuse was beyond the power of bishops to amend. Nor were such practices confined to outlying areas or to the sixteenth century. Most of the rectories belonging to the Dean and Chapter of Worcester were leased in Charles I's reign.[4] In 1639 the sheriff of Hampshire reported to the Council that most of the incumbents of the county, whether because of non-residence or for some other reason, had leased their livings, rectories and vicarages alike, except some poor vicarages which were not assessed for Ship Money.[5]

It was in Hampshire that the rector of Harting ('a poor ignorant man') was persuaded by the recusant patron of the living to pass a lease of it, by which he received only £4 or £5 a year whilst the lessee secured nearly £300. In 1631 the Dean of Winchester was still trying to undo the harm wrought by this lease made over twenty years earlier.[6] At the beginning of Elizabeth's reign Sir Thomas Stanley was granted a ninety-nine years' lease of Winwick rectory by the parson, whose name curiously enough also happened to be Stanley. This lease was challenged in James I's reign, but when a compromise was finally patched up in 1626–8, the rector still got only £225 per annum from 'one of the fattest

---

[1] Kennett, op. cit., appendix, pp. 20–23.

[2] Strype, *Whitgift*, i. 407; cf. iii. 174.

[3] Ibid. ii. 313.

[4] Ed. T. Cave and R. A. Wilson, *The Parliamentary Survey of the Lands . . . of the Dean and Chapter of Worcester* (Worcestershire Historical Soc., 1924), pp. xxvii.

[5] *C.S.P.D., 1639*, p. 32.   [6] *The Diary of John Young*, p. 93.

parsonages in England', whilst the heirs of the lessee were left with about £500 a year.[1]

In Hertfordshire the rector of Shenley was presented to the church courts in 1627 for ploughing on a saint's day. His rectory had been leased for ninety-nine years in 1569 (with the bishop's consent!), and the incumbent was left with only £20 a year, from which he had to pay first-fruits and tenths.[2] A similar ninety-nine years' lease of tithes passed by the Dean and Chapter of Chichester in Elizabeth's reign meant that in seven Sussex parishes there had been no preaching during the sixty years before the civil war.[3] The vicar of Baddow Parva, Essex, in about 1637 leased his living for twenty-one years to a gentleman. There was in consequence no minister, and the parishioners had to hire neighbouring clergy-men to supply the cure.[4] In 1638 the minister of Croston assigned his tithes to the Earl of Derby, in return for £50 cash and an annuity of £13. 6s. 8d. He felt that £50 was inadequate, but he had left the sum to be fixed at the Earl's discretion, so he had no remedy. In 1650 the vicarage was valued at £379. 13s. 4d. a year.[5]

In Northamptonshire in 1641 Sir John Wake was reported to hold the parsonage of Piddington 'by colour of some old lease from St. John's Hospital in Northampton', though no one knew when, if ever, the lease was due to terminate. This was 'no lawful vicarage, but a church robbed by strong hand'. Sir John held the rectory, the glebe, and all the tithes, to an estimated total value of almost £300. There was not even a resident curate, 'only Sir John keeps a minister in his house . . . whom he sends to Piddington at times'.[6]

The last story is to be treated with caution, since it comes from a propagandist source. But the other examples are less suspect. They suggest yet a further warning against assuming that the minister necessarily benefited even where the nominal revenue of

---

[1] Ed. A. Clark, *The Life and Times of Anthony Wood* (Oxford Hist. Soc., 1891–1900), i. 151–2; J. E. Birley, *The Life of a Lancashire Rector during the civil war* (1877), pp. 5–6.   [2] Urwick, *Nonconformity in Hertfordshire*, pp. 458–60.

[3] C. Thomas-Stanford, *Sussex in the Great Civil War* (1910), pp. 294–5. If the man who in about 1651 reported the story to the Sussex Committee had got the dates right, this lease must have been granted after the statute of 1571 prohibiting leases for more than twenty-one years or three lives. See above, p. 30.

[4] H. Smith, op. cit., p. 253; cf. *C.S.P.D.*, *1637–8*, p. 362 (49 years' lease in Somerset).

[5] Ed. J. H. Stanning, *Royalist Composition Papers for Lancashire* (Lancashire and Cheshire Record Soc., 1892), p. 140; *Minutes of the Committees for Plundered Ministers*, p. 259. For Derby's revenue from tithes, see Stanning, pp. 126, 130.

[6] *A Certificate from Northamptonshire*, pp. 3–4; see other examples on pp. 6–7.

his living improved proportionably to the rise in prices. And they show once again how the gentry were controlling and exploiting the church. When, as often happened, bishops or deans and chapters shared the income from their impropriate rectories with lessees to the detriment of the vicar, we are reminded once again of the deep economic divisions which contributed to prevent the church presenting a united front to its despoilers.

In the days before the establishment of a funded national debt, indeed, the leasing of tithes (or the purchase of an impropriation) offered a convenient, safe, and not unprofitable form of investment. In some cases the lease was a fig-leaf covering an outright transfer, as with the 2,000 years' lease of the tithes of Smithfield, Warwickshire.[1] Such a lease presumably dates from the early days of the Reformation. But later even so prudent a financier as Sir Arthur Ingram found it worth his while to lease tithes from a Cambridge college.[2] Sir John Bramston's mother in her widowhood depended largely upon a lease of the tithes of St. Botolph's without Aldersgate, left her by her husband. She paid £20 per annum to the Dean and Chapter of Westminster for this lease, and sub-let it to William Kirby for £120, retaining for herself the rent of two houses worth about £30 a year. Kirby's receipts were estimated by the vicar in 1638 at about £200. The vicar himself got only some £71 in all, out of which he had to pay £20 to a curate. It is hardly surprising that during the revolution tithes proved difficult to collect in this parish.[3]

IX

So in the century after the dissolution the *average* money value of benefices may have increased four or five times, thus apparently roughly keeping pace with the rise in prices. But this average figure conceals the fact that some rectors had got much richer, whilst the real incomes of many vicars and curates, and even of some rectors, had fallen sharply. It does not tell us whether the profits of any given benefice were collected by the incumbent or by a lay impropriator or farmer. Unless special remedies were adopted, the legally established incomes of urban rectors and

[1] Ed. S. C. Ratcliff and H. C. Johnson, *Warwickshire Quarter Sessions Order Book, 1637-50* (Warwick County Records, 1936), p. 219.
[2] *Hist. MSS. Commission, Report on MSS. in various collections*, viii. 51.
[3] Sir J. Bramston, *Autobiography* (Camden Soc., 1845), p. 16; T. C. Dale, *The Inhabitants of London in 1638* (1931), p. 209.

vicars might be infinitesimal. The wealth of ministers, particularly in towns, might decline relative to that of the more important members of their congregations even where it did not decline absolutely.

Taking all this into account, it seemed vital to responsible members of the hierarchy, if the church was to maintain its position in society, to get behind tithe agreements, to recover personal tithes, and to obtain for ministers something approaching a genuine tenth of the wealth produced in the country. By the law of God and nature, Dr. Cowell declared, no custom which prevented this ought to last any longer than the parson approved of it. Tithes, argued Bishop Carleton, were better than stipends because they were not affected by fluctuations in the price level: 'howsoever the price of things rise or fall, the minister hath his part with his people in all estates by tithes'. That was in God's mind when He ordained the payment of tithes. 'It would much trouble the wisest to name a stipend that would be sufficient at all times.'[1]

But for the full realization of God's intentions tithes should be paid in kind, or rates of commutation should vary with the general price level. 'With what conscience', Dr. Tillesley asked Selden and his readers, 'may a man retain his tithe, and pay for it but a penny or a halfpenny, which is now xiid. or iis.? And why should the tenth be less worth than any other of the nine parts are?'[2] Hence the continued attempts of the clergy to overthrow all tithe agreements, as by the bill of 1584 for true answering of tithes.[3] Bancroft wanted the restitution of tithes in kind (as well as of traditional fees) and the abolition of *modi*, and he felt that even these drastic measures might not solve the church's economic problems unless all exemptions from tithe were ended and some impropriations could also be recovered.[4]

To those who thought like Bancroft, the whole development described by Tillesley, whatever its causes, was wrong: it should be put right as a mere matter of equity. 'We enfeeble our bodies', wrote Richard Montagu eloquently, 'beat our brains, and burn out the very lamp of our lives, for other men; and yet it is thought fit we should live upon alms.' But there was also a positive moral obligation on laymen to see that the wrong was righted: for

---

[1] Cowell, op. cit., s.v. 'Tithes'; Carleton, op. cit., p. 27.

[2] R. Tillesley, *Animadversions upon M. Selden's History of Tithes* (1619), p. 224.

[3] Sir Simonds D'Ewes, *Journals of All the Parliaments during the Reign of Queen Elizabeth* (1682), pp. 335–72.

[4] Usher, op. cit. ii. 256–7, 332–3.

tithes were due by the law of God. 'Let your bounty alone', Montagu continued, 'restore us our own, to which we have eternal right.'[1]

In the sixteen-thirties serious attempts were made to revise *modi* to the advantage of tithe collectors. A wealthy pluralist, Meric Casaubon, raised the rate of tithe for marsh and pasture lands in Minster, Kent, from 1*s*. 2*d*. an acre to 1*s*. 6*d*. This increase, he claimed, was less than the rise in prices since the rate had been fixed. The vicar of Dartford raised the tithe which he claimed on marsh land by 6*d*. an acre. The farmer of two other vicarages in Kent 'unconscionably racked and improved . . . the tithes'.[2]

To many laymen the rights did not seem so exclusively on one side as they did to Montagu. Nobody ever likes paying rent or taxes: the desire to avoid an increase, however 'equitable', needs no explanation. But the *effectiveness* of the opposition, in what we are usually led to believe was a religious and minister-ridden society, calls for comment.

In the first place, the whole mode of thought of protestantism contributed by its stepping-down of the status of the priest. He was no longer the indispensable mediator between man and God, superintending the miracle of the mass. Inward grace and repentance, not sacraments and formal good works, opened the doors to heaven. Sermons were more important than ceremonies. Payment of tithes became a statutory duty because it had lost its moral compulsion: and their legal as opposed to divine right basis further diminished the moral sanction behind tithes. Bishop Carleton found it necessary to argue at some length that tithes were not 'properly ceremonial' and so not abolished under the Gospel.[3] The destructive implications of protestantism went far.

Secondly, those most successful in evading the real burden of tithes were precisely those who were prospering most in the century and a half before 1640—citizens of London, industrialists, sheep-farmers, lessees, market-gardeners, not to mention those whose wealth was won outside England—merchants, fishermen, pirates, plunderers of Ireland and America, investors in trading or

---

[1] Montagu, op. cit., pp. 403–4. Montagu's own dogged, and ultimately successful, hunt for promotion, shows his determination to make the most of this 'eternal right'. (See Ornsby, op. cit. i, *passim*.)

[2] Larking, op. cit., pp. 105–9, 235, 155–6; cf. pp. 206–26.

[3] Carleton, op. cit., pp. 12–17; cf. Brian Walton's analysis summarized on p. 278 below; also Hooker, *Ecclesiastical Polity*, ii. 442–57; Comber, op. cit. i. 242; ii. 158.

colonial ventures. Those sectors of economic activity which produced the biggest profits would have been hardest hit if the tithing
system had been recast as the ecclesiastics wished it to be.

Yet the margin between success and failure in these sectors was
still very narrow. Much business activity, whether overseas trade
or industrial enterprise, was still highly speculative. In new
industries, where monopolies had to be bought and therefore
courtiers bribed, heavy initial capital outlay was essential. In the
older industries government interference (as in the Cokayne
project) or a monopoly might bankrupt many small men. For
traders, privateers, and pirates the cost of ships and armaments
was heavy and continually increasing. The switch-over from arable
to pasture, from corn-growing to market-gardening, also called
for considerable expenditure. And interest rates were high. To
the business man it would have seemed outrageously unfair to be
asked to pay full tithes on increased profits resulting from capital
investment for which (except in the case of enclosure of the waste)
no allowance was made. It was the age of accumulation of capital: if
you could take care of the pence, the pounds would take care of themselves. Wise investment at the right time would bring in large profits.
But whilst many succeeded, the debtors' jail awaited others.

In the rural areas it was the yeomen and middling husbandmen,
those who would have liked to extend their farms to meet the
steadily expanding demand for wool and food, who were most
conscious of the burden of tithes, most radical in their opposition
to them. This opposition was no doubt as old as Christianity in
England; but the sixteenth-century economic developments made
such men especially conscious of tithes as a burden. Men richer
and more powerful could drive a bargain with the minister, and
might themselves collect tithes as impropriators; so their attitude
towards tithes was ambiguous. But the yeomen and husbandmen
knew no such inhibitions. Once experience and the new critical
spirit had shattered their traditional belief that regular payment of
tithes was essential to worldly prosperity, they might easily be
brought by their own observation to hold that the opposite was true.[1]

It was also those who most benefited by the new ways of making
wealth who enjoyed the greatest relative immunity from taxation
because of the failure of old taxes like the subsidy to tap their new
wealth.[2] The royal attempt to draw on such wealth, by forced

[1] *The Husbandmans Plea*, sig. A^v.   [2] Dietz, op. cit., *passim*; cf. pp. 87–89 above.

loans, benevolences, Ship Money, roused opposition precisely similar to that produced by the episcopal attempt to increase revenue from tithes. Here again we find deep economic roots for the unity of Puritan and parliamentarian opposition. In both church and state a drastic financial reorganization was necessary: the civil war was fought to decide which element in society should control and profit by that reorganization.

The struggle for tithes, or rather for the *status quo* which the ecclesiastical politicians would have liked to upset, was therefore a life and death matter to many a hard-working yeoman and crafts-man, improving landlord or overseas trader; and no less so to the humble copyholder or journeyman, who in this matter would follow the lead of his betters. It was one form of the struggle for the growing surplus being produced in the sixteenth century, a struggle which went on between laymen not less than between parsons and laymen, even in tithe disputes. Dr. Purvis has drawn attention to a sudden and startling increase in tithe litigation between laymen after the dissolution of the monasteries.[1]

To the ecclesiastical politician the refusal to recognize the iniquity of out-of-date *modi decimandi* was stupidly sinful; but to many a layman the maintenance of the *modus* was essential to his economic survival. Selden, the Sussex yeoman's son, was not fighting a private war with his 'so much applauded *History of Tithes*':[2] he had a class behind him.

X

Nor was the controversy confined to England. Inevitably, any really radical movement of social protest in medieval society, such as that of the Lollards in England or the Taborites in Bohemia, had wished to bring the priest under the control of the community, to pay him a stipend. What was new in the sixteenth century was the coalescence of this popular social protest with the perennial attempts of the landed class to plunder the church. This helps to explain the dual strand which runs all through protestantism, its combination of 'democracy' and 'oligarchy', of 'individualism' and 'collectivism'; the fear of anabaptistry in the orthodox, the conviction, sincerely held by English presbyterians

[1] Purvis, op. cit., p. viii.
[2] Montagu, op. cit., sig. A3–3ᵛ. See below, pp. 136–7.

in the sixteen-forties, that toleration was a work of the devil; John Lilburne's equally sincere belief that he was following in the steps of the protestant martyrs. The Calvinist conception of the church itself was ambiguous: in one sense it comprised the whole of society, in another sense it consisted of the elect minority only. It was as contradictory as Locke's conception of 'the people'.[1]

But the working out of these contradictions lay far ahead. The idea of paying a stipend to the priest was older than protestantism, but it was with the protestants that it became relatively respectable. Luther had declared that tithes belonged to the state, although he later modified his position sufficiently for Lancelot Andrewes to claim him and Melanchthon as defenders of tithes. 'Calvin, Martyr and Bucer', the Bishop of Winchester had to admit, 'go another way'. In England, he thought, it was 'the devourers of church revenues', who 'whisper up and down in corners', challenge tithes in this old age of the world, 'this eating and drinking age', and talk of a stipend.[2] Selden himself pointed out that some of the reformed churches had abandoned the whole traditional principle of tithing and adopted a system of paying ministers stipends.[3] Men knew that tithes had helped to finance the Dutch war of independence against Spain.

In 1547 it had been intended that all bishops' lands should be seized by the king, and that bishops should receive stipends from the crown. This proposal was revived by Dr. Henry Hooke in 1630, who wanted bishops to be allowed £1,000 a year each. Hooke, although orthodox in his theology, had already lost the favour of court and bishops by preaching against non-residence; he thought that ministers should not be J.P.s, nor bishops privy councillors.[4] Two years later Richard Spink of St. John's College,

---

[1] C. Hill, 'Puritans and the Poor', in *Past and Present*, no. 2; C. B. Macpherson, 'The Social Bearing of Locke's Political Theory', in *Western Political Quarterly*, vii, no. 1.

[2] L. Andrewes, *Of the Right of Tithes* (1647 translation), p. 26; R. B. Schlatter, *Private Property* (1951), p. 84.

[3] Selden, *Works*, iii. 1177. Not that this automatically solved the economic problem. Sir Benjamin Rudyerd in 1628 expressed himself as scandalized by the poverty of the stipendiary ministers in the reformed churches of Germany (Manning, *Memoirs of Rudyerd*, p. 136). For allegations of the poverty of the state-salaried ministers in the Netherlands, see Heylyn, *History of the Presbyterians*, pp. 137–8, and Comber, op. cit. ii. 189. For stipends in Scotland, see J. Knox, *History of the Reformation* (1949), ii. 30–31.

[4] *C.S.P.D., 1629–31*, p. 280; *1625–49*, p. 71; C. Stephenson and F. G. Marcham, *Sources of English Constitutional History* (1938), pp. 468–9.

Cambridge, condemned non-residency and 'approved the act of the great-grandfather of the king of Sweden in taking away the revenues of the churches and making them all stipendiary'. Mr. Spink was sent down in disgrace: in due course he recanted most submissively.[1] In 1634 a commission was appointed to look after all the English colonies, with Laud at its head. Among its duties was to establish a clergy supported by 'tithes, oblations and other profits'.[2] It was rightly supposed that ministers in the New World would not be endowed with tithes by the free will of the Puritan emigrants. The tendency of radical protestant thought was in the opposite direction.

Earlier, Bishop Carleton had found it necessary to attack the theory that if the minister got a 'competent maintenance' instead of tithes, that met God's requirements. Every man', he pointed out, 'will take upon him to define a competent maintenance'.[3] The phrase 'a competent maintenance' became indeed almost a hall-mark of Puritanism. It was a double-edged phrase, since it implied a wish to augment livings as well as a rejection of tithes by divine right. It also contained the idea of *equalizing* the remuneration of ministers, and so concealed an attack on the position of bishops, deans, and other dignitaries.[4] And once the minister's automatic claim to a tenth was abandoned, Carleton was right to suppose that there was no logically defensible half-way house between that and the voluntary principle, dependence of clergymen on the good will of their flocks. Some ministers, indeed, to avoid the hazards and animosities of collecting tithes were willing to agree with their parishioners on *modi* which were virtually indistinguishable from stipends. This was risky, to them and especially to their successors: it led to direct economic dependence. Calibute Downing, noting the practice, hoped it would never become general 'as long as this kingdom is a monarchy, for it is a mystery of free cities and democracies'.[5]

There were wide political implications, then, and it was a matter on which 'the churches abroad' had experience to offer. The very

---

[1] *C.S.P.D., 1631–3*, pp. 334, 553.   [2] Gardiner, *History of England*, viii. 167.
[3] Carleton, op. cit., pp. 1–3, 22ᵛ; cf. Robartes, op. cit., p. 132; Fuller, *Collected Sermons*, i. 430; Stock, op. cit., pp. 223–4.
[4] W. H. Frere, *A History of the English Church, 1558–1625* (1904), p. 248; cf. A. Smith, op. cit. ii. 453–7.
[5] C. Downing, op. cit., p. 91. Cf. J. Burckhardt, *Reflections on History* (1943), pp. 102–4.

idea of paying stipends to ministers could be made to sound subversive. Heylyn hinted darkly that, as the revolutionary war in the Netherlands had been financed by tithes, so Englishmen were encouraged to believe that 'if the Parliament prevailed in the present [civil] war, they should pay no tithes at all'.[1] And in fact these problems were settled not by theological or antiquarian arguments, but by the blood and iron of the civil war—though not in the way Levellers and Quakers hoped and Heylyn pretended to fear.

XI

So the two sides diverged. The parliamentarians saw economic popery in the Laudian schemes for reorganization; the hierarchy saw voluntaryism and republicanism lurking behind the Puritan demand for a competent maintenance. The important question before 1640 was how and where tithe cases were to be decided. If they went before the church courts, as the bishops wished, any *modus* would be called in question which did not give the incumbent an 'equitable' tenth. If they went before the common-law courts a 'rank *modus*' would be disallowed because too large: no *modus* would be disallowed because too small.[2]

The church courts insisted that producers should notify the minister when hay had been mown, or corn harvested: the common-law courts did not care if the corn or hay rotted in the fields, provided the parson's share had been lawfully separated from the other nine-tenths.[3] 'One while, the parson sueth the parishioner for bringing home his tithes; another while, the parishioner sueth the parson for not taking away his tithes in time.'[4] The common-law courts, unlike the church courts, allowed no tithe of agistment on sheep fatted for the market, since the parson would get a tithe of their wool (7 Car. I). The common-law courts decided that fallow was tithe-free (7 Jac. I); but in 15 Car. I (under the ascendancy of Laud) Sir Robert Berkeley ruled that if an occupier left his land fallow in order to prejudice the minister, the latter might sue *in the church courts* for it.[5] Motives are difficult to ascertain, but the ecclesiastical courts would no doubt be severer with delinquent

---

[1] Heylyn, *Historical and Miscellaneous Tracts*, i. 177.
[2] See p. 97 above.
[3] Gibson, op. cit., pp. 710–11, 719–21; cf. p. 91 above.
[4] T. Nashe, *Pierce Penilesse his Supplication to the Devil*, in *Works* (1904), i. 189.
[5] Gibson, op. cit., pp. 717, 709.

laymen than the common-law courts. Hostility to the clergy must have gone far before a husbandman would thus cut off his nose to spite his minister's face.

The common-law courts, as we have seen, issued prohibitions to stop ministers carrying forward claims on small livestock from one year to another. Prohibitions were also issued to check clerical attempts to tithe bricks (18 Eliz.) and coal (13 Jac. I), as well as to remove trial of the validity of customs and *modi decimandi* from the church courts. To the prejudices of common-law judges, moreover, we must add the prejudices of common-law juries, which would almost invariably be composed of interested parties, tithe-paying laymen. If such men had to pronounce upon customs of tithing fish or lead or 'old mills', or to decide what land was 'waste and barren', ministers' claims were likely to get short shrift.[1]

But tithe causes still formed a large part of the business of the ecclesiastical courts.[2] In the seventeenth century Coke and others began to insist that prohibitions should be used to bring *all* suits about tithes or impropriations before the common-law courts, or (in cases affecting London tithes) before the Lord Mayor of London.[3] In these courts tithes would be treated as a form of property like any other. Men, even the ministers of God, must keep covenant: and custom once established would validate a *modus decimandi*, whether or not it gave the minister 10 per cent. of what his parishioners produced. Those who plead prescription, said Thomas Adams, could 'undo the poor ministers in these terrene courts', even though their plea would be damned in the courts of God.[4] A Puritan like Stoughton argued in 1604 that suits concerning tithes or wills should be handed over to the common-law courts: 'the customs of payment of tithes', Ridley retorted, 'are triable only at the ecclesiastical courts.'[5] But even Falkland, a royalist in the civil war, thought there was nothing sacred about the right of bishops' courts to try tithe cases.[6] It was only after

---

[1] Gibson, op. cit., pp. 707–8, 712; Bohun, *The Law of Tithes*, pp. 119–20, 360; Hughes, op. cit. (3rd ed.), pp. 282–5. See pp. 86, 89, 94, 96–98, 104 above.

[2] Cf. Fletcher, op. cit., p. 48; F. G. Emmison, 'Abstract of the Account Book of the Archdeacon of Huntingdon's Court', *Transactions of the East Herts. Archaeological Soc.* viii. 28–29.

[3] For the jurisdiction of the Lord Mayor, see Chapter XII.

[4] Adams, *Gods Bountie*, in *Workes*, p. 864.

[5] W. Stoughton, *An Assertion for true and Christian Church-Policie* (1604), pp. 90–103; Ridley, op. cit., pp. 148–51, 259–61.

[6] Rushworth, op. cit. iv. 186.

the abolition of episcopacy that ingenious radicals began to argue
that the church courts alone had jurisdiction in tithe suits, and
therefore that the right to collect tithes had been abolished with
them.[1]

We should not, however, imagine that all laymen appealed to
the common-law courts, all parsons to the church courts. In each
case men would go where they thought they were most likely to
win a verdict favourable to their interests. Many laymen were
recipients of tithes: and there were tithe disputes between vicars
and clerical rectors. Common-law procedure required only one
witness to establish a custom, ecclesiastical courts two.

The rival jurisdictions, moreover, could be used for delay, or
to confuse the issue.[2] In 1621 the Master of the Court of Wards
reported to the House of Commons a tithe suit between a ward
and a parson. Both had been committed to prison, the parson by
the Court of Wards, the ward by Chancery: 'and this proceeds
because there is no difference set between the jurisdiction of courts'.
Cranfield asked for remedial legislation, but unsuccessfully.[3] In
the sixteen-thirties the rector of Fiskerton, Lincolnshire, brought
a suit in the church courts against a farmer whom he accused of
withholding tithes from 550 acres of land. The farmer obtained
a prohibition, and the case was transferred to the common-law
courts. When a jury returned a verdict against him, the farmer got
a consultation, and the case reverted to the church courts. The
decision went against him there too, and by this time he had died;
but his heirs, undaunted, appealed to the Court of Arches. At this
stage the exhausted rector asked Laud to intervene.[4] On such
terms it was hardly worth suing for tithes at all against a rich
parishioner. Even after Thomas Gataker had got an Exchequer
decree recognizing his right to tithe from houses in Rotherhithe,
he still thought it safer to accept an offer of £40 from his parishioners in lieu of those tithes than to face the hazards of bringing
further suits: the possibilities of delay were not yet exhausted.[5]

Various statutes of Henry VIII and Edward VI authorized the
ecclesiastical courts, in case of non-payment, to award double the

---

[1] *The Husbandmans Plea*, pp. 62–66.   [2] Usher, op. cit. ii. 63–66, 276.
[3] E. Nicholas, *Proceedings and Debates in the House of Commons in 1620 and 1621*
(1766), i. 44. For complaints of withdrawal of cases from church to common-law
courts, see Ridley, op. cit., pp. 146–8, 180–1.
[4] *C.S.P.D.*, *1640–1*, pp. 343–4.
[5] Gataker, op. cit., pp. 48–50. See p. 114 above.

value of the tithes in dispute, over and above·the original sum
due. In 29 Eliz. an ingenious lawyer persuaded the common-law
courts that under 2 & 3 Ed. VI, c. 13, action of debt lay at
common law where tithes had not been properly set out. In such
an action treble damages could be recovered, and henceforth
there were many such cases.[1] But since costs could be recovered
in the church courts, a verdict there was often more advantageous
to the recipient of tithes, especially in suits over tithes of small
value, where common-law costs were likely to be prohibitive.[2] In
the Exchequer Court only the single value of the tithes was
recoverable.

prohibitions

Common-law prohibitions could be issued in tithe cases on a
great variety of grounds, of which the following are some of the
chief: (i) if prescription was pleaded in attempting to establish a
modus, or where there was a written *modus*, or where the existence
of a *modus* was in dispute; (ii) if the bounds of a parish were in
dispute; (iii) if it was claimed that the lands were tithe-free as
former monastic lands, or as reclaimed waste; (iv) if the things
sued for were not tithable at common law (and we have seen how
many commodities this included); (v) if it was claimed that tithes
had been taken after parishioners had separated the minister's
tenth from the remaining nine parts—unless the suit was between
two ecclesiastics; (vi) if there had been irregular procedure in a
spiritual court; (vii) if a church court disallowed proof by one witness.[3] It was a poor lawyer who could not get a prohibition with
all those possibilities before him.

Where there was no written agreement the common law, so
respectful of contract, would be unsympathetic to clerical claims.
Men performed their covenants made: but where there is no
covenant, as Hobbes said, there can be no injustice.[4] Once a case
was transferred to the common-law courts 'the truth may be
overborne', Bancroft sadly warned the privy council in 1605, 'and
poor ministers still left unto country trials, there to justify the
right of their tithes before unconscionable jurors in these cases'.
The whole weakness of the church's position, as he saw it, was that
'contentious persons' knew only too well 'their own strength with

[1] Bohun, *The Law of Tithes*, pp. 355–6; Sheppard, op. cit., pp. 70–71.
[2] Coke, *First Part of the Institutes*, p. 159; *Second Part of the Institutes*, p. 651;
The Husbandmans Plea, p. 69; Rayner, op. cit. I. lxii–lxiii; Sheppard, op. cit., pp. 70–71.
[3] Degge, op. cit., pp. 271, 276–80, 293, 303.
[4] Hobbes, *Leviathan*, p. 74.

jurors in the country'. However well directed by the judge, Montagu agreed sourly, juries 'will be sure to understand the evidence for the party whom they favour, and go against the parson for his tithe'. That is why Bancroft, and Laud after him, wished to 'break the back of prohibitions'.[1] In 1606 it was reported that the king had consented 'to put a restraint upon prohibitions'.[2] James was at pains to deny what he admitted was the common belief that he was 'an enemy to all prohibitions, and an utter stayer of them'; but he spoke with feeling against their employment to the detriment of ministers' claims to tithes.[3]

'Many ministers have grown of late more troublesome to their parishioners', said the common-law judges in 1605, since they were no longer 'content with what was usually paid'. Thereby they brought custom and profits into the spiritual courts. 'Were it not for the prohibition' the clergy 'would overthrow all pre-scriptions and compositions that are for tithes, which doth and would breed such a general garboil amongst the people as were to be pitied and not to be permitted. And where they say there be many statutes that take away these proceedings from the temporal courts, they are much deceived.' Bancroft wanted the church courts to have the right of 'interpreting all statute laws concerning the clergy': the judges replied that this right belonged to them.[4] Whatever his subjective motives, Coke was no more conducting a mere personal battle than was Selden. The squabbles over juris-diction affected matters of great substance for men of property.

Hence the Ecclesiastical Commission was the battleground, since in it the bishops attempted to create an overriding authority. In 1606 the common-law judges stated that the Commission might not examine laymen on oath, except in matrimonial causes. They denied its right to imprison. In 1607 they denied its compe-tence to try tithe causes at all.[5] Oaths were a crucial point in the disputes. Putting a man on oath was thought to be the only rapid way of getting at the truth. About 1569 it was proposed that

---

[1] Cardwell, *Documentary Annals*, ii. 94–95; Laud, *Works*, iv. 138–41, v. 351; Montagu, op. cit., pp. 89, 119. Juries, Montagu thought, were equally prejudiced against lords in cases affecting commons or copyholds. Remarks like Bancroft's and Montagu's help us to grasp how far—doctrinal Puritanism apart—the established church was from enjoying the sympathy and respect even of the propertied class.

[2] Cardwell, *Synodalia*, p. 589.

[3] Ed. C. H. McIlwain, *The Political Works of James I* (1918), pp. 312–13, 336.

[4] Coke, *Second Part of the Institutes*, pp. 610–11.

[5] Frere, op. cit., p. 358.

section 9 of 2 & 3 Ed. VI, c. 13, should be repealed, and that 'bishops should be empowered to give any man a corporal oath and to examine him thereupon concerning the true payment of his personal tithes'. All men of property would share the common lawyers' objection to such procedure, and this 'article for government and order in the church' was 'not allowed'.[1] The common-law courts could still require a man to give evidence about his own liability to tithe, as the Quakers found to their cost.[2] But they were mostly vulgar men of small property.

With or without the power to put on oath, excommunication was always the church's ultimate sanction, in economic causes no less than in spiritual: it was, wrote Helwys, 'of . . . especial use of profit in that by the power thereof are brought in all duties, tithes and court fees'.[3] The end of excommunication as an effective sanction was not one of the least significant consequences of the revolutionary period.

This is no place for a full analysis of the reasons for the alliance between common lawyers, parliamentarians, and Puritans. It is, however, worth noting how far back it goes. Bishop Cooper already found it necessary to rebuke Martin Marprelate because his attitude meant that 'the whole state of the laws of this realm will be altered. For the canon law must be utterly taken away. . . . And matters of tithes, testaments and matrimony, judgments also of adultery and slander, etc., are in these men's judgments mere temporal, and therefore to be dealt in by the temporal magistrate only.'[4]

In many respects the alliance was one of convenience. Mere sordid questions of fees inclined lawyers and judges to like seeing causes brought before their courts. But it goes far deeper than that. The 'liberalization of the common law', of which Mr. Wagner has written,[5] suggests a real community of interest between business men and at least a section of the legal profession. Nor is there anything surprising in this. The lawyers were largely drawn from the same groups as merchants and improving lessees. They had similar interests in money-making, in not being ruled by old-fashioned

---

[1] Strype, *Annals*, 1, part i. 563.
[2] S. Fisher, *Works* (1679), p. 441.
[3] Helwys, op. cit., p. 20.
[4] Cooper, op. cit., p. 66.
[5] D. O. Wagner, 'Coke and the rise of economic liberalism', in *Econ. Hist. Rev.* vi. 30–44.

clerics or new-fangled civilians. 'If bishops and their courts were
overthrown', wrote a pamphleteer in 1641, people would be freed
from paying tithes, 'which is the secret thing which our common
freeholders and grand-jury-men do so much aim at.'[1] Behind the
conflict of courts lurked questions affecting economic interests:
what mattered was not where one got justice, but what sort of
justice one got.

From one point of view it was 'just' that the parson should
receive his fair tenth: that was the point of view of the church
courts and the bishops, of conservatives. From the other point
of view it was 'just' that men should abide by covenants freely
entered into; that industry should not be penalized to succour
improvident non-producers; that parsons should have no claim
on the community for services which they rendered incom-
petently and whose value was anyway dubious: that was the
point of view of the lawyers, of advocates of economic freedom,
of radicals.

The spokesmen of the church claimed that God from the beginning had 'a right in every man's goods', and that He gave tithes
to the church out of this right.[2] Now this is a denial of that claim
to absolute property rights which business men, with the help of
the common lawyers, were trying to establish. The crown's right
to collect feudal dues, of irregular incidence, also limited absolute
property rights. The Commons negotiated for the abolition of
these dues in 1610, abolished them in 1646, and got this abolition
confirmed in 1660. Similarly the crown's right to tax without the
consent of Parliament was attacked as an infringement of property:
and was abolished by the revolution. Tithes had the advantage of
being relatively certain in their incidence: but tithes claimed as
part of God's right to 10 per cent. of every man's goods infringed
the absolute sanctity of property that the revolution was to secure.

I have over-simplified and sharpened the outlines of the conflict:
but that is what it was about. Neither Coke's dismissal nor Selden's
recantation could stop the wheels of industry going round.

So the first and most obvious clerical policy—revision of the
modi—came up against solid hostility especially from the men of
substance in town and country, from the jury class, abetted by
the common lawyers and supported by the humbler artisans and

---

[1] *A Certificate from Northamptonshire*, p. 14.
[2] Carleton, op. cit., p. 5ᵛ.

farmers. The tremendous effort made by the ecclesiastical courts, pressed on by Bancroft, to revise *modi decimandi* in an upwards direction was frustrated by the issue of prohibitions by the common-law judges. The battle between Bancroft and Coke ended in an indecisive compromise in 1611; neither ecclesiastical nor common-law courts established a monopoly over tithe disputes. But in such circumstances the church's failure to win victory outright was equivalent to defeat, since the whole trend of development of society was against it. The creeping invasion of the common-law courts had advanced too far to be driven back. Tithes remained a form of property, and Selden could ask with assumed naïveté, 'To whom it belongs more to write the *History of Tithes* than to a common lawyer?'[1] Laud had to start the struggle all over again. But already wide support, of a decidedly non-theological kind, had been won for Puritan policies among those 'common freeholders and grand-jury-men' who opposed episcopal jurisdiction for economic reasons.

[1] Selden, *Works*, iii. 1073.

VI

IMPROPRIATIONS

You say they [tithes] were taken away from idle drones and
fat-bellied monks. . . . From the unworthy they were taken, from
the worthy they are detained. But to whom are they given?
Possidebant Papistae, possident rapistae. Those kept some good
hospitality with them, these keep none.

T. ADAMS, *Mans seede-time and Harvest*, in *Workes*, p. 638

The supreme magistracy, by robbing the greatest part of parish
churches and selling away all impropriated benefices to the
nobility and gentry, and they covetously retaining them in their
possession, have made the churches and ministry base, contemptible and beggarly.

The Model of a Presbyterian Government (1646), p. 28

I

OPPOSITION to tithes was one thing: opposition to impropriations another. The clergy wanted to enforce and increase tithes: the radicals and sectaries wanted to abolish
them. But others among the critics of the church themselves
collected tithes as impropriators or lessees. So when we come to
consider the resumption of impropriations as a possible solution
to the economic problems of the church, we find different attitudes.
The clergy thought impropriations *'radix omnium malorum* in this
realm'.[1] The gentry felt otherwise. And those who disapproved
of tithes altogether had no sympathy for clerical aspirations to
recover impropriations.

Originally, in theory at least, the parish priest had been supported by voluntary contributions from his parishioners because
he performed social functions which they valued. But at an early
date tithes had become a charge enforced by law. They tended
to be disposed of by the landlord, the patron of the church: it was
indeed with a view to attracting this additional payment from

[1] Strype, *Annals*, I, part i. 479.

the peasantry that he had made land available to be built upon.
Tithes might also be appropriated to a bishop, a monastery, or a
dean and chapter. The national ecclesiastical hierarchy was an
essential part of the national feudal hierarchy, standing above
but maintained by the village communities.

The parish priest retained close connexions with the villagers, to
whom socially he often belonged. But bishops and monasteries were
more remote, undistinguishable by the peasant producer from lay
landlords. They performed their pastoral functions by hired
deputy, who often neglected his traditional duty to provide hospitality and charity. This 'invention', Spelman thought, 'gave the
wound unto the church whereof it bleedeth at this day'.[1] Certainly
in such circumstances tithes ceased to be payments manifestly
made in return for services to the community, and became barely
distinguishable from rent, whether paid in kind or money. Peasant
opposition to tithes—e.g. that of John Ball and the Lollards—was
thus part of the general opposition to the exaction of a surplus to
maintain landlords and the hierarchy of functionaries in church
and state. Ball would have allowed tithes where 'the party that
should give the same were richer than the vicar or parson that
should receive it'.[2]

At the dissolution the purchasers or grantees succeeded not only
to the monastic estates but also to tithes and patronage rights
appropriated to those monasteries. For those who had to pay the
tithes, the change was probably not very noticeable. Even before
the Reformation monastic tithes had normally been farmed by
laymen: the dissolution was indeed made possible by the fact that
the monks had become mere rentiers, had abandoned their
managerial functions to laymen. But, as in so many of the events
of the Reformation, an apparently slight social rearrangement was
pregnant with vast consequences. It was not merely that 'the
noise of the dissolution' encouraged many laymen 'to withdraw
their tithes'. Statutes could be passed to enforce their payment.[3]
But more fundamental changes took place in mental attitudes.
The common lawyers came to think of the vicar not as collecting

[1] Spelman, *The Larger Treatise concerning Tythes*, in *English Works*, i. 138; R. A. R.
Hartridge, *A History of Vicarages in the Middle Ages* (1930), esp. pp. 122–3, 156–61,
198–9, 208; Kennett, op. cit., pp. 15–32, 78–117.
[2] R. H. Hilton and H. Fagan, *The English Rising of 1381* (1950), p. 99. Contrast the
more radical *urban* opposition to tithes referred to earlier (pp. 79–80).
[3] Coke, *Second Part of the Institutes*, p. 648, referring to 27 Hen. VIII. c. 20.

tithes to which he had a right, but as receiving an allowance from
the impropriator by contract or even (if there was no contract)
as an act of grace. (This rejection of divine right has its affinities
with the Puritan idea that the minister should receive 'a competent maintenance'.)

Moreover, from the point of view of the theoretical justification
of tithes, the replacement of the monastic appropriator by the
lay impropriator made a world of difference. The layman, like his
monastic predecessor, allowed the vicar only a small fraction of
what came in as tithes. In endowed vicarages the vicar got the
small tithes: in unendowed vicarages he got a stipend. But 'the
monks supposed that they did something for the husbandman that
he could not do for himself for the tithes that they received of him;
and the husbandmen in those ignorant times supposed that they
had some spiritual benefit by paying of tithes'.[1] The monastery
had at least been an ecclesiastical body, and had provided charity
as well as prayers. But when tithes were pocketed by a layman
their character as rent or tribute was made manifest, and the
successors of the monasteries soon shook off even their statutory
obligations to provide hospitality.[2]

Owners and farmers of impropriations claimed exemption
from all local rates except the poor rate, to which they had been
expressly declared liable by the statute of 1601.[3] When impropriators were authorized to sue for tithes in the ecclesiastical courts,
and those courts were instructed to call in the help of J.P.s where
necessary to enable the impropriator to collect his tithes, the church
courts had become rent collectors for laymen.[4] Stoughton in
1604 used the fact that the common-law courts had jurisdiction
over the property rights of impropriators to argue that all tithe
suits should be handed over to those courts. The distinction
between tithe and rent was virtually obliterated. Tithes lost their
sacred character.[5]

---

[1] *The Husbandmans Plea*, p. 55; cf. Stock, op. cit., p. 228.
[2] Fuller, *Church History*, ii. 166, 212.
[3] G. W. Prothero, *Statutes and Constitutional Documents, 1558–1625* (3rd ed., 1906),
p. 104; E. Cannan, *The History of Local Rates in England* (1896), p. 59; Ratcliff and
Johnson, op. cit., pp. 68, 165, 187, 214. The payment of constables' levies by impropriators began to be enforced in Warwickshire only after 1640 (ibid., pp. 73–75,
165). See p. 197 below.
[4] Coke, *First Part of the Institutes*, p. 159; Degge, op. cit., pp. 272–3.
[5] W. Stoughton, op. cit., pp. 90–103. This pamphlet was reprinted in 1642. See
also p. 125 above.

A contemporary parallel suggests itself: the stimulus to socialist ideas by the fact that, in many branches of industry, the owner-manager, himself taking a direct part in productive activities, has been succeeded by absentee shareholders, coupon-clippers, who render no visible services (beyond contributing capital) in return for the profits which they receive.

It had once been possible to justify tithes by the argument that they paid for communal functions—for the village boar or bull or dovecot which the priest kept, for the hospitality and charity which it was his duty to dispense, as well as for his spiritual services to the community. But no impropriator could pretend that the community received any return for the tithes which he collected. Crowley made precisely this point in his epigram: 'Of laymen that take tithes.' Justice gave judgment that:

> Seeing he made that private
> That common should be,
> He shall have this justice
> By judgment of me:—
>
> Those poor men, that by the tithes
> Should be relieved,
> Shall have all his goods
> Among them divided.[1]

Moreover, the church as a whole lost in financial flexibility. It might have been possible to draw upon *appropriated* tithes to augment vicars' incomes to meet the rise in prices: it was more difficult to use impropriations for this purpose. When Laud tried to do so, he found it easiest to begin with impropriations held by ecclesiastics.[2] In this sphere, as in that of poor relief, the significance of the dissolution of the monasteries was that it prevented the church being able to cope with an emergency that still lay ahead.

The manifest assimilation of tithes to lay property made possible a new intellectual freedom in regard to them. A divine right to tithes remained plausible so long as tithes went mainly to ecclesiastics; but the divine right of lay impropriators to a tenth of all

---

[1] Ed. J. M. Cowper, *Select Works of Robert Crowley* (1872), pp. 39–40. Cf. p. 124, where Crowley pleads for the restoration of tithes to the poor. Robert Burton was opposed to 'private men' holding impropriations or exercising patronage: such things, he believed, should be in the hands of 'common societies, corporations, etc.' (op. cit. i. 102).

[2] See Chapter XIV below.

wealth produced was a less defensible proposition. Selden's *History of Tithes* (1618) came as the climax to a good deal of lay speculation on the subject. And not only laymen denied a *jus divinum* to tithes. Selden himself quoted with relish 'a book written in behalf of all the clergy, especially of the bishops . . . and printed by public authority, and by the late Queen Elizabeth's printer, in the 32nd year of her reign', wherein 'it is expressly affirmed that it is an error of the papists to hold that tenths and offerings are in the church *jure divino*'. By Selden's time such views were becoming unfashionable, and he knew it: but he could have quoted Bacon to show that the choice between tithes and stipends was a matter of convenience, not necessity.[1]

Selden's book took the controversy from the realm of right to the realm of fact. It established that tithes had not become a regular institution until after the Christian church had become part of the state apparatus of the Roman Empire. Since that date tithes had been collected in varying ways in different countries at different times, and their enforcement could be regarded as depending wholly upon the discretion of the civil magistrate. The conclusion which some drew (and, though Selden expressed pious horror, there can be no doubt that he intended them to draw it) was that what the civil magistrate had instituted he could modify, or even abolish.

In England appropriated tithes, tithes paid to a bishop or monastery, existed before parochial tithes, said Selden: the universal right of the incumbent to the tithes arising in his parish was not established until about 1200. The endowments of parish churches had originated from the gift of lay landlords. Before about 1200 'the incumbent as really, as fully, and as immediately received the body of his church, his glebe, and what tithes were joined with it, in point of interest from the patron's hand, as a lessee for life receives his lands by the lessor's livery. . . . The bishop indeed had the usual consecration of the incumbent, but nothing at all to do with the disposition of the church or endowments.' 'Every man, questionless, would have been the unwillinger to have specially endowed the church, founded for the holy use chiefly of him, his family, and tenants, if withal he might not have had the liberty to have given his incumbent, there resident, a special and several maintenance, which could not have been,

[1] Selden, *Works*, iii. 1395; Bacon, *Works*, x. 125; cf. Perkins, *Works*, iii. 555.

had the former community of the clergy's revenue still remained.'[1]

The parochial system, that is to say, was the creation of lords of the manor. This new historical vision was breath-taking in its attractions for the gentry. 'All, evermore left in the hands and at the wills and disposing of lay owners and landlords, to give tithes as they would and if they would.' Such, Montagu thought, was the effect of Selden's *History*. 'Are you able to devise . . . any way more to prejudice us in our right, or means more effectual to avow and establish sacrilege?' Even those who had not read his book believed that 'Master Selden was unanswerable; and had given the clergy such a blow in their claim for tithes as was irrecoverable'.[2]

Selden's daring book was suppressed, and he himself was forced to express regret for publishing it:[3] but his ideas were no more to be suppressed than Galileo's. 'Never a fiercer storm fell on all parsonage barns since the Reformation', said Fuller.[4] The storm was fierce and the ideas could not be suppressed because Selden's arguments suited the interests of too many people. Henry Burton noticed that some ministers used the denial of a divine right to tithes to justify near-simoniacal practices. They claimed to buy not the living, the cure of souls, but the temporal maintenance.[5] And after the Restoration an Anglican divine had to admit that 'since the beginning of our late sacrilegious civil war', Selden's *History* 'hath been the armoury to which all sectaries and coveters of the church revenues have resorted for instances and arguments against this sacred maintenance of the clergy'.[6] Selden's researches into the history of tithes were not just an academic exercise: they had been stimulated by very real and pressing problems of the society in which he lived.

---

[1] Selden, *Works*, iii. 1152–4, 1124, 1209–10. Note the sly emphasis on *residence*.

[2] Montagu, op. cit., pp. 19, 21. 'Never was tract bent . . . more maliciously and dangerously against the church's inheritance', declared Montagu. Selden was 'the most capital enemy, of a man of your rank and ability, unto the church' (ibid., pp. 16, 20). Montagu apparently expected enmity from those of lesser rank and wealth. The vigour of his attack on this occasion may perhaps help to explain the violence with which his later indiscretions were exploited by the House of Commons.

[3] Selden, *Works*, iii. 1371–1457.

[4] Fuller, *Church History*, iii. 260. See also Fuller's *Appeal of Injured Innocence*, in *The History of the University of Cambridge* (1840), pp. 537–40.

[5] H. Burton, op. cit., p. 9.

[6] Comber, op. cit. i, Preface, sig. A2v–A3.

II

Impropriated tithes were for all practical purposes a piece of lay property, which could be bought and sold, leased, used for marriage settlements and (subject to the limitations of the Statute of Mortmain) devised.[1] Sixteen years' purchase was given by Thomas Adams as the current price for an impropriate rectory.[2] Sir John Holles in 1598 thought 20 years' purchase an excessive price. He was ready to offer 15, with $18\frac{1}{3}$ as his maximum.[3] But he was a hard bargainer. One rectory and manor bought by a London clothworker in 1631 for £1,050 was worth £126. 6s. six years later.[4] This suggests the very cheap rate of $8\frac{1}{3}$ years' purchase, unless the property had been drastically 'improved' in the intervening period. In 1647 it was stated that an impropriator would pay no more for his tithes than would be paid as fine for a 21 years' lease.[5]

Through impropriations parishioners might be able to gain a say in running their own affairs. The parish of St. Sepulchre's, London, held the rectory in fee-farm of the crown.[6] The parish of St. Bride's leased the impropriation from the Dean and Chapter of Westminster for £40 per annum. In 1638 they claimed that they collected no more than £160 a year in tithes, and that they had recently paid a fine of £240 for a 21 years' lease. But the transaction was still manifestly to their advantage. The church of St. Edmund's in Salisbury had been conveyed as a lay fee to trustees for the parishioners. It was argued in 1633 that the church was legally exempt from the jurisdiction of the bishop. This was important since Henry Sherfield, recorder and late M.P. for the city, was defending himself in the Star Chamber for having taken down windows in the church on the instructions of the vestry. He claimed that the parishioners had lawful power to take such action, notwithstanding the bishop's prohibition. The Star Chamber fined Sherfield £500, a sentence which would be noticed by impropriators.[7]

The impropriator's rights were founded on statute and were enforceable at common law.[8] From his point of view, the vicar's

---

[1] Strype, *Annals*, II, part ii. 157. For mortmain, see pp. 273–4 below.
[2] Adams, op. cit., p. 1060.
[3] *Portland MSS.* (Historical MSS. Commission), ix. 66–67.
[4] Kennett's annotated copy of *The Case of Impropriations*, appendix, pp. 3–7.
[5] *The Husbandmans Plea*, p. 77.   [6] Stearns, op. cit., p. 36.
[7] Rushworth, op. cit. ii. 154; Gardiner, *History*, vii. 254–8.
[8] Henry VIII, said Pearson, had to make new laws to enforce payment of tithes

claim to small tithes, or the obligation to pay a curate, were unpleasant burdens attached to the property, to be evaded or discharged as cheaply as possible. In 1578 the Bishop of Bath and Wells interfered to stop a peer converting a rectory into an impropriation and settling a stipend of £30 per annum on the vicar. 'If this should be brought into a custom', he wrote to Burghley, 'there are few benefices of any value but would be reduced to little or nothing.'[1] In one case which came to light in 1637 a Lincolnshire impropriator presented his grandson and heir to the living, and the latter took steps to make over to his grandfather his rights in the tithes, glebe, and vicarage.[2]

Utterly inadequate incomes might be allowed to ministers by impropriators who were themselves making handsome profits. As early as 1563 the Speaker of the House of Commons complained that this practice was a principal cause of the shortage of preaching ministers.[3] Parker's secretary in 1563 drew up a paper in which he expressed the pious hope 'that in all towns of this realm, the proprietaries may increase the exility of the vicarage by augmenting the living: so that the people be not unserved or defrauded of a reasonable minister . . . as very many towns be, where such impropriations be seen'.[4] One suggestion was that impropriators should find four sermons a year in their churches, on penalty of a fine of 13*s*. 4*d*. for every sermon omitted.[5] In 1576 Grindal complained to Elizabeth 'this church of England hath been by appropriations . . . spoiled of the livings, which at the first were appointed to the offices of preaching and teaching. . . . So as at this day, in my opinion, where one church is able to yield sufficient living for a learned preacher, there be at least seven churches unable to do the same.'[6]

Grindal had put his finger on the economic root of the evil, and of the Puritan opposition to it: this was in a letter defending prophesyings. But what could he do? When complaint came in of lack of preachers in Richmondshire in 1580, in Northumberland in

---

to impropriators, 'they having no law whereby to recover them, the Pope's law not reaching the lay-parsons' (op. cit., p. 22; cf. Selden, *Works*, iii. 1273–5).
[1] Lysons, *A View of the Revenues of the Parochial Clergy of this Kingdom* (1824), p. 41.
[2] *C.S.P.D.*, *1637*, pp. 206–7.
[3] Sir J. E. Neale, *Elizabeth I and her Parliaments, 1559–81* (1953), p. 99.
[4] Strype, *Annals*, 1, part i. 524.
[5] Kennett, annotated copy of *The Case of Impropriations*, p. 167.
[6] Strype, *Grindal*, p. 565.

1595, in each case the explanation was the number of royal impropriations in those parts.[1] Elizabeth, finding the benefices in one part of Lancashire 'swallowed up in impropriations', and the people consequently 'extremely backward in religion', endowed four stipendiary preachers with £50 a year each to supply the preaching needs of this politically unreliable area. Bacon suggested that the scheme might be extended to 'other corners in the realm', and non-preaching ministers might be made to contribute towards it. But the proposal was not taken up.[2] John Penry had thought rather similarly in 1587 that it would be a great advance if 'the tenth part of every impropriate living in Wales' were bestowed on a preaching minister.[3] But Wales, like Yorkshire and Northumberland, had to wait for the Interregnum.

In 1609, or thereabouts, a Puritan survey of Essex noted that the vicar of Broomfield, whose living was worth £35 a year, had never preached in twenty years; the vicar of Bulmer, with £40, was also a dumb minister, who was non-resident because hiding from his creditors.[4] At Theydon Bois there had in 1650 been no vicar 'for these many years'.[5] 'Our vicar is no preacher', said the churchwardens of Westhampnet, Sussex, in 1625, adding sympathetically 'and that because his living is small. We have not our monthly sermons, as we should, but some sermons we have, as he is able to prepare them.'[6] Laud noted in 1635 the Bishop of Gloucester's report that his diocese was 'very full of impropriations, which makes them fall upon popular and factious courses. I doubt this is too true', the Archbishop told the king sadly, 'but it is a mischief hard to cure in this kingdom.'[7] The roots of opposition to the established church went too deep down into society for the Court of High Commission to be able to dig them up.

Many examples could be given where vicars had to live on a tiny fraction of what the impropriator received. Thus the rectory of Leigh, Lancashire, was in 1636 worth £632 a year to the lay rector, 50 per cent. more than the capital sum for which it had been

[1] Peck, op. cit., p. 94; Strype, *Whitgift*, ii. 313.
[2] Bacon, *Works*, x. 124, xi. 254.
[3] Arber, *An Introductory Sketch to the Martin Marprelate Controversy* (1895), p. 65.
[4] *A Viewe of the State of the Clargie within the Countie of Essex*, pp. 16–17.
[5] H. Smith, op. cit., p. 273.
[6] Johnstone, *Churchwardens' Presentations, Archdeaconry of Chichester*, p. 105. The vicarage was worth £7. 4s. 4d. in the King's Book.
[7] Laud, *Works*, v. 336.

bought two generations earlier. The vicar got £18. 1s. 4d. per annum, plus a house valued at another £10. From this princely income he had to pay £4 annually to an assistant, and £1. 10s. in taxes, so that he had £12. 11s. 4d. net left. Rather naturally, he complained to Laud as soon as he thought he could get a hearing.[1] Two west-country vicars, each claiming to receive less than £30 a year, told Laud that their lay rectors got £400 a piece.[2] William Crashawe, writing of the East Riding of Yorkshire in 1605, referred to impropriations worth from £100 to £400 a year, where the minister had only £8, and 'with much ado £10 more was obtained for a preacher'. The rest went 'to the feeding of kites and cormorants'.[3] Many impropriations in the East Riding were in the hands of absentee southerners, who either had grants from the king exempting them from charges for repairs, or else met their obligations only under expensive legal pressure. In the early seventeenth century there were endless complaints of decayed churches in impropriated parishes: the same gentleman was often presented several times.[4] (Enclosure rather than impropriation was no doubt the real cause: a pre-Reformation ballad told how

> Great men maketh nowadays
> A sheepcot in the church.[5]

But the replacement of monastic landowners by laymen at least did nothing to slow down the enclosure movement.)

Henry Burton also agreed with Crashawe that many impropriated parishes were so inadequately provided for that they 'necessarily devolved upon some poor £10-man', and on men paid less than that in more than half the cases in his experience. Naturally this made the creation of a satisfactory preaching clergy impossible. Petitions from Kent in 1640-1 provide a large number of examples.[6] The terrier of Boxted, Essex, said in 1610 that the impropriator 'hath stripped the vicarage stark naked, without

---

[1] J. E. Worsley, *The History of the Parish Church of St. Mary at Leigh* (1870), pp. 19-22. See also p. 329 below. This vicarage was valued at £9 in the King's Book.

[2] *C.S.P.D., 1635*, p. 544; *1637-8*, p. 606.

[3] Crashawe, *Epistle to Sir John Savile*, loc. cit. See also *Minutes of the Committee for Plundered Ministers, passim*.

[4] Ornsby, op. cit. i. 94, 82; R. H. Skaife, 'Extracts from Visitation Books at York', in *Yorkshire Archaeological Journal*, xv. 224-41, *passim*.

[5] Tawney and Power, *Tudor Economic Documents* (1924), iii. 19.

[6] H. Burton, op. cit., pp. 126-7; Larking, op. cit., pp. 115-239, *passim*. For other examples see *V.C.H., Lincolnshire*, ii. 63.

glebe, wood, hay or corn'. Another Essex terrier of the same date, for Ugley, described how the vicar had been dispossessed of his dwelling house, some 45 acres of glebe and all the corn since the purchase of the rectory by Sir William Maynard: the vicarage had been decreased to mean value and the inhabitants rendered homeless. Many other examples could be given.[1]

In 1641 it was said that nearly half of Northamptonshire's 326 benefices were impropriate, and the vicarages 'commonly left so small and destitute, that there is not sufficient means left to a minister to buy books, nor to keep hospitality'. Poor vicarages were 'abridged and despoiled' under pretence of long leases made before the statue of 1571, and by *modi decimandi* in lieu of tithes in kind. The nave of one impropriate church in Cambridgeshire had been pulled down, the lead, stone, timber, and bells sold; another church in Northamptonshire was turned into a kennel for greyhounds, the steeple into a pigeon house.[2] There is much evidence to show that propaganda stories of 'the whole parish, church, steeple, bells and all' being swallowed up at enclosure[3] were not wildly exaggerated.

At Kidbrook, Essex, where there was no endowed vicarage, the church was entirely demolished, and the rectory existed merely to provide extra profits for the lord of the manor. In 1604 James I granted both manor and rectory to the Earl of Mar.[4] At the depopulated village of Little Gidding the church was used as a hay-barn and pig-sty until the Ferrars bought the manor in 1625. Both the churches of which George Herbert was incumbent were so dilapidated that he spent considerable sums on their repair.[5] The chancel of Upmarden church, Sussex, was 'so undecently and beastly kept . . . that through the pigeons' dung and other filth in the same' the worshippers in 1625 were 'enforced to stop their noses or carry

---

[1] Newcourt, op. cit. ii. 79, 614; cf. pp. 49, 65, and *C.S.P.D., 1633–4*, p. 548.

[2] Laud, *Works*, v. 367; *A Certificate from Northamptonshire*, pp. 2–6.

[3] Shakespeare, *Pericles*, Act II, scene i. Mr. F. W. Bateson is surely right when he suggests that Shakespeare's 'bare ruined choirs, where late the sweet birds sang' is more likely to refer to churches dilapidated because of enclosure than to dissolved abbeys (*Essays in Criticism*, iii. 8). The adverb 'late' would hardly be applied to a period two generations earlier; but parish churches recently stripped of their roofs and falling to ruin would not have been difficult to find in 1593. For churches 'decayed' in consequence of depopulation in the sixteenth and seventeenth centuries, see Beresford, *Lost Villages*, pp. 63–65, 99–101, 176, 297, 308–13, 322, 341–87; *C.S.P.D., 1636–7*, p. 65.

[4] Lysons, *Environs of London*, iv. 341–2.

[5] Gardiner, *History*, vii. 263; I. Walton, *Lives*, pp. 278–9, 291.

flowers in their hands to prevent the ill smell thereof'. But the impropriator, so the vicar alleged, said that the church should fall to the ground before he would repair it.[1] Laud instructed his Vicar-General 'to enquire after such impropriations whose cure is not well served'; and we have Sir Nathaniel Brent's sober account, during his visitation of Lincoln, of finding Lord Castleton's bailiff in the middle aisle of Saxby church, busy melting the lead he had stripped off the roof; and of other ruined churches.[2]

Many equally circumstantial reports of 'decayed' and deliberately destroyed churches in impropriate parishes can be found in Laud's annual accounts of his Province. Not there, but in the State Papers, is a list of ten decayed impropriate churches in the diocese of Canterbury: four of the impropriations belonged to the Archbishop himself.[3] There are also lists of ruined churches in Lincolnshire (1605), Rutlandshire (1605, 1619, 1640), Buckinghamshire (1637), Warwickshire (1638).[4] In 1641 the inhabitants of a depopulated parish in Rutlandshire used the decayed state of their church as an excuse for refusing to pay tithes.[5] 'The charitable man', wrote a contributor to *News from any whence*, 'dreams of building churches, but starts to think the ungodlier courtier will pull them down again.'[6] Notable in all these accounts is the connexion between enclosure, depopulation and the decay of churches; just as we observed the deleterious effects of enclosure on ministers' revenues.

[1] Johnstone, op. cit., pp. 96–97; cf. other examples at pp. 69 and 103. See ibid., p. 65 and *passim* for church buildings 'in decay'.

[2] Laud, *Works*, vii. 645; Gardiner, *History*, viii. 111; *V.C.H., Lincolnshire*, ii. 62; *C.S.P.D., 1635*, p. xxxiv. For other examples see *C.S.P.D., 1637*, p. 491; *1638–9*, pp. 52–53; W. H. Hale, *Precedents in Causes of Office against Churchwardens and others* (1841), p. 7 and *passim*; Purvis, *Tudor Parish Documents*, pp. 39–45 (18 out of 61 churches in two deaneries presented for dilapidations in 1595–6); *V.C.H., Suffolk*, ii. 45–46; ed. C. Jenkins, 'The Account Book of the Archdeacon of Taunton', in *Somerset Record Soc. Pubs.* xliii. 72 and *passim*; R. F. B. Hodgkinson, 'Extracts from the Account Books of the Archdeacon of Nottingham', in *Trans. of the Thoroton Soc.* xxxi. 129–34; S. A. Peyton, *The Churchwardens' Presentments in the Oxfordshire Peculiars of Dorchester, Thame and Banbury* (Oxfordshire Record Soc.), p. 27 and *passim*; J. F. Williams, *Bishop Redman's Visitation, 1597* (Norfolk Record Soc.), pp. 10–20.   [3] *C.S.P.D., 1633–4*, p. 551.

[4] *V.C.H., Lincolnshire*, ii. 59; *V.C.H., Rutlandshire*, i. 151–3; *V.C.H., Bucks.* i. 324–6; *C.S.P.D., 1638–9*, p. 86.

[5] *Hist. MSS. Commission, Fourth Report*, p. 110.

[6] 'Newes from the bed', by R.S., in *The Miscellaneous Works . . . of Sir Thomas Overbury* (ed. E. F. Rimbault, 1890), p. 197.

Nor were remedies easy to find. *The Reformation of the Ecclesiastical Laws* tried to define the duties of impropriators to maintain churches in repair; but it never became law. Bancroft equally failed to lay the burden on impropriators.[1] In 1619 all the bishops were instructed to exhort the clergy to call upon the people to contribute to repairing dilapidated churches.[2] Sometimes ecclesiastical courts instructed impropriators to undertake repairs.[3] But, as Laud explained to an unsympathetic House of Lords in 1629, impropriators had a habit of taking out prohibitions if they were presented for allowing churches to fall into decay. He and Bishop Neile of Winchester 'desired some course might be taken in this by the judges, and shewed some vile abuses which were complained of in the High Commission, but forthwith a prohibition was granted'. Their lordships, however, sagely considered that the stay of prohibitions was a matter to be entered upon only with the greatest caution, and appointed a committee 'to consider of these things'. Saye and Sele and other anti-episcopalians insisted that the committee should also take pluralities and non-residence into consideration.[4] They were determined that the economic problems of the church should not be solved merely at the expense of impropriators. It was only after the dissolution of Parliament that Charles I ordered the bishops to take special care for the repair of decayed churches (charging the inhabitants); to use the power of the ecclesiastical courts for this purpose; and instructed the judges not to interrupt the course of law by the too easy granting of prohibitions.[5]

III

The total number of impropriated livings was estimated by the bishops in 1603 at 3,849. This is virtually identical with the figure of 3,845 (out of a total of 9,284 livings) given by Spelman in a work published posthumously in 1646.[6] The distribution of impropria-

[1] *Reformation of the Ecclesiastical Laws*, pp. 80–82; cf. p. 149 below.

[2] D. Wilkins, *Concilia* (1737), iv. 460–1.

[3] Hale, op. cit., p. 85.

[4] Journal of Lord Mountagu, in *Buccleuch MSS., Montagu House* (Hist. MSS. Commission), iii. 338.

[5] Rushworth, op. cit. ii. 28. See Chapter XIV below.

[6] Spelman, *English Works*, i. 35. This (*An Apology of the Treatise De non Temerandis Ecclesiis*) was probably the source from which a pamphleteer quoted by Miss James in *History*, N.S., xxvi. 4) took his figures. The *Valor Ecclesiasticus* gives 3,347

tions seems to have been very unequal. Heylyn said that in London there were 189 impropriations in 623 parishes.[1] In the diocese of Chester the figure was given as 133 ('and those the best') out of 248; in the diocese of Hereford and the county of Northampton, nearly half.[2] In Kent 140 parishes out of 252 were impropriate; in Yorkshire the proportion was as high as 63 per cent.—392 out of 622.[3] William Crashawe said that almost 100 out of some 105 parishes or parochial chapels in the East Riding of Yorkshire were impropriate.[4] In the see of Lincoln there were many poor impropriations belonging to the bishop. Wales was another area in which impropriations abounded.[5]

A paper drawn up in 1588 with Whitgift's approval estimated the annual loss to the church through impropriations at £100,000; Hooker put it at £126,000.[6] If these guesses are at all correct, the loss was from £25 to £35 in each impropriated parish. Its restoration would have gone far to solve the economic problems of the church at one stroke, without resort to the Puritan solution of a total expropriation of bishops, deans, and chapters.

But even more important than the large sums that they pocketed was the control over the church which the gentry wielded through impropriations, leasing of tithes, and patronage. Five-sixths of the benefices in the country, declared a committee of bishops in 1604, were controlled by laymen, including the crown; and the crown's share was diminishing as lands were perforce sold. In the dioceses of York, Norwich, Rochester, and Lincoln, of 2,323 benefices laymen controlled 1,987 (of which the crown 493); ecclesiastics, including Oxford and Cambridge colleges, 336. Here the ratio is six-sevenths to one-seventh. The grip of laymen seems to have been strongest in the south-east.[7]

---

vicarages out of 8,838 parishes; the Archbishop of Canterbury's Register 3,227 out of 8,803 (*C.S.P.D., 1634–5*, p. 381). See also Fuller, *Church History*, iii. 362, and Collier, *Ecclesiastical History*, ix. 362–3. Canon Foster, *The State of the Church*, p. lv, corrects Usher's error about the number of impropriations.

[1] Heylyn, *Cyprianus Anglicus* (1668), p. 185.

[2] White, op. cit., p. 267; Browne Willis, op. cit. ii. 37; *A Certificate from Northamptonshire*, p. 2.

[3] *V.C.H., Kent*, ii. 89; A. H. Thompson, *The English Clergy and their organization in the later Middle Ages* (1947), p. 115.

[4] Crashawe, *Epistle to Sir John Savile*, loc. cit.

[5] Browne Willis, op. cit. i. 500; Ecton, op. cit., p. vii.

[6] Strype, *Whitgift*, i. 535; Hooker, *Works*, iii. 404.

[7] Usher, op. cit. i. 111, 95; Foster, *The State of the Church*, p. lvi.

So long as the gentry were a socially united class their control of the church did not contribute to political tension. But in the two generations before the civil war a substantial number of lay-men began to use their patronage and influence over the rank and file of the clergy to have a particular kind of doctrine and discipline preached. Lay patronage made Puritanism an issue within the church. Sale of the right of next presentation modified control of the church by landed patrons: a moneyed man could sometimes buy his son's way into the church, as we have seen. But the fact that oligarchical control was tempered by the poverty of some of the oligarchs was hardly sufficient to justify the system.[1]

IV

Through impropriations and leases, then, much of the increase in the value of livings, which should have accrued to ministers, was diverted into the pockets of landlords and farmers. 'Dumb dogs' were the natural result: the impropriator or farmer rarely allowed enough to the vicar for him to be a 'learned minister'.

The Puritan opposition, from 1572 onwards, steadily argued in favour of the restoration of impropriations. They were papistical survivals: 'as popish abbeys stole them, so a popish state kept them'.[2] Penry attacked impropriations as the main cause of non-residents and dumb dogs in his beloved Wales.[3] By impropriations, said Crashawe, 'above any other one means . . . an ignorant and unteaching ministry is set over a great part of our people, which is the source and fountain of all other evils in our church'. At the dissolution of the monasteries this abuse could have been cured; now there seemed to be no remedy 'unless the king's majesty vouchsafes to take the matter into his hands, to heal the wounds that he never made'.[4] The restoration of impropriations, Crashawe had declared pessimistically in 1605, 'is a work for God himself,

---

[1] See above, pp. 64–65.

[2] Crashawe, loc. cit. Appropriations, Kennett thought, were 'a badge of the Norman Conquest' (op. cit., p. 23). The idea, though not the phrase, occurs in a Digger-influenced pamphlet, *No Age like unto this Age* (1653), p. 18. Cf. Stock, op. cit., pp. 228–9; Stillingfleet, op. cit. I. xi.

[3] Penry, *An Exhortation unto the Governors and People of Her Majestys country of Wales* (1588), quoted in J. Waddington, *John Penry* (1858), p. 32.

[4] Crashawe, *Sermon Preached at the Crosse, Feb. xiv, 1607*, pp. 169–70.

for if man could do it, so many Parliaments would not have slipped it, but some of them would have eternized itself with this honourable name to all posterities, THE PARLIAMENT THAT RE-STORED IMPROPRIATIONS'. 'But till that or some other course as good be taken', he continued, 'it is both unseasonable and un-reasonable to complain of the ignorant, or to crave a learned ministry. . . .' Whitgift had said almost the same thing in 1601.[1]

A favourite suggestion of Puritans and M.P.s throughout our period was that poor but preaching vicars should be given an opportunity of leasing the tithes of their livings: this, it was argued, would solve all their economic problems. The vicars, Stoughton suggested in 1604, should not pay fines, but should be charged two or three times the old, unimproved rents. This would be no hardship to either party, for 'men experienced in these affairs of this life know that the profits arising out of churches appro-priated, unto the farmers thereof, are commonly six, eight or ten times more worth, by just estimation, than are the old rents, payable unto colleges, hospitals and other like places'.[2] The proposal, included in the Millenary Petition, and introduced as a bill in the 1621 Parliament, was never accepted.[3] It shows, among other things, what contemporaries thought of the profits of lessees.

It was all very well for Puritan ministers to advocate restoration of impropriations: but the shrewder among them knew, as Stoughton's elaborate proposals show, that there was no simple solution. The gentry of England were not going to abandon their property in impropriated tithes and patronage, any more than they had been willing to restore monastic lands under Mary. 'This is a certain and sure principle', Whitgift declared in 1575, 'that the temporalty will not lose one jot of their commodity in any respect to better the livings of the church; and therefore let us keep that we have; for better we shall not be, we may be worse, and that I think by many is intended.'[4] Matthew Hutton, Archbishop of York, told Bancroft before the Hampton Court Conference that he thought impropriations were confirmed by law, and therefore

---

[1] Crashawe, *Epistle to Sir John Savile*, loc. cit.; Kennett, op. cit., p. 171.
[2] W. Stoughton, op. cit., pp. 136–62.
[3] E. Nicholas, op. cit. i. 345. See pp. 250–1 below.
[4] Kennett, op. cit., appendix, pp. 20–23.

that bona-fide purchasers 'may keep them with a safe conscience; and the parishioners are bound in conscience, as to the parsons, so to the appropriators, to pay their tithes truly, though they be never so wicked men'. 'I wish', he added sadly, 'better provision were made for godly preachers. But how it may be done, I leave that to his majesty' and to the government.[1]

Ridley summed up the hierarchy's viewpoint when he said that the return of impropriations 'might well be wished'; but 'in so far as they are perplexed and intricated by the laws of this land, with private men's states, it would be hard to be performed: for the changing of them would be much like as if a man should move one stone in a vaulted work, where the taking of one stone away is the jeopardy of the whole building.' 'But yet', Ridley concluded grimly, 'let those to whom this doth appertain consider whether in this it were better to please God than man.'[2]

Impropriations, in fact, formed one of the sensitive points in the alliance between parliamentarian gentry on the one hand and Puritan ministers and the more radical laymen on the other. Spokesmen of the hierarchy were quick to take advantage of this. Bishop Cooper pointed out that Martin Marprelate was in effect demanding abolition of the laws 'whereby impropriations and patronages stand as men's lawful possessions and heritage':[3] and the point must have gone home. Bancroft especially enjoyed driving in wedges. 'The clergy factious', he declared in his one surviving sermon, preached in 1589, 'do contend that all livings which now appertain to the church ought of right to be employed for the maintenance of their presbyteries, and that rather than they should want, the old spoil of the abbeys and such religious houses should be restored again unto their use. . . . The lay factious on the other side are of a far contrary opinion', urging that ministers should follow the apostles' example of poverty. Behind the demands of 'the clergy factious', Bancroft warned 'the lay factious', lurked Anabaptist social heresies. 'I beseech you, upon what grounds do you stand? . . . You ought to be ashamed to open your mouths ever hereafter against the present government of the church, and for the new platform, until you can be contented to be so far from coveting the goods of the church as that

---

[1] Strype, *Whitgift*, iii. 394.
[2] Ridley, op. cit., p. 214.
[3] Cooper, op. cit., p. 67.

you are both willing and ready to deliver out of your hands such spoils and preys thereof as you have already.'[1]

Sixteen years later Bancroft, as Archbishop of Canterbury, told his bishops that he hoped some course would be taken against 'such as have all the best ecclesiastical livings in the land, named impropriations: and yet make no conscience in suffering them to be served with very simple curates'.[2] But his scheme for raising a subsidy to buy in impropriations, put forward in the Parliament of 1610, came to nothing.[3] All parties, in fact, tended to advocate a restoration of impropriations until there was any prospect of it actually happening. Then it was at once revealed how many vested interests were involved. Revenue from leases of royal impropriations was considerable. It was argued forcefully in the Parliament of 1586 that a restoration of impropriations would mean heavy financial loss for the crown.[4] The Puritan policy in this respect, Elizabeth was advised by her Council a few years later, was 'an opinion against the revenues of the crown'.[5]

I have come across only one instance in which the economic lot of the incumbent of a royal living was bettered, and then it was not thanks to the crown. The tithes of the unendowed vicarage of West Ham, Essex, were regularly leased until in 1638, by a complicated financial transaction, William Blower bought out the lessee. Blower, who was father and predecessor of the incumbent, also compensated the crown for endowing the vicarage with tithes. In 1650 it was worth £60 in consequence, a substantial increase over the pension of £39. 13s. 8d. previously paid from the Exchequer.[6] But such examples were rare: to many vicars the crown must have seemed no less of an economic enemy than other impropriators. The vested interests of the gentry, the financial solvency of crown, bishops, deans and chapters, university colleges, all stood in the way of reform.[7]

---

[1] Bancroft, op. cit., pp. 24–29. The same argument that the Puritan demands threaten the property interests of noblemen and gentlemen was employed by the author of *Certen slaunderous speeches against the present Estate of the Church of Englande* (1583–5): a point which reinforces Dr. Peel's attribution of this tract to Bancroft (*Tracts ascribed to Richard Bancroft*, pp. 59–60). The argument was also used in the House of Commons in 1587 by Sir Christopher Hatton, whose chaplain Bancroft then was (Frere, op. cit., p. 246).

[2] Kennett, op. cit., p. 177.

[3] Usher, op. cit. ii. 257.

[4] Strype, *Whitgift*, iii. 190–3.

[5] Strype, *Annals*, IV. 197.

[6] Lysons, *Environs of London*, iv. 264–5.

[7] This point was made as early as 1550, by Thomas Lever (op. cit., p. 31).

V

The position of Oxford and Cambridge was crucial. Almost exactly 100 grants of tithes to universities and colleges are recorded in the century between the Reformation and the Long Parliament.[1] Only the universities could train and turn out a learned ministry. But any suggestion that the learned ministers there trained should receive augmentations from impropriations cut at the root of college finances, since nearly all colleges depended on impropriated tithes for a large part of their revenues. Short of a drastic and wholesale reorganization, it was difficult to escape from that vicious circle. James I, at the beginning of his reign, had the admirable intention of devoting royal impropriations to the augmentation of ministerial stipends, and urged the universities to follow his example. Whitgift, in great alarm, pointed out that this 'will be in time the overthrow of the universities and of learning', and he and Bancroft succeeded in discouraging James from so embarrassing a step.[2] The profound hostility to the universities shown by religious and political radicals in the sixteen-fifties was directed primarily against their teaching: but this economic point should also be borne in mind.

Elizabeth at the beginning of her reign had exchanged some of her impropriations for more desirable bishops' lands: and thus the bishops too acquired a vested interest in preserving impropriations. They wept: but they took. Cox lamented: 'It will be unto us a grievous burden to take benefices impropriated, because we are persuaded in conscience that the parishes ought to enjoy them, in such sort, and for such godly ends, as they were appointed for at the beginning.'[3] His remedy would appear to have been in his own hands!

Mr. Grove's figures, not necessarily complete, show bishops holding impropriated tithes in 417 parishes, deans and chapters in 309, colleges and other ecclesiastical corporations in 107.[4] Ecclesiastical impropriations should therefore not be underestimated in accounting for the support which presbyterian ideas

---

[1] Grove, op. cit., part iii, *passim*.

[2] Usher, op. cit. i. 301–2, 339.

[3] Strype, *Annals*, I, part i. 146 (complaints of Cox and Grindal); Strype, *Grindal*, p. 42; Strype, *Whitgift*, i. 144–6; Rowse, *Tudor Cornwall*, p. 330 (rectories sold back to the Dean and Chapter of Exeter in 1585). See also pp. 46–48 above.

[4] Grove, op. cit., part iii, *passim*.

received among the clergy. Presbyterianism, we are often told, was the creed of a small group of clerical intellectuals, encouraged by influential laymen with interested motives. But many of the ministers themselves did not lack an economic motive. Complaints from Kent in 1640–1 reveal a wide divergence between the exiguous stipends paid to curates or vicars in unendowed vicarages and the receipts from tithes which were shared between the lessee and the bishop, dean and chapter, or college. The sober parliamentary surveys of church lands confirm the shrill petitions to the Long Parliament.[1]

A glaring example was the vicarage of Hornchurch, Essex. This was worth £800 a year to the Warden and Fellows of New College (or their farmers), whilst the vicar received only £55 per annum from the small tithes, and the parishioners had to pay for preaching ministers at two chapels within this large parish. The rectory of Rickling, leased by the Dean and Chapter of St. Paul's, was worth £80; but it had been empty for many years, and the church was very much decayed, because the vicar's maintenance was only £28 a year.[2] The Dean and Chapter of Chichester kept the parsonage house of Singleton, in Sussex, 'in decay' for many years, despite repeated presentations by the churchwardens that it was their duty to repair it.[3] In 1638 Laud was collecting information from poor vicars in Lincolnshire. He learnt that the vicar of Hogsthorpe received a pension of £10 from the Bishop of Lincoln; the vicar estimated the impropriation to be worth £90. The vicar of Alford got £19. 16s.; the impropriation, again belonging to Bishop Williams, was said to be worth £80.[4] The chaplain of Chapel-en-le-Frith received only £4. 6s. 8d. from the Dean and Chapter of Lichfield, and so became dependent upon 'the people's gratuity'.[5] The system asked for, and got, scandalous and non-preaching ministers. Nathaniel Fiennes indeed suggested in February 1641 that it concerned the bishops in their profits that there should be 'good store of cheap curates' to 'furnish the cures of such places whereof they have the impropriations'.[6]

[1] Larking, op. cit., pp. 115, 124–31, 141–6, 179, 189–90, 201–3, 233–9; Bodington, op. cit., *passim*.

[2] H. Smith, op. cit., pp. 249–50, 284.

[3] Johnstone, op. cit., pp. 12, 104.   [4] *C.S.P.D., 1637–8*, pp. 173, 176.

[5] Bunting, op. cit., p. 59. See p. 293 below. See also Newcourt, op. cit. ii. 493, 518–19, for quarrels over tithes between clerical rectors and vicars.

[6] Nalson, op. cit. i. 759.

The hierarchy, then, was largely maintained by revenues to which even some bishops thought the parochial clergy had a more equitable claim. The point had been made in a piece of Puritan doggerel in 1584:

There is one church in Lancashire, that called is by name Whalley,
Which has belonging thereunto nine other churches, I dare say,
All in my Lord of Lambeth's hands, yet most of them have not by year
Past £6 both by meat and way. How can a preacher live well there?

Pluck first the beam from your own eyes, and so shall you the clearer see.[1]

Lancashire became one of the traditional strongholds of presbyterianism.

A paper approved by Archbishop Whitgift denounced as 'prejudicial to the revenues of the church' the Puritan view that the holding of impropriations was sacrilege, and that they should be restored.[2] 'The church' in this context appears to mean the hierarchy and the universities, to the exclusion of the parishes. Even Laud, who did regard impropriations as sacrilege, extended rather than diminished this abuse by establishing impropriated livings as perpetual *commendams* for bishoprics. How much more prudent the action of Bishop Williams, who bought good finable lands from neighbouring gentlemen for the bishopric of Lincoln! Episcopal impropriations must have helped—to say no more—many a minister to ask himself whether the New Testament really did authorize prelatical bishops.

Nor is this merely a sordid economic afterthought of the historian. In Edward VI's reign Crowley had remarked that in 1549 'unworthy curates' would not have been able to stir the simple people up to revolt if the higher clergy had not in so many parishes intercepted the tithes which should have maintained a preaching ministry.[3] The point was noted by no less official a person than Dr. Ridley. The bishops, he grumbled, are 'brought into obloquy, as though they detained the due provision of the parochial church from it, and are set in a way ready to be overthrown if every bird have his own feather again'.[4] To ask for

---

[1] *The Seconde Part of a Register*, i. 273. Sir George Clark suggests 'mete [measure] and weigh' for 'meat and way'.

[2] Strype, *Whitgift*, ii. 17; cf. iii. 237.

[3] Crowley, op. cit., p. 140. The Norfolk rebels had demanded a resident preaching clergy, as had the German peasants in 1525.   [4] Ridley, op. cit., p. 210.

one's own feather again was, after all, not so very unreasonable, even if it came from the cap of a bishop. Puritanism, for some of the ministers, was a knife and fork question. There were divisions of interest within the ranks of the clergy, which existed in their own right, not merely as a reflection of the political attitudes of patrons. The laity could sympathize unreservedly with poor vicars in parishes impropriated by bishops or ecclesiastical corporations. A petition presented to Parliament from Nottinghamshire in 1641 spoke of the 'engrossing of tithes into the revenues of bishops and cathedrals, the churches where such impropriations are being the worst provided for ministry and maintenance'.[1] The bishops prevented godly laymen enjoying a preaching clergy, not only by depriving Puritan ministers but also by swallowing up the substance of those who retained their livings.

VI

So though on paper the economic problems of the church could easily have been solved by the restoration of impropriations, in practice cure was less simple than diagnosis. The property rights of impropriators, no less than of lay patrons, were an obstacle in the path of reform. Everybody would agree, Bacon said, in *wishing* that impropriations should be restored; but it was equally clear that this could not be done. For men's property in them was guaranteed by act of Parliament, 'and the restitution must of necessity pass their hands, in whose hands they are in interest and possession'.[2]

Hooker, Norden the surveyor, Robert Burton, Quarles, Chillingworth could call for restitution from their intellectual armchairs.[3] But kings, bishops, peers, and members of the House of Commons—those who would have to take the effective decisions—were all interested parties. Ridley indulged in the harmless reflection that it would have been better if all appropriated tithes had been restored to incumbents at the dissolution of the monasteries. Selden, not quite so harmlessly, and choosing his adjectives

[1] [Anon.], *A Petition presented to the Parliament from the County of Nottingham* (1641), p. 8.

[2] Bacon, *Works*, x. 125.

[3] Hooker, *Works*, iii. 404; J. Norden, *The Surveyors Dialogue* (1618), p. 77; R. Burton, op. cit. i. 102; F. Quarles, *Enchiridion* (1856), p. 133; W. Chillingworth, *Works* (1838), iii. 201–3.

with care, thought 'every good man' wished that at the dissolution impropriations had been used 'for the advancement of the church, to a better maintenance of the labouring and deserving ministry, to the fostering of good arts, relief of the poor, and such other good uses'.[1] There seems to have been very little voluntary restoration of impropriated tithes before Charles I's reign. The publicity given to one of the few known cases—that of Staplegrove, near Taunton, restored by Lord Chief Justice Dier *in Mary's reign*—suggests that it was rare. And even in this case the family retained the patronage. The same was true of Serjeant Benlowes's dissolution of the impropriation of Great Bardfield, Essex, also in Mary's reign. The chantry which he endowed was dissolved again under Elizabeth; and his great-grandson, the poet, still retained the advowson.[2]

In rather a different category, and equally exceptional, was Joseph Hall's recovery of the endowments of Wolverhampton collegiate church from the recusant Leveson family whilst he was vicar of Waltham. For Hall brought a legal action in which it was proved that the documents by which the family claimed the perpetual fee-farm were forgeries.[3]

The proposals for recovering impropriations made in the sixteen-twenties and -thirties will be considered later.[4] They sprang on the one side from an opposition attempt to acquire piecemeal influence in the church, rather than to solve its economic problems as a whole; and on the side of the government and its supporters they were the first tentative essays at a newly aggressive policy, evolved in very different international circumstances.

One section of the gentry, then, as impropriators, collected tithes; they did not wish to see tithes abolished, especially as they were well placed for evading or reducing to a minimum their own liability to pay. The most convinced opposition to tithes came from those lower in the social scale, who were not themselves likely to own or lease impropriations, and who were not powerful enough to drive a personal bargain exempting them from payment. In the countryside, where the burden of tithes fell heaviest,

---

[1] Ridley, op. cit., p. 212; Selden, *Works*, iii. 1338.

[2] Newcourt, op. cit. ii. 29; Kennett, annotated copy of *The Case of Impropriations*, p. 140; H. Jenkins, *Edward Benlowes* (1952), p. 2.

[3] Lloyd, *Memoires*, p. 414; T. F. Kinloch, *The Life and Works of Joseph Hall* (1951), p. 25.

[4] See Chapters XI and XIV.

this social group, the yeomen and farmers, formed the backbone of the radical opposition to tithes in the sixteen-forties and -fifties, whether it was expressed by the spokesmen of Cromwell's army, by the Levellers, the Anabaptists, or the Quakers; or by the 5,000 Hertfordshire men who signed *The Husbandmans Plea* in 1647.

This became a deep line of cleavage in the revolutionary period. Many of those whom we call 'Presbyterians', those parliamentarians whose outlook in political, social, and religious matters was relatively conservative, were personally interested in the preservation of tithes because this affected their own pockets directly, as well as because they approved in general of the maintenance of an established church. There was a natural alliance between these gentlemen and ministers of the establishment, whatever form the state church took. It was the more radical groups which wanted tithes either to be abolished, or to be used in the Scottish manner for constructive public purposes, such as education and poor relief.

These divergences of interest were obscured before 1640 by unity in opposition: but we should not forget them. They must have existed in the breasts of many Puritan ministers, who found themselves in alliance with impropriators on the one hand, and with enemies of tithes on the other. The way of godliness was narrow.

VII

Even this brief analysis will suggest a whole series of different and sometimes contradictory reasons why men should object either to the payment of tithes at all, or to episcopal schemes for their reorganization and increase.

1. First there was plain greed on the part of laymen, especially (for the reasons I have given) of those who hoped to profit by the new ways of making money, and of those for whom the margin between success and failure was narrowest. Bishop Cooper was undoubtedly partially right when he said that the Puritan attack on the landed wealth of the church 'doth very well justify the covetous and uncharitable dealings of many parishioners, which partly by violence, partly by crafty means, detain from the ministers their portion of tithes appointed by the law. This doctrine giveth good countenance to corrupt patrons, who will not bestow their benefices but by composition of a good part of the fruits to

their own use and commodity.'[1] There was also the growing sense of absolute property rights. Any limitation of such rights, whether by the priest's claim to God's tenth, or by the king's claim to arbitrary taxation, was resented. There is something Lockean in the way this is expressed in a pamphlet of 1647: 'We have a natural right unto our goods gotten by the daily labour of our hands: and so we have a right unto our crop of corn, as it is the fruit of our proper stock of money and year's labour.' No people can give either king or Parliament a right 'to dispose of themselves, their houses, lands, goods, liberties and labours'.[2] The lawyers' opposition, personified by Coke and Selden, derived its strength both from the hostility of the average sensual layman to paying tithes, and from the theory of a natural right to property.

2. It could be convincingly argued that tithes had a distorting effect on the national economy. They represented a 10 per cent. tax on commodities in universal demand, especially as food and for industry. Before the statute of 1549 freed newly cultivated land from tithe, this was a serious barrier to the expansion of agriculture. Even after that date tithes still penalized tillage in comparison with pasture, thus forcing England to import grain and encouraging depopulating enclosure. The system of assessing tithes on small livestock, beginning to pay in kind on the seventh bird or animal, also discouraged expansion of production: so did the custom of rendering tithe-milk only where there were at least seven calves. Even though 'the least and leanest' was always given as tithe, it was often cheaper for the small peasant to kill birds and beasts above six than to rear them.[3] The dependence of poor vicars on small tithes set their economic interests in opposition to those of the national economy as a whole. The hierarchy could not help the poorer clergy by effecting a large-scale financial reorganization: they merely encouraged them in hanging on to their legal claims to tithes. In so far as they received effective support under Laud, the authority of the government was thrown against agricultural improvement.

The recipient of tithes was a sleeping partner, reaping where others sowed. He risked no capital, yet claimed 10 per cent. not

[1] Cooper, op. cit., p. 163. Note that the Bishop here justifies tithes by the law, not by divine right.

[2] *The Husbandmans Plea*, pp. 86–87.

[3] Cowell, op. cit., s.v. 'Tithes'; Stillingfleet, op. cit. i. 312; Collier, op. cit. vii. 356; Fuller, *The Holy State* (1841), p. 85. Cf. the first epigraph to Chapter IX below.

merely of profits but, in some spheres, of gross takings. In those days of narrow margins between success and bankruptcy, this was a real deterrent to capital investment in agricultural improvements, experiments with new crops like hemp and flax. Claims to tithe could not always be enforced in practice: but the uncertainties, the rival jurisdictions, were terrifying to all but the richest farmers. The combination of recurrent friction, expensive litigation, uncertainty and the 10 per cent. levy which might represent 50 per cent. or more on profits: all this made tithes a veritable 'mill-stone round the neck of would-be agricultural improvers' in the seventeenth century. On this nearly all the agricultural writers agree.[1]

The claims of tithe-owners also put obstacles in the way of any economic improvement which affected, or was thought to affect, the interests of landowners. Sir Hugh Myddelton's plan to replenish London's water supply by 'the New River' in James I's reign met with this sort of opposition. Bishop Dove of Peterborough (1601–30) used his influence against the draining of the Fens.[2] At best, tithes were a highly regressive form of taxation, which, as Adam Smith was to argue convincingly, fell most heavily on those whose land was least productive.[3] As late as 1680 a pamphleteer complained that tithes, by raising costs, hampered the English fishing industry in competition with the Dutch.[4]

3. The reluctance of laymen to pay tithes, and the desperate attempts of ministers to collect and increase them, produced friction. 'The parson against the vicar, the vicar against the parson, the parish against both and one against another, and all for the belly.'[5] Richard Greenham, towards the end of Elizabeth's reign, attributed the 'great hatred' which had 'sprung up from the people' against ministers, to the fact that the latter were more diligent in collecting tithes than in dispensing hospitality.[6] It was

---

[1] Venn, op. cit., p. 100; M. James, in *History*, N.S., xxvi. 2, and references there cited; Pearson, op. cit., p. 66; J. W[orlidge], *Systema Agriculturae* (1669), p. 39; *Britannia Languens* (1680), in J. McCulloch, *Early English Tracts on Commerce* (1856), p. 367; A. Smith, op. cit. ii. 487–9. Smith points out the advantages of *modi* from the producer's point of view.

[2] S. Smiles, *Lives of the Engineers* (1874), i. 72; White, op. cit., p. 407. See also p. 37 above.   [3] A. Smith, op. cit. ii. 486.

[4] *Britannia Languens*, loc. cit.

[5] Edward Dering, preaching before Elizabeth in 1570, quoted in Haller op. cit., p. 13; cf. Hakewill, op. cit., p. 605.

[6] R. Greenham, *Works* (1612), p. 698.

noted that Abbott, the seventeenth-century Archbishop who showed least enthusiasm for ecclesiastical-economic reform, 'was never incumbent on any living with cure of souls', and therefore not 'acquainted with the trouble of taking tithes'.[1] Baxter 'escaped the offending of the people' by leaving the collection of his tithes to others, and never resorting to lawsuits against the poor.[2] But not everybody had Baxter's saintliness—or his rich wife. Selden puts the layman's case: 'A parson goes to law with his parishioners; he says for the good of his successors, that the church may not lose its right; when the meaning is to get the tithes into his own pocket.'[3]

Quarrels then were innumerable, and they increased under Laud. The hierarchy's attempt to improve the financial position of vicars at the expense of impropriators is discussed below.[4] By the sixteen-thirties both the reluctance of many laymen to pay tithes at all, and the determination of the clergy to enforce and increase their payment, had gone far. On 12 December 1630 forty-five persons were haled before the single consistory court of Wimborne Minster Peculiar in consequence of tithe disputes; on 18 April 1639 there were sixty-one persons before the same court for refusing to meet clerical demands for tithes.[5] In 1637 we find parishioners in another Dorset parish, Witherstone, clubbing together to defeat their minister.[6] This state of warfare must have had a cumulative effect in getting the clergy and the church a bad name. Volumes of lay irritation with the whole system are summed up in Milton's contemptuous reference to 'the ignoble hucksterage of piddling tithes'.[7] How much more satisfactory, Selden delicately insinuated, was the payment of regular stipends as in many of the reformed churches.[8] Though difficult to assess accurately, these conflicts must have created a highly unfavourable

---

[1] [George Sandys], *Anglorum Speculum* (1684), p. 798.

[2] Ed. M. Sylvester, *Reliquiae Baxterianae* (1696), i. 95.

[3] Selden, *Table Talk*, p. 223.

[4] See Chapter XIV.

[5] Fletcher, op. cit., p. 48. By far the largest number of citations before this court, Canon Fletcher tells us, was for tithe offences.

[6] *C.S.P.D., 1637*, pp. 96, 243.

[7] Milton, *Prose Works*, ii. 417–18.

[8] See p. 122 above. Even in Elizabeth's reign there had been itinerant Puritan ministers, dependent on voluntary contributions, who ('to please the people') taunted the beneficed clergy with their unapostolic behaviour (*Tracts ascribed to Richard Bancroft*, p. 58).

climate of opinion for Laud's attempts to solve disputed questions
in the clergy's favour. Again and again we find ministers in the
sixteen-thirties appealing to the Council in tithe disputes and
getting their cases referred to a committee of which Laud was
invariably the leading member.[1] So the government itself was
involved in the church's attempt to escape from the decisions of
juries, and therefore shared the odium of what was regarded as an
attack on property rights. And there was the further conflict of
interest between vicars and appropriating bishops, deans and
chapters, and colleges, as well as between vicars and lay rectors.

4. The older tradition, that tithes were communal property
held in trust by the minister, still survived: but it was a recollection rather than a reality. In a few parishes the parson might still
keep a dovecot, or even a bull or boar to service the village cows
or pigs: but this lost its point in enclosed villages, the inhabitants
of which would nevertheless have to pay tithes on livestock. At
Berwick, Suffolk, the minister in 1622 had leased the dovecot
out:[2] it had become his private property, not the property of the
community.

The parson was also traditionally expected to dispense hospitality and poor relief. Crowley was prepared to envisage the
expropriation of impropriators, so greatly did he disapprove of the
diversion of communal property from charitable purposes.[3] But
as poor relief ceased to be a parochial and became a national
concern, financed by taxation rather than by charity, the parson
felt himself less personally responsible: and this social justification
for his maintenance at the public expense also lost its validity.
John Penry, in a letter written from prison to the Earl of Essex in
1593, urged that tithes should be 'restored again unto the subjects',
and a smaller tax imposed for the queen's benefit.[4] In Scotland
Knox had almost incited to non-payment of tithes, telling the
commonalty that they might 'withhold the fruits and profits which
your false bishops and clergy most unjustly receive of you, until
such time as they be compelled faithfully to do their charge and

---

[1] *C.S.P.D.*, *1637–8*, pp. 396, 568; *1638–9*, pp. 208, 383, 469, 62, 396; and *passim*.
See also below, pp. 327–8.

[2] S. O. Addy, *Church and Manor* (1913), p. 409.

[3] See p. 135 above.

[4] *The Notebook of John Penry, 1593*, p. 89. The most forceful exposition of this
tradition, which is also interesting evidence of its survival, is to be found in W.
Cobbett's *History of the Protestant Reformation*, and others of his works.

duties', by preaching, *inter alia*.[1] In the first four centuries, Selden reminded his readers, 'the whole church, both lay and clergy, . . . lived in common'.[2] There are social overtones in all these comments, which point forward to the radical opposition to tithes of the sectaries during the revolutionary years.

(5.) 'In former ages', said Dr. Crompton in 1601, 'impropriations were given to the spirituality, and then no pluralities were allowed; but spiritual men having now the impropriations taken from them, they cannot keep that hospitality which is required, for which one benefice of small cure, especially with wife and children, sufficeth not.'[3] Ministers, that is to say, were being thrust—largely by impropriations—between two stools. They were too poor to carry out either their medieval duties of charity and hospitality, or their modern duties of preaching. The minister earned his tithes by preaching: so even Bishop Carleton and George Herbert thought.[4] But what if he did not preach? Here the argument became circular, spokesmen of the hierarchy urging that a preaching clergy was possible only if ministers were better paid, the opposition replying that they would pay more when, and only when, they got competent preachers.

This point was made by the Norfolk rebels in 1549, by the *Admonition to Parliament* of 1572, and on many later occasions. 18 Eliz., c. 11, followed Knox by authorizing parishioners to refuse tithes to non-resident ministers if the bishop refused to punish them. In 1604 the House of Commons passed a bill allowing parishioners to withhold tithes from any minister inducted after the date of the act who could not produce testimony to his moral conduct and ability to preach, either from his university or from six preachers in his own county.[5] Naturally this bill was rejected by the Lords. The logical conclusion of paying tithes only to those whose preaching gave satisfaction was that drawn by the sectaries: ministers should be chosen and paid by congregations.

(6.) The more developed principle of theological voluntaryism was propounded by Barrow: ministers should live on pure alms. Burghley countered by asking the question asked so often during

---

[1] Knox, *Letter to the Commonalty of Scotland*, in *History of the Reformation of Religion in Scotland* (1832), p. 406.

[2] Selden, *Works*, iii. 1096.   [3] Kennett, op. cit., p. 167.

[4] Carleton, op. cit., pp. 26, 36; G. Herbert, 'Charms and Knots', in *Works* (1941), p. 96.

[5] Gardiner, *History*, i. 179–80. See p. 225 below.

the revolution: 'But how if the people will not give?' 'Such people are not the people of God', was Barrow's conclusive if unconvincing answer.[1] Tithes, Henry Jacob thought in 1616, were not absolutely unlawful if paid voluntarily; but it was not lawful to pay them under legal compulsion.[2] Here refusal of tithes fused with opposition to the whole idea of a state church. Tithes imply an established church: acceptance of Christianity by the state implies tithes.[3] Advocates of adult baptism and voluntaryism naturally reject compulsory tithes.

Before 1640 this type of sectarian opposition was no doubt confined to a small minority: men like Cartwright and Travers were in favour of tithes. It is, however, hinted at even by Selden: 'So liberal, in the beginning of Christianity, was the devotion of believers, that their bounty, to the evangelical priesthood, far exceeded what the tenth could have been.'[4] And in fact the substitution of common-law right for *jus divinum* did mean, as Selden's indignant opponent Tillesley put it, that 'the church hereby must be fain to leave God's interest, and rely on man's bounty'.[5] The bounty of seventeenth-century man, in this respect, could not be relied on.

In 1646 a pamphleteer was arguing that if a minister cannot make it infallibly appear to me that he is of right my minister (i.e. that he has been called to that position, and has not been imposed by external authority) in the same way as a man can prove that he is my servant, then he has no more right to tithes than a servant would have to his wages. Here the special relationship between the priest and his parishioner has been entirely replaced by voluntary contract of the ordinary business type. Otherwise, 'why may not a carpenter or tailor be put upon every parish, whether the parish will or no, as well as a minister?'[6] Divine right was well and truly dead when men could write like that.

---

[1] Arber, op. cit., p. 46; cf. Carleton, op. cit., pp. 1–3. Barrow's answer may, of course, be convincing to one who does not believe in the necessity of a state church.

[2] [H. Jacob], *A Confession and Protestation of the Faith of Certaine Christians* (1616), sig. C7ᵛ.

[3] Browne, *An Answere to Master Cartwright* (1585?), in *The Writings of Robert Harrison and Robert Browne*, p. 449; Carleton, op. cit., p. 21.

[4] Selden, *Works*, iii. 1096. Note the delicate emphasis on 'evangelical': a preaching clergy. Such subtle Aesopian writing, of which Selden was a master, is a joy to read: but Selden's own recantation reminds us of the real risks involved.

[5] Tillesley, op. cit., 'To the Reader'.

[6] [Anon.], *Tyth-Gatherers, no Gospel Officers* (1646), p. 14.

7. The reluctance of Englishmen to pay tithes in our period might thus have many explanations, not all of them theological; but it could conveniently be expressed in terms of anti-popery. Fuller quoted Luther's Latin to make a point which was clear to all official Anglican spokesmen from Luther's time to Fuller's: 'Unless some of the spoils had remained which we snatched from the Pope, all the ministers of God's word must have perished through hunger; for if their maintenance had depended on the contributions of the people, they would indeed have had only a miserable and mean pittance. Our sustenance, therefore, is indeed derived from the spoils of Egypt, which had been collected together under the Papacy.'[1] Such remarks make one appreciate the wisdom of discussing the affairs of the church in a language which most laymen could not understand. It was an unfortunate, an embarrassing truth that the protestant Church of England could not subsist without the popish device of tithes; but laymen found it intolerable when the leaders of that church seemed bent on recovering *all* the spoils which the Pope had enjoyed. If Laud's economics were popish, what did it matter that he had controversies with Fisher the Jesuit? Antichrist, said Milton, was Mammon's son.[2]

VIII

Here, then, were many reasons for union against the bishops under the blanket slogan of 'No popery!' And as many for dissension after the bishops had been got rid of, and men faced the problem of bringing order into the chaos of ecclesiastical economics. The medieval system of appropriation had broken down, for the church no less than for the crown. The last opportunity to patch it up vanished after the Parliament of 1610, which Bancroft had tried to persuade to agree to a drastic reorganization of ecclesiastical finance, just as Cecil had tried through the Great Contract to place the crown's revenue on a new basis.

The king and those lay landowners who in the Reformation Parliament shared out the lands of the church destroyed more than they knew. In the short run it profited them greatly: but Sir Henry Spelman had grasped a profounder truth than he under-

[1] Fuller, *The Holy State*, p. 220.
[2] Milton, *Prose Works*, ii. 402.

stood when he argued that sacrilege never pays. His laborious attempts to show that individual families inheriting monastic lands came to bad ends are beside the point: it was the traditional social order, handed down from the Middle Ages, that was destroyed. That is the true historic irony of the four generations between 1529 and 1640. Those landed families which survived did so by moving over to a kind of economic activity very different from that which had predominated before the dissolution: and they developed new political attitudes. 'O the great judgments of God!' exclaimed Charles I's secretary of state, the near-papist Windebank, to the Pope's representative in England. 'Henry VIII committed such sacrilege by profaning so many ecclesiastical benefices in order to give their goods to those who being so rewarded might stand firmly for the king in the lower house; and now the king's greatest enemies are those who are enriched by these benefices.'[1]

The despoilers of the monasteries and the enclosers of common lands both helped to disrupt the old social order, though as land-owners they were exactly the class which might have been ex-pected to defend it. Contemporaries were right to see these two groups as sacrilegious offenders against God, who would punish them and their posterity on earth as well as in the hereafter.[2] During the revolutionary period it was forcibly shown that land-lords' property rights were no more sacred in the eyes of the lower orders than the church's property had been in theirs. Why, after all, should monastic, episcopal, and cathedral lands alone be vulnerable?

There is an agreeable dialectic about the transitions. First, tithes are assimilated to lay property, lose their divine sanction, and so become liable to lay criticism (Selden). But because priests defend them as due *jure divino*, they still have to be attacked by quasi-religious arguments. A divine right, a Christian liberty, *not* to pay tithes had to be evolved. But opposition to tithes was also economic. And since tithes *were* after all virtually indistinguish-able from rent to those who paid them, why should liberty be confined? Members of the Long Parliament foresaw that those

[1] Gardiner, *History*, viii. 137.
[2] J. Dod and R. Clever, *A plain and familiar Exposition of the Ten Commandements* (19th ed., 1662), p. 78. 'This enclosing doth but exclude them and theirs. . . . God plagues their sins both in themselves and their houses.' See above, pp. 23-24.

who refused tithes would soon refuse rents : and they were right.
The confiscation and sale of bishops' and cathedral lands was a
transfer *within* the propertied class; it left the structure of society
untouched. But the abolition of tithes would have meant the
downfall of the established church, with all that this involved in
political terms for the ruling class, and of impropriations and the
patronage system, with all that that would have involved economically for the gentry. The same gentleman who was evading or
compounding for tithes in one parish might be collecting them in
the next.

No wonder so many of the propertied revolutionaries began to
draw back when they saw what gulfs were opening before them!
No tithes, no rents; attacks on church property produced attacks
on property as such; sovereignty of Parliament led to sovereignty
of the people. It was a pity, many of the men of 1640 must have
thought, that one thing leads to another. Bancroft's logic in his
sermon at Paul's Cross had not convinced their grandfathers; but
the logic of events ultimately led the men of property to support
the restoration of church and king; and Charles II found himself
with a government composed largely of men who had been in
arms against his father.

IX

It would be too large a subject to discuss the solutions arrived at
during the revolution to the problems here indicated, and the new
conflicts to which they gave rise. Here these solutions may be
briefly listed. First, ministers' revenues were augmented from
bishops', deans' and chapters' lands, and from *royalists'* impropriations. This did not provide adequate stipends for all ministers,
but it greatly improved the lot of many of them; and it left intact
the property rights of those impropriators who had chosen the
parliamentary side.

Secondly, the common law triumphed over the church courts;
Coke finally vanquished Bancroft, as thoroughly as Selden did
those who had silenced him. Nor was the position reversed after
1660 in so far as the security of lay property was concerned; though
parsons lost their augmentations. The church courts never effectively recovered their jurisdiction, since the High Commission
was not restored; and excommunication ceased to be a serious

sentence. Coke's interpretation triumphed in the disputed areas of tithe jurisdiction, as in almost every other sphere. In 1732 Bohun was able to justify the publication of his *Tithing Table* by the reflection that the *Tithing Table* published in 1635 'falls vastly short of the mark it aimed at, as being founded chiefly on opinions and decisions of the canon and civil law', which were of no present use in determining the rights of tithes. For tithes were 'now generally confessed to be mere lay chattels, and consequently determinable according to the rules prescribed by our common and statute laws'.[1] So complete was the victory that Bohun could write, in words which Selden might have envied, 'how can a matter of custom, which is private common law, be determined in any other manner than by a jury at common law?'[2]

Thirdly, although tithes were not abolished (as the radicals wished), claims to them by divine right were virtually abandoned. Selden noted that the Oxford divines, forced to set aside *jus divinum*, found 'the best argument for their tithes' in his *History*, 'a book so much cried down by them formerly'.[3] Selden himself had claimed long before that 'never was there so much human law positive for the payment of whole tithes observed to public view' as in his *History*.[4] He must have smiled grimly when he received a letter from the Rev. Dr. Langbaine, Provost of Queen's, an ardent royalist and episcopalian, saying: 'I am not out of hopes but that work . . . which was looked upon as a piece that struck deepest against the divine, will afford the strongest arguments for the civil right: and if that be made the issue, I do not despair of the cause.'[5] It had, however, taken a revolution to make that the issue, to displace divine law by human contract.

Fuller, writing in 1655, tells a story of his uncle Bishop Davenant in the days when he was vicar of Oakington, which helps to explain how churchmen came to accept the new position. An Anabaptist refused to pay tithes, on conscientious grounds, since he could find no Scriptural authorization for them. Davenant replied that he had conscientious scruples about allowing the Anabaptist to retain the other nine-tenths of his property. The

[1] Bohun, *A Tithing Table*, sig. A3–A3ᵛ.
[2] Bohun, *The Law of Tithes*, pp. 390–1.
[3] Selden, *Table Talk*, p. 209. Selden may have been thinking of Heylyn: see his *Historical and Miscellaneous Tracts*, i. 172.
[4] Selden, *Works*, iii. 1072.
[5] Selden, *Table Talk*, p. xxvii.

Anabaptist appealed to the law as the guarantor of his property:
and so had to accept the vicar's claim that the law also guaranteed
his tithes. The worse argument, Fuller concluded, proved the
better for his apprehension.[1] When church courts were abolished,
divine right went with them; for now tithe claims could only be
enforced at common law.

'Men perform their covenants made': Ireton in the Putney
Debates, and Hobbes in *Leviathan*, were only summing up for the
propertied class a truth that they were continually learning from
their own experience: that inviolability of contract was the
foundation of the new social order, the beginning of bourgeois
political justice, as divine right had been of the preceding order.
Yet the consequences, from the hierarchy's point of view, were
not altogether desirable. 'Though the civil right make men pay
them well out of fear,' Comber noted, 'yet none ever paid them
so fully and freely as those who believe in the divine right; which
is the main reason why the principal batteries of the church's
enemies are raised against that.'[2] It may also be the main reason
why ecclesiastics defended divine right as long as they could.

The church had to accept the new order, *faute de mieux*. Many
ministers cast nostalgic glances backwards; but even the restoration of church courts in 1660 could not restore divine right. By
1735 a common lawyer could write that personal tithes 'were
never due in England of common right; never otherwise than by
special custom in some particular parishes; and are lost and gone
for ever where an immemorial, uninterrupted custom for the
payment of them cannot be proved'.[3] As an historical statement,
that might perhaps be improved on: but its implication for practice in the writer's day is accurate enough.

Tithes, then, survived in 1660. The men of property in town
and country were best placed to evade full payment. Their
main burden fell on the poorer classes in the countryside. For
political reasons it seemed desirable to the new ruling class to
retain a state church: and no system of taxation could be easily
devised which would fall so disproportionately on the lower
orders as tithes. The Leveller and Quaker movement for their

---

[1] Fuller, *Church History*, p. 171; Bailey, *Life of Fuller*, p. 67.

[2] Comber, op. cit. ii. Preface, sig. a 3ᵛ.

[3] Sir Michael Foster, *An Examination of the Scheme of Church Power laid down in the Codex Juris Ecclesiastici Anglicani*, pp. 100–1. I quote from the reprint of 1840, Tracts for the People.

total abolition was therefore side-tracked and defeated. (George Fox was not alone in thinking this to be Oliver Cromwell's greatest treachery.) Feudal dues were abolished and replaced by an excise: thus landowners saved their own pockets at the expense of the mass of consumers. For exactly similar reasons tithes were retained though (or because) they normally took away half the husbandman's profit. They also provided a discriminatory tax upon non-conformists (mainly drawn from the middle and lower classes) who were forced to pay for the maintenance of a church to which they did not belong as well as of that to which they did.

It is not perhaps irrelevant to compare and contrast the French Revolution. The *cahiers* of 1789 asked for the abolition of tithes, among other reasons because of the vast number of legal cases they engendered: only ecclesiastical *cahiers* demanded their retention. *Cahiers* also asked that impropriators should be compelled to give curés a stipend adequate for them to live decently and exercise charity.[1] The ecclesiastical-economic problems in the two revolutions were decidedly similar: so were the solutions proposed. Not so, however, the results; for in France tithes and impropriations were abolished together in August 1789. That early and lasting success for the policy advocated in vain in England by Levellers and Quakers is a measure of the greater radicalness of the French Revolution; of the triumph in France of the peasantry over lay impropriators as well as over the church.

[1] See documents in Albert Soboul's *1789: l'an I de la liberté* (Paris, 1939), pp. 49, 51, 164.

VII

PARISH FEES

> They teach for gain and preach for hire, . . . and they do this by
> the authority of the governing power. A man must not take a
> wife, but the priest must give her him. If he have a child, the
> priest must give the name. If any die, the priest must see it laid in
> the earth. If any man want knowledge or comfort, they teach
> him to go to the priest for it; and what is the end of all this,
> but to get money?
>
> GERRARD WINSTANLEY, *The New Law of Righteousness* (1649), p. 44

I

THE Reformation saw the end of some voluntary offerings,
but other fees and dues were made obligatory by 2 & 3 Ed. VI,
c. 13. Christening and churching of women cost from 4*d.*
to 11½*d.*, 1*d.*–2*d.* only if the child died. Mrs. Chidley, giving us
a rare glimpse of the woman's point of view, complained that fees
had also to be paid for the priest's blessing during pregnancy.
Marriage cost from 1*s.* to 4*s.* with banns, 3*s.* to 6*s.* by licence
without banns. Burials normally ran from 2*d.* to 1*s.* 4*d.* in the
churchyard, 2*s.* to 2*s.* 8*d.* with coffin, 3*s.* outside Wells cathedral.
Spelman quotes examples running up to 6*s.* For 'strangers' dying
in the parish a considerably higher fee had to be paid. In London
it cost 7*s.* or 8*s.* to bury a child, Mrs. Chidley tells us.[1]

'Some fifteen or sixteen shillings will bestow him honestly',
said Wiggen in Peele's *Old Wives Tale*; and the sexton confirmed
the estimate.[2] Burial in the church, which at least one Elizabethan
bishop thought should be reserved for 'those of the best sort of
the parish',[3] cost 6*s.* 8*d.* and upwards, £1. 6*s.* 8*d.* in Wells cathedral, £5 at Chester; but there might also be a much heavier charge

---

[1] Katharine Chidley, *The Justification of the Independent Churches of Christ* (1641),
p. 57.

[2] In *Minor Elizabethan Drama* (Everyman), ii. 146.

[3] Kennedy, op. cit. iii. 152. The bishop was Middleton of St. David's: he expected
10*s.* to be paid. Cf. W. Habington, *Poems* (ed. K. Allott, 1948), p. 47.

for the ground. Spelman gives 20*s.* and 26*s.* 8*d.* as charges confirmed by bishops as 'laudable customs', with others not so approved running up to £10. He mentions even rents for graves, at £1 to £4 per annum; one parson threatened to foreclose by pulling down the monument on a grave for which the rent was in arrears. In one parish Spelman says 6*s.* 8*d.* was due to the parson for burials in his church, even when he left it to the curate to officiate; and the latter claimed an extra 10*s.* for this, as well as 10*s.* for a sermon, 'though there be none'. The hearse cloth was normally regarded by the minister as his perquisite.

Bells for a funeral or a marriage would cost an extra 1*s.* or more, according to the dignity of the peal. At Chester cathedral the ringers got 3*s.* 4*d.* for the great bell, only 8*d.* for the fourth bell; but the Dean and Chapter had £1 in each case for allowing the peal. A pamphlet of 1641, though propagandist, neatly and accurately takes up all these points: 'So much for burials, so much for the knell, so much for the grave; for the corpse more, if coffined; more yet, if in such a churchyard; more than that, if in the church; higher yet, if it be in the chancel; beyond all these, if buried with torches and sermon, and mourning with attendance; but it is put upon the highest strain, if it be a stranger.'[1]

Easter offerings at communion seem to have been standardized at 2*d.*, sometimes with an extra 1*d.* for the clerk. There might be additional fees for bread and wine at communion, sometimes graded because 'the better sort' got superior wine. Other charges, such as pew-rents, went into parish funds: the 4*d.* or so paid by those who could afford it for a licence to eat meat on statutory fish days went into the parson's pocket.[2]

[1] [Anon.], *The Curates' Conference*, in *Harleian Miscellany* (1808–11), i. 498.

[2] For lists of church fees see *C.S.P.D., 1637–8*, p. 176; *MSS. of the Dean and Chapter of Wells* (Hist. MSS. Commission), ii. 419; *Sussex Archaeological Soc. Collections*, xxv. 154; Bunting, op. cit., pp. 123–4; Hale, *A Series of Precedents and Proceedings . . . extracted from the Act-Books of the Ecclesiastical Courts in the Diocese of London* (1847), p. 221; W. E. Buckland, *The Parish Registers and Records in the Diocese of Rochester* (Kent Archaeological Soc., 1912), p. 21; R. V. H. Burne, 'Chester Cathedral after the Restoration', in *Chester Archaeological Soc.'s Journal*, xl. 38–39; Spelman, 'De Sepultura', in *English Works*, i. 184–6; ed. W. Cunningham, *Common Rights at Cottenham and Stretham*, *Camden Miscellany*, xii. 252; T. E. Gibson, *A Cavalier's Notebook* (1880), pp. 263–4; J. C. Cox, *The Parish Registers of England* (1910), pp. 99, 120; S. L. Ware, *The Elizabethan Parish in its Ecclesiastical and Financial Aspects* (Baltimore, 1908), pp. 78–82; J. S. Purvis, *Tudor Parish Documents of the Diocese of York* (1948), p. 74; *V.C.H., Lincolnshire*, i. 62; E. Trotter, *Seventeenth Century Life in the Country Parish* (1919), p. 43.

Without attaching too much weight to them, let us consider the kind of accusation made by parishioners against their ministers when the assembly of the Long Parliament had opened their mouths. The pluralist and non-resident vicar of Tenterden was charged with extorting 12*d*. for ringing the great bell at burials, a fee never heard of till his day. The fee for marriage had been raised from 1*s*. 6*d*. to 2–4*s*. The curate now expected 10*s*. for a funeral sermon, the vicar 20*s*. for hire of the pulpit if a stranger preached. The vicar of Dartford was also accused of doubling marriage fees and the cost of funeral sermons.[1] Similar accusations were made against the vicar of Christ Church, London, who was the brother of Lord Keeper Finch. He exacted 20*s*. and upwards for funeral sermons, his parishioners said, 'himself seldom preaching any of them'. On one occasion he had £5 in advance for a funeral sermon, but refused to preach it because he was not also given a pair of gloves. Another time he received £13. 5*s*. 6*d*. to allow someone else to preach at a funeral in his church. He took up to £10 or £12 for burials, they alleged, and would not suffer the ground to be broken until he had been satisfied. He charged 10*s*. for christenings, 3*s*. 4*d*. for administering communion to a dying woman (being drunk at the time). His pulpit, he was alleged to have said, was his shop, and he must improve it to the utmost. It had been asserted, on an earlier occasion, that when Finch *did* preach, a collector stood at the door crying 'Pray remember the minister'.[2]

Finch's replies were singularly lame: so lame indeed that they failed to convince even Walker, who supposed he was 'in some part guilty'.[3] Finch admitted taking 20*s*. for funeral sermons from 'the most able sort', but claimed that he took less from those of inferior rank. He did not specify how much less. No one, he thought, had *proved* that he took £5 for a funeral sermon which he did not preach: the money was for the ground and other (unnamed) church duties. He demanded fees only as his predecessors had done. He did not say his pulpit was his 'shop' but his 'livelihood'. He denied swearing *frequently*; and to the accusation that he had administered the communion whilst intoxicated Finch

[1] Larking, op. cit., pp. 230, 235; cf. Johnstone, *Churchwardens' Presentments*, p. 94.
[2] [Anon.], *The Petition and Articles . . . exhibited in Parliament against Edward Finch* (1641), *passim; C.S.P.D., 1637*, p. 519.
[3] Walker, *Sufferings of the Clergy*, i. 72.

replied with feeling: "'Tis an hard matter to swear positively when a man is drunk.'[1] The House of Commons Committee on Religion found him guilty, among many other things, of foul extortion.

Similar accusations of exacting unwarranted sums of money for attendance at funerals, of raising fees 400–500 per cent. within seven years, were made against William Grant, vicar of Isleworth, a protégé of Goodman of Gloucester. Grant also denied taking more than the accustomed fees, but Parliament thought him guilty and sequestered him.[2] Brian Walton, whom we shall meet again later, was also accused by his parishioners at St. Martin Orgar's of increasing fees on his own initiative and to his own profit; of appropriating other parish property, with the connivance of the higher ecclesiastical authorities; and of many other misdemeanours. He was deprived.[3]

II

Mortuaries—the second-best beast (or garment if there was no beast), the best being seized by the lord as a heriot—were regulated by 21 Hen. VIII, c. 6, wherever they were customary at that date. Those who were fortunate enough to die leaving goods worth less than 10 marks (all debts paid) were exempt; 3s. 4d. was charged on movable goods and chattels worth between 10 marks and £30; 6s. 8d. on £30–40; 10s. on £40 and over. In certain areas (e.g. Wales), mortuaries were not customary; in other areas they had 'decayed'.[4] Where they had ceased to be due by custom the minister had no legal right to collect them, declared Coke;[5] but he often tried. In 1629 the parishioners of St. Oswald's, Chester, instituted legal proceedings against their vicar for demanding and

---

[1] E. Finch, *An Answer to the Articles preferred against Edward Finch* (1641), pp. 2–18. See p. 301 below.

[2] [Anon.], *The Petition of the Inhabitants of Isleworth (Middlesex . . .) against William Grant, Minister of the said Parish* (1641), *passim*; Grant, *The Vindication of the Vicar of Isleworth* (1641), *passim*; Lysons, op. cit. iii. 108.

[3] [Anon.], *The Articles and Charge Proved in Parliament against Dr. Walton* (1641), pp. 5–12; Matthews, *Walker Revised*, pp. 47, 61. See below, pp. 180, 277–8.

[4] Degge, op. cit., pp. 252–4; Strype, *Whitgift*, i. 441; Rowse, *The England of Elizabeth*, p. 431. Usher was wrong in thinking that mortuaries had been abolished at the Reformation, but right to suppose that their 'decay' and the cessation of other dues was a severe blow to churchmen (op. cit. i. 233). Laud approved Bramhall's sabotage of an act of the Irish Parliament aimed against mortuaries (*Hastings MSS.*, iv. 61–62).

[5] Coke, *Second Part of the Institutes*, p. 491.

taking a mortuary of 10s. 'and having grown otherwise very troublesome'.[1] In 1634 the vicar of Rype, Sussex, was taking mortuaries of 6s. and 10s., not only from his own parishioners, but also (illegally) from travellers who died while passing through the parish. The vicars of Stanton Lacy, Shropshire, were receiving mortuaries at the higher rate down to 1643, and again after 1660.[2] In North Wales, we are told as late as 1686, friends of a dead man made offerings in money 'according to their own ability and the quality of the person deceased. This custom proves a very happy augmentation to some of the very poor vicars, and is often the best part of his maintenance.' A similar custom had prevailed in at least one Oxfordshire parish.[3]

III

The maintenance of the fabric of the church was coming to be paid for by the church rate, levied on every occupier of land or inhabitant of the parish. Visitation fees, due from churchwardens on attendance at the archdeacon's court, also had to be paid for out of the rates, and took a considerable share of the parish income.[4] Parishioners, moreover, were liable for wages (sometimes paid in kind) as well as fees to the parish clerk. At the end of Elizabeth's reign there was a typically outrageous proposal to grant a monopoly for appointing or 'surveying' parish clerks. Whitgift opposed this attempt to set up a nation-wide patronage racket with the argument that 'they receive their fees and accustomed wages of the parishioners; therefore a stranger cannot be obtruded well upon them; for if any of another's appointment be their clerk, they will think it hard measure that they should be forced to maintain him'.[5] Disputes over the election of parish clerks and over their wages were perennial, the clerks running for support to the ecclesiastical courts or to the bishop.

Attempts were made to settle such disputes by regulation. Bancroft in the diocese of London in 1601, followed by the Canons of 1604 for the whole country, laid it down that the parish clerk was to be nominated by the minister, not elected by the parish; and

---

[1] R. V. H. Burne, 'The History of Chester Cathedral in the Reigns of James I and Charles I', loc. cit., p. 20.   [2] Cox, op. cit., p. 125.
[3] J. Aubrey, *Remains of Gentilisme and Judaisme* (1881), pp. 23–24 (additions by White Kennett).   [4] Trotter, op. cit., pp. 28, 35; Usher, op. cit. ii. 33.
[5] Strype, *Annals*, iv. 63.

that clerks should 'receive their ancient wages, without fraud or diminution, either at the hands of the churchwardens . . . or by their own collection, according to the most ancient custom of every parish'.[1] But the most ancient customs were disputable. From 8 Jac. I the common-law courts maintained the parishioners' right to elect their clerk wherever such a right could be proved to have existed before the Canons. They regularly issued prohibitions in order to assert their jurisdiction.[2] Often conflicts over the right to elect concealed quarrels about fees. Thus in 1624–5 a dispute between vicar and parishioners of Hackney was only settled when the parishioners elected the vicar's nominee as their clerk, on condition of good behaviour and not exacting fees higher than those *now* listed in a table in the chancel.[3] These disputes acquired a new importance as the policy of the hierarchy began to diverge widely from that which would have been approved by the elected officers in many parishes. The bishops, Leighton alleged, were trying to turn parish clerks into 'the eyes of their spiteful courts'.[4]

As usual, the many disagreements came to a head under the rule of Laud. In 1636 the parish clerks of London were empowered by a new charter of incorporation to collect their own wages. Two years later, still in difficulties, their Company decided to appeal to Laud or the Privy Council for help. Laud raised the matter with the bishops during the Convocation of 1640, pointing out how injuriously parish clerks were chosen, 'to the disturbance and vexation of the clergy'. The bishops agreed to ask the Attorney-General to find some suitable remedy.[5] Probably in consequence of this, the parish clerks received another charter, under which each clerk was empowered not only to collect his own wages but also *to sue for them in the church courts*. Churchwardens were forbidden to collect clerks' wages, but ordered to present in the bishop's court all those who refused payment.[6]

There was a terrific uproar about this charter. In a pamphlet of 1641 one curate urges another to turn parish clerk, since a clerk's place in London is worth £200 or more a year. 'Oh! their

---

[1] Kennedy, op. cit. iii. 345; Cardwell, *Synodalia*, p. 298.
[2] Hughes, op. cit. (1st ed.), ii. 115–18; Gibson, op. cit., pp. 240–1.
[3] J. Christie, *Some Account of Parish Clerks* (1893), pp. 170–1; cf. Hale, *A Series of Precedents* . . ., p. 250.
[4] Leighton, op. cit., p. 137.   [5] Nalson, op. cit. i. 365.
[6] Christie, op. cit., pp. 171–2.

fees come in sleeping or waking. . . . Some of them rule the whole parish, and parson and all.'[1] The clerks' opponents petitioned Parliament, against the incorporation, against the authorization to collect wages, and against the right of appeal to the church courts, all of which they believed to be illegal without Parliament's sanction.[2] The House of Commons agreed that the levying of rates by parish clerks for their wages was illegal. It infringed the property rights of the subject, and anyway the clerk was a lay officer with whom the church courts had no business to meddle.[3] After the Restoration the common-law judges accepted the view that the parish clerk was a temporal officer, whose office was a freehold; they refused to enforce the jurisdiction of the church courts in disputes in which he was involved.[4]

There were, then, two possible sources of friction arising from fees. The first was between clergy and parish; the second between vestry and parishioners. In parishes where revenue from tithes was non-existent or very small, ministers were entirely dependent on fees. It was contrary to all the laws of God and nature, said a paper of 1629 defending the existing position, that the clergy should do all their work for nothing.[5] Parsons, therefore, having lost other sources of income, clung desperately to their fees, and tried where possible to raise them.

Beaumont and Fletcher's *The Spanish Curate* (1622) has some pleasing passages that clearly reflect English and not Spanish conditions. The vicar and his sexton complained bitterly of the failure of their parishioners to die, marry, and beget children often enough:

> To have a thin stipend, and an everlasting parish:
> Lord, what a torment 'tis!

And the vicar told his parishioners 'Ye have neither faith nor money left to save ye'. When the vicar threatened to leave, his parishioners promised to try to do better in the way of dying and begetting children. It is significant that this minister was a keen

---

[1] *The Curates' Conference*, pp. 498–9.

[2] *Hist. MSS. Commission, Fourth Report, Appendix*, p. 54.

[3] Ed. Notestein, *The Journal of Sir Simonds D'Ewes*, pp. 281–2, 436; cf. p. 112, and N. Wallington, *Historical Notices of events occurring chiefly in the reign of Charles I* (1869), i. 151.

[4] S. and B. Webb, op. cit., p. 33.

[5] *C.S.P.D., 1625–49*, p. 330. This paper was probably sent to Laud by Richard Manwaring. See p. 186 below.

advocate of the traditional sports, whilst his parishioners 'had Puritan hearts awhile, spurned at all pastimes'.[1]

On the other hand, vestries which were responsible for assessing and levying the church rate (and which for that reason tended during our period to become select and co-optative) also had views on these matters. London select vestries, especially, drawn from the richer parishioners, saw a solution to the parish's financial problems by raising fees, pew-rents, &c. In 1633 the vestrymen of St. Botolph's without Bishopsgate were hauled before the Star Chamber on a charge of conspiracy and combination to assume the royal power in imposing burdens on the subject, by increasing their church fees by 300 per cent., and prosecuting those who refused to pay at the new rates. They were accused of denying burial to the foreman of a jury which had inquired into these extortions.[2] That such practices were fairly general is clear from Spelman's *De Sepultura*.[3]

The quarrels to which fees gave rise furnished yet another source of economic dissatisfaction with the parochial system; and since the practices of vestries and ministers were often officially sanctioned by bishops or their chancellors, the odium reflected back upon the hierarchy. It was one more reason for desiring an economic reorganization, a definition of authority, and for believing that if this was to be done in the spirit desired by laymen of property, a necessary preliminary was the abolition of the hierarchy.

IV

In yet another minor but significant sphere we can see how the breakdown of the traditional system of appropriation for parish expenses led to its replacement by contracts, to the advantage of the self-assertive moneyed class. From the end of the fifteenth century there are examples of parish revenues being supplemented by pew-rents. These became more frequent from the mid-sixteenth

---

[1] Act II, scene 1; Act III, scene 2.

[2] S.P. 16/255/51. The vestrymen were also accused of allowing persons chosen by the parishioners as scavengers, constables, or questmen to buy themselves off. Cf. S.P. 16/298/31, 85; 16/301/19, 53–4; 16/302/34—similar charges in St. Martin Orgar's, Brian Walton's parish. (I owe these references to the kindness of Dr. G. E. Aylmer.)

[3] Spelman, *English Works*, i. 183–6.

century, in consequence no doubt of the new emphasis on preaching. We can see the change taking place in two Reading parishes.
At St. Lawrence's in 1573, since collections and chantry lands now
no longer paid for the maintenance of the church, the parishioners
agreed that all women to whom seats had been allotted should pay
for them. By 1607 the wedge had been driven home, and the
whole church was divided up into pews hired out at differential
rates. At St. Mary's from 1581, to augment the parish stock and
maintain the church because rents were very small, differential
pew-rents were introduced.[1] At St. Edmund's, Salisbury, receipts
from pews rose from £2. 0s. 6d. in 1589 to £4. 14s. 10d. in 1622–3,
and had trebled again by 1641–2 to £13. 9s. 0d. Spelman speaks of
pew-rents running from 15s. to £4.[2] Even for outdoor sermons,
at St. Paul's Cross and outside other cathedrals, a charge was made
for seats.[3]

In some churches pews were allotted for life only: in others
the right to a pew was annexed to the payment of rates, to the
right to be buried in church (a social distinction), to the holding
of property in the parish, or to an ecclesiastical office such as
churchwarden. Special pews were allotted to municipal authorities
—and their wives. But the right to build a pew might also be sold
for cash down: and purchasers would vie with one another in
ostentatious construction. A pew was a valued possession, a mark
of social status. Earle's 'she precise hypocrite' 'knows her own
place in heaven as perfectly as the pew she has a key to'.[4] The poor
were reminded of their place by being seated on forms, which at
St. Edmund's, Salisbury, had FOR THE POOR written on them in
great red letters.[5]

Light is perhaps thrown on lower-class sectarianism by the
regulations of Stepney parish church (1627–32) that no servants
were to sit in the pews, and that their occupants were to be
placed 'according to their several ranks and qualities'. Stepney
was a very radical area during the revolution. But such measures

---

[1] Cox, *Churchwardens' Accounts* (1913), p. 188; Ware, op. cit., pp. 80–81.

[2] Cox, op. cit., pp. 67–69; Spelman, *English Works*, i. 185. Differential rates were
also charged at Shenfield, Essex (W. J. Pressey, 'Some seating experiences in Essex
churches', in *Essex Review*, xxxv. 8).

[3] Sir T. Browne, *The Antiquities of Norwich*, in *Works* (Bohn edition, 1852), iii.
301.

[4] Morley, op. cit., p. 194.

[5] Cox, op. cit., pp. 69, 192; cf. T. Pape, *Newcastle-under-Lyme in Tudor and early
Stuart Times* (1938), pp. 271–2.

were economic as well as social, for the finances of Stepney parish depended on pew-rents. The grant of a faculty by the Bishop of London (Laud) to hold three pews tended 'to the impoverishing of the parish'.[1] When Thomas Farnell, gentleman, of Grays Thurrock, Essex, was presented in 1623 'for that he hath taken two seats or pews to his own use . . . in which the better sort of the parishioners did sit', the objection was that it caused not only shortage of space but also refusal to pay parish and church duties.[2] John Donne allowed his churchwardens at St. Dunstan's to allot seats, taking 6s. 8d. himself for each parishioner so placed.[3]

The hierarchical principle was still very strong in this society. The churchwardens of St. Ebbe's, Oxford, were at pains to assure ecclesiastical authority that they 'disposed of seats . . . according to the degrees and qualities of the parishioners'. They placed new-comers to the parish 'higher or lower in the said church than their predecessors in such houses did sit, according to their estates and reputations'. There was trouble when a cobbler and ale-bearer 'did remove themselves . . . out of the seat used by them . . . into a higher seat there, not so fit for them as their said former seat, because that in show of the world they now sit above their betters'. The show of the world was what most mattered. When the vicar and churchwardens of Banbury put a mere shepherd into the pew of Mr. Thomas Bennett, the latter complained to the church court.[4] Even higher authority might be called in. When one gentleman of Charnes, Staffs., seated 'his ploughman' in a pew claimed by another gentleman, the affair was brought before the Star Chamber in 1632, which 'misliked and condemned' the affront.[5] Bishop Goodman thought it matter for boast that in his Berkshire parish of West Ilsley no parishioner 'did claim a property in the seats, . . . but being free from pride and bred up in humility they did place themselves, still preferring the eldest or those who paid the greatest rent and rates in the parish'.[6] Humility was the virtue of the poor rather than of the rich.

A secular authority like the corporation of Newcastle-under-Lyme was no less anxious that men and women should keep their due places in church, and differentiated sharply between those who

---

[1] G. W. Hill and W. H. Frere, *Memorials of Stepney Parish* (1890–1), pp. 122, 125–6, 135–6.   [2] Hale, *A Series of Precedents*, p. 249.

[3] *Times Literary Supplement*, 16 September 1955.

[4] Peyton, op. cit., pp. xxxii, 199.

[5] Rushworth, op. cit. iii, Appendix, pp. 45–46.   [6] Soden, op. cit., p. 113.

had a right to a particular pew and the poor who had to make do with forms.[1] Typical of the ruling-class attitude towards priorities in religious matters was Lord Dorchester's suggestion to his bishop that the pulpit in his parish church might be moved to facilitate the construction of pews for Lady Dorchester and her women.[2] As Dorchester was secretary of state at the time the bishop was likely to agree. A faculty was granted by the Archbishop of Canterbury, with the approval of the Bishop of Bangor, for Sir Thomas Holland of Anglesey to pull down the chancel wall of his church and build an aisle to house a pew for his family.[3]

Disputes over pews fell within the jurisdiction of the church courts. They strictly maintained social status. Thus in 1577 the London Consistory Court ordered that the inhabitants of one parish should attend another parish church, every parishioner there 'to be placed according to his degree'.[4] Similar orders were issued for Kingston-upon-Thames in 1585, for Walden, Essex, in 1594. In 1605 Bancroft's Commissary found that at Adisham, Kent, 'some of the meaner sort' sat 'in the highest pews', whilst others of better ability were placed very low. He selected five parishioners whom he ordered to 'place and displace' in such a way that every man might be seated 'as beseemeth his degree and wealth'.[5] An almost identical case occurred at Great Chesham two years later. There too 'some of the meanest account had gotten the best seats, and would sit with persons of far better reckoning'. The Commissary directed the minister, churchwardens, and two gentlemen to see that new pews were built and to reseat the people 'more decently and conveniently, according to their respective dignities, states and conditions'. Some of the parishioners resented this, and opposed the arrangements made. The High Commission had to be called upon to intervene several times before they submitted.[6]

This was an insubordinate area. There was a dispute about pews in the parish church of Rickmansworth in 1637. Laud intervened

---

[1] Pape, op. cit., pp. 215, 224, 260, 271–2, 285.
[2] D. Mathew, *The Age of Charles I* (1951), p. 160.
[3] *C.S.P.D., 1639–40*, pp. 309–10.
[4] Hale, *A Series of Precedents*, p. 158.
[5] Pressey, op. cit., pp. 4–5; Addy, op. cit., pp. 416–19.
[6] J. W. Garnett-Pegge, 'Richard Bowle's Book', in *Records of Bucks.* ix. 332–46. I am indebted to Mr. John Bowle for drawing my attention to this case.

with the same object of insisting that parishioners should 'be placed in the church according to their conditions, qualities and degrees'.[1] The parish authorities of Monks Eleigh, in the Deanery of Bocking, received a similar commission in 1638 to seat parishioners 'according to their degrees and fashion'; 'according to their several conditions, qualities and estates' was the phrase used to St. Mary's church, Dover, in the following year.[2] Bishop Bridgman, who was also parson of Wigan, advised that parish likewise to rank the best in the highest seats.[3] In 1635 Sir Nathaniel Brent ordered the destruction of a gallery at St. Pancras's church, Chichester, which had been built 'to receive strangers'. At the same time the minister was made to confess his error in being 'too popular in the pulpit'.[4] Next year, at Great Yarmouth, the Bishop's Commissary ordered the removal of some pews in the parish church and a reduction in the size of others.[5]

At Chester a storm raged from 1624 to 1640 between the mayor and corporation on the one hand and the Bishop and Dean and Chapter on the other. Laud got Charles I to intervene, although it was no business of his, the Province of York being outside his jurisdiction.[6] At Durham the seats of the mayor and corporation, of the wives of the Dean and prebendaries and of other women of quality, were removed from the cathedral choir at the king's command; and Laud gave instructions for similar action to be taken at York and Salisbury, with Charles's approval.[7] Charles issued general orders for the removal of pews from cathedral churches, and this was carried out at Lichfield and Worcester, though in the latter instance Laud was forced to compromise.[8]

[1] Laud, *Works*, v. 500–1.

[2] E. G. Breton, 'Seventeenth century church discipline', in *History Teachers' Miscellany*, iv, no. 2, p. 28; W. E. Tate, *The Parish Chest* (1946), p. 90.

[3] Bridgeman, op. cit., p. 273; *Kenyon MSS.* (Hist. MSS. Commission), p. 54.

[4] *C.S.P.D., 1635*, pp. xlii–xliii.

[5] *Hist. MSS. Commission, Fourth Report, Appendix*, p. 311. For other disputes see R. F. B. Hodgkinson, 'Extracts from the Account Books of the Archdeacon of Nottingham', *Transactions of the Thoroton Soc.* xxx. 21–24, xxxi. 134–6; C. Jenkins, 'The Account Book of the Archdeacon of Taunton', *Somerset Record Soc. Pubs.* xliii. 101, 141; Pressey, op. cit., *passim*.

[6] Burne, 'The History of Chester Cathedral in the Reigns of James I and Charles I', loc. cit., pp. 16–18, 23–24.

[7] Ornsby, op. cit. i. 216, xxix; *C.S.P.D., 1633–4*, p. 72; *Wilts. Notes and Queries*, i. 23.

[8] Wilkins, op. cit. iv. 519; *C.S.P.D., 1635*, p. xxxvi; *1639–40*, pp. 79–80, 129–30; Laud, *Works*, v. 324–5.

One of the articles which his parishioners presented against Brian Walton in 1641 was that he 'appropriates to himself divers pews in the church', and that he cut pews up to make way to the altar.[1] A chapel in Tothill Fields, built in the sixteen-thirties, was in large part financed by profits from pews.[2] In 1634 Dr. Duck, Chancellor of the diocese of London, faced with the fact that a chapel at Knightsbridge, newly built by the inhabitants, had no endowment, ordered that such persons should be placed in the several seats as should most conduce to the maintenance of the curate, the repair of the chapel, and the relief of the poor: i.e. that pews should be put up to auction.[3]

In all these cases the important thing for our present purposes is the attitude of the ecclesiastical authorities and the government. The church courts enforced subordination and degree. They interfered to see that pews were disposed of by ministers, or by ministers and churchwardens. Profitable galleries were pulled down, to the detriment of parish finances. Bishops granted faculties which interfered with parochial arrangements. The High Commission ordered pews to be pulled down for whose erection the bishop's consent had not been obtained.[4] Dignity was impaired. Dr. Lambe, it was alleged in 1621, cited a former mayor of Northampton before him for erecting a pew, with the consent of minister, churchwardens, and parishioners, but without, presumably, a faculty from the bishop. The man lost his pew, which he had built at a cost of £3 for himself, his children, and servants; and it was given, the House of Commons was told, to 'three of the stubbornest fellows in the town', one of whom was subsequently presented for incontinence with two women.[5]

Thus faculties granted in church courts were cutting across the older tradition that churches were the property of the community and its lord: that the right to a pew went with property in the parish.[6] The ultimate cause of the disruption was the money power. The newly-rich were buying their way into social prominence. Church courts were trying to take advantage of this,

---

[1] *The Articles and Charge proved in Parliament against Dr. Walton*, p. 11.

[2] Newcourt, op. cit. i. 722, 923.

[3] Ibid. i. 694. Pew-rents continued to be charged by the nonconformist sects after 1660, were indeed the main source of their ministers' revenue.

[4] *C.S.P.D., 1639*, p. 337.

[5] Notestein, Relf, and Simpson, op. cit. vi. 473–6; cf. iii. 260.

[6] Addy, op. cit., pp. 416–32.

whilst parishes regarded pew-rents as their property, a heaven-sent solution to their growing financial difficulties. At St. Botolph's without Bishopsgate the churchwardens claimed to have collected pewage money to the extent of £30 'time out of mind'. It went to pay for the repair of the fabric and to poor relief as well as to pay the parish clerk's wages. But after the incorporation of the parish clerks, the clerk of St. Botolph's claimed the whole sum for himself, and threatened parishioners with processes in the church courts when they opposed him. The parish appealed to the Long Parliament against him.[1]

So, as in almost every sphere we look at, there were conflicts of jurisdiction over cases involving allocation of pews, or of the money received from pews. In Coke's time the common-law courts held that the ordinary could not displace a man who, time out of mind, had occupied a pew and kept it in repair. They would support old-established customs by which churchwardens and the major part of the parish disposed of seats in the church; and they would issue prohibitions if the ordinary tried to assert his jurisdiction.[2] But prohibitions virtually ceased in the sixteen-thirties. The government, especially under Laud, intervened in local quarrels to ensure that the increasingly important revenue from pew-rents went to the ecclesiastical and not the lay local authorities. Thus church fees and pew-rents figure among the many subjects in dispute between the vicar and the town of Plymouth in the sixteen-thirties. The vicar alleged that the mayor (the corporation being patron of the church) sold pews at £1. 10s. and £2. 10s. and pocketed the proceeds. The Star Chamber entrusted the disposal of pews to the vicar and churchwardens, and insisted that no more seats were to be disposed of to private families.[3] Among the accusations which the Nottinghamshire petition of 1641 made against the bishops was that they fined parishes 'excessively, without limit, for not altering of seats'.[4]

The issues then were complex—financial and social as well as doctrinal. At Adderley, Shropshire, there was a feud between the Needham and Corbet families. The Corbets had a family pew. The Needhams wished to outdo them by building a chapel in the

---

[1] *Hist. MSS. Commission, Fourth Report, Appendix*, p. 54. See p. 175 above.

[2] Hughes, op. cit. (1st ed.), ii. 113; Rolle, op. cit. ii. 288; Gibson, op. cit., p. 222.

[3] S.P. 16/355/168-9. I owe this reference to Dr. G. E. Aylmer.

[4] *A Petition presented to the Parliament from the County of Nottingham*, p. 4.

opposite transept to house an even more magnificent pew. In 1625 the bishop hesitated to grant a faculty: in 1637 Laud gave it. Sir John Corbet was later an opposition member of the Long Parliament—and a presbyterian elder.[1]

Other forms of government intervention had financial consequences. Thus Laud forced two London parishes to pull down pews which had been erected above the communion table. This arrangement suggested that the pulpit rather than the altar was the centre of worship, and Laud attacked the churchwardens for placing their seats 'above God Almighty and above Christ in his own house'. The churchwardens of St. Austin's, who were no doubt blissfully unaware of the theological implications of what they had done, replied timidly that they had no room for their parishioners, and that anyway they had only been obeying the instructions of their vestry. This soft answer, however, was far from turning away episcopal wrath. 'The power of vestries and churchwardens', cried Bishop Bowle at this point; 'this is to hatch a lay presbytery!'[2]

V

The system of church fees originated in the same society as appropriated lands to maintain its ecclesiastics. They provided, with a rough and ready equality, payment for ministers according to services rendered. But the satisfactoriness of the system depended on certain assumptions, most of which could no longer be made in our period.

1. A flat rate of charge for compulsory services could be justified in a medieval town or village community where differences in income level (if we except the lord) were inconsiderable; but with the rapidly growing economic differentiation of the century before 1640, fees weighed relatively very heavily on the poor. Marriage without publication of banns, for instance, would cost an agricultural labourer more than a week's wages, whilst for a City merchant it would be a bagatelle. Even for the rich the constant exaction of small sums must have been a great nuisance.

2. Differential fees, on the other hand, emphasized a social inequality of which the Puritans disapproved. It seemed perfectly

---

[1] F. A. Hibbert, 'Adderley and its Church', in *Transactions of the Shropshire Archaeological Soc.* xlvi. 123–4; cf. *C.S.P.D., 1635*, pp. 500–1.

[2] Stephenson and Marcham, op. cit., p. 470.

natural to Hooker that at burial 'some men's estate may require a great deal more [honour] according as the fashion where he dieth doth afford'.[1] George Wither, on the other hand, heartily disliked the practice of burying men inside the church, a custom which, he thought,

> Did first arise . . . to gain
> Some outward profit to the priestly train.[2]

We may compare Cartwright's objection to funeral sermons 'at the request of rich men, and those which are in authority, and are very seldom at the burial of the poor', by which 'there is brought into the church, contrary to the word of God, an acceptation of persons, which ought not to be'.[3]

3. A conventionally loyal Anglican layman like Spelman, no less than Bishop Bowle, bitterly resented the recent practice of vestries in constituting themselves 'a parliament', in which 'a dozen or sixteen private persons (I will not meddle with their trade or quality)' introduced new financial customs. Spelman, as his social sneer suggests, was attacking the attempts of bourgeois vestrymen to balance the parish's budget by increasing fees or pew-rents. But he admitted that their authority usually received official sanction (for a price); and Spelman's eloquent denunciation could be taken as applying to the *system* rather than to abuses of it:

The grave is the only inheritance that we are certainly born to, the inheritance which our grandmother the Earth hath left to descend in gavelkind among all her children. Shall one enter, and hold another out, or drive him to pay a fine *pro adeundo haereditate*, as they say in the feudal law, or *pro ingressu habendo*, as we in the common law? Is our tenure base like a copyhold *ad voluntatem domini*, and not rather noble by frankalmoign, free from all payments and services? How do the dead rest from their labour, if they be vexed with payments? . . . No ground in the kingdom is now sold so dear as a grave.[4]

---

[1] Hooker, *The Laws of Ecclesiastical Polity*, ii. 403.

[2] Wither, *Brittans Remembrancer*, i. 268. Wither continues, in lines which throw some light on popular iconoclasm during the revolution:

> Thence was it that our churches, first of all,
> Were glaz'd with scutcheons like a herald's hall;
> And that this age in those depainted sees
> So many vain and lying pedigrees.

[3] Quoted in Hooker, loc. cit.

[4] Spelman, *English Works*, i. 185–6.

The language is old-fashioned; but there lurks in it the doctrine of the equality of all mankind. The Levellers would soon be developing this doctrine to ends very different from those of Sir Henry.

4. The whole fee system assumes that parson and clerk serve a real community, are known to its members and know them, and that there are recognized times and seasons for collecting. This remained true in those village communities where the parson was not an absentee, but was ceasing to apply in London and the larger towns, where neighbourhood counted for far less than in rural society. Voluntaryism, the selection of a congenial congregation which paid a pastor an agreed stipend, ultimately proved to be the way of creating religious communities in the urban world of free contract.

5. The irritation caused to the wealthy laity would be intensified by the readiness of parsons to appeal to the church courts, and of those courts, backed up by the High Commission, to enforce their claims.[1] Fees can be collected when the overwhelming mass of the congregation accepts as necessary the services for which they provide. But fees for baptism, marriage, and burials had been challenged by Wyclif 250 years earlier, and often since. By the beginning of the seventeenth century many members of many congregations—often influential members—had doubts about their lawfulness. A man who had scruples about infant baptism or the wording of the marriage service would doubly resent having to pay a fee for a ceremony which he was not allowed to omit. Even where there was no objection to the particular service rendered, there might be criticism of the expenditure which church fees went to finance. Those who disapproved of the vestments of the clergy, and of the adornment of churches, would hate paying fees which were spent on such 'costly and dear-bought scandals and snares' rather than on education or on preaching ministers. That such things 'ought to be many and over-costly, no true protestant will affirm'.[2] A principal objection to the Laudian ritual was its expense.

6. So far we have talked of men of principle, of intellectual conviction. But there were other men in the world, and other motives. Relations between laity and clergy deteriorated as

---

[1] See *C.S.P.D.*, *1637*, p. 539, for reference to the High Commission of the case of a powerful and litigious man who refused to pay church rates.

[2] Milton, *Prose Works*, ii. 402.

Not want to pay!

worldlings learnt the economic advantages of a scrupulous conscience. The process would be cumulative, and not necessarily
intellectually dishonest. Once other ladies of Barking learnt that
Mrs. Jane Minors, when urged to come and be churched after
giving birth, answered 'It is a ceremony' and refused either to
come or to pay the fee,[1] they too would begin to ask themselves
why they should pay for a service which they could not refuse,
however much they might dislike it. They might well begin to
devote more thought to ways and means of evading payments
which had hitherto been accepted as inevitable. Similar objections
on principle to baptism and other ceremonies would beget similar
doubts. So a new 'climate of opinion' developed. Between disinterested principle and conscious hypocrisy there are many stages
of self-deception.

7. Finally, the system is acceptable if no alternative exists or
can be conceived. Consumers will not purchase commodities at
a price fixed by the seller and in quantities laid down by him if
alternative sources of supply are open. The Church of England
was not only a monopoly supplier, it also used legal coercion to
make men buy, like the salt monopoly in France. Members of the
English tax-paying community had thought a good deal about
monopolies in the first four decades of the seventeenth century,
and few had a good word to say for them. Most of the stolid
passive resistance to payment of fees came from those social
groups which also favoured free trade. The church's monopoly
in the Middle Ages may never have been entirely effective; but at
least there was then no serious challenge to it from members of
the propertied class. But now there was. The semi-legal existence
of Catholic congregations after the Reformation brought home to
men the possibility of choosing one's church; and sectarian congregations sprouted in the main urban centres in the decades
before the revolution. It was long before perfect competition
between the different churches was established; but the dangerous
and disruptive idea that it was possible already existed in men's
minds by the beginning of the seventeenth century. It is, perhaps,
not too rash to suggest that the ideas of consumers' choice, free
trade, and free contract in religion arose first and were most influential in circles which were already accustomed to those ideas
in their economic life.

[1] Hale, *A Series of Precedents*, p. 216. This was in 1597.

Fees, like tithes, were a financial device evolved in medieval agrarian society. They were ill-adapted to the requirements of an urban industrial civilization.[1] Again as with tithes, two events accelerated the realization of this fact—the Reformation and the price revolution. The effect of the rise in prices is obvious. The economic and theological changes of the Reformation (cessation of belief in purgatory, masses for the dead, confession, &c.) deprived parsons of a number of fees which they had previously received, and at the same time encouraged men to speculate about the legitimacy of other fees.

The consequences were put clearly in a letter from the Royal Court of Guernsey to Elizabeth. (In Guernsey the Reformation had been very radical and Calvinist; but the point would apply to a lesser degree in England.) In former times, the letter said, ministers' livings consisted mainly of fees for acts done 'after the superstitious order which they called the rites of the church, for which each household paid a good sum yearly; they are greatly diminished now that we have godly preachers, so that three benefices can scarcely maintain one minister'. They therefore asked for permission to levy contributions for the maintenance of ministers.[2]

The issues are here neatly summarized and foreshortened. Cheapness was one of the advantages of a protestant church: but should godly ministers therefore be allowed to starve? The combined effect of Reformation and rise in prices had been so to disorganize the old system of financing the clergy that the only alternative solutions appeared to be pluralism or maintenance augmented by the state and paid for by taxation. The issue was never posed as clearly in England as in Guernsey, but it lies behind all piecemeal attempts at reform before 1640. 'The labourer is worthy of his hire', cried Dr. Manwaring in an eloquent protest against a commission which was proposed in 1629 'to abolish or innovate on the just and laudable custom of obventions, commonly called church dues.' If receiving such dues be simoniacal, then all the clergy are guilty of simony.[3]

---

[1] See above, pp. 77–80, 156–7.

[2] A. J. Eagleston, *The Channel Islands under Tudor Government, 1485–1642* (1942), pp. 77–78. The letter appears to date from the fifteen-eighties.

[3] *C.S.P.D., 1625–49*, p. 330. The attribution to Manwaring is uncertain. But see ibid., *1631–3*, p. 262, for an undoubted letter from him to Laud on the same subject.

Nor did the attack all come from one side. Ecclesiastics had dreams of getting back behind the Reformation and the price revolution in this sphere too. Bancroft hoped to get oblations paid 'as heretofore at marriages, burials and feast days, . . . for the betterment of ministers' livings'.[1] One of the articles of impeachment against Bishop Wren of Norwich alleged 'that he assumed to himself an arbitrary power to compel the respective parishioners in the said diocese to pay great and excessive wages to parish clerks', threatening the recalcitrant with the High Commission.[2] This was yet one more issue on which battle was joined in response to an attack from the clergy, led by Laud.

[1] Collier, op. cit. vii. 352. See pp. 246–7 below.
[2] Rushworth, op. cit. iv. 355; C. Wren, *Parentalia* (1700), p. 113.

VIII

ECCLESIASTICAL TAXATION

No one order of subjects whatsoever within this land doth bear
the seventh part of that great proportion which the clergy
beareth in the burdens of the commonwealth. No revenue of
the crown like unto it, either for certainty or for greatness.

HOOKER, *The Laws of Ecclesiastical Polity, in Works*, iii. 401

Tyranny and kingship were not things personal, but . . . there
was a deputation and concatenation of tyrants throughout the
whole nation, whereby the burthens of war and peace were
unequally supported, the manors of courtiers, demesne lands,
forests, parks, warrens, tithes, bishops' lands, with the whole
endowment both of church and court, either exempt from all
public contributions, or assessed in that disproportion as is not
now suitable for England free.

Declaration of the Commissioners for the monthly assessment in
Yorkshire, in *Daily Intelligencer*, 18–25 February 1652

I

THE Reformation had freed ministers from the heavy and
arbitrary burdens of papal taxation. But royal taxes were not
light. From 1559 onwards, first-fruits and tenths were again
paid to the crown on all vicarages worth £10 and upwards in the
Valor Ecclesiasticus, and on all rectories of £6. 13s. 4d. and upwards.
In England 1,895 vicarages and 1,083 rectories were exempt from
taxation.[1] The payment of the first year's income on promotion
to a benefice was similar in its economic incidence to the purchase
of a lay office in the state: a lump sum down (normally paid over
the first two years) entitled the payer henceforth to take the annual
emoluments of the benefice or office. Too rapid promotion in the
church was, therefore, a dubious advantage, unless one was
allowed to retain one's previous benefice as well as the new one.

[1] Collier, op. cit. ix. 362. For other exemptions, including university and college
estates, see Cardwell, *Synodalia*, p. 568. Tenths brought in an average of £11,000 a
year (Dietz, op. cit., p. 394).

From the point of view of the court, a shuffle round of bishops was always a possible way of raising revenue in a crisis, bringing in fees as well as first-fruits.[1] From the other point of view, payment of first-fruits in respect of a benefice seemed to give an economic reason for retaining that benefice at least until the payer had recouped himself: and so provided a psychological justification for pluralism among the higher and court clergy.

Clerical taxation was calculated on the valuation recorded in the King's Book. It took no account of any increase in the value of livings, whether from tithes paid in kind or from voluntary augmentations paid by parishioners or patrons. Increase of either kind came very unequally in different parishes, so that the existing assessment of taxation became more and more inequitable. Such augmentations, therefore, had for the parson the equivalent effect of tax-free allowances today. This fact would considerably increase their value to him, and his economic dependence on the contributors would be the greater.[2]

There were various projects for reassessing the values of livings for taxation. In 1584–5 Whitgift managed to prevent the appointment of a commission for this purpose. He argued that the clergy were already so poor that an increase in taxation would be intolerable and would merely lead to accumulation of arrears: 'for every waterman on the Thames earneth more by his labour than the greater part of several ministers in England should do by their benefices.' Clerical incomes, 'standing upon the tithes of corn and wool chiefly', fluctuated from year to year. When subsidies were granted, the clergy paid a third more than the laity, for 'temporal men, for the most part, are not valued but, either in lands or goods, to the tenth part of their known ability: the poor divine having his living valued to the utmost in all duties to her Majesty, and other common charges far passing'. The object of the proposed commission, the Archbishop hinted, was to make the clergy afraid to enhance the value of their livings, and so to bring them into greater dependence on the laity.[3]

Whitgift scotched the project, but it recurred. In 1610 Coke declared from the bench that all taxes and dues paid to the king should be assessed on the actual value of benefices, not on the

[1] Stone, op. cit., p. 29; cf. p. 17 above.
[2] See Chapter XIII below.
[3] Strype, *Whitgift*, i. 403–8, iii. 171–6.

value rated in the King's Book.[1] The price revolution had worked to the advantage of the richer clergy, as it had to the advantage of the richer London householders.[2] There was no more, if no less, case for stepping up London tithe-payments than there was for reassessing the clergy to taxation. But our period was the great age of projects, which were themselves the product of the economic situation. Many people made, or were believed to have made, windfall profits; many people, including the government, wanted large sums quickly; much confusion had been caused by the rapid shifts in economic relations. So almost any project would be considered if it promised to raise money by tapping unearned increments or by exploiting somebody's financial difficulties or improvidence.

The proposal of a national reassessment of church livings was revived in 1621 by 'an ancient grave lawyer', who suggested to James I that a considerably increased revenue from first-fruits and tenths could be raised if all spiritual preferments ('which now in the King's Books passed at under-rates') were brought up, or nearly up, to their full value. James, after referring the proposal to Cranfield, decided not to proceed with it—a resolution which Fuller attributed to the king's love for parsons. The bishops showed their gratitude to Cranfield by the support they gave him when he was impeached by the House of Commons. The suggestion was revived in Charles I's reign and again rejected.[3]

The valuation in the *Valor Ecclesiasticus*, in addition to being inaccurate, was also very inequitable as between vicars and rectors. For the value of vicarages was computed as if the great tithes were included: so that taxation fell as heavily on the vicar (if his living was worth more than £10 a year) as if he had been the rector. 'This', observed Kennett dryly, 'was an injustice so apparent that it could never have been established into a law if the nobility had not thought they were themselves more likely to be appropriators than vicars of a church.'[4]

The clergy (with the same exemptions for poorer livings) also paid subsidies.[5] These were usually voted at the same time as

---

[1] Usher, *The Rise and Fall of the High Commission* (1913), p. 208.

[2] See Chapter XII below.

[3] Fuller, *Church History*, iii. 290; Goodman, op. cit. i. 327–9.

[4] Kennett, *Parochial Antiquities* (1695), p. 632; cf. Heylyn, *Cyprianus Anglicus*, p. 119; Strype, *Whitgift*, i. 407, 500; iii. 174.

[5] In 1640 vicars whose benefices were worth between £8 and £10 in the King's Book were to pay 6s. 8d. (Nalson, op. cit. i. 536).

Parliament granted lay subsidies, and at the same rate, though clerical subsidies were voted independently by Convocation. But since 1540 their votes had been confirmed by Parliament. In Elizabeth's reign the clerical subsidy was normally paid at the rate of 6s. in the pound on the value of the benefice in the Queen's Book after tenths had been paid—i.e. at the rate of 5s. 5d. in the pound net assessed value. In the seventeenth century, when the practice of granting multiple subsidies became common, the rate was normally reduced to 4s. (i.e. 3s. 7d.) in the pound. Thus together with tenths, most ministers in the seventeenth century were paying tax at the rate of 5s. 7d. in the pound on *all* their assessed income in most years.[1] What mattered, therefore, was the relationship between real and assessed income. The lower ranges of clerical incomes were exempt, and in 1609 the poorer clergy were relieved from paying taxes on their glebe, which in certain areas would be a substantial help.[2] But for the middle-ranking clergy (and especially vicars) the rate of taxation was relatively stiff.

Ministers were exempt from fifteenths and tenths, but not from other direct taxes—e.g. forced loans, benevolences, contributions in lieu of military service (due until 1662 from 'spiritual promotions or pensions' of £30 a year and upwards, as well as from any freehold property a minister might hold as estate of inheritance).[3] And of course they had to pay their share of indirect taxes with the rest of the population.

In the matter of benevolences the clergy were peculiarly susceptible to pressure through the bishops, who assessed them. The latter would be well squeezed themselves; they were often closely associated with government policy and sympathized with its objects; and they had reasonably accurate information about the revenues of their clergy.[4] A clerical benevolence needed no confirmation from Parliament; it was paid directly to the king, who accounted for it to nobody; and payment was enforced by ecclesi-

---

[1] Dietz, op. cit., pp. 394–6.　　　　[2] Usher, *Reconstruction*, ii. 264.

[3] Prothero, op. cit., p. 162; Gibson, op. cit., p. 15. For a justification of the taking of taxes for military purposes from the clergy, see Ralegh, 'A Discourse of Tenures', in *Collectanea Curiosa* (ed. J. Gutch, 1781), i. 66–68. It was contrary to medieval papal theory, though not to the practice of medieval English governments.

[4] See Goodman, op. cit. ii. 157–60 (a benevolence in 1614, wrongly described as a forced loan by Tanner in *Constitutional Documents of the Reign of James I*, 1930, pp. 362–3); Cardwell, *Documentary Annals*, ii. 141–5 (a benevolence in 1622); and Laud, *Works*, vi. 558–9 (a benevolence in 1639).

astical penalties, including excommunication.[1] Forced loans, however, seem to have been out of the bishops' control: the Archbishop of York wrote to Burghley in 1598: 'I wish there had been
more indifferency in the direction of the privy seals: for I know
some clergymen that are not worth so much as they are assessed
to land, and yet they must pay tenths and double subsidy. . . .
Some did allege, that at the last loan they were left unpaid, some
two, some three years.'[2]

So Whitgift, Harrison, Hooker, and James I were right in saying
that the clergy contributed proportionately far more than the laity
in taxation.[3] This can be shown in relation to the subsidy alone.
Thus in 1628 five lay subsidies brought in £275,000, five clerical
subsidies £94,000.[4] Moreover, as Harrison also pointed out, 'the
laity may at every taxation help themselves, and so they do through
consideration had of their decay and hindrance', whereas the
clergy might not; though their revenues necessarily fluctuated in
accordance with those of their parishioners.[5] Thus whereas the
yield from one lay subsidy declined from nearly £150,000 in 1563
to £55,000 in 1628, the clerical subsidy decreased only from some
£25,000 or £26,000 in the fifteen-eighties to nearly £19,000 in
1628. The decline is entirely accounted for by the fact that the
rate of assessment had been reduced from 6s. to 4s. in the pound.
Meanwhile the number of subsidies granted at one time had
substantially increased.[6]

These rather remarkable figures are worth pausing over. They
suggest, in the first place, that the clergy as a whole were assessed
much more severely than the laity. If we guess that there was one
clergyman for every 500 of the population we shall probably not
be far wrong;[7] and yet this 0·2 per cent. paid more than 25 per cent.

[1] Cardwell, *Synodalia*, p. xiii.

[2] Strype, *Annals*, IV. 446. In 1598 the archbishops, bishops, and four deans contributed more than one-third of their combined yearly assessed income to the
queen (Usher, *Reconstruction*, i. 225).

[3] W. Harrison, *A Description of England* (1876), pp. 24–26; Hooker, *Works*, iii.
401; Goodman, op. cit. i. 329. For Whitgift, see p. 189 above.

[4] Dietz, op. cit., pp. 393–5.   [5] Harrison, op. cit., pp. 24–25.

[6] Dietz, op. cit., pp. 392–6. The point was noted by Heylyn in *Cyprianus Anglicus*,
p. 119.

[7] Gregory King's estimate in 1696 was 10,000 clergymen in a population of 5½
millions. But by that date there were also large numbers of nonconformist ministers
functioning side by side with the clergy of the established church. A pamphlet of
1646 said there was 'not above one clergyman to every 500 men and women'
(*Tyth-Gatherers, no Gospel officers*, sig. A2ᵛ).

of the principal direct tax. The figures on which this calculation is based are extremely rough and ready; but even allowing a very large margin of error indeed, the disparity would still remain striking. Laud was not far out when he claimed that three clerical subsidies were a burden equivalent to 50–60 lay subsidies.[1]

The inequality was not offset by the exemption of ministers from parliamentary fifteenths and tenths, since they paid ecclesiastical tenths. Calibute Downing, after a rather specious argument that the real value of clerical incomes had fallen by 50 per cent. since the Reformation, was on safer ground when he suggested that lay wealth was increasing far more rapidly than the rate of taxation, whilst taxation of the clergy, by remaining constant whilst their real incomes had at least not increased, hit them proportionately much harder. The clergy, he declared, was 'constantly the most beneficial state of this realm to the crown, both in ordinary and extraordinary revenues, *ceteris paribus*'.[2] One of the arguments put forward in 1641 for the retention of deans and chapters was the large sums the clergy paid in taxation, 'greater in proportion than any other estates and corporations in the kingdom'.[3]

Moreover, within the ranks of the clergy themselves the distribution of taxation was inequitable. The worst-paid ministers of all were exempt from taxation; but the highest ranks of the profession were generally believed to be seriously under-assessed. The lands of Oxford and Cambridge and their colleges were exempt before the civil war.[4] Taxation was not assessed on fines. So the big ecclesiastical landowners, bishops and deans and chapters, paid nothing on a large part of their income. But fines came in irregularly: Whitgift used this among other arguments to build up a case for saying that bishops were *over*-assessed.[5] Their regular annual incomes had indeed not advanced beyond those recorded in the *Valor Ecclesiasticus* to the same extent as those of most rectors. But there were compensations. Each bishop collected taxes within his own diocese, and fixed the proportions at which

---

[1] Laud, *Works*, vii. 622. Cf. Birch, op. cit. ii. 236, and the passage from Hooker quoted at the head of this chapter.

[2] Downing, op. cit., p. 65. Cf. Laud, *Works*, vi. 431.

[3] Fuller, *Church History*, iii. 422.

[4] Cardwell, *Synodalia*, p. 568; Fuller, *History of the University of Cambridge*, p. 239; Prothero, op. cit., p. 36.

[5] Strype, *Whitgift*, i. 406; iii. 173.

clerical benevolences were to be paid.[1] This arrangement was hardly likely to work to their detriment. Archbishops also had the customary right to demand, on installation, a benevolence of one-tenth from the clergy in their province.[2]

Further, even more important in creating divisions within the clergy was the fact that ministers continued to pay first-fruits and tenths on the basis of the *Valor Ecclesiasticus* of 1535. Most clerical incomes had risen between that date and 1640; but they had risen very unequally, as we have seen. In so far as ministers were able to increase their revenues substantially over what the King's Book recorded, this extra income would be untaxed. Rectors in corn-growing areas, and all those who received their income largely in kind; ministers with augmentations or lectureships financed by voluntary contributions—all these were relatively prosperous; clerics with fixed money incomes, Harrison declared, might think themselves lucky if, after paying all dues and taxes, they retained two-thirds of their nominal stipends.[3] The apparently discriminatory severity of the *rate* of taxation of clerics was no doubt intended to allow for the fact that the King's Book did not represent the true position; but its effect was to widen the gap between those who had and those who had not been successful in adding a substantial tax-free augmentation to their taxable income.

Subsidies, wrote Heylyn, 'must needs fall exceeding heavy on many poor vicars in the country, whose benefices are for the most part of small yearly value, and yet rated very high in the King's Books (according unto which they are to be taxed) . . . I knew several vicarages, not worth above £80 *per annum*, which were charged higher than the best gentlemen in the parish, whose yearly revenues have amounted unto many hundreds.'[4] Laud thought two ministers out of three would have to borrow in order to pay three subsidies. It was to lighten the burden of subsidy payments on poor vicars that Laud sought the assistance of the Duke of Buckingham in 1624, to the extreme indignation of the Archbishop of Canterbury that laymen should be encouraged to interest themselves in matters of clerical taxation.[5]

[1] Prothero, op. cit., pp. xxxv–xxxvi; Goodman, op. cit. ii. 157–60.
[2] Hodgkinson, op. cit., pp. 45–46.
[3] Harrison, op. cit., p. 24; cf. pp. 108–17 above.
[4] Heylyn, *Cyprianus Anglicus*, pp. 119–20. For an example, see Larking, op. cit., pp. 149–50.
[5] Laud, *Works*, iii. 150; vii. 622–3; Heylyn, loc. cit.

Finally, tenths, as Harrison somewhat sourly reminds us, had originally been devised by the Pope, and before 1534 were neither annual nor compulsory payments, being voted by Convocation from time to time.[1] Their payment to the king, together with first-fruits, deprived both of their character of internal ecclesiastical taxation, devoted to clerical objects, and made them indistinguishable from ordinary lay taxes. Some of the Puritans proposed to relieve ministers from 'first-fruits, tenths, subsidies, etc.' altogether.[2]

For all these reasons, then, there was a strong case to be made out for the reorganization and reassessment of clerical taxation. There was a no less powerful case for reorganization of general taxation; but that raised questions of state power which were only to be solved by the civil war. Ecclesiastical taxation raised more complex questions: (1) redistribution of taxation more equitably within the church; (2) redistribution as between laity and clerics; (3) the relation of Convocation to the House of Commons. The taxes paid by the clergy were now merely part of the national fiscal system, and no longer in any sense taxation of a separate estate for its own internal purposes. The church's right to tax itself by its own representatives was purchased at the price of a heavy over-assessment. If this was evened out, did any case remain for Convocation's separate right to tax the clergy? It was, of course, convenient for the crown that the clergy should be treated as a separate estate for fiscal purposes: it got thereby a revenue that was 'certain, continual and seldom abated'.[3] But it was of dubious advantage for ministers themselves, and was the survival of an out-of-date conception of society that no longer corresponded to social realities.

II

As the constitutional conflict between crown and Commons developed, there was added the further threat of a use of the church to help the king to establish his financial independence. Thus in 1614, after Parliament had refused to vote supplies and had been dissolved, Convocation granted a benevolence from the clergy. In 1624 Convocation voted four subsidies, unconditionally,

---

[1] Harrison, op. cit., pp. 22–24; Dietz, op. cit., p. 394.
[2] Strype, *Whitgift*, ii. 17; *Tracts Ascribed to Richard Bancroft*, p. 31.
[3] Harrison, op. cit., p. 26.

at a time when Parliament was imposing strict conditions. This 'much troubled' the Commons, and bred distaste, 'being contrary to the usual form (which was to go together and in the same manner)'. In 1639, when Charles asked for a general contribution which was a benevolence in fact if not in name, and so a breach of the Petition of Right, the clergy contributed over two-thirds of the meagre £35,000 which trickled into the Exchequer. Finally in 1640, when the Short Parliament had been dissolved, Convocation voted six subsidies as a benevolence, with excommunication as a sanction against those who refused to pay.[1] Even without this deliberate use of ecclesiastical taxation to finance non-parliamentary government, the church was clearly such an important institution that it was no less necessary for Parliament to control it than to control the rest of the machinery of government: and this could not be done so long as the church was financially independent.

In Ireland Wentworth persuaded the clergy in 1640 to agree to a reassessment of benefices, to bring the King's Book valuation up to one-sixth of the full value. This he expected would double the returns on a clerical subsidy.[2] Such a change would only bring the relationship of taxable to true value up to the English level; but it suggested interesting possibilities.

In England Ship Money recognized the need for all-round financial reorganization. One of the great novelties of this tax was its inclusion of the clergy within a single national system of taxation.[3] Charles laid it down that no incumbent should be rated at more than one-tenth of the land rate of the parish of his cure—an attempt to adjust the balance between parson and tithe-payers.[4] It appears, however, that Ship Money nevertheless fell especially heavily on vicars and tithable land: yet another wedge driven between the government and the lesser clergy to whom it looked for support. Certainly the opposition to Ship Money seems to have been stronger in the countryside than in the towns.[5]

---

[1] Birch, op. cit. i. 323–4; Tanner, op. cit., pp. 362–3; ed. N. E. McClure, *Letters of John Chamberlain* (1939), ii. 558; Gardiner, *History*, ix. 7, 25, 143. In 1640 Convocation relied on a precedent of 1587, when the clergy had granted Elizabeth a benevolence over and above the subsidy confirmed by Parliament.

[2] Knowler, op. cit. ii. 402.

[3] Dietz, op. cit., p. 396.

[4] Heylyn, *Cyprianus Anglicus*, p. 321.

[5] W. B. Willcox, *Gloucestershire, a study in local government, 1590–1640* (1940), pp. 126–7, 233. Cf. *C.S.P.D., 1639*, p. 32: complaint from the sheriff of Hampshire that

Ship Money broke down in face of the opposition of the moneyed classes; but this particular aspect of it was taken over, under different political circumstances, by the parliamentary assessment of the sixteen-forties. The lands of Cambridge colleges were taxed by the townsmen to pay for the civil war;[1] and henceforward separate clerical taxation played no part in the English fiscal system.

III

In local taxation similar problems arose. The poor-law act of 1601 had put an end to a long dispute by specifically stating the liability of parsons and vicars, tithes and impropriations, to the poor rate.[2] But quarrels continued. Laud was accused at his trial of expressing a wish to see ministers free from all local taxes. His defence was that he had spoken only of taxes levied for failure to apprehend a robber. Laud claimed that he had been told by Lord Keeper Coventry that ministers were exempt from such taxes because they were not bound to keep watch and ward.[3] But, of course, the mere legal rights and wrongs were not the only elements in the situation. The City of Exeter in 1624 was helpless before Dr. Gooch, the bishop's chancellor, 'a man mighty in authority, high in dignity, rich in revenue', who was 'excepted from all payments whatsoever, confronting the city and daring you to do your worst, with haughty menaces. . . .'[4]

It was only after the fall of the ecclesiastical *power* that such situations could be ended and the position rationalized. In 1647 we find the Warwickshire Quarter Sessions insisting that a vicar's tithe and glebe were liable to 'all taxations and levies for all matters whatsoever', and that they should be levied according to the true value of the land. Similarly the judges rejected the claim of farmers of an impropriation to be exempt from all local levies except the poor rate.[5] Attempts to exempt the clergy from local taxation after the Restoration were unsuccessful, and it came to be an accepted

nearly all livings of sufficient value to be assessed for Ship Money were leased to laymen.
  [1] Fuller, *History of Cambridge*, p. 239; C. H. Firth and R. S. Rait, *Acts and Ordinances of the Interregnum* (1911), i. 90, 134.
  [2] See p. 134 above.   [3] Laud, *Works*, iv. 166–7.
  [4] *City of Exeter MSS.* (Hist. MSS. Commission), p. 161.
  [5] Ratcliff and Johnson, op. cit., pp. 162, 207, 238; 165, 187, 214.

common-law principle that ministers were included in any provision for local taxation voted by Parliament unless the statute specifically exempted them.[1] The clergy had ceased to be a separate and unique estate: they had become one of many groups of professional men.

[1] Gibson, op. cit., pp. 21–22.

IX

SOCIAL AND ECONOMIC STATUS OF THE CLERGY

We rob the church, and what we can attain
By sacrilege and theft is our best gain.
In paying dues, the refuse of our stock,
The barrenest and leanest of our flock,
Shall serve our pastor . . .
Men seek not to impropriate a part
Unto themselves, but they can find in heart
T' engross up all; which vile presumption
Hath brought church-livings to a grand consumption. . . .
   No marvel, though instead of learned preachers
We have been pestered with such simple teachers,
Such poor, mute, tongue-tied readers, as scarce know
Whether that God made Adam first or no . . .
But patrons think such best, for there's no fear
They will speak anything they loathe to hear. . . .
   But most of us do now disdain that place,
Accounting it unworthy, mean and base;
Yea, like to Jeroboam's priests, we see
They of the lowest of the people be.

GEORGE WITHER, *Abuses Stript and Whipt* (1613), Of the Vanity, Inconstancy
and Weakness of Men, Satire IV, Of Presumption

Where the nation is in a state of prosperity, the wives and
children of clergymen will, and may reasonably, expect to bear
some proportion to other people, and not to live in so mean
a condition as to be objects of contempt to persons of other
professions. Besides, common justice, as well as natural affection,
obliges clergymen to make the best provision they can for their
wives and children, that they may not be exposed to poverty and
contempt when they are dead.

Sir Isaac Newton's Tables (6th ed., 1742), p. 96

ALMOST every economic development we have considered so far—commutation, impropriation, leasing of tithes, 'decay' of fees and offerings, inequitable distribution of taxation—contributed to impoverish a large section of the clergy. The glebe was often swallowed up, either at enclosure or as part of a simoniacal bargain with a patron. Parsonage houses were allowed to fall into disrepair. Clerical marriage made the parson with a wife and children to support more conscious of his poverty. If the clergy was not a celibate caste set apart from the rest of mankind, then the church was a profession which must compete with others. A seventeenth-century archbishop had asserted, in defending his thesis for the degree of Bachelor of Divinity, that though 'the end of theology is to gain souls, the end of the theologue, subordinate to the first and architectonical end, is for an honest maintenance and sustentation'.[1]

But ministers had only a life-interest in their benefices. There was no provision for their widows at death, or for their families on deprivation. These family encumbrances may help to explain their marked reluctance to be ejected from their cures—e.g. in 1604. In 1638 the Archdeacon of Gloucester gave fear of losing their livings as the only reason for the conformity of 'divers' ministers.[2] This consideration goes far to account for the rapid and absolute collapse of the hierarchy in 1640. The strength of the ruling group in the church had always been more apparent than real, except in so far as the power of the government stood behind them.

As married men, Bishop Cooper tells us, ministers had a greater need to accumulate money than other freeholders, so as to be able to give marriage portions to their children and leave provision for their widows. So far from expecting them to be less acquisitive than lay property-owners, he implies, we should expect them to be more so.[3] Clerical marriage necessitated pluralism, Dr. Crompton argued in the Parliament of 1601.[4] In an age when any court

---

[1] Hacket, op. cit. i. 25. Fuller arrived at similar conclusions in *The Holy State*, pp. 222-3.

[2] Laud, *Works*, v. 359.   [3] Cooper, op. cit., p. 114.

[4] D'Ewes, *Journals*, pp. 639-40.

favourite expected jobs to be provided for his friends and relations, when the family was a tightly-knit economic unit with many ramifications, this seemed sound enough logic. But it was a recent, a post-Reformation problem, caused by the new status of legitimacy given to parsons' families, and a consequent rise in the demands of parsons' wives. 'Most honest women of sober and good behaviour', continued the Bishop of Winchester, whose own wife was anything but that, 'are loath to match with ministers . . . because they see their wives so hardly bested when they are dead. They that are not moved with this', he added, 'have but cold zeal toward the gospel.'[1]

There were indeed occupational hazards in being a parson's wife in the sixteenth century. The minister who 'sold his wife to a butcher' in Mary's reign[2] was responding in an exceptional way to a difficult situation: but it was long before ladies could be sure that the situation would not recur. Under Elizabeth, as Cooper hinted, marriage was made as difficult as possible for the clergy, and the parson's wife continued to be in an equivocal position as long as the Virgin Queen was Supreme Governor of the church. The lady of a minister's choice had to be approved by his bishop and by two J.P.s before he might marry her. He must also have the consent of her parents or kinsmen, or in default of them (and this is significant of the expected social status of clerical wives) 'of her master or mistress where she serveth'. Wives or 'other women' were not permitted to reside in cathedral or college precincts during Elizabeth's reign.[3]

Harrison thought that marriage made hospitality easier for ministers,[4] and so perhaps in one sense it did. Wives and children certainly added to the parson's available labour supply. A good marriage, moreover, to a yeoman's or rich craftsman's daughter, might be an economic godsend. As Mr. Brooks points out, a wife approved by two J.P.s was likely to be a good manager.[5]

---

[1] Cooper, loc. cit.

[2] Ed. J. G. Nichols, *The Diary of Henry Machyn* (Camden Soc., 1848), p. 48.

[3] Cardwell, *Documentary Annals*, i. 192, 273–4. Certificates of permission to marry ceased to be issued to ministers, in the diocese of Lincoln, about the middle of James I's reign (Foster, *State of the Church*, p. xxi). Cf. J. O. W. Haweis, *Sketches of the Reformation* (1844), pp. 73–79. For correspondence between J.P.s about a minister 'desirous to marry a maid dwelling in the same parish', see *Losely MSS.* (ed. A. J. Kempe, 1836), p. 254. [4] Harrison, op. cit., pp. 33–34.

[5] F. W. Brooks, 'The Social Position of the Parson in the 16th century', in *Journal of the British Archaeological Soc.*, 3rd series, x. 37.

We should probably differentiate, here as so often, between village parsons, for whose farming additional hands were an economic advantage, and ministers in towns, for whom dependents were more likely to be a liability. Beyond that guess it is unsafe to go until we have more evidence.

Charity and hospitality were felt to be the special duties of ministers. Spokesmen of the hierarchy did not fail to emphasize this when defending their revenues against Puritan attack. Thus in 1584 the bishops answered criticisms made in Parliament by stating that prices were two or three times what they had been fifty years earlier, 'and yet as great or greater hospitality looked for'.[1] Standards naturally varied. In the rich rectory of Houghton, Durham, the Puritan Bernard Gilpin, the Apostle of the North, used to entertain all his parishioners to dinner every Sunday from Michaelmas to Easter (the hard time of the year), down to his death in 1583. But he found it a great and increasing financial strain, and few indeed of the clergy can have lived up to his example.[2]

Defenders of the clergy complained that 'many English ministers . . . may preach of hospitality, but cannot go to the cost to practise their own doctrine;' and yet 'hospitality is expected. . . . The poor come to their houses as if they had interest in them.'[3] On the other hand, the introduction of a compulsory poor rate relieved the clergy of part of the burden of relieving the poor: and at the same time undermined their unique position in the parish, and deprived them of one justification for their tithes.[4]

II

In 1585 Whitgift stated that half the benefices with cure in the country were worth less than £10 in the Queen's Book, and most of these were below £8. His figures were correct, and they helped him to defeat a bill for the abolition of pluralities.[5] The figures in

---

[1] Cardwell, *Documentary Annals*, i. 433. .

[2] Gilpin, op. cit., pp. 194–5. Richard Baxter seems, however, to have thought in 1656 that £40 out of an income of £90 might be spent on charity: it would be a severe but not impossible standard (ed. R. Parkinson, *Autobiography of Henry Newcome*, 1852, p. 344).

[3] Fuller, *The Historie of the Holy Warre*, p. 38; *The Holy State*, p. 219.

[4] See pp. 159–60 above.

[5] Strype, *Whitgift*, i. 371. 4,543 out of 8,803 livings were worth less than £10 in the *Valor Ecclesiasticus* (Collier, op. cit. ix. 362–3).

the *Valor Ecclesiasticus*, as we have seen, certainly do not tell the whole story; but there were some losses as well as gains. Convocation's petition of 1587 declared that rising costs, the difficulty of collecting tithes, the decay of offertories, the need to gratify patrons, together with enclosure, had halved the real value of the sums recorded in the Queen's Book.[1] 'Carnal men', noted Dod and Clever, 'are never more witty in anything than in withholding [the minister's] due allowance and relief.'[2]

There can be no doubt that many livings were terribly inadequate, especially in towns and the outlying areas. 'So many livings', said Dr. Gooch in the Parliament of 1621, 'yield but £3, £4, £5, £8 or £10 maintenance'.[3] These figures can be confirmed. In 1599 the Bishop of Carlisle reported that in his diocese no vicar or curate had more than £6. 13s. 4d. towards all charges.[4] The vicars of ten churches annexed to the chapter of St. David's got from £2 to £10. 13s. 4d. a year.[5] In 1634 over half the livings in the Isle of Man were worth less than £4 apiece.[6]

Nor was this true only of the outlying regions. In Essex, about 1609, Pentlow could only get a reading minister, since it offered a mere £8; the rectories of St. Rumbald, Colchester, at £5, and Brunden at £8, were vacant.[7] In 1637 it was reported that St. Mary's, Stamford, was difficult to fill at £12.[8] In three Kentish parishes impropriated to the Archbishop of Canterbury two ministers got £10 apiece, a third £13 'and no house'.[9] As late as 1649–50, before parliamentary augmentations had been received, the vicarage of Royston, Herts., was worth only £5; in Wiltshire, Slaughterford was £4, Bilstone £6, Avon and Seagrey £10 each, Ditchbridge £11.[10] In Essex again, Marks Tey was £2; Manningtree, a market town, only £3 per annum, the inhabitants having in

---

[1] Strype, *Whitgift*, i. 500; cf. iii. 171, Manning, op. cit., pp. 135–6.

[2] Dod and Clever, *Ten Commandements*, p. 214. Cf. the first epigraph to this chapter.

[3] Notestein, Relf, and Simpson, op. cit. iv. 432.

[4] White, op. cit., p. 388; cf. Usher, *Reconstruction*, i. 220.

[5] T. Richards, *The Puritan Movement in Wales, 1639–53* (1920), pp. 5–6.

[6] Trevor-Roper, op. cit., p. 189.

[7] *A Viewe of the State of the Clargie*, pp. 16, 38.

[8] *C.S.P.D., 1637–8*, p. 563. See p. 297 below. The curate of King's Walden, Herts. also had a stipend of £12 (A. Kingston, *Hertfordshire during the Great Civil War*, 1894, p. 6).

[9] Larking, op. cit., pp. 179, 189, 195; cf. p. 143 above.

[10] Urwick, *Nonconformity in Herts.*, p. 810; Bodington, op. cit. xli. 1–10. Chapel-en-le-Frith was worth £4. 6s. 8d.: see p. 293.

the past maintained a lecturer at their own expense. Four churches in Colchester could only muster £13. 16s. 8d. between them, though this extreme poverty may be partly due to the siege of 1648. Even the vicarages of Newport at £18, and Rickling at £28 were 'so small that no man will accept thereof'.[1] In the city of Worcester four rectories and one vicarage totalled £32. 8s. 4d. between them; and in the same county the vicarages of Grimley (£3), All Saints, Evesham (£5. 6s.) and Great Malvern (£8) stand out.[2]

What hope could there be of getting a learned minister for such sums? Most of the parishes listed found it difficult enough to fill the living at all. The Bishop of Bangor complained sadly in 1638 that 'by reason of the poverty of the place, all clergymen of hope and worth seek preferment elsewhere'.[3] But there were many bad spots in wealthier dioceses; and towns generally suffered. Throughout our period these facts were observed with monotonous regularity—by Latimer, Jewell, Parker, Grindal, Sandys, Sir Benjamin Rudyerd, Laud. 'The basest sort of the people', lamented the *Admonition to Parliament*, were made ministers:[4] how many times was that cry repeated in the following seventy years!

Yet at the same time the Reformation, and the rise of an educated laity, had put a premium upon preaching. Many men were coming to think of the delivery of sermons as the minister's main function, of the sermon as the normal means by which God spoke to the hearts of men. This revolutionized their conception of the educational standard required: and the traditional attainments of the clergy fell lamentably short of these new expectations. Yet how could any improvement be effected without increased clerical incomes? A university education was very expensive, and it opened the door to more lucrative professions than the church. Books were expensive too, and were becoming a conventional necessity. We may discount Sir Edward Dering's estimate in 1641 of £600 as 'but a mean expense in books' for a minister, which would 'advance but a moderate library.'[5] It may be contrasted with

[1] H. Smith, op. cit., pp. 311, 316–19, 284.

[2] Urwick, *Nonconformity in Worcestershire*, pp. 163–71.

[3] Laud, *Works*, v. 359.

[4] Latimer, *Sermons* (Everyman ed.), pp. 194–5; Jewell, *Works*, ii. 999–1000, 1012; M. Parker, *Correspondence* (1853), pp. 120–1, 311–13, 373–4; Strype, *Grindal*, p. 60; E. Sandys, *Sermons* (Parker Soc., 1842), pp. 154–5; Whitgift, *Works*, i. 316.

[5] *Sir Edward Dering Revived* (1660), p. 70.

the books valued at 13*s*. 4*d*. left by the parson of Grainsby forty years earlier. Yet even in his case books formed nearly 8 per cent. of his estate as shown in his will; and by the end of the sixteenth century nearly all ministers in Lincolnshire left some books.[1]

In Elizabeth's reign £30 came to be taken as the minimum competence for a minister. Anything less, Harrison thought, could not maintain a mean scholar, let alone a learned man; although Whitgift told the queen that not one in twenty of the benefices in the country was worth £30 clear.[2] There are not 600 livings in the whole of England competent to maintain a preaching minister and his family, declared spokesmen of the hierarchy in 1584, 1588, and 1601.[3] In 1587 the Puritans recommended £100 per annum as a goal to be aimed at if satisfactory ministers were to be secured. The smaller livings went to wandering ministers, prowling 'up and down like masterless hounds, being glad to serve . . . for a piece of silver and a morsel of bread'.[4] Bancroft referred in 1605 to curates 'who are content to serve for ten groats a year and a canvas doublet'. A year or two later an Essex curate was reported as serving for £5. 6*s*. 8*d*. and his diet: he was 'dumb'.[5] Despite government hostility to mere gentlemen keeping chaplains, the Archbishop of York recommended in 1637 that curates at poor stipends should be allowed to serve in gentlemen's houses provided they used the Prayer Book.[6]

Curates indeed, as we have seen, were the worst off of all clerics.[7] Their stipends were at the mercy of their employers, and some bishops could always be found to ordain 'mean men' to undertake the most menial clerical tasks. Delinquent curates in the East Riding of Yorkshire were in 1626 thought too poor to be worth proceeding against in the Archdeacon's Court.[8] Scandalous and non-preaching curates, at £5–20 a year, were denounced in many Kentish petitions in 1641.[9] No less significant were the reports

---

[1] Brooks, op. cit., p. 32.

[2] Harrison, op. cit., p. 22; Collier, op. cit. vii. 259.

[3] Strype, *Whitgift*, i. 381, 536; ii. 445. Standards had risen slightly since Grindal declared (1576) that at most one church in eight yielded a sufficient living for a learned preacher; Dr. James's figure in 1601 was 1 in 15 (Grindal, *Remains*, 1843, p. 383).

[4] *The Seconde Parte of a Register*, ii. 209.

[5] Wilkins, op. cit. iv. 414; *A Viewe of the State of the Clargie*, p. 23.

[6] *C.S.P.D., 1636–7*, p. 411; cf. Stock, op. cit., pp. 224, 229, 234.

[7] See p. 113 above.

[8] Ornsby, op. cit. i. 94.

[9] Larking, op. cit., pp. 115, 124–5, 145–6, 195, 203, 229–30.

from parishes which sympathized with their curate. John Streat-
ing, M.A., of Ivychurch, after twenty-six years as a curate and
many promises of preferment, was earning £30 a year on a living
farmed for over £200 a year. He had won golden opinions from
his parish, but not, apparently, from his ecclesiastical superiors.
Even the curate of Ore, whose stipend was £8 a year, seems to
have had the sympathy of his parishioners when, 'choosing rather
to steal meat for himself and his than to beg or starve', he was
convicted on a charge of felony. The inhabitants pointed out with
some asperity that the impropriator, Sir Robert Honeywood,
owned fourteen or more impropriations as well as this one.[1] In
1643 the heavily-indebted Sir Thomas Dawes was paying his
'almsfolk and curates' according to a sliding scale based on the
price of corn.[2] Adam Smith did not class curates with almsfolk,
but he compared their pay with the wages of journeymen.[3]

The result of poverty was that some of the rank-and-file clergy
were still very ignorant by the standards beginning to prevail in
urban lay society. In 1551 more than half the ministers in the
diocese of Gloucester could not repeat the Ten Commandments;
more than one in ten did not know where they were to be found.
One in twelve could not name the author of the Lord's Prayer,
ten out of 311 could not repeat it. At least one of the ministers
who was ignorant of the commandments was still holding his
living in 1576.[4] In 1583 it was reported of the vicar of Blidworth,
Notts., that he was apt to confuse Jesus with Judas.[5] The Injunctions of 1559 made special provision for 'such as are but mean
readers' and therefore might have difficulty even in stumbling
through a Homily unless they had read it through once or twice
beforehand.[6] In 1577 Bishop Barnes of Durham asked his clergy
to make a special study of St. Matthew's Gospel, and the following
year he examined them on it. Of 195 ministers who were set the
task, less than one-third had completed it.[7]

---

[1] Larking, op. cit., pp. 151–4.

[2] Ed. V. B. Redstone, 'The Diary of Sir Thomas Dawes', in *Surrey Archaeologica
Soc. Collections*, xxxvii. 4, 13–14.

[3] A. Smith, op. cit. i. 148–9.

[4] F. D. Price, 'Gloucester Diocese under Bishop Hooper, 1551–3', in *Transactions
of the Bristol and Gloucestershire Archaeological Soc.* lx. 100–3, 123–5.

[5] Peyton, op. cit., p. xviii.   [6] Cardwell, *Documentary Annals*, i. 199.

[7] Ed. J. Raine, *The Injunctions and other Ecclesiastical Proceedings of Richard Barnes,
Bishop of Durham* (Surtees Soc., 1850), pp. 70–79; cf. Strype, *Grindal*, p. 174, and
Hoskins, *Essays*, p. 19, for examples of unlearned ministers.

By the end of the century things had improved to the extent that most ministers had been to a university, whether or not they had taken a degree. Popery had been rooted out of the universities, and the acute shortage of clergy of the early years of Elizabeth had been met somehow. In the diocese of Worcester the percentage of graduates among ministers rose from 19 in 1560 and 23 in 1580 to 52 in 1620 and 84 in 1640.[1] But still the ministry failed to attract enough learned men; barely half the beneficed clergy in the country, including some who had degrees, were licensed to preach in 1603, and in areas like Staffordshire and Wales the proportion was much lower.[2] This lack of preachers may have been due to nonconformity as well as to incapacity: deprivations for Puritanism were creating clerical unemployment whilst the shortage of preaching ministers remained.

The picture must not be overdrawn. Or rather, we must remember not to be deceived by contemporary generalizations about 'the clergy'. There was a great deal of poverty among the rank-and-file clerics, but there were others who did very well out of the church. Many livings had a real value far above that which appeared on paper. The cathedral and court clergy, the pluralists, had nothing to complain of; the simoniacal clerics who bid briskly for some livings knew what they were doing. A minister was beginning to have a certain social status which, for a plebeian, might count for more than the actual cash value of a living. But when all is said about the fortunate few who were chosen, there remain the many who were called: and they are the subject of this chapter. Just as Hooker thought that a 'mean gentleman' would not change places with many bishops, so he believed that 'a common artisan or tradesman of the City' could be compared 'with ordinary pastors of the church'.[3] For we must, above all,

[1] Miss Barratt's figures. For Oxford (an exceptional diocese because of its university) the percentages were 38 in 1560, 50 in 1580, 80 in 1620, and 96 in 1640. In Devon in 1561 20 per cent. had degrees (Rowse, *Tudor Cornwall*, p. 324). In 1592–3 less than one-third of the clergy in the dioceses of York and Chester were graduates, 49 per cent. in Norwich; in Lichfield in 1602–3 the figure was 24 per cent. (H. W. Saunders, 'A List of the clergy of Norfolk and their status, 35 Eliz.', in *Original Papers of the Norfolk and Norwich Archaeological Soc.* XVIII, part i, 81–82; J. C. Cox, 'An Elizabethan Clergy List of the Diocese of Lichfield', in *Derbyshire Archaeological and Natural History Soc. Journal*, vi. 158. I owe these last references to the kindness of Miss Barratt.)

[2] Usher, *Reconstruction*, i. 241; Pape, op. cit., pp. 29–30; Richards, op. cit., pp. 9–10; Dodd, op. cit., p. 40.

[3] Hooker, *Works*, iii. 405; cf. p. 189 above.

distinguish between the towns and the agricultural villages. In the towns clerical poverty was often the greatest, wife and family were a liability, and yet the standards of living and education set by the richer classes were rising fast. In corn-growing villages the wealth of some rectors may often have advanced whilst the majority of their parishioners were being impoverished.[1] But Tudor and early Stuart England was dominated by the standards and values of the urban bourgeoisie and the gentry. The failure of most of the clergy to keep up with the advancing prosperity of these classes was not compensated for by the fact that in many villages the economic gap between parson and peasant was being widened.

III

Poverty, by general consent, bred contempt. Richard Stock could see no reason 'why the great and rich men of the world should contemn the ministry for their children as too base a thing, and not fit for their sons'. But he admitted that 'mean men will now abuse them in words and contemn as far as they can for the law of man, . . . if they teach cross to their humours'. Stock's assurance that God would honour ministers though man did not was perhaps small consolation.'[2]

Divinity was no profession for the upper classes. All the nobility, and all the gentry 'in a manner', said Stockewood carefully in 1579, shunned 'this high office of preaching and ministry of the word of God'; only the 'meaner and poorer sort' were left.[3] 'Hath not this despising of the preachers almost made the preachers despise preaching?' Silver-tongued Smith asked in 1590. '. . . They which would study divinity above all, when they look upon our contempt and beggary and vexation, turn to law, to physic, to trades, or anything rather than they will enter this contemptible calling.'[4] Some of the nobility and gentry, wrote Richard Bernard in 1607, 'wish their children anything, worldly lawyers, fraudulent merchants, killing physicians . . .' rather than '(as they call them)

---

[1] Brooks, op. cit., pp. 35–36.

[2] Stock, op. cit., p. 131.

[3] John Stockewood, *A very fruiteful Sermon preached at Paules Crosse* (1579), p. 17; cf. Strype, *Annals*, I, part i. 538. Bishop Jewell said young men designed for the church changed to become prentices, physicians, lawyers (*Works*, i. 1012).

[4] Ed. J. Brown, *The Sermons of Henry Smith* (1908), p. 43.

priests'. Consequently, 'the basest of the people and lowest sort' become ministers, '. . . because the wise men of the world, men of might and the noble, hold it derogatory to their dignities'.[1] 'Politic men', said Thomas Adams, 'begin apace already to withhold their children from schools and universities; . . . knowing they may live well in whatsoever calling save in the ministry.'[2]

'This age', wrote the ward of a bishop in 1622, for her unborn child's eye, holds the ministry 'a most contemptible office, fit only for poor men's children, younger brothers and such as have no other means to live'. 'For God's sake be not discouraged with these vain speeches', she continued piously;[3] but alas! they were not altogether vain. Bishop Hall spoke feelingly of 'those notorious contempts which are daily cast' upon the clergy.[4] When George Herbert decided to take orders, a friend tried to dissuade him on the ground that it was 'too mean an employment, and too much below his birth and the excellent abilities and endowments of his mind'. The saintly Herbert accepted the imputation, and merely replied that 'though the iniquity of the late times have made clergymen meanly valued, and the sacred name of priest contemptible: yet will I labour to make it honourable'.[5] *The Priest to the Temple* contains a chapter entitled 'The Parson in Contempt'. There Herbert speaks of 'the general ignominy which is cast upon the profession', for which 'he must be despised'.[6] James I in 1616 regarded it as 'a sign of the latter days drawing on' that 'great men, lords, judges, and people of all degrees from the highest to the lowest', despised churchmen.[7]

The overwhelming majority of the clergy came from the middle and lower classes of society, and could have come from nowhere else. The Rev. Anthony Grey, who subsequently became 8th Earl of Kent, was a very remarkable exception. He continued to officiate as minister after succeeding to the peerage: the only change was that he ceased to be molested for his nonconformity.

---

[1] R. Bernard, *The Faithfull Shepheard* (1607), pp. 3–5.

[2] Adams, op. cit., p. 1060. Cf. the first epigraph to this chapter.

[3] Elizabeth Joceline, *The Mother's Legacy* (1894), pp. 4–5. Mrs. Joceline was the grandchild of and had been ward to William Chaderton, Bishop of Lincoln. The child, perhaps fortunately, turned out to be a daughter.

[4] Kinloch, op. cit., p. 67.

[5] I. Walton, *Life of Herbert*, in *Lives*, p. 277; cf. Selden, *Table Talk*, pp. 128–9.

[6] Herbert, *Works*, p. 268.

[7] *Political Works of James I*, p. 330.

Holy aristocrats like Herbert or Grey did not get very far in the church. They were eccentrics.[1]

Scandalous livings cannot but have scandalous ministers, Sir Benjamin Rudyerd told the House of Commons in 1626 and again in 1628. 'Men of worth and of parts would not be marked up to such pittances' as 5 marks or £5 a year. 'Though the calling of ministers be never so glorious within, yet outward poverty will bring contempt upon them, especially among those who measure men by the acre and weigh them by the pound, which indeed is the greatest part of men.'[2] 'The greatest part of men': and, as Bishop Cooper reminded us, of women. Whilst so much money was to be made at the bar, or in business, or (with luck) at court, why should men choose the church as a career? Another future bishop described the highest hopes of 'a young raw preacher': 'his friends and much painfulness may prefer him to £30 a year; and this means to a chambermaid, with whom we leave him now in the bonds of wedlock.'[3] Many were less fortunate. The revenues of poor vicars, Laud reported as a general complaint in 1634, 'are scarce able to feed and clothe them'. Most dangerous of all, Laud continued, was the fact that 'the vicars in great market towns, where the people are very many, are for the most part worst provided for'.[4] It was there that lecturers were set up by popular subscription, to preach doctrines agreeable to the subscribers; and it was there that it was most damaging for the hierarchy to lose control of public opinion.

All parties agreed on the facts. Many livings remained vacant for long periods. A faithful preaching ministry was impossible, said a pamphlet of 1641, until there was a tolerable maintenance in every parish.[5] Even in the sixteen-fifties, after many livings had been substantially augmented, Pearson could still ask the clergy

why they suffer not only so many villages, country towns and parishes, but even great and populous cities and market towns and whole corners

---

[1] Fuller, *Worthies*, i. 488–9. See pp. 28–29 above. Mr. C. H. Mayo listed seventeen 'near relations of peers who entered holy orders in the 17th century' (*English Hist. Rev.* cxlv. 258–9). All but four of them took orders after 1660, and most were younger sons holding family livings. James Montagu was the only bishop among them: and he was little better than a Puritan. But Mr. Mayo missed, for instance, Edward Finch, brother of Charles I's Lord Keeper, for whom see pp. 170–1 above.

[2] Manning, op. cit., pp. 135–6.

[3] Earle, *Microcosmographie*, in Morley, op. cit., p. 160.

[4] Laud, *Works*, v. 327.

[5] *A Certificate from Northamptonshire*, p. 8.

of counties to lie destitute, who never could get any other minister than a poor vicar or reading curate? They will presently answer me, 'There is no maintenance, without that they cannot live.' If I ask them farther, 'Why there is no maintenance?' they will tell me, 'It is either a city or market town, to which belongs no land, and so no tithes; or otherwise the people have converted their arable lands into pastures, and their tithe is of small value, and will not afford a maintenance.' . . . Is not a third part of the nation in this condition? And must they never have a minister?[1]

IV

Under Elizabeth, and even later, ministers were fair game for greedy bishops and greedy courtiers. There was no one to protect them except perhaps their patron, and he was far more likely to join in the scramble for pickings. Thus Harrison: 'Every small trifle, nobleman's request or courtesy craved by the bishop, doth impose and command a twentieth part, a three-score part, or two pence in the pound, etc., out of our livings.'[2] Such behaviour by their ecclesiastical superiors was conducive to Puritanism in the lesser clergy.

But the worst offenders, by general consent, were 'the church-robbers whom we falsely call patrons of the church'.[3]

Not a few also find fault with our threadbare gowns [Harrison continued] as if not our patrons but our wives were causes of our woe. But if it were known to all, that I know to have been performed of late in Essex—where a minister taking a benefice (of less than £20 in the Queen's Books so far as I remember) was enforced to pay to his patron 20 quarters of oats, 10 quarters of wheat and 16 yearly of barley, which he called hawks' meat; and another let the like in farm to his patron for £10 by the year, which is well worth forty at the least—the cause of our threadbare gowns would easily appear: for such patrons do scrape the wool from our cloaks.

That is why weavers, peddlars, and glovers have been made ministers, for the learned refuse such matches.[4] Every ploughboy knows that patrons sell benefices by one subtle device or another,

---

[1] Pearson, op. cit., p. 63.

[2] Harrison, op. cit., p. 22.

[3] Greenham, op. cit., p. 846. The whole eloquent passage, pp. 846–7, is worth consulting.

[4] Harrison, op. cit., pp. 34, 26. Note how important renders in kind still were.

said a pamphlet of 1585.[1] 'Patrons maintain themselves with those tithes which the people give', declared Sandys in a sermon preached before Elizabeth, 'and ministers have what the patrons leave.'[2] Even a future bishop found his living 'gelded' of £10 by the patron.[3] 'Every gentleman thinks the priest mean', said Thomas Adams, 'but the priest's means hath made many a gentleman'; and he asked: 'Having full gorged themselves with the parsonages, must they pick the bones of the vicarages too?' 'They were taken into the church for patrons, defenders; and they prove offenders, thieves: for most often *patrocinia, latrocinia.*' The clergy got 'leavings, not livings'.[4]

Patrons sell benefices, farm them out, give them to boys, serving men, &c., said Dering in 1570; they present 'their falconer, their huntsman, their horsekeeper or any other such-like, so as he can reasonably read English', said Stockewood in 1579.[5] Harrison referred in similar vein to 'the covetousness of the patrons, of whom some do bestow advowsons of benefices upon their bakers, butlers, cooks, good archers, falconers and horsekeepers, instead of other recompense for their long and faithful service'.[6] A patron, said Peacham, will refuse a living to his chaplain, on the grounds that he has promised it to his 'butler or bailiff, for his true and extraordinary service; . . . when the truth is, he hath bestowed it upon himself, for fourscore or an hundred pieces'.[7] 'The ringleader of the nonconformists' in Cheshire during James's reign rebuked 'such . . . as, being entrusted with the lands and livings of the church, . . . do notwithstanding turn their patronage into pillage.'[8] Bishop Carleton agreed that patrons, so far from

[1] *A Lamentable Complaint of the Commonalty, by way of Supplication, to the High Court of Parliament, for a Learned Ministery*, quoted in Cowper, *Select Works of Robert Crowley*, pp. xxx–xxxi.

[2] Lysons, *A View of the Revenues of the Parochial Clergy*, p. 49.

[3] Kinloch, op. cit., pp. 22–23, 181; Joseph Hall, *Works* (1808), I. xxxii–iv.

[4] Adams, *The Forrest of Thornes*, and *Heaven and Earth Reconciled*, op. cit., pp. 1060, 119; cf. Stock, op. cit., pp. 143, 224, 234.

[5] Dering is quoted in Haller, op. cit., p. 13; Stockewood, op. cit., p. 40. Latimer had made similar charges against patrons: see his *Sermons* (Parker Soc.), p. 290; also Bernard Gilpin, *A Sermon preached . . . before King Edward VI*, in Gilpin, op. cit., pp. 269–72.

[6] Harrison, op. cit., pp. 26–27. An amusing scene in *The Return from Parnassus* (1601 or 1602) illustrates the standards of learning and piety expected by a patron (Act III, scene i).

[7] Peacham, *The Compleat Gentleman* (1634: I quote from the reprint of 1906), p. 31.

[8] Hinde, 'Life of Bruen', quoted in Nicholas Assheton's *Journal*, p. 21; see also pp. xviii–xix.

defending their church's right, 'look on whilst every one maketh haste to carry away the spoils, one inviting another as to a common prey'.[1]

There is a certain recurrent similarity of phrase in these accounts which makes one suspicious of them. From the days of Nashe and Greene complaints of clerical corruption became almost common form. The universities seem to have been turning out more graduates than the church could absorb. Such unemployed intellectuals had no less inducement than Puritans to exaggerate the abuses which made their entry into the clerical profession difficult, or which reduced its remuneration. There was an eager public for such attacks, the public which had enjoyed Martin Marprelate. Not necessarily Puritan in any doctrinal sense, it was a public which had grown up in the anti-clerical tradition of middle-class protestantism: it had a keen eye for economic sharp practices in others.

So we should discount literary evidence on this point. Nevertheless, many of the facts which the pamphleteers allege can be confirmed from other sources. Here are two examples from Essex. In August 1609 Henry Smith, lord of the manor of Langford Hall and patron of Langford rectory, held a manor court at which he seized a house and an acre of ground which (for anything the churchwardens could find out to the contrary) had been in the use of the rector and his predecessors time out of mind. The parson was unwilling to contend with his patron, and agreed to recognize the latter's right to the property on condition of being allowed to occupy the house himself at a rent of 1s. a year. In consequence he did not sign the terrier in which this fact is reported: it was presented by the churchwardens only. At Parndon Parva two terriers were drawn up within three days of each other in 1610. One of them recorded that the patron had stripped the rectory of 1½ acres of glebe and converted it into copyhold: the other did not.[2]

We should be chary of taking the Elizabethan Puritan surveys entirely literally, since they have an obvious axe to grind. Nevertheless, where we can check them, they often appear surprisingly accurate; and they would have defeated their own object had they been demonstrably fictitious. Their lists of clergymen who had

---

[1] Carleton, op. cit., p. 31. Cf. the first epigraph to this chapter.
[2] Newcourt, op. cit. ii. 362, 463; cf. p. 275 and Lysons, *Environs of London*, iv. 408.

been serving men, pedlars, tailors, grocers, linen-drapers, fish-
mongers, sow-gelders, painters, interlude-players, or 'the old
bishop's butler' correspond very closely to the accounts of the
pamphleteers (by no means all of whom were Puritans), and must
have had some foundation in fact.[1] Bishop Cooper did not deny
Martin Marprelate's charge that Aylmer gave his porter the
living of Paddington; he only said that many other Elizabethan
bishops had made similar presentations, and that the porter was
a God-fearing man.[2]

The situation may have improved in the seventeenth century,
as a result of a rise in general educational standards, of the stable
establishment of protestantism at the universities, and possibly
of a general change in the attitude of the landed classes towards
the church, which showed itself in growing prudence and restraint
by patrons as well as by the crown. But at the Hampton Court
Conference Bishop Bilson still found it necessary to exculpate
bishops for the 'insufficiency of the clergy' and to put the blame on
'lay patrons who present very mean men'.[3] And Robert Burton
described, with an eloquence that cannot be entirely literary, how
greedy patrons drive parsons to trade; others have to fawn on
their patrons and adopt their opinions. Patrons are griping,
covetous, simoniac, hypocritical; they despise learning. Merit is
rewarded with a living only by accident or miracle. In Burton's
ideal commonwealth lay patronage would be abolished.[4] The
writer's feelings became so strong that he prudently veiled them
in Latin as he continued

What can we expect when we vie with one another every day in
admitting to degrees any and every impecunious student drawn from
the dregs of the people who applies for one? . . . This is that base and
starveling class, needy, vagabond, slaves of their own bellies, worthy
to be sent back to the plough-tail, fitter for the pig-sty than the altar,
which has basely prostituted the study of divinity. These it is who fill
the pulpits and creep into noblemen's houses. . . . They subscribe to
any opinions and tenets contrary to the word of God, only so as not
to offend their patrons and to retain the favour of the nobles and the
applause of the masses, and thereby acquire riches for themselves.[5]

---

[1] *The Seconde Parte of a Register*, ii. 89–174, *passim*; Pierce, op. cit., p. 261; *A Viewe
of the State of the Clargie*, pp. 18–38.
[2] Cooper, op. cit., pp. 42–43.
[3] W. Barlow, *The Summe and Substance of the Conference* (1604), p. 53.
[4] R. Burton, op. cit. ii. 191–2; i. 36, 42, 102, 311–22.   [5] Ibid. i. 327–8.

That was in part the conventional railing of the Schools, in part social disgust. But the *tone* of the complaint is significant. The poverty of the church allows ministers from the lower classes to creep in, and they come easily under the control of patrons. The same means which gratify the aristocracy also win them popular applause.

Everywhere there was resentment at the bad treatment of ministers by their social superiors. 'No copyhold', declared Robartes in 1613, 'is in that thraldom wherein most patrons do hold the benefices whereto they do present.'[1] 'The great men', said a preacher in 1635, 'do send God's messengers upon their base errands, place them below their serving men, esteem them below their parasites.'[2] That was one reason why men of Milton's calibre disdained to go into the church, to 'subscribe slave'. In the sixteen-thirties bishops found themselves forced to ordain 'very mean ministers' 'to supply cures as mean'.[3] The uncharitable indeed suggested that bishops deliberately ordained 'cheap curates' in order to supply the meanly-paid cures of their own impropriations'.[4] At all events, they did ordain them. A conservative parliamentarian pamphlet of 1646 asked indignantly 'Who . . . did prefer the basest of the people to be priests of the high places, namely court flatterers, ambitious bribers, importunate beggars, simoniacs, and slaves to great men's lusts, but the supreme magistracy, licentious nobility, profane gentry and covetous patrons of benefices?'[5] By that date the ministers were enjoying their revenge.

The Reformation had deprived the church of many of those rewards which had attracted men of talent and ambition to her service. White Kennett even wondered whether the Elizabethan government had not pursued a deliberate policy of keeping the clergy poor so that they should be dependent on the crown: a similar reflection had occurred earlier to Sir Thomas Wilson.[6] Certainly, as a profession compared with other professions, the church did not hold out good prospects to the worldly-wise. Yet

---

[1] Robartes, op. cit., p. 133.

[2] Jasper Fisher, *The Priests Duty and Dignity* (1636), quoted in J. Brown, *John Bunyan*, p. 7.

[3] Laud, *Works*, v. 330.

[4] Nathaniel Fiennes, speech in the House of Commons, 9 Feb. 1641, in Nalson, op. cit. i. 759; see p. 151 above.

[5] *A Modell of the Government of the Church under the Gospel, by Presbyters . . .* (1646), p. 27; cf. F. Osborne, *Advice to a Son* (1896), pp. 10, 106 (first published 1656).

[6] Kennett, op. cit., p. 171; Wilson, op. cit., p. 38.

many who might have entered the church because they believed they had a vocation were excluded as nonconformists. When Laud wished to improve the financial and social position of ministers he found he had a great deal of history to contend with.

V

One natural consequence of the poverty of ministers was that they engaged in by-employments, some of which were held to bring discredit on the profession. By 21 Hen. VIII, c. 13, ministers were forbidden to take lands to farm, or to buy or sell in the way of merchandise. The ban on leasing was a great grievance. Henry Burton urged that the statute should be repealed, since it was illogical to forbid ministers to purchase farms so long as laymen were free to purchase livings.[1] But when the House of Commons in 1621 and 1625 discussed bills whose object was to enable ministers to take leases, members were anxious to ensure that parsons 'may occupy no more than will be sufficient for their house-keeping, lest they become farmers'.[2]

Wills show ministers acting as farmers. A Leicestershire parson who died in 1580 left a horse, a gelding, five cows, and five pigs: his estate (£41. 16s.) was less than that of the poorest husbandman who left a will. His successor, who died in 1625, shortly after the House of Commons had finished discussing farming parsons, was a substantial mixed farmer, leaving nearly five times as much as his predecessor.[3] In 1586 the vicar of Tuchbrooke, Warwickshire, gave 'himself wholly to the plough and cart, whence he is many times called to burial and churching'.[4] In Norwich diocese in 1597 the rector of Nacton ('a swearer, curser and brawler') and the curate of Boughton also used 'all kinds of husbandry'. The rector of Semer worked at harvest time 'only in his hose and shirt'.[5] In Lincolnshire at the end of the sixteenth century wills show that 'practically every parson was a farmer'.[6] The vicar of Liddington, Rutlandshire, was stated in 1634 for many years to have

---

[1] H. Burton, op. cit., pp. 119–20.
[2] Notestein, Relf, and Simpson, op. cit. iii. 431–2; ed. Gardiner, *Debates in the House of Commons in 1625*, p. 66.
[3] L. A. Parker, op. cit., p. 54.
[4] *The Seconde Parte of a Register*, ii. 167. There are other examples here.
[5] J. F. Williams, *Bishop Redman's Visitation, 1597*, pp. 20–21.
[6] Brooks, op. cit., p. 34.

'busied himself in sordid employments, and served a thatcher with straw, and helped the thatcher to sow his house, and thereby acquired good skill in that faculty . . . to the . . . disgrace of his priestly function'. Worse still, 'for sundry years past he has omitted or neglected to wear the surplice, but only one old threadbare coat with four skirts'. Here (and perhaps in other cases too) one suspects that poverty rather than Puritanism was the reason, for the vicar, Robert Rudd, appears to have had old-fashioned views, including a dislike of capitalist farmers and of men who changed their calling.[1] In 1639 the curate of Flass, Durham, 'cast his mind wholly upon his earthly plough, being a man devoted to Ceres, and only solicitous after worldly business'.[2]

The Protestation which every Elizabethan clergyman had to sign on admission to a cure included a clause whereby he promised that he would 'not openly intermeddle with any artificers' occupations, as covetously to seek a gain thereby' if his living was worth £6. 13s. 4d. or upwards per annum.[3] (There was scope for casuistic evasion in the words 'openly' and 'covetously'.) In Elizabeth's reign the intention was chiefly to exclude artisans from the ministry, or at least to see that they abandoned their crafts on ordination. In this the Protestation was not successful. We have it on Burghley's authority (1585) that the Bishop of Lichfield and Coventry made seventy ministers in one day, for money: tailors, shoemakers, and other craftsmen.[4] Such men almost certainly continued to exercise their craft: entering the ministry for them was rather like purchasing an annuity. 'A glover or a tailor will be glad of an augmentation of £8 or £10 by the year, and well contented that his patron shall have all the rest, so he may be sure of this pension.'[5]

Examples are easy to find. In 1586 the Rev. Thomas Milles of Badeley was described as 'a digger of coals, wherein he toils for his maintenance'.[6] Dr. Hoskins gives instances from Leicestershire, at about the same date, of ministers who were day labourers

[1] D. Mathew, *Social Structure in Caroline England* (1948), pp. 44–45; *The Age of Charles I*, pp. 195–6. Rural poverty in this part of Rutlandshire had led three years earlier to overtures from a shoemaker of Uppingham to one of Rudd's poor parishioners for an agrarian rising (Bland, Brown, and Tawney, *English Economic History, Select Documents*, 1914, p. 390).

[2] Ed. J. C. Hodgson, *Six North Country Diaries* (Surtees Soc., 1910), p. 8.

[3] Cardwell, *Documentary Annals*, i. 296; cf. pp. 264, 270.

[4] Pierce, op. cit., p. 110.   [5] Harrison, op. cit., p. 26.

[6] *The Seconde Parte of a Register*, ii. 172.

or husbandmen.¹ In Lincolnshire in 1605 we find one clergyman
who was a gardener, another 'a common buyer and seller'; and
others following divers crafts.² In Essex a year or two later there
were alleged to be 'a seller of books in markets', who also wheeled
a barrow as labourer in sea-wall works (his living was worth
£7); a horse and cow leech; two graziers; a reputed blacksmith;
four usurers; six who were or had been in prison for debt or were
absent evading the ircreditors.³ In the sixteen-thirties a Somerset
rector leased his rectory for forty-nine years to secure a debt of
£350.⁴ An M.P. in 1621 said he had the names of twenty tradesmen made ministers in Devon. In 1626 Sir Benjamin Rudyerd
told the House that he knew of two ministers who kept ale-
houses for want of means; many other examples could be given.⁵

Bishop Wren of Ely admitted in 1636 that he had inhibited
four ministers in his diocese from preaching. One of them,
he said, had been a draper, another a weaver, a third a tailor.⁶ But
not only Puritans followed menial occupations: Jonathan Skynner,
one of those put in by Bishop Wren himself in place of a 'godly
honest man' whom he had outed, was alleged in the Commons to
have 'followed mechanical works and almost all sorts of husbandry'.⁷ Robert Burton tells us that many doctors took orders in
hope of a benefice; whilst on the other hand 'many poor country
vicars, for want of other means, are driven to their shifts, to turn
mountebanks, quacksalvers, empirics, and if our greedy patrons
hold us to such hard conditions as commonly they do, they will
make most of us work at some trade, as Paul did, at last turn
taskers, maltsters, costermongers, graziers, sell ale as some have
done, or worse'.⁸ Richard Baxter in his youth knew of two 'poor

¹ Hoskins, *Essays*, pp. 19–20.
² *V.C.H., Lincolnshire*, ii. 58–59; cf. Brooks, op. cit., p. 34, for a suspected horse-
dealer.   ³ *A Viewe of the State of the Clargie*, pp. 17, 23–36.
⁴ *C.S.P.D., 1637–8*, p. 362. In 1604 the Prolocutor of the Convocation of
Canterbury had been arrested for debt: twenty years later the Convocation of York
had to ask that the Dean of Chester should be free from arrest for the same reason on
his way to and from Convocation (Usher, *Reconstruction*, i. 347; Burne, 'The History
of Chester Cathedral in the Reigns of James I and Charles I', loc. cit., p. 7).
⁵ Notestein, Relf, and Simpson, op. cit. iii. 432. Birch, op. cit. i. 82–83; ed. J. C.
Atkinson, *Quarter Sessions Records* (North Riding of Yorkshire Record Soc.), ii. xiv–
xv; Halley, op. cit. i. 115; Shaw, op. cit. ii. 336; W. M. Palmer, 'The Vicarage as
alehouse and smithy', in *History Teachers' Miscellany*, iv, no. 11, 167.
⁶ Heylyn, *Cyprianus Anglicus*, p. 309.
⁷ Ed. Notestein, *The Journal of Sir Simonds D'Ewes*, p. 201. This was after Wren's
translation to Norwich.   ⁸ R. Burton, op. cit. i. 36.

ignorant curates' in neighbouring parishes, one of whom made his living by cutting faggots, the other by making ropes.[1]

So the 'mechanic preachers' of the revolutionary decades were not quite such a novelty as their enemies pretended. Some of the Elizabethan Puritans already thought by-employment good in principle. *An humble supplication* to the queen in 1584 said:

> The bishops forthwith ask, what shall our curates do,
> Or what allowance shall they have to live upon?
> We say we think it best that out of hand they go
> To their old trades or learn some occupation.
>   Then did they storm with angry mood, saying that we
>   Would have all vicars through the land beggars to be.[2]

This view, however, was that of the Anabaptists rather than of Cartwright and the majority of early Puritan propagandists.[3]

The lay preachers of the years after 1640 were craftsmen who believed that they had a call to preach the gospel, and did not do it for money: many of the poor vicars before 1640 regarded both their clerical and their non-clerical occupations as means of scraping together a pittance. 'It were to be wished', wrote Milton in 1659, that ministers 'were all tradesmen; they would not then so many of them, for want of another trade, make a trade of their preaching; and yet they clamour that tradesmen preach.'[4]

In London and the great cities, the most appropriate by-employment was a lectureship endowed by the congregation or some other body. There was, apparently, some pressure upon ministers to take up such work, and as the rewards were often considerable, it was easy by this means for them to come under the economic influence of the wealthier citizens.[5]

VI

Chillingworth depicted in eloquent words the realities of the economic dependence of a parson on his patron: and he is hardly likely to exaggerate, since his connexions were not with the opposition:

Consider in what a miserable state the church must be . . . when those

---

[1] *Reliquiae Baxterianae*, i. 80.   [2] *The Seconde Parte of a Register*, i. 268.
[3] Cartwright's ideas on the subject are quoted in Whitgift's *Works*, iii. 432–7.
[4] Milton, *Prose Works*, iii. 28.
[5] Heylyn, *Cyprianus Anglicus*, p. 282; Rushworth, op. cit. ii. 269. See also below, pp. 277, 300–1.

to whom you have committed your souls in trust . . . shall through
want and penury be rendered so heartless and low-spirited that for fear
of your anger, and danger of starving, they shall not dare to interrupt
and hinder you when you run headlong in the paths which lead you to
destruction; when, out of faint-heartedness, they shall not dare to take
notice, no, not of the most scandalous sins of their patrons; but, which
is worst, be the most forward officious parasites to soothe them in their
crimes . . ., be the most ready to tell you that those possessions and
tithes which have been wrested out of God's hands are none of God's
due . . ., that their right is nothing but your voluntary alms and charitable benevolence.[1]

Sir William Petty inclined to the view that 'religion best flourish-
eth when the priests are most mortified'.[2] The English parochial
clergy could not complain of insufficient mortification. But their
dependence meant that divisions within the landed class, among
lay patrons, were reflected in the rank-and-file clergy: the seamless
robe of the church was rent. So whilst the crown and probably the
majority of lay patrons continued to prefer 'to appoint men who,
although ignorant, were safe politically, rather than to take the
risk that the man with learning might prove troublesome',[3] a
growing group of patrons found themselves in alliance with an
intellectual aristocracy of learned clergy. Such ministers could see
little hope either of their own advancement in endowments or
self-respect, or of the advancement of learning or piety, except
through a drastic reorganization of the church which could only
be carried through by parliamentary action. The alliance corresponded to real interests on both sides.

VII

In the generation before 1640, then, the clergy were dependent,
yet potentially powerful. Both groups, government and opposition, needed their support and feared their enmity. The ministers
themselves, whether they were 'the dregs of the people' seeking
lucre, or men with high Christian principles who wished to put
them into practice, needed patrons. Where were they to find them?

[1] Chillingworth, *Works*, iii. 201–2. Cf. Selden's remarks about the origins of
tithes in England, quoted on pp. 136–7 above.
[2] *Treatise of Taxes*, in C. H. Hull, *Economic Writings of Sir William Petty* (1899), i.
79.
[3] Usher, *Reconstruction*, i. 209.

Some looked to the parliamentary opposition for support and loaves and fishes. Others looked to Laud and the government, both for immediate preferment ('the Arminians hold all the best benefices in the kingdom') and because of Laud's known desire 'to relieve the poor and depressed condition of many ministers', whose 'sordid and shameful aspect' seemed to him to give great advantages to those that were popishly inclined. But Laud went beyond merely wishing to give economic assistance to the nineteen clergymen out of twenty who, he thought, had no decent garment to put on;[1] he also encouraged the parson 'to hold up his head in the presence of the county families',[2] and did so deliberately by trying to augment the independent authority of the church.

The traditional attitude was that of John Williams. In 1631 a peer considered that he had reason to complain to the Bishop of Lincoln of the Rev. Mr. Pestle, who had been suing his parishioners and had spoken ungratefully of his patron. Williams replied that he could not stop a vicar suing for his tithes, 'but for his carriage towards your lordship, if it shall appear he hath but slented upon your good lordship out of his pulpit, or given the least cause of offence in that kind upon the people, I will make him an example unto all that county for his beastly ingratitude, and (if any proofs come home in that kind) deprive him of his living, as he well deserves'.[3]

Abbott, like Williams, browbeat the lesser clergy, and would listen to any country gentleman who had a complaint to make against a minister; Laud irritated nobles, gentry, and citizens by backing up the clergy.[4] The mayor of Arundel, Prynne tells us, was fined and censured by the High Commission in 1634 for imprisoning a drunken clergyman for the night.[5] Laud intervened

---

[1] D. Lloyd, *Memoires*, p. 268. Lloyd was reporting his own conversations with Laud. Cf. Laud's *Works*, v. 327.

[2] Gardiner, *History*, viii. 122.

[3] B. Dew Robert, *Mitre and Musket* (1938), pp. 126–7. The wily Williams was careful not to commit himself about the particular accusations; but his general attitude is clear enough. 'Slent' means 'to fall obliquely', and so 'to make sly hits or gibes' (*Oxford English Dictionary*).

[4] Collier, op. cit. viii. 67; Heylyn, *Cyprianus Anglicus*, pp. 242–5. With Laud's attitude we may contrast that of Cromwell. When Richard Byfield responded to a similar accusation from his patron by appealing to Williams's great kinsman, the Lord Protector rebuked the patron in words that brought tears to his eyes, and so restored peace (Palmer, op. cit. ii. 446).

[5] [Prynne], *A Breviate of the Prelates intollerable usurpations* (1637), pp. 164–5.

at York, Durham, Salisbury, to support the cathedral clergy
against the civic authorities.[1] We may compare the 'wicked
injustice' of the Laudian Bishop Corbett in failing to back up Sir
Simonds D'Ewes against the 'wicked malice' of his 'unhappy
minister'.[2] Secretary Coke boasted in 1636 that the clergy had been
shielded from 'rich encroaching neighbours and patrons'.[3] If any
man indicted a priest of any crime, said Prynne, 'he hath ere the
year go about such a yoke of heresy laid in his neck that it maketh
him wish he had not done it'.[4] We must recall that the parsons
who obtained the most spectacular promotion under Charles I
were those, from Sibthorpe and Manwaring downwards, who
preached that resistance to arbitrary taxation entailed damnation.

So, given the social subservience of so many ministers, we can
understand why the opposition gentry disliked the idea of clergymen being put into the commission of the peace: for ministers
dependent on Puritan gentlemen were not likely to be appointed.
In Northumberland and Durham, it was alleged in the Parliaments
of 1614 and 1621, the clergy and their dependents were in a
majority on the commission.[5] It was, Leighton thought, 'a dis-
graceful affront to the nobility, judges and gentry, as though they
were not worthy or fit for the places'.[6] Under Laud large numbers
of parochial ministers were put into the commission, 'to the great
grievance of the country in civil affairs', complained May, 'and
depriving them of spiritual edification'.[7] 'The inferior clergy',
observed a protégé of Laud's, 'took more upon them than they
had used to do, and did not live towards their neighbours of
quality, or their patrons themselves, with that civility and con-
descension they had used to do; which disposed them likewise
to a withdrawing their good countenance and good neighbourhood from them.'[8] Hyde was almost quoting the Root and Branch
Petition's reference to 'the encouragement of ministers to despise
the temporal magistracy, the nobles and gentry of the land'.[9]

[1] Laud, *Works*, vii. 343; Ornsby, op. cit. i. xxix, 216; Bridgeman, op. cit., pp.
302–3, 406–8.

[2] D'Ewes, *Autobiography* (1845), ii. 102–3.   [3] Laud, *Works*, v. 128.

[4] *A Breviate of the Prelates intollerable usurpations*, p. 31.

[5] *Commons' Journals*, i. 482; E. Nicholas, op. cit. i. 365; Notestein, Relf, and Simpson, op. cit. ii. 319, 333–4.

[6] Leighton, op. cit., p. 129.

[7] T. May, *The History of the Parliament of England* (1647), i. 23.

[8] Clarendon, *History of the Rebellion* (ed. Macray, 1888), i. 130; cf. Soden, op. cit.,
p. 233.   [9] Gardiner, *Constitutional Documents*, p. 138.

Worst of all was the careless talk which accompanied the Laudian operation, as when Bishop Wren, son of a London merchant, said in the High Commission that he 'hoped to live to see the day when a minister should be as good a man as any Jack Gentleman in England'. 'To such a height of infatuation had a petty blaze of mistaken honour elevated this high flier', commented the royalist L'Estrange, adding truthfully 'the Presbyterians were gainers by all this.'[1] It was Wren and Bishop Pierce of Bath and Wells whom Clarendon described as having 'with great pride and insolence provoked all the gentry, and in truth most of the inhabitants, of their dioceses'.[2]

This was getting the worst of both worlds, and neatly illustrates the impossible situation in which the government found itself. It was opposed by a heterogeneous alliance comprising Puritans and common lawyers, advocates of parliamentary sovereignty and advocates of free trade. Against this alliance the clergy were the surest prop of the old order; loyalty to the church proved the most reliable cohesive on the royalist side in the civil war. Yet under the Laudian régime the church found itself more and more isolated from public opinion in the country, and the government had to take ever more drastic steps to elevate the prestige of parsons as such, to increase their social and political importance. In doing so it ran up against the prejudices of its own lay supporters. When the Long Parliament met, it was the *House of Lords* which, without waiting for legislation, took the initiative in putting clergymen out of the commissions of the peace. The Commons followed up by asking the Lord Keeper and the Chancellor of the Duchy to leave all ministers out when the commissions were renewed.[3] The confirmatory Clerical Disabilities Act came a year later.

---

[1] H. L'Estrange, *The Reign of King Charles* (2nd ed., 1656), p. 144; W. Lilly, *Several Observations on the Life and Death of King Charles I* (1651), in F. Maseres, *Select Tracts* (1815), i. 162–3.

[2] Clarendon, op. cit. ii. 272. Cf. p. 29 above.

[3] *Commons' Journals*, ii. 79.

X

PLURALISM AND NON-RESIDENCE

To desire that every parish should be furnished with a sufficient
preacher, and to desire that pluralities be forthwith taken away,
is to desire things contrary.

BACON, *Certain Considerations touching the better pacification and edification
of the Church of England*, 1604, in *Works*, x. 124

I

THERE was nothing new about ecclesiastical pluralism or
absenteeism. In the days when royal servants had been
mainly clerics, pluralism and non-residence had kept them
without disturbing the royal revenue. The change-over to lay
administrators came gradually after the Reformation, and was
financed by expanding perquisites and fees rather than by introducing regular salaries. But many ecclesiastical functionaries
remained—bishops, heads of colleges, royal chaplains, as well as
civil servants—whose regular revenues would have had to be
substantially augmented were it not for the convenient device of
pluralism. The contemporaneous fall in the purchasing power of
fixed incomes aggravated the problem. Pluralism was reduced
after the Reformation, but it was difficult to abolish.

Traditional habits of non-residence, however, appeared in a
new light when preaching came to be regarded as the essential
task of the minister. For this put the relationship of the absentee
minister, the hired curate, and the congregation on a different
footing. The curate was not paid the salary of a scholar, presumably because he could not preach. The minister guilty of 'that
fearful sin of non-residency'[1] thus seemed to be swallowing the
emoluments of his benefice without earning them by preaching
the word, and without even providing a competent deputy. He
was robbing his parishioners of that most valuable of all things—

---

[1] Thomas Taylor, *A Commentary Upon the Epistle of St. Paul written to Titus* (1658),
p. 526; cf. p. 117.

spiritual food. The matter had looked rather different when all that was required was a duly ordained priest who could perform the prescribed rites and ceremonies.

About the facts of pluralism and non-residence there was little disagreement. Some thought they were unavoidable evils, and that any attempt to remedy them might bring worse disasters on the church. Men differed about their causes and their cure: but their existence was generally admitted. At a conference on the Prayer Book between Puritans and official clergy, held about 1585 in the presence of Leicester, Walsingham, the Archbishop of Canterbury and other bishops, non-residence and pluralities were 'disallowed of by all judgments and needed no debating'.[1]

A series of acts of Parliament, with increasingly severe penalties, show how unavailing legislation was to check pluralism. 21 Hen. VIII, c. 13, punished non-residence with a fine of £20 for each offence, half to the king, half to the informer. 13 Eliz., c. 20, cancelled leases of livings made by non-residents and confiscated a year's profit of the living for each offence, to be distributed among the poor of the parish. Five years later (18 Eliz., c. 11) it was enacted, dangerously enough, that if the bishop did not sequester the living of a non-resident minister, parishioners might withhold payment of tithes. Non-residence was defined in 1571 as eighty days' absence in a year.

The Puritan surveys present statistics of pluralism and non-residence which may not be entirely accurate, but which stand up well to examination and comparison with official estimates. One survey of 1586, covering nine counties, gave 565 parsons in 1933 livings as double-beneficed and non-resident. Less than one church in four had a resident preaching minister.[2] Official figures from the diocese of Lincoln in 1576 show 77 parish ministers out of 466 as pluralists. This omits all consideration of cathedral preferments, and it is amongst the cathedral clergy that there was probably most pluralism. At least one in eight of the ministers was non-resident: less than one in six was licensed to preach.[3] In the diocese of Norwich there were in 1593 112 pluralists among 484 ministers.[4] Usher's estimate for the whole country in 1603 was

[1] *The Seconde Parte of a Register*, i. 283. Cf. Penry, *A Treatise wherein is manifestlie proved, that reformation and those that sincerely favor the same, are unjustly charged to be enemies unto hir Majestie and the state* (1590), sig. D2 sqq.

[2] D. Neal, *History of the Puritans* (1837), i. 310.

[3] Foster, *Lincoln Episcopal Records, 1571–84*, pp. 333–4.   [4] Saunders, op. cit., p. 82.

1,000 pluralists, holding between them 2,500 benefices.[1] This would leave at least one out of every six parishes without a resident incumbent. But this or any other guess based on either Puritan or episcopal surveys is likely to under-estimate, since they may miss combinations of benefices in different counties or dioceses—the worst type of pluralism, since it inevitably meant non-residence.[2]

The hierarchy made attempts to remedy the situation, so far as this was possible without fundamental reorganization. The canons of 1571 forbad ministers to hold more than two benefices, and insisted that they must be within 26 miles of each other. This was later extended to 30 miles, the canons of 1604 adding that a curate must be supplied for the living in which the pluralist did not reside.[3] The latter provision was easy to break, but the 30 miles rule seems to have been fairly well observed. In the diocese of Lincoln in 1603 the benefices of 67 out of 90 pluralists were within 10 miles of each other. Only 4 were over 30 miles apart.[4] The 30 miles limit also seems to have been observed in the dioceses of Norwich, Oxford, and Worcester.[5] But by limiting pluralism this canon in a sense legitimated it.

Deprivation of Puritans complicated the problem. It was difficult to find ministers to fill vacant benefices. A minister in Essex, it was said, reported to his bishop in 1584 that within the compass of 16 miles there were 19 silenced preachers and 22 non-residents. For this tactless juxtaposition of figures he was summoned before the High Commission.[6] But it remained true that there could have been more preaching ministers if the hierarchy's policy had been different. Pluralism may have been slightly reduced in the last two decades of the sixteenth century; but it remained scandalous. In the diocese of Lincoln there were 140 pluralists in 1585, 90 in 1603.[7] And in the seventeenth century the

[1] Usher, *Reconstruction*, i. 211. Mr. Rowse thought that in Devon and Cornwall something like one-third of the benefices were held in plurality in 1561, and that at least one in every five was held by a non-resident (*Tudor Cornwall*, p. 324). This is better than the 30 per cent. of absentees in Oxfordshire in 1520 (Coulton, *Mediaeval Panorama*, 1945, p. 156).

[2] I am indebted to Miss Barratt for drawing my attention to this point. She believes that Usher's neglect of it vitiates many of his conclusions. But at least he does not over-estimate.

[3] Cardwell, *Synodalia*, pp. 128, 145, 150, 271.

[4] Foster, *State of the Church*, p. 459.

[5] Information from Miss Barratt's thesis.

[6] Neal, op. cit. i. 282.

[7] Foster, *State of the Church*, p. lxiii; cf. Hoskins, *Essays*, p. 22.

price paid for an increase in the number of preaching ministers seems to have been a sharp rise in the number of pluralists. Cases of pluralism increased from 18 to 33 in the dioceses of Oxford and Worcester between 1600 and 1640, and by the latter date one in five of the clergy held a second living.[1]

II

It is important to distinguish between various causes of pluralism which were often deliberately confused. Many benefices were extremely badly endowed, and for this impropriation was usually to blame. Such was the defence of pluralism regularly advanced by the bishops and their spokesmen. Thus Dr. James said in the Commons in 1601 that so far from pluralism having brought corruptions into the church, it was poverty made the corruption, which would be taken away if competent livings were given to every minister.[2] If pluralism had been confined to the union of ill-endowed benefices within the thirty miles laid down by the canon, this defence might have been valid. The author of *A Certificate from Northamptonshire* thought the clergy would be content to forgo pluralism 'if the poor vicarages and other poor livings might be made competible [competent], or enjoy their full tithes, and the small rates [i.e. *modi*] taken away throughout the whole kingdom'.[3]

But it was notorious that in fact the bishops themselves, the cathedral clergy, heads and fellows of Oxford and Cambridge colleges, and what one may term 'court clergy' like John Donne were the worst pluralists, and probably the most numerous.[4] Horse and armour for national defence, Whitgift argued in 1601, were provided almost exclusively by the pluralists among the clergy. Deaneries, archdeaconries, prebends, and most offices in collegiate churches were exempted from the limitations on pluralism which 21 Hen. VIII, c. 13, imposed. The statute also allowed some groups of clergymen to purchase dispensations to hold two livings

[1] By 1650–2 there were only four cases of pluralism—a remarkable reversal of the trend (Miss Barratt's thesis).
[2] D'Ewes, *Journals*, p. 640.
[3] *A Certificate from Northamptonshire*, p. 8.
[4] Cardwell, *Synodalia*, pp. 446–7; I. Walton, *Lives*, p. 55. Usher, *Reconstruction*, i. 210–11, gives examples of episcopal pluralism. For pluralism in Oxford, see Laud, *Works*, v. 197, 207–8.

with cure of souls worth £8 and over a year. These included chaplains to members of the royal family, to peers, to bishops, and to
certain state officers; brothers or sons of peers or knights; doctors
and bachelors of divinity or law. There was no limit to the number
of livings which might be held by royal chaplains. So the right to
pluralism was first and foremost a social privilege: its abolition
would for this reason be prejudicial to the nobility and gentry,
declared Whitgift.[1] The privilege could also be bought. Dispensations from the canon of 1571 were available for those with money.
Grindal tried to abolish or reduce their number; but total abolition
of pluralities would have led to loss of revenue to the crown: so
large was the trade in dispensations.[2]

Naturally official spokesmen justified the system from which
they benefited. Insistence on residence in parochial cures, said
the bishops in 1584, would be 'very prejudicial for grave men
required for government in the universities', and would overthrow
residence in cathedral churches, colleges, and deaneries.[3] 'If every
one shall have but one benefice', asked a defender of the hierarchy
in 1588, 'what difference shall be between a doctor in divinity and
a scholar?'[4] When Bishop Cooper argued in the following year
that ministers would not devote themselves to their pastoral duties
unless they retained 'their ample and large livings', it is clear that
he was not thinking of the poorest cures.[5] Many of these learned
preachers, Stoughton observed, 'gallop from place to place, and trot
from parish to parish', feeding none of their flocks satisfactorily.[6]

'Most of the grosser instances of non-residence', writes Dr.
Hoskins, of Leicestershire, 'occur among the wealthier clergy, who
often lived hundreds of miles from parishes from which they drew
handsome incomes.'[7] In the Puritan Survey of Essex, made about
1609, whose accuracy we have seen confirmed from other sources,
71 pluralists were listed. Only 12 of them received less than £100
from their combined livings. Forty-seven received sums ranging
from £100 to £540, whilst in the remaining 12 cases the facts are
not given fully enough to be certain, but most of them probably
got over £100.[8] Between 1617 and 1631 the son of Bishop Bayley

[1] Collier, op. cit. vii. 262.   [2] See below, p. 232.
[3] Cardwell, *Documentary Annals*, i. 434.   [4] Cardwell, *Synodalia*, p. 576.
[5] Cooper, op. cit., p. 135.   [6] W. Stoughton, op. cit., pp. 245–6.
[7] Hoskins, *Essays*, p. 21. His examples include the Master of Christ's College,
and a chaplain to the Countess of Cumberland.
[8] *A Viewe of the State of the Clargie*, pp. 9–15, 17–21.

of Bangor held 10 preferments.[1] At Canterbury in 1634 the Dean and 8 prebendaries held between them 15 livings and 5 chapels; at Exeter the Dean and 9 members of the chapter held 19 benefices and one donative, in addition to 5 archdeaconries.[2] The prebendaries of Salisbury admitted to having at least two benefices each, and they confessed that 'we have been defective, but especially in preaching at those churches where we receive rents and profits'.[3] At Durham, at about the same period, Cosin had two rich livings, an archdeaconry, and a prebend: he retained these when he became Master of Peterhouse and Dean of Peterborough. Another prebendary of Durham held three benefices, two prebends, and an archdeaconry.[4]

From such persons the episcopate was recruited. It was therefore easy for the parliamentarians to mock at the ecclesiastical careerists who 'heap up by hook or crook three or four fat livings, they seldom preach at any of them, nor keep residence or hospitality, but hoard up full bags, skulk at the court, ingratiate themselves with those in greatest grace, and when the chair is void, they bring out their bags, and so are the only qualified men for such a dignity'.[5] The complaint, though propagandist, only exaggerates: it does not invent.

The most convincing evidence of the pluralism of bishops and cathedral and court clergy is to be found, ironically enough, in Walker's *Sufferings of the Clergy*. Walker naïvely emphasizes, time and again, how the wicked parliamentarians despoiled men of two or three rich livings in order to establish a single minister in each of them. Thus, to give only a few examples, Matthew Nicholas, who had the advantage of being brother to a clerk of the council, was Dean of Bristol, canon of Salisbury, and held a prebend at Westminster, a rectory, two vicarages, and a hospital: he also leased a rectory and manor from the Dean and Chapter of

---

[1] Richards, op. cit., p. 6. For Bayley see p. 310 below.

[2] *Hist. MSS. Commission, Fourth Report, Appendix*, pp. 125, 136; cf. p. 128. Matters were no better at Canterbury a decade later, if we are to believe a petition against bishops from the citizens of that town quoted in Richard Culmer's *Cathedrall Newes from Canterbury* (1644), pp. 1–2. For the pluralism of John Young, Dean of Winchester, from 1616 till the abolition of his office, see his *Diary*, pp. 6, 19, 47. For Heylyn see p. 255 below. Other examples of pluralism among the cathedral clergy may be found in Soden, op. cit., pp. 93–94, 110.

[3] *Wilts. Notes and Queries*, i. 17.   [4] Ornsby, op. cit. i. 185.

[5] [Prynne], *Lord Bishops none of the Lords Bishops* (1640), sig. E2ᵛ. 'Those in greatest grace' is presumably an oblique reference to Laud.

Salisbury.[1] William Cotton, son of a former Bishop of Exeter, was Chanter and canon of Exeter, and was in possession of two Devon rectories worth £800 per annum; his brother was Archdeacon of Totnes, canon, and held three rectories.[2] Michael Hudson, royal chaplain, held three rectories whose total value was some £800 a year, and a hospital as well.[3] Richard Marsh, chaplain at various times to both archbishops and to the king, held an archdeaconry, two or three prebends, and two or three vicarages, one worth £200 a year. In 1644 he was made Dean of York as well.[4] Bishop Bowle of Rochester gave his nephew Richard Chase two livings, together worth £400–600. One to live on, one to finance his litigation, as Mr. Chase cheerfully explained to the inhabitants of the parish in which he did not reside but in which he was trying to raise the *modi decimandi*.[5]

In 1640 some three-quarters of the cathedral clergy and one-quarter of the university clergy, at least, held parochial livings in plurality. 'Receptacles for drones and non-residents', was Sir Benjamin Rudyerd's description of cathedrals even whilst defending them;[6] 'a nest of non-residents, an epicure college of riot and voluptuousness', added Sir Edward Dering with the same benevolent intention.[7] In July 1641 the heads of Cambridge colleges petitioned against a bill to oblige the clergy to reside on their benefices. The livings which they held, the reverend pluralists declared, with less than academic regard for truth, were of such small value that men of sufficient parts would not accept them by themselves, so that the future possessors would be exposed by the bill in question not only to want but also to disesteem.[8]

In Wales, which Dr. Richards describes as 'a land of pluralism and non-residents' in the early seventeenth century, the fattest pickings were enjoyed by Englishmen who never visited the country, and by a small group of rich Welsh clerics with influential connexions.[9] The same was true of Ireland, where 'some

---

[1] Walker, op. cit. ii. 3; Matthews, *Walker Revised*, p. 378.
[2] Walker, op. cit. ii. 24, 26, 217; Matthews, op. cit., p. 111.
[3] Walker, op. cit. ii. 269; Matthews, op. cit., p. 252.
[4] Walker, op. cit. ii. 82–83; Matthews, op. cit., p. 395. Cf. pp. 21–23 above.
[5] Larking, op. cit., pp. 206, 210, 214, 219. I am indebted to Mr. John Bowle for drawing my attention to this reference to his forbears.
[6] Matthews, op. cit., p. xiv; Manning, op. cit., p. 189.
[7] *Sir Edward Dering Revived*, p. 87.
[8] *Hist. MSS. Commission, Fourth Report, Appendix*, p. 89.
[9] Richards, op. cit., pp. 6–7.

would take the liberty, though possessors of several livings, to reside at none of them at all'; and where at the beginning of the seventeenth century an archbishop held three bishoprics and 77 other benefices. By comparison the archbishop who in Strafford's time held a mere 16 livings, and even the bishop who held 23, were reformed characters.[1]

Simony begat non-residence and non-residence begat simony: so at least Henry Burton argued. 'For first, a simonist, after the payment of his first purchase, is commonly enforced to live privately, to let out his parsonage to farm, defrauding the poor of their hospital relief, and go skulk in some corner of the city or other, and then thrust himself into some lecture: there he gathers up his crumbs again', and tries to accumulate enough capital to buy still higher preferment.[2]

A main source of pluralism was that permitted under 21 Hen. VIII, c. 13, to chaplains of peers and court officials. Such chaplains were often distinct from the clergyman whom a great personage kept in his family as minister or tutor, and who was little more than a personal servant. (Though a household chaplaincy might offer a refuge for a displaced Puritan, since noblemen's chaplains were exempt from ecclesiastical jurisdiction.) But a magnate often nominated a minister his chaplain in order to qualify him to become a pluralist. Dukes were allowed 6 chaplains, marquises and earls 5, and so downwards on a graded scale, with archbishops permitted 8, bishops 6. So the total number of chaplains which members of the House of Lords could license was formidable.

In 1621 some M.P.s wanted to repeal those clauses of this statute which licensed pluralism, except for royal chaplains, on whose number there seems to have been no restriction.[3] 'I should think', Bacon observed tartly, 'that the attendance used and given in your Majesty's court, and in the houses and families of their lords, were a juster reason why they should have no benefice than why they should be qualified to have two'.[4] The legally permitted

---

[1] Ed. E. S. Shuckburg, *Two Biographies of William Bedell* (1902), p. 44; Gardiner, *History*, i. 390; J. Bramhall, *Works* (1842), 1. lxxix–lxxxii, lxxxix–xc; H. O'Grady, *Strafford in Ireland* (1923), i. 529. Cf. R. Parr, *Life of Usher* (1686), ii. 453; Knowler, op. cit. i. 187–9.

[2] H. Burton, op. cit., p. 105.

[3] Notestein, Relf, and Simpson, op. cit. v. 99.

[4] Bacon, *Works*, x. 123.

qualifications for non-residence, a Sub-Committee reported to the Commons in 1625, had been of late years greatly increased by the increase of the nobility.[1] It does indeed appear that between 1625 and 1627 more men obtained dispensations to hold livings in plurality on the ground that they were chaplains than for any other reason.[2]

Laud and Charles tried to restrict the practice by ordering that only men of high rank should have chaplains, and they conformable men. This device, Prynne thought, not only deprived the gentry of ever-present godly influences, but also made young divinity students 'more dependent on, more obsequious to, the bishops, and less dependent on the nobility, gentry, people'. But such orders not only aroused resentment: they proved difficult to enforce.[3] 'It is not in the bishop's power', John Davenport told Lady Vere in 1633, 'to take from you what is settled upon the nobility and others by Magna Carta, the right and power of entertaining chaplains.'[4] So by judicious use of such privileges the landed class extended its hold over the clergy, a hold to which eloquent testimony is borne by countless dedicatory prefaces, funeral sermons, &c. 'The transferring of the power of dispensation in this case from the Pope, and scattering it amongst the nobility and others', said Sir Simon Degge, was contrary to the interest of the poorer clergy and the church.[5] It was another factor dividing the clerical ranks.

III

When a bill for the abolition of pluralities was introduced into the House of Commons in 1584 Whitgift opposed it for the following reasons: (i) it would take away the royal prerogative of granting dispensations; (ii) it would reduce the royal revenue, since half the payments for dispensations came to the crown; (iii) by

---

[1] Gardiner, *1625 Debates*, p. 21. The Sub-Committee proposed to moderate and regulate these qualifications; but that expropriatory clause was afterwards omitted. They also suggested that the king be thanked for reducing the number of his chaplains.

[2] I owe this information to Miss Barratt.

[3] Laud, *Works*, v. 340–1, 344, 357, 365; Heylyn, *Cyprianus Anglicus*, pp. 201–2; Prynne, *Canterburies Doome*, p. 384. Prynne clearly thought that ministers must be dependent on somebody; the great question was, on whom?

[4] Ed. I. M. Calder, *Letters of John Davenport* (1937), p. 40.

[5] Degge, op. cit., pp. 33–34; cf. Haller, op. cit., p. 381.

depriving learned men of due reward it would lead to an unlearned ministry;[1] (iv) even if all benefices had a sufficient maintenance, learned ministers could not be provided for one-third of them; (v) heads of Oxford and Cambridge colleges, and (vi) deans and chapters depended on pluralities for revenues; (vii) it would increase the number of 'the factious and wayward sort'; (viii) it would discourage 'the best sort of the clergy' and encourage the 'factious and contentious'.[2]

It is fairly clear that it was the poorer parochial clergy whom their Archbishop regarded as factious. The 'best sort' are heads of colleges and cathedral clergy maintaining 'convenient hospitality' on the spoils of non-residence. The bill, Convocation declared, with remarkable emphasis on the economic motive behind theological conviction, would drive 'the younger sort of students' to 'other seminaries, where they may hope for more encouragement'. Despite this dark hint of the lurking dangers of popery, the bill passed the Commons; it was defeated in the Lords by the bishops' vote.[3] Exactly the same fate befell a similar bill in 1589, which would have enforced the canon of 1571 by prohibiting pluralism except in the case of two small and adjacent livings, and would have compelled residence.[4] Similar bills failed in 1601, 1604, 1610, 1621, and 1624, as did bills 'against the universities [and] pluralities' in 1625. The Sub-Committee on Religion of 1625 said that pluralities and *commendams* were great hindrances to the instructing of the people in the true knowledge and service of God, and hinted that the number of non-resident chaplains was increasing, whilst the universities were full of grave and able ministers unfurnished of livings.[5]

The bishops' attitude was simple and unchanging. 'The best gifts deserve the best rewards', they said. To suggest that livings should not be combined when the total income would amount to over £40 was to 'deal covertly to pull away religion'. To limit the holding of prebends to two was very unreasonable, and would

---

[1] Usher seems to me to exaggerate the significance of this real point when he writes: 'Without pluralities the church could not have retained those learned and efficient men upon whom rested the whole weight of the ecclesiastical fabric' (*Reconstruction*, i. 220; cf. p. 239).

[2] Strype, *Whitgift*, i. 380–1; cf. Cardwell, *Synodalia*, pp. 573–4.

[3] Strype, *Whitgift*, i. 384; Neal, op. cit. i. 296.   [4] Pierce, op. cit., pp. 106–8.

[5] [Ed. Birch], *The Court and Times of Charles I* (1848), i. 39 (the Rev. Joseph Mead Sir Martin Stuteville, 2 July 1625); Gardiner, *1625 Debates*, p. 21.

'discourage men from the ministry and make a beggarly clergy'. 'For most of these dignities are decayed within these last 50 years very much', owing to heavy taxation and the rise in prices.[1] The argument was repeated almost word for word by opponents of the bill against pluralism in the Commons in 1621. 'But it was answered that it would rather encourage men, because by this law every man might hope to obtain one' living.[2]

In 1610 Bancroft expressed to James I the *non-possumus* episcopal attitude in the words 'for the bill that is in hand against pluralities, it is the same that, for above 40 years, from parliament to parliament, hath been rejected; and that very worthily'.[3] Later in the same year Bancroft caused inquiries to be made into pluralism, but this seems to have been mainly window-dressing, demonstrating the activity of the bishops, 'to the end that notice thereof may be had throughout your diocese before the next session of parliament'.[4] Since Bancroft had held some eight rectories and prebends as Bishop of London, and resigned them only upon becoming Archbishop,[5] his defence of pluralism and non-residence was natural enough: but the argument that poverty of benefices and the need to provide preachers made pluralism a necessary evil hardly carried conviction in his mouth. William Browne spoke for many when, anticipating Milton, he wrote of

> The prelate in pluralities asleep,
> Whilst that the wolf lies preying on his sheep.[6]

Almost every Elizabethan bishop held several livings *in commendam*: Hughes of St. Asaph had sixteen, and from his time the Archdeaconry of St. Asaph was regularly held by the bishop. In 1576 the Bishop of Carlisle held *in commendam* a rectory worth £120–140 per annum, paying the vicar £14. 13s. 4d.[7] Grindal and Bacon queried the practice,[8] but *commendams* survived them. They were attacked by the Millenary Petition and in the Parliament of

---

[1] Cardwell, *Documentary Annals*, i. 431–5.
[2] Notestein, Relf, and Simpson, op. cit. iv. 342–3.
[3] Quoted by Lord Nugent, *Memorials of John Hampden* (1899), p. 175.
[4] Cardwell, *Documentary Annals*, ii. 120–2 (the Archbishop of Canterbury to the bishops).
[5] Pierce, op. cit., pp. 106–8; Usher, *Reconstruction*, i. 28, 34, 114. Cf. the bishops' remarks on the necessity of plural holding of prebends, quoted on p. 228 above.
[6] W. Browne, *Poems* (Muses Library, n.d.), i. 220.
[7] Strype, *Annals*, ii, part ii. 56; Ecton, op. cit., p. 341; Pierce, op. cit., p. 100.
[8] Pierce, op. cit., p. 59; Bacon, *Works*, x. 125; cf. xii. 352.

1614. Episcopal pluralism became a first-class political issue when Sir Edward Coke was dismissed from the bench for refusing to obey the king's order to suspend judgment against the Bishop of Lichfield and Coventry, who held (by royal authority) a living *in commendam*. As Whitgift had foreseen, the royal prerogative was involved. But even without the publicity of this case, men would have noticed that Williams, when Bishop of Lincoln and Lord Keeper, also held the Deanery of Westminster, three rectories, three prebends, as well as a Chanter's and a Residentiary's place at Lincoln. They did not, he pleaded, bring in more than £1,000 a year clear; and they did not stop him putting forward a scheme for the drastic reduction of pluralism, so that only very learned men should obtain dispensations.[1]

In a great potentate like Williams, or a careerist civil servant like Bancroft, such behaviour is hardly surprising. But when John Bridgman became Bishop of Chester, he took care to retain the living of Wigan, which was one of the richest in the country:[2] and even a relatively virtuous prelate like the Calvinist Joseph Hall of Exeter and Norwich was a rector, a prebendary, an archdeacon, and a dean as well as a bishop.[3] On the opposite theological wing, Montagu combined the Bishopric of Chichester with the rectory of Petworth, which at £600–650 a year was comparable with Wigan. Brian Duppa, who succeeded Montagu at Chichester and Petworth, had previously held three vicarages whilst Dean of Christ Church, and was prebendary of Salisbury and Chancellor of the diocese as well. Manwaring held Stanford Rivers in Essex (estimated by Walker to be worth £200 per annum) *in commendam* with St. David's, and two more rectories were added in 1637. He had previously held Stanford Rivers in plurality with St. Giles in the Fields, Muckleston, Staffordshire (another rich living), and Mugginton, Derbyshire; and was Dean of Worcester. Goodman of Gloucester held a prebend and at least two rectories *in commendam*.[4] Even Laud clung on to his benefices in the country

---

[1] *Cabala* (1654), i. 55, 85; Hacket, op. cit. i. 123. Williams devised this scheme during Prince Charles's absence in Madrid, as one of a series of contrivances to sweeten the Spanish marriage in public opinion.

[2] McClure, op. cit. i. 161–3; *C.S.P.D., 1638–9*, p. 523; Bridgeman, op. cit., *passim*.   [3] Kinloch, op. cit., pp. 25–26.

[4] Knowler, op. cit. i. 462, 507; ii. 152; Walker, op. cit. ii. 88; ed. Sir G. Isham, *The Correspondence of Bishop Brian Duppa and Sir Justinian Isham, 1650–1660* (Northamptonshire Record Soc., 1955), pp. xxi–xxii; *D.N.B.*, s.v. Manwaring; Soden, op. cit., pp. 141, 116, 290, 310. Cf. pp. 308–10, 316–17 below.

and his prebend at Westminster on becoming Bishop of St. David's. Both he and Manwaring must have encountered certain geographical difficulties in performing their various pastoral functions.

Laud's explanation is perhaps to be found in a letter of 1637 to Bishop Bedell, who was trying to get rid of pluralism in his Irish diocese: 'I wish as heartily as you that there were a dissolving of pluralities, especially in bishoprics. But, as the times are, this cannot well be thought on, till the means of the church there be so settled as that men may be able to live in some sort answerable to the dignity of their calling. For poverty draws on contempt; and contempt makes clergymen unserviceable to God, the church and the commonwealth.'[1] The words were applicable to England as well as to Ireland. It was for similar reasons, 'as the times now go', that Laud in 1635 opposed another project by Williams that one-fortieth of the revenues of non-residents should be allotted to the poor.[2]

The hierarchy could not seriously oppose pluralism. For as Ames put it: 'Pluralism, non-residence . . . are practised in the bishops' palaces; and not only the Court of Faculties but most bishops do gain by them.' Everybody deplored pluralism in words (and especially, like Williams, when out of office). But, said Ames, if the bishops really wanted reform, they would have begun with themselves, or would 'have harkened unto parliament-remedies of wise and careful physicians, which have been often prescribed, prepared, tendered and almost applied'.[3] Compared with the solutions proposed by Parliament before 1640, and actually carried out during the revolutionary period, the hierarchy never began to tackle the problem.

The government did as little about it as the bishops. James I detested pluralism, he assured Parliament in 1610: 'Yet it cannot be expected at our hands that we should in this, more than in any other cases, abridge any of our loving subjects of that which they have in express words granted unto them by the laws of this our realm.' Even if vested property interests could be disregarded, he added, it would not be convenient to abolish pluralism until livings had been augmented.[4] From that circle there appeared to be no escape. Preaching against non-residence was a sure way to

[1] Laud, *Works*, vii. 374–5.					[2] Ibid. vi. 427, 431.
[3] Ames, op. cit., p. 416.					[4] *Lords' Journals*, ii. 658.

lose favour at court, however orthodox the theology of the preacher.[1]

Laud's phrases, 'as the times are', 'as the times now go', show the helplessness of conservatives in face of developments which they disliked but could not control. 'As the times were', pluralism could be abolished only by a complete economic reorganization; and the forces were so nicely balanced that this was impossible until the fundamental issues of power in the state had been settled. Then 'parliament-remedies' could be applied without opposition.

The evidence for non-residence accumulates in the last decade of the old régime. At Bradford, a place of 10,000 inhabitants, Lord Keeper Finch presented a vicar who only visited his cure once. When the inhabitants tried to appoint a schoolmaster to do some of his work, they were overruled by the Archbishop of York.[2] Parishioners of Nerquis and Treythin complained to the Bishop of St. Asaph in 1632 that they had had no regular services for years: things were in the same state eight years later.[3] The inhabitants of three Oxfordshire villages petitioned in 1641 against their pluralist and non-resident vicar, who paid his curates inadequately and got rid of a preaching minister whom the parishioners were prepared to maintain.[4] Curates, said a pamphlet of the same year, 'are worse dealt with by the rich double-beneficed men than the children of Israel by the Egyptians'.[5]

The system was ceasing to work satisfactorily. Congregations could not get what they wanted even by paying for it. Henry Ainsworth was not the only separatist to draw the conclusion that there was no remedy to be found within the established church for 'the many souls ... miserably famished by dumb, negligent and non-resident priests, evil beasts and slow bellies'.[6]

The traditional system of appropriation inherited from the Middle Ages was breaking down. A total financial reorganization lay far ahead; pluralism and non-residence were the pitiful hand-to-mouth compromise evolved by greedy men for their own ends, and supported by frightened conservative ·ecclesiastics in order to maintain what they believed to be the dignity of the church.

---

[1] *C.S.P.D., 1625–49*, p. 71.
[2] *Hist. MSS. Commission, Fourth Report, Appendix*, p. 46.
[3] Ibid., *Sixth Report, Appendix*, p. 424.
[4] Ibid., *Fourth Report, Appendix*, p. 97. Cf. p. 227 above.
[5] *The Curates' Conference*, p. 496.
[6] H. Ainsworth, *Counterpoyson* (1608), pp. 183–5.

IV

The economic changes of the century before 1640, then, worked in many ways to produce divisions within the ranks of the clergy:

1. Divisions in the landed class itself were reflected through landlords' rights of presentation, and the influence of patrons and impropriators on their vicars and curates—of the squire on the parson.

2. The rise in prices caused a sharp differentiation between (say) rectors in corn-growing areas, who were able to collect their tithes in kind and might be relatively prosperous; and vicars in sheep-farming areas, whose tithes had been partially commuted and who might be badly off. All clerics in towns were liable to find themselves in difficulties. Marriage aggravated their problems.

3. Poverty, among other things, led to pluralism, and pluralism stimulated jealousies among ministers. Those who were not lucky enough, or well enough connected, to obtain more than one living, might sympathize with Puritan denunciations of pluralism and non-residence for interested as well as disinterested motives.

4. In the first half of Elizabeth's reign there had been a shortage of ministers, especially of 'learned' ministers; in the seventeenth century, with Oxford and Cambridge fuller in relation to the population of the country than they were to be for 250 years, and concentrating on the production of clerics, the danger was much rather of clerical unemployment. 'Some bishops of the poorer sees', wrote Heylyn, 'for their private benefit, admitted many men promiscuously to Holy Orders.' These indigent clerks, Heylyn continued, became either chaplains or schoolmasters in gentlemen's houses, or stipendiary lecturers.[1]

Heylyn's remark is significant in many respects, coming as it does from a staunch defender of episcopacy. He admits the existence of a poorer clergy of dubious qualifications; there is a causal association in Heylyn's mind between poverty and chaplaincies and lectureships; and he admits that there is episcopal corruption. Pluralism reduced the number of jobs: that was an inducement for a young graduate to turn Puritan, when a lectureship might be found for him, or a post in the household of an opposition magnate; but then his Puritan connexions would debar him from any living except one in the presentation of a

[1] Heylyn, *Cyprianus Anglicus*, p. 253.

member of the opposition: and so the clergy were lined up into two camps. In 1633 Laud procured an order from the king that no bishop was to ordain a minister until he had a title.[1]

5. The over-production of graduates itself has economic causes, if we press back far enough. For it sprang from that endowment of grammar schools and colleges by merchants which is such a feature of the century and a half before the revolution. As they prospered they put their money into education, an educational system already partially wrested from the dead hand of the church. They hoped to create a society in which careers would be open to the talents: in particular they wished a preaching ministry to carry the gospel into all corners of the kingdom, to the greater glory of God and the greater security of protestantism. But when these eager, learned, able, poor, and ambitious young men came on to the market, what did they find? Vicarages of £5 and upwards a year; pluralism by the richer clergy; critics of this régime silenced; dumb dogs not purged. A state is speedily brought to necessity, Bacon was noting in his *Essay of Seditions and Troubles*, 'when more are bred scholars than preferments can take off'.[2] 'Preferments' under Bancroft and Laud did not 'take off' as many scholars as a different ecclesiastical policy might have done. At the same time, a growing opposition group of gentry and citizens was offering alternative employment to young men prepared to live by their talents, whether in cures in their presentation, the income augmented where necessary; or in domestic chaplaincies; or in lectureships in market towns, the best-paid of all, the most influential, and those least controlled by bishops. John Preston, Professor Haller reminds us, preferred a popular lectureship at Cambridge to a bishopric.[3]

Here again we note the contradictions in the situation. The way in which they were financed bound most of the clergy to the old landed order: yet the economic attitudes and social connexions of the bishops lost them the sympathy even of those landlords who were to fight for Charles I in the civil war. The root cause of the poverty of parsons was lay impropriation: yet a group of impropriators became the patrons of a clerical party which attacked those

[1] *C.S.P.D., 1633-4*, p. 212.

[2] Bacon, *Works*, vi. 410.

[3] Haller, op. cit., pp. 40, 73-74. The ease with which a clerical proletariat lends itself to faction was noted by Roger Coke, *A Detection of the Court and State of England* (1694), i. 348-9; ii. 127-8.

bishops who were trying (so far as was possible without fundamental reorganization) to improve the economic situation of the
parochial clergy. Meanwhile the bishops themselves could not
preserve a solid front in support of the lesser clergy against those
gentlemen who were busily screwing the last penny out of their
church. For many of them, ties with local landowners were far
stronger than professional loyalty to Canterbury.

There was no future for the church unless its revenues could be
reorganized: and propertied laymen already had sufficient control
of the church *from within*, as well as sufficient political power, to
prevent that reorganization being carried out by Laudian ecclesiastics in a conservative, backward-looking manner. More accurately, they could prevent it so long as the government could not
dispense with parliaments altogether, and could not reduce the
common-law judges to acceptance of its policies: we always come
back to that fundamental issue of political power. But Laud's
power in the sixteen-thirties was illusory, because insecurely
based; and its overthrow was absolute. Even the restoration of the
church in 1660 saw the tacit abandonment of every attempt to
resume church property secularized at the Reformation, or to
increase tithe payments; friction between parson and squire was
ended by the complete subordination of the former to the latter.

V

What solutions were possible, short of wholesale reorganization?
Laud won one victory. 21 Hen. VIII, c. 13, allowed livings worth
less than £8 a year to be held in plurality without licence. By what
Bacon called an innovation introduced into the laws and government, common-law juries decided at the end of Elizabeth's reign that
the £8 referred to the true value of the benefices. This, said Bacon,
frustrated the intention of the statute, 'for there is no benefice of
so small an improved value as £8 by that kind of rating'.[1] But it
was not until Laud's ascendancy that the judges, in Drake *v.* Hill
(8 Car. I) ruled that the £8 meant value as shown in the King's
Book, and not true value. In 1637 they declared that this interpretation of the statute was established, 'although', they added

---

[1] Bacon, *Works*, xiii. 93; Gibson, op. cit., p. 945; Hughes, op. cit. (1st ed.) i.
98–102.

significantly, 'diversity of opinions have been therein before'.[1] Clearly Laud's domination had led to the victory of the clerical 'opinion', even in the common-law courts.

That was a valuable gain. Pluralism was extended, free of charge, beyond the very poorest of the clergy. But how inadequate to the problems involved; and how ignoble this encouragement of pluralism must have seemed to those who envisaged a preaching minister in every parish! Laud's victories were more fatal to him than his defeats.

The hierarchy, then, in this as in other spheres, could only patch up: it could not reorganize. It was only with the Long Parliament's Scandalous Ministers' Committee and Preaching Ministers' Committee that a beginning was made with the collection of factual information on pluralism, absenteeism, inadequate livings, and non-resident clergy *as interrelated problems*. And all pluralism was summarily forbidden. A ballad of 1641 shows contemporary realization that this measure would help poorer ministers and penalize especially the university and court clergy:

> At great preferment I aimed,
>   Witness my silk;
> But now my hopes are maimed.
>   I looked lately
>   To have lived stately,
> And a dairy of bell-ropes milked:
>   But now, alas! myself I must not flatter;
>   Bigamy of steeples is a hanging matter;
>   Each must have one, and curates will grow fatter.
>   Alas, poor scholar!
>   Whither wilt thou go?[2]

---

[1] Sir George Crooke, *Reports* (1683), iii. 456; Stillingfleet, op. cit. i. 99–100. This decision, unlike many of those made by the judges of the period of Laudian influence, remained valid after 1660.

[2] Quoted in the *Diary of John Rous* (ed. M. A. E. Green, Camden Soc., 1856), p. 116. See p. 227 above for evidence of the effectiveness of this Parliament's measures against pluralism.

PART III

The Church Triumphant

We begin to live here in the Church Triumphant.

JAMES HOWELL to Lord Deputy Wentworth,
16 March 1635 (Knowler, op. cit. i. 522)

XI

THE FEOFFEES FOR IMPROPRIATIONS

If it were possible, it were to be wished that there were set up some lights in all the dark corners of this kingdom, that might shine to those people that sit in darkness and in the shadow of death. One way is, *To have a competent maintenance*: to devise it for the poor ministry, that they might live by the gospel that preach the gospel: so by this means there might be a church world without end.

R. SIBBES, *Experience Triumphing, or the Saints Safetie*, a sermon in *The Saints Cordials* (1629), p. 83

I

THE economic problems which we have outlined seemed to call for a national policy of augmenting small stipends. The opportunity of using impropriations for this purpose was lost at the Reformation. Cranmer similarly failed under Edward VI to prevent chantries being sold to private individuals; he had hoped, if they could have been preserved till the pious king came of age, to use them as a fund for augmentation. The Catholic Mary handed over all tenths, impropriations, and other spiritual rents and pensions due to the crown, to build up a fund for the augmentation of small livings and better maintenance of the clergy. But in 1559 the first bill proffered in the House of Lords was one for restoring these dues to the crown to help to meet its 'huge, innumerable and inestimable charges'.[1] The Convocation of 1563 proposed that an act of Parliament should be passed to raise every living to £20; but apart from suggesting that the money necessary should be assessed where it might most conveniently be laid, Convocation was prudently inexplicit on the question of ways and means.[2] A government bill in the Parliament of the same year proposed to lay the charge upon impropriators, or in non-impropriate parishes to levy a tax upon householders. Rather naturally it failed to pass

[1] Burnet, op. cit. iii. 60; Strype, *Annals*, I, part i. 53, 83.
[2] Strype, *Annals*, I, part i. 514.

in the Commons, as did another bill of the same sort in 1581.[1] The tug-of-war between gentry and parsons had begun.

But the economic problem remained. By 1604 the increase of ecclesiastical incomes had become, in Mr. Usher's view, 'the main question of reform'.[2] But how? Bacon made a shrewd point when in 1603 he wrote: 'We must take heed that we desire not contraries; for to desire that every parish should be furnished with a sufficient preacher, and to desire that pluralities be forthwith taken away, is to desire things contrary, considering *de facto* there are not sufficient preachers for every parish; whereto add likewise that there is not sufficient living and maintenance in many parishes to maintain a preacher, and it makes the impossibility yet much the greater.'[3]

The only resolution of this contradiction, the Puritan and parliamentary opposition thought, was by means of a drastic reorganization. But at whose expense? Could full tithes be restored? If not, the operation must be financed from some other source. What source? Here views differed again. Some wanted to see impropriated tithes restored to the church and to charitable purposes; others wished the whole expense of reorganization to be borne by the bishops and cathedral clergy. This was substantially a division between the clerical and landlord wings of the opposition: and it was the steady policy of the bishops and their allies to drive wedges in at this weak spot.[4] The effect of the Puritan policy, declared a tract attributed to Bancroft, would be that 'noblemen and gentlemen must surrender out of their hands their impropriations and such their possessions as did heretofore belong to the abbeys; cathedral churches must be overthrown: bishops' livings are to be altered: and all must be conferred to the supply of such wants as might hinder the dignity of their worshipful senate in any place'.[5]

One extreme of policy was that laid before the House of Lords by Bancroft in 1610. It proposed that all predial tithes should be paid in kind; that the oath should be restored in suits about personal tithes; that mortuaries should be restored, and that

[1] Read, *Mr. Secretary Cecil and Queen Elizabeth*, p. 271.
[2] Usher, *Reconstruction*, i. 229.
[3] Bacon, *Works*, x. 124.
[4] Usher, *Reconstruction*, i. 53, 339–42, 349–53; ii. 54–55, 123, 246–8, 255–7.
[5] *Tracts Ascribed to Richard Bancroft*, p. 59. 'Their worshipful senate' is a presbyterian consistory.

oblations should be paid as of old at marriages, burials, feast days, and communion. Exemptions from tithe should be abolished for former monastic lands, for all lands withdrawn from tillage in the preceding sixty years, whether they were pasture or park land; and for lands recovered from sea or fens. Occupiers of lands in depopulated parishes should pay tithe to the nearest poor parson. Small benefices should be united; and all benefices should be discharged of pensions to laymen. Glebe lands should be restored, and never henceforth leased to patrons or lords of manors. Curates in chapels of ease should be maintained at the expense of their congregations, not of the parson or vicar.

Lay patrons should be made to take an oath against simony as well as ministers, and should forfeit their patronage rights if convicted of simony. It should be declared simony to sell an advowson as well as a particular presentation. Tithe should be paid in kind on new or disputed crops and commodities, such as woad, hops, roots, coals and other minerals, lime-kilns, brick-kilns. Ministers should be allowed to lease lands. A fund should be raised, by parliamentary taxation, for buying in impropriations; and when bought they should be in the gift of the bishops. Alternatively, impropriations with no endowed vicarage should be declared void; and bishops should be authorized to augment the maintenance of vicars at the expense of the impropriators or lessees. Chancels in impropriate churches, everywhere in decay, should be repaired. It was also proposed at the same time that all commutations affecting garden produce, fruit, vegetables, &c., should be abolished; and that tithe should be paid in kind on wood, milk, and other commodities in dispute.[1]

This vast programme was aimed at giving ministers something like an equitable tenth of the total produce of the country, and at recovering impropriations. If it could have been carried out it would have solved the economic problems of the church. It would have made possible the payment of stipends which would attract and maintain an adequate ministry in all parishes. But the policy was far too radical in its attack on vested interests ever to be carried out as a whole: and it is not even certain that the hierarchy and the government had no reserves in their enthusiasm for establishing learned and possibly independent-minded ministers in all parishes.

[1] Collier, op. cit. vii. 352–8.

The other logical extreme of policy was equally impossible of realization without a social upheaval. This was to abolish bishops, deans, and chapters, and use their revenues to finance a preaching ministry, the establishment of schools, and poor relief. These proposals, made in the first *Admonition* of 1572, continued to be advanced regularly until the Long Parliament began to put them into operation. It was an attractive programme. Bishop Cooper found it worth discussing seriously, 'such common obloquies is in all men's mouths' against the bishops. But both he and Bancroft regarded, or pretended to regard, the criticisms and proposals merely as a smoke-screen behind which land-grabbers hoped to advance on the property of the church.[1]

There were, no doubt, many who were more interested in acquiring church lands for themselves (or for the government in order to reduce taxation) than for the advancement of piety and learning. Whitgift in 1585 refused to commit himself to support for the revolutionary Netherlands because 'some of calling have openly given it out that these wars must be maintained by the dissolution of cathedral churches, which God forbid'.[2] That suggests a connexion between ecclesiastical and foreign politics which is worth pondering.

Bancroft declared flatly that 'the hope which many men have conceived of the spoil of bishops' livings, of the subversion of cathedral churches, and of a havoc to be made of all the church's revenues, is the chiefest and most principal cause of the greatest schisms that we have at this day in our church'.[3] It was a palpable hit. Such 'havoc' was, naturally, opposed by the hierarchy in the seventeenth century, and by the government, which believed the maintenance of the church as established to be necessary to its own secure existence.

Behind the proposal for the abolition of bishops lurked even more radical projects for the abandonment of the appropriation of lands to maintain the church, and its replacement by a principle better suited to a society that was coming to be based on wage-labour—by payment of salaries. Martin Marprelate argued that 'no prince or magistrate by God's word may lawfully assign lands to the ministers of the church to live on, but ought to set them to pensions'. Bishop Cooper was profoundly shocked. 'Almost a

---

[1] Neal, op. cit. i. 312; Cooper, op. cit., p. 117.
[2] Strype, *Whitgift*, i. 436.   [3] Bancroft, *A Sermon*, pp. 23–24.

flat heresy,' he called it, 'as dangerous as many branches of the Anabaptists' errors.'[1] Dangerous it was, heretical it might be: but it was difficult to counter by rational argument.

Between these two logical extremes, then, of an upgrading of tithes and a resumption of secularized church lands, or of the confiscation of the property of the hierarchy, compromise solutions were being sought in the decades before 1640.

The debate, we must recall, was not carried on in a vacuum. Stipends had replaced tithes in some continental protestant countries. In Scotland the *First Book of Discipline* had required the restoration of impropriations to the parishes. The Revolt of the Netherlands had been financed, in part, by the sale of church lands, and 'confiscated church livings', it was noted, remained an important part of 'the revenue of this state'.[2] The French Huguenots also sold church property, partly to finance military expenditure; but some of the proceeds were distributed among the poor. This part of the operation helped to alienate some of the nobility: it was recorded by Davila in his *History*, Mr. Hampden's *Vade Mecum*.[3]

The strength of the opponents of the English hierarchy was that they were prepared to accept piecemeal reforms, anything that would weaken the position of the bishops even if it fell short of what the reformers thought ideally desirable. The bishops, on the other hand, were forced into a merely negative, *non-possumus* attitude. A few benefices were united here and there, for instance, by Montagu in his diocese of Norwich; or pluralists were shifted so that their livings were within easy reach of one another. Whitgift, when leasing impropriations, sometimes reduced the fine in order to add £10 or so to the curate's wage where it was very small.[4] But bishops and ecclesiastical corporations did little to divest themselves of their impropriations, as we have seen. A bishop like Robert Abbott of Salisbury could bully his Dean and Chapter into disgorging £500 for the repair of the fabric of the cathedral, after their covetousness had 'filled their purses with that which should have stopped the chinks in the walls'.[5] But he

---

[1] Cooper, op. cit., p. 122.

[2] Overbury, 'Observations upon the state of the XVII Provinces' (1626), in *Miscellaneous Works*, p. 227.

[3] H. C. D'Avila, *The History of the Civil Wars of France* (1678), p. 137.

[4] *V.C.H., Suffolk*, ii. 46; Paule, op. cit., p. 38.

[5] Fuller, *Abel Redivivus*, p. 549.

was so notorious a Puritan that there had been great opposition to his being made a bishop at all, even though he was elder brother to the Archbishop of Canterbury. A virtuous character like Dr. Willet might persuade the Dean and Chapter of Ely to augment the stipends of three vicars of impropriate parishes; but his biographer's enthusiasm suggests that this was a rare achievement.[1] And such tinkering was all that could be done.

By contrast the Puritan and parliamentarian schemes were possible of achievement. A studiously moderate Puritan petition to the Parliament of 1584, with a view to establishing a preaching ministry, asked for:

1. 10 per cent. of the revenues of cathedrals, bishops, and other churchmen with great revenues, to be devoted to scholarships for the universities;

2. the wages of choristers and musicians in cathedral and collegiate churches to be diverted to augment the stipends of resident ministers;

3. the prebends of cathedrals to be reserved for preaching ministers.

If these measures proved insufficient,

4. bishops should pay stipends to preaching ministers from their own revenues;

5. impropriations should be used;

6. last of all, a tax should be levied in the parishes if otherwise sufficient stipends could not be raised.[2]

The Millenary Petition of 1604 put forward similarly moderate-seeming and practicable proposals: (1) Impropriated tithes annexed to bishoprics and colleges were to be demised only to resident preaching ministers, and at the old rent. (2) Lay impropriations were to be taxed one-sixth or one-seventh part of their *value*, the proceeds to maintain a preaching minister.[3] The preparatory instructions for the Puritan spokesmen at the Hampton Court Conference told them to endeavour to obtain a competent maintenance for ministers by the union of small parishes, by getting rid of unreasonable tithing customs, or by help from

---

[1] Peter Smith, 'Life and Death of . . . Dr. Andrew Willet', prefixed to Willet's *Synopsis Papismi* (1634), sig. B4ᵛ. Various augmentations by bishops, from Hooper of Gloucester onwards, are recorded in Kennett's annotated copy of *The Case of Impropriations*, pp. 136–7, 156 sq. See also Ducarel, op. cit., p. 4.

[2] Strype, *Annals*, III, part ii. 279–81.

[3] Fuller, *Church History*, iii. 195. Cf. p. 147 above.

impropriations: either by causing rectories held by colleges, bishoprics, and cathedral churches to be leased only to the preaching minister serving the cure, or by some other convenient way.[1]

In 1604 the Commons asked for augmentations to all livings worth less than £20 per annum.[2] In 1614 and 1621 bills were introduced into the lower house to enable the bishop and the judges of assize 'to rate a reasonable living to a preaching minister' out of impropriations.[3] Another bill providing for the leasing of the impropriations of bishops, cathedrals, and colleges to vicars, at a favourable rent, was rejected: one argument against it was that it would 'take away the livings' of the present farmers.[4] The Puritan Earl of Huntingdon wanted to have augmentations discussed in the Parliament of 1624.[5] In the following year the Commons' Sub-Committee on Religion proposed a comprehensive scheme for augmenting ministers' revenues from impropriations, which they wished to have discussed with the Lords; but the House did not accept this part of their report. In the debates £50 was mentioned as a desirable minimum stipend, to be raised in part by a parochial rate, since the whole charge should not be laid upon impropriations; and there should be no meddling with *modi decimandi*.[6] Sir Benjamin Rudyerd pressed for the use of impropriations to augment the livings of poor vicars in the Parliaments of 1626 and 1628, drawing the House's attention on the latter occasion to the generosity of James I in causing churches to be planted all through Scotland with £30 per annum. In 1628 the bill 'for the better maintenance of the ministry' was 'stayed' in the Commons, on the odd ground that it was 'against the church'.[7]

It is worth emphasizing two points about these proposals. First, the steady recurrence of certain fundamental demands, in particular the suggested use of the lands of the hierarchy to finance

[1] *Montague MSS.* (Hist. MSS. Commission), pp. 32–33. The suggestion that small parishes should be united and redivided had been made in the Convocation of 1555 (Cardwell, *Synodalia*, p. 447). It was not to be acted on seriously until after 1640.

[2] Gardiner, *History*, i. 179.

[3] Notestein, Relf, and Simpson, op. cit. vii. 640; ii. 301. See below, p. 321.

[4] Ibid. ii. 330; iii. 105; iv. 271; vii. 243–4.

[5] Ed. Lady De Villiers, *The Hastings Journal of the Parliament of 1621, Camden Miscellany*, xx. 36.

[6] Gardiner, *1625 Debates*, pp. 21–22, 26–27. The last two pages seem to contain the Diarist's summary of the debate.

[7] Manning, op. cit., pp. 104–5; *C.S.P.D., 1628–9*, p. 164.

a preaching ministry. The Long Parliament was realizing the hopes of two generations of reformers when it introduced its drastic solutions. Secondly, the moderation and practicability of the specific proposals laid before Parliament and king. The hierarchy was not called upon to make all the sacrifices: impropriators and parishioners were, if necessary, to make their contributions. If the establishment of a preaching ministry had been all that was at stake, then compromise should have been easy. But the bishops, probably rightly, saw the proposals as the thin end of a very large wedge. So they set 'the ministry', whose maintenance was to be augmented, against 'the church', from which the maintenance was to be extracted; and so 'the church' came to signify 'bishops' impropriations' rather than 'a preaching ministry'. The import of this would hardly be lost on would-be reformers.

The reforming proposals were, indeed, usually associated with schemes for equal remuneration of ministers and for a consistorial system which would have deprived the hierarchy of its independent control of the church (under the crown) and instituted some degree of lay control on the Scottish model. Hence, however modest the economic proposals, disciplinary aspirations were believed to lurk behind them which would have involved a transfer of power. Control of the church through lay participation in consistories, or through the subordination of the hierarchy to the sovereignty of Parliament, were two alternative paths to the same goal.[1]

II

There is the less need to deal in detail with the major attempt of our period to restore impropriations to the church, since the activities of the Feoffees for Impropriations have been fully discussed in a recent article by Miss Calder.[2] But a few points may be made in relation to our theme.

The Feoffees made the greatest single attempt to put into practice the Puritan alternative solution for the economic problems of the church and the provision of a well-paid preaching clergy.

[1] Strype, *Annals*, III, part ii. 279–93.
[2] Isabel M. Calder, 'A 17th Century attempt to purify the Anglican Church', in *American Historical Review*, liii, no. 4. Cf. also H. A. Parker, 'The Feoffees of Impropriations', *Transactions of the Colonial Soc. of Massachusetts*, xi, and E. W. Kirby, 'The Lay Feoffees', *Journal of Modern History*, xiv, no. 1.

But it proved impossible to do even so much as that without being involved in what the government, not altogether unreasonably, regarded as a conspiracy against the established order. So what began as an example of reform without tarrying for the magistrate, by private enterprise, ended in frustration at the hands of the government, in serious financial losses affecting many prominent London citizens; and must have forced many men to conclude that the way of peaceful reform without a change of government was barred to them. The Feoffees began to work on a programme inherited from fifty years of Puritan activity: they ended by training some of the men of 1640–9.

The establishment of a fund for the purchase of impropriations had been suggested by Stoughton in 1604,[1] and by Bancroft in 1610. About 1620 a scheme was mooted for buying them in, at eight to ten years' purchase, by means of taxes and subsidies.[2] In 1621 Richard Montagu had heard that men were beginning to bequeath money to buy in impropriations and restore them to the church: a scheme of which he approved.[3] Attorney-General Noy dated the existence of the Feoffees for Impropriations as a society from the tenth year of King James—i.e. 1612–13.[4] It may be that they had begun to function informally before 1625–6,[5] when we first have evidence of their activities.

That date is not without its significance. Heylyn noted that the project began 'when Preston governed the affairs of the Puritan faction'.[6] The brief honeymoon between Buckingham and the parliamentary opposition was over: the Duke no longer discussed with Preston the use of dean and chapter lands to maintain a preaching ministry. Yet men's minds were full of the problem. In 1624 Henry Burton had supplicated Parliament to pass an act for the allotment of a certain portion of all impropriations to the maintenance of a minister, especially where there were unendowed or poorly endowed vicarages.[7] But the Parliament of 1625 failed to work out an acceptable scheme for augmenting the livings of poorer ministers.[8] It was clear that there was no hope of getting the desired changes from on top by legislative action.

---

[1] W. Stoughton, op. cit., pp. 148–60.
[2] *Rutland MSS.*, *Belvoir* (Hist. MSS. Commission), iv. 212–13.
[3] Montagu, op. cit., p. 94. [4] Rushworth, op. cit. ii. 150.
[5] F. Rose-Troup, *John White, the Patriarch of Dorchester* (1930), p. 247.
[6] *Cyprianus Anglicus*, p. 209. [7] H. Burton, op. cit., pp. 127–8.
[8] Gardiner, *1625 Debates*, pp. 21–27.

The Feoffees' project was to tackle the problem piecemeal, from below. Contributions were solicited to a fund from which impropriations were to be bought and used to augment the incomes of ministers. The twelve Feoffees were 'men of public callings . . . and men of noted zeal, in the opinion of the world (such as it was)': that is the testimony of an enemy. Many London preachers stirred up 'the rich and well-affected to contribute liberally to this so religious an act; . . . and amongst the last counsels given to the dying . . . this was never forgotten'.[1]

In fact £6,361. 6s. 1d. was contributed to the Feoffees between 1625 and 1633, in sums varying from 6s. to £500. £1,554. 13s. 4d. was raised to increase the stipends of lecturers at St. Antholin's, London, of whom more anon. The total collected, as Miss Calder remarks, compares very favourably with the stocks raised by the Providence Island Company.[2]

Real estate was bought by or bequeathed to the Feoffees in fourteen counties—mainly impropriations, but also leases of tithes and other properties. The Feoffees bought 'at or under 12 years' valuation'.[3] By 1633 the members of the group held 31 church properties and patronage in 18 counties. At least 18 vicars, curates, or lecturers had been installed in livings in 11 counties, including 6 or more lecturers in London. Hugh Peter, no doubt with some exaggeration, spoke later of 'forty or fifty preachers . . . maintained in the dark parts of this kingdom' by 'that famous, ancient, glorious work of buying in impropriations'.[4] Something like 10 per cent. of the total sum raised seems to have been used for the augmentation of livings (to the extent of £20–60 a year per recipient) or to establish lectures (at £20–30 per annum). The Feoffees appear also to have lent money, at the favourable rate of 5–6 per cent.[5]

Before considering the significance of these achievements, it is worth looking at the persons involved. One witness to the standing and reputation of the Feoffees has been quoted. Peter Heylyn, who led the attack on the Feoffees, is another hostile but

---

[1] [Anon.], *A Letter from Mercurius Civicus to Mercurius Rusticus*, in *Somers Tracts* (2nd ed., 1809–15), iv. 583. This pamphlet has been attributed to Samuel Butler, apparently without authority.

[2] Calder, op. cit., pp. 763, 767.

[3] Fuller, *Church History*, iii. 362.

[4] H. Peter, *Gods Doings and Mans Duty* (1645), p. 43.

[5] Calder, op. cit., pp. 768, 763.

well-informed observer, since his uncle, Alderman Rowland Heylyn, was a Feoffee for six years. Heylyn tells us that the Feoffees were 'chief patrons of this growing faction' (i.e. of the Puritan-parliamentary opposition), and that they were appointed 'by a secret combination of the brotherhood, to advance their projects'. Amongst them 'there was not one man that wished well to the present government'.[1] From 1629 Laud had his eye on them.[2]

The original 12 Feoffees included 4 ministers, 4 lawyers, and 4 merchants. One of the ministers and one of the lawyers died and each was replaced by another of the same profession. In 1626 the Sheriff of London was added, and replaced on his death in 1633 by the then Lord Mayor of London. Of the 16 persons thus directly involved, 7 were adventurers in the Massachusetts Bay Company, and George Harwood was its Treasurer;[3] another of the Feoffees, Christopher Sherland, was an original member of the Providence Island Company. Gabriel Barbour, one of the largest contributors, was also a member of the Providence Island Company. Many of the Feoffees had also been associated with the Dorchester and New England Companies. Interlocking matrimonial alliances bound them to one another and to other opposition leaders.[4]

The ministers were a significant group. Richard Sibbes (died 1635), Preston's predecessor as lecturer at Trinity church, Cambridge, had been since 1617 the famous preacher at Gray's Inn, and was also Master of the Puritan St. Catherine's Hall, Cambridge. In his will he left a ring to his 'dear and worthy friend, Mr. John Pym'.[5] John Davenport was vicar of St. Stephen's, Coleman Street, the 'Faubourg St. Antoine' of the English Revolution. He himself, like a number of his parishioners, was a member

---

[1] J. Barnard, *Theologo-Historicus, . . . the Life of . . . Peter Heylyn* (1683), pp. 147–50; Heylyn, *Examen Historicum* (1659), pp. 208–9. Heylyn himself held, in plurality, more than one rich preferment (Walker, op. cit. ii. 90).

[2] Rushworth, op. cit. ii. 8.

[3] Harwood's brother, Sir Edward, was a member of the Virginia and Providence Island Companies, and a shareholder in the Somers Island Company, as well as being one of the four standing colonels of the English contingent in the Low Countries (A. P. Newton, *Colonizing Activities of the early Puritans*, 1914, pp. 69–70).

[4] Rose-Troup, op. cit., pp. 61–63, 111, 117; *The Massachusetts Bay Company and its Predecessors* (1930), pp. 131–62.

[5] Z. Catlin, 'Dr. Sibbs his Life' (1652), in *Antiquarian Communications presented at Meetings of the Cambridge Antiquarian Soc.* i (1859), 260.

of the Virginia and Massachusetts Bay companies. Though for security reasons Davenport's name did not appear in the Massachusetts Bay patent, he was very active in the Company's affairs. Davenport had been *elected* by his parishioners in 1624. For this reason, and because he 'was reported to be factious and popular', and 'to draw after him great congregations of common and mean people', his bishop reported him to Secretary Conway for the king's views. 1624, however, was the year of Preston's ascendancy over Buckingham: the Duke intervened to get Davenport's nomination confirmed.[1] After the expropriation of the Feoffees Davenport emigrated, first to the Netherlands, then to New England, where he was a figure of some significance.

Sibbes and Davenport were entrusted by Preston with the preparation for the press of his London sermons. The two of them, together with a third Feoffee, William Gouge, and Thomas Taylor, were reprimanded by the Star Chamber in 1627 for appending their names to a circular asking for contributions for persecuted protestants in the Upper Palatinate.[2] They were clearly in the habit of working together. Gouge was first lecturer and then rector of St. Anne's, Blackfriars. He was also *elected* minister, though originally introduced by 'some of the better sort of the inhabitants'. Citizens flocked from all parts to hear his sermons, together with many 'pious and judicious gentlemen of the Inns of Court', so that the church had to be enlarged. There was scarce a lord, lady, or citizen of quality in or about the City that was piously affected, his son assures us, but they sought his acquaintance.[3] Gouge replaced Richard Stock as Feoffee: Stock until his death in 1626 had for thirty-two years been rector of Milton's father's church, All Hallows, Bread Street.

Both the lawyers who survived until 1640 were M.P.s in the Long Parliament, and both were supporters of Pym. John White, the Winthrops' family lawyer, who perhaps drafted the Massachusetts Bay charter, represented the radical constituency of

[1] F. B. Dexter, 'Sketch of the life and writings of John Davenport', in *Papers of the New Haven Colony Historical Soc.* ii (1875), *passim*; Davenport, *Letters*, *passim*. See p. 296 below.

[2] Dexter, op. cit., p. 216; Prynne, *Canterburies Doome*, p. 362.

[3] S. Clarke, *A Collection of the Lives of Ten Eminent Divines* (1662), pp. 95–117, *passim*; Haller, op. cit., pp. 67–69. It is not without its significance for the social affiliations of the Feoffees that both Gouge and the last clerical Feoffee, Offspring, signed a Presbyterian petition deprecating the use of violence against Charles I just before his execution. By that date Sibbes was dead and Davenport in New England.

Southwark, and was an active Root and Branch Puritan;[1] Samuel Browne, whose mother was a St. John, thus making him a member of the Cromwell cousinry, sat for a group of Devon boroughs: he was later to be an Independent. Another lawyer, Sir Thomas Crew, had been Speaker of the Commons in 1623 and 1625, being chosen in the former year against the wishes of the government.[2] Among figures later politically prominent we may mention Hugh Peter, who collected money for the Feoffees until he had to leave England in 1629.[3] Bishop Goodman adds that William Prynne 'was a principal man' among those 'employed for the buying of impropriations'.[4]

The activities of the Feoffees took forms which their composition and backing might have led us to expect. They 'had sundry agents and messengers whom they employed about that business, and that both far and near'.[5] When they purchased an impropriation, they did not normally[6] restore the tithes to that parish: they used them to augment the stipend of a minister of whose opinions and preaching abilities they approved. There might happen to be such a minister in the parish to which the impropriated tithes belonged. If there was not, there were various means by which the incumbent might be got rid of. At Hertford and at Dunwich he was 'wearied' out. At Cirencester the vicar was offered the 'next Easter book and £30'.[7] Or he might be persuaded to accept a lecturer. If none of these expedients would serve, the tithe-revenue would be diverted to another parish. In one case where a lady gave £500, the Feoffees specifically inquired whether, if the lecturer was 'disturbed' by the incumbent of that parish, the allowance might

[1] J. H. Hexter, *The Reign of King Pym* (1941), pp. 79–82.

[2] Prynne, *Canterburies Doome*, p. 385; Parker, op. cit., p. 272; Roger Coke, op. cit. i. 166; Hacket, op. cit. i. 176; ii. 18.

[3] *Gods Doings*, p. 43. See *C.S.P.D., 1645–7*, pp. 587–8, for a letter (wrongly dated) from Peter to Vicars, which shows him deeply involved in the Feoffees' activities. There must be some mistake in the statement made by the editor of Lady Brilliana Harley's *Letters*, that Thomas Pierson, rector of Brampton Bryan, was one of the Feoffees. Pierson's friendship for Perkins, however, and his general outlook, renders it likely that he supported the scheme. (Ed. T. T. Lewis, *Letters of the Lady Brilliana Harley*, Camden Soc., 1854, pp. xv–xvii.)

[4] Goodman, *The Two Great Mysteries of Christian Religion*, sig. a3ᵛ.

[5] Clarke, *A Collection of the Lives*, p. 110. The Feoffees also acted in areas with which they were personally familiar—e.g. Rowland Heylyn was instrumental in getting an advowson in Shrewsbury, his birthplace (*C.S.P.D., 1634–5*, p. 377); John Geering operated in Gloucestershire (Heylyn, *Examen Historicum*, p. 210).

[6] Heylyn says never (*Cyprianus Anglicus*, pp. 210–12).

[7] Kirby, op. cit., p. 15.

be diverted to serve for the maintenance of like purposes else-where: and one suspects that this was a routine inquiry. The rather naïve reply received in this instance was that 'no doubt' they could procure a licence from the bishop, which the incumbent, being insufficient, could not gainsay.[1]

The purchased impropriations thus remained lay fees; though now they were in the hands of a powerful corporate body with vast patronage, which had a secure economic grip over its mini-sters. Pensions might be withdrawn, lectures removed, 'at the will and pleasure of the patrons if they grew slack and negligent in the holy cause: which fastened a dependence on them to the very last'. Thus, to quote what a pamphleteer assures us were 'Mr. Foxley's own words', they hoped to 'establish the Gospel by a perpetual decree'.[2]

The Feoffees were accused of preferring to appoint temporary curates and lecturers rather than vicars, for whom episcopal approval would have been necessary. But when Laud suggested this at his trial, the managers for the Commons replied: 'None were recommended to officiate or preach at any of the purchased impropriations but by special licence of the bishop in whose [diocese?] they were.'[3] Part of their funds, the Exchequer judg-ment against them declared, was given to schoolmasters; Laud added that they subsidized young university students so as to win them over to their side.[4]

They were further accused of using their funds to support silenced ministers. One of their nominees, Heylyn alleged, had been ejected from four lectureships by four different bishops, and finally suspended from the ministry by the High Commission.[5] The Feoffees even maintained the widows and children of the ejected, 'than which', Heylyn caustically commented, 'there could not be a greater tie to unite men to them, and make them sticklers in the cause'.[6] Less responsible contemporary propagandists asserted that the Feoffees tried to purchase the headship of a college in Oxford, 'for the first training up of their novices in their

---

[1] *C.S.P.D., 1645–7*, pp. 587–8.
[2] Heylyn, *Cyprianus Anglicus*, pp. 211–12; *A Letter from Mercurius Civicus to Mercurius Rusticus*, p. 584. For Foxley, see p. 260 below.
[3] Prynne, *Canterburies Doome*, pp. 538–9.
[4] Rushworth, op. cit. ii. 152; Laud, *Works*, iv. 304.
[5] Heylyn, *Examen Historicum*, pp. 210–11.
[6] Heylyn, *Cyprianus Anglicus*, p. 212.

mysteries'; and also to buy 'a commissary's place . . . so that even if honest churchwardens should present their ministers' the latter would be secure from ecclesiastical censures.[1] Bishop Goodman further alleged that the Feoffees' agents 'did tempt bishops with bribes, with no interest but to accuse them; and to me in particular they sent 20 angels, in the business of Cirencester'.[2] Goodman perhaps generalizes too easily from his own case: there were good reasons for thinking him the most bribable of all the bishops.

In William Strode's play, *The Floating Island* (1636), Melancholico, who may be intended for Henry Burton, says:

> The godly
> Are in distress; the wicked, that usurp
> The children's-right, do here grow fat and prosper. . . .
> Verily unless that conscientious lawyer,
> Good Memor, from rebought impropriations
> Had thus deducted and distributed
> The better part to us distressed brethren,
> Affliction some, and some devotion,
> Had brought us to despair.[3]

As has been seen, a special fund was formed for purchasing impropriations in order to raise the maintenance of six lecturers at St. Antholin's to £30 a year each; and an augmentation of £10 a year was given to the rector, Charles Offspring, himself one of the Feoffees.[4] St. Antholin's, formerly a Huguenot church in which the full Genevan discipline was exercised, stood at this time in a very special relationship to the City authorities; from 1622 the Chamber of London had been contributing £40 a year towards

[1] Christopher Dow, *Innovations unjustly charged upon the Present Church and State, Or an Answer to the Most Material Passages of a Libellous Pamphlet made by Mr. Hen. Burton and intituled 'An Apologie of an Appeale &c.'* (1637), p. 211; *A Letter from Mercurius Civicus*, p. 584; Sir William Dugdale, *A Short View of the Late Troubles in England* (1681), p. 37.

[2] Goodman, *The Two Great Mysteries*, sig. a3ᵛ. The Feoffees had purchased the impropriation of St. John the Baptist in Cirencester, in Goodman's diocese, and appointed Alexander Gregory as curate. But they had had some difficulty in getting rid of the previous incumbent (Calder, op. cit., pp. 764, 768; and see above, p. 257).

[3] Strode, op. cit., p. 198. Memor may be intended for Samuel Browne. Cf. Habington's reference to those who 'buy up for the silenc'd Levites all The rich impropriations' (Habington, *Poems*, p. 62).

[4] Calder, op. cit., p. 767. An impropriation was bought for this purpose at Presteign, in Radnorshire and Herefordshire (ibid., p. 766; Parker, op. cit., p. 270).

the maintenance of morning lectures there, a grant which was discontinued only in 1630, apparently because the right to nominate lecturers had passed to the Feoffees.[1]

It had been no part of the Feoffees' original scheme to establish lecturers in London, which was hardly one of the 'dark parts of this kingdom' in need of preachers. In fact St. Antholin's seems to have been used as a training ground for young ministers, who after winning their spurs there were sent out to livings augmented by the generosity of the Feoffees.[2] At All Hallows, Bread Street, formerly Stock's church, £20 per annum was also allocated to a lecturer who had been *chosen by the parishioners* in 1632. Since Davenport and Gouge had also been elected by their congregations, there can be no doubt that this was a matter of policy. The money subscribed in 1629 by 'persons unknown' to found a lectureship at St. Botolph's, Aldgate, may also have come from the Feoffees.[3]

Certainly the Feoffees tended to appoint men of radical religious views. Among their nominees was Zachary Simms, lecturer at St. Antholin's and then curate at Dunstable, who emigrated to New England after the Feoffees' suppression; Julius Herring, lecturer at Shrewsbury, went to Amsterdam; John Archer, lecturer at St. Antholin's and subsequently vicar at Hertford, was suspended in 1638 for being absent for over a year: presumably he too had emigrated.[4] Thomas Foxley, lecturer at St. Antholin's, clerk to the Feoffees and a defendant in the case brought against them, was imprisoned by the Privy Council in 1639 for seditious preaching. Laud had not forgotten him, and charged him with having tried 'to bring the bishops under the Feoffees' girdles'.[5]

[1] Heylyn, *History of the Presbyterians*, p. 250; *C.S.P.D., 1628–9*, p. 495; D. A. Williams, op. cit., pp. 4–8.

[2] 'St. Antholin's . . . did, *in spiritualibus*, answer to the Artillery Garden, being a place to train up their young emissaries' (*A Letter from Mercurius Civicus*, p. 583).

[3] Kirby, op. cit., p. 12; see p. 301 below.

[4] Calder, op. cit., p. 768; Urwick, *Nonconformity in Herts.*, pp. 524–5; *C.S.P.D., 1637–8*, p. 563.

[5] Fuller, *Church History*, iii. 362; Laud, *Works*, iv. 100–1; Prynne, *Canterburies Doome*, pp. 387–8. It was Foxley whose sermon in St. Antholin's on the duties of servants to masters sent the truant William Kiffin back to his master, John Lilburne, and made him want to hear more Puritan ministers. London employers thought better of Foxley than Laud did: his parishioners petitioned for his restoration to his lectureship in 1640, as soon as they dared; the Long Parliament voted him damages against Laud (Orme, *Remarkable Passages in the Life of William Kiffin*, 1823, p. 3; *Hist. MSS. Commission, Fourth Report, Appendix*, p. 36).

Attorney-General Noy observed that the Feoffees specialized
in supplying preachers for boroughs which were represented in
the House of Commons.[1] This at a time when the government was
busy remodelling charters of parliamentary boroughs in the hope
of being able to secure an amenable Parliament one day. At
Huntingdon these attempts were resisted by Oliver Cromwell in
1630; and three years later the Mercers' Company set up a lectureship there.[2] Gouge's son and biographer admitted that the Feoffees
concentrated on cities and market towns. Heylyn adds that in
such market towns 'the people had commonly less to do [!], and
consequently were more apt to faction and innovation than in
other places'. The object of the Feoffees, he thought, was to
influence the people to elect burgesses hostile to monarchy and
episcopacy.[3] The accusation that the Puritans concentrated their
propaganda efforts on populous towns goes back at least to
1585.[4] It could be argued that town parishes were most in need
both of augmentations and of a preaching ministry; but the
possible effect on the return of M.P.s was certainly a curious
coincidence.

The real danger of the scheme lay in its success. In addition to
the lump sums contributed, we are told, promises of annual contributions and of legacies had been received; and others had
pledged themselves to contribute to each impropriation bought.
The publicity given by the Feoffees' trial, the same source assures
us, increased the subscriptions; and 'not a week before we were
suppressed', a lady sent a promise of £1,000. Many testators who
had left money to the Feoffees had to alter their wills after the
suppression.[5]

These are the claims of a partisan. But other contemporary
remarks about the financial success of the Feoffees seem dis-
proportionate to their recorded assets. Thus Fuller says that it
was believed that 'within fifty years, rather purchases than money
would have been wanting unto them'; and Prynne confirms that
'in a very few years' they would in all probability have bought up

---

[1] Calder, op. cit., p. 771. [2] See below, p. 271.

[3] Clarke, *A Collection of the Lives*, p. 111; Heylyn, *Examen Historicum*, p. 201:
Cyprianus Anglicus, p. 209. Cf. *A Letter from Mercurius Civicus*, p. 583.

[4] *Tracts ascribed to Richard Bancroft*, p. 57.

[5] George Harwood, *The Life and Death of Sir William Harwood* (1642), quoted in
Kennett's annotated copy of *The Case of Impropriations*, pp. 184–5. Christ Church,
Southwark, was built from money left to the Feoffees (Calder, op. cit., pp. 774–5).

impropriations 'in most of the great towns and noted parishes
. . . of England'. Laud, Fuller adds, feared that they would become
'the prime patrons, for number and greatness of benefices. This
would multiply their dependants, and give a secret growth to
nonconformity'.[1] It was, Laud said at his trial, 'a cunning way,
under a glorious pretence, to overthrow the church-government
by getting to their power more dependency of the clergy than
the king and all the peers and all the bishops in all the kingdom
had'. 'They were the main instruments for the Puritan faction to
undo the church', he noted in his *Diary* as he triumphed over their
suppression.[2] Prynne was really making the same point from the
opposite side when he attributed the suppression to Laud's
'enmity to preaching'; the Archbishop, Prynne thought, 'would
rather keep people in ignorance than see them instructed with the
gospel's light'.[3]

So the Feoffees were haled before the Exchequer Court and
suppressed, thanks, the House of Commons later alleged, to
violent pressure from Laud, and despite John White's offer to
allow the Archbishop to consider and approve or amend their
plans. It was argued against the Feoffees in their trial that they
had illegally functioned as a body corporate without ever being
incorporated; they had 'usurped upon the king's regality' in
forming themselves 'into a body and society', said the judgment given against them.[4] Behind this technical point is the
fact that the Feoffees were taking upon themselves the political
and economic reconstruction of the church not only without
authorization from the government, but in a way which conflicted
with its policy. 'We know the beginning', said Sir John Denham
in passing sentence; 'but the end what it may be if they should go
on we do not know; it may be transcendent.' They would ultimately make a hierarchy of their own and weaken the bishops'
power, added Cottington. In time, the judgment declared, the

---

[1] Fuller, *Church History*, iii. 362, 371–2; Prynne, *Canterburies Doome*, p. 385.

[2] Laud, *Works*, iv. 303, iii. 216–17; cf. Heylyn, *Examen Historicum*, p. 211. Note
who Laud thought the clergy *ought* to be dependent on. Casual remarks like this
reveal the closeness of the relationship between the church hierarchy and a traditional
aristocratic framework of society. Laud was in fact very nearly quoting the judgment
given in the Exchequer Court against the Feoffees (Rushworth, op. cit. ii. 152).
Prynne, we saw above (p. 232), thought ministers must be dependent on somebody.
The only question was, on whom?

[3] Prynne, *Canterburies Doome*, p. 385; cf. p. 537.

[4] Ibid., pp. 385–7, 539; Rushworth, op. cit. ii. 151.

Feoffees would draw to themselves 'the principal dependence of the clergy . . . in such measure, and on such conditions, as they should fancy, thereby introducing many novelties of dangerous consequence, both in church and commonwealth'.[1] The judgment also accused the Feoffees of misapplying the funds subscribed; against which we may set the fact that Alderman Heylyn himself gave an impropriation, as well as Gouge's son's statement that the Feoffees were £1,000 out of pocket, and Davenport's solemn assertion that he had lost by the scheme. The Feoffees' assets were confiscated to the king's use.[2]

significance

III

But though the scheme came to nothing, its effects were prodigious. It had offered the first focus outside Parliament for grappling with a national problem. In one sense it was a harbinger of the great voluntary societies, modelled on the joint-stock company, through which public opinion in England has so often made itself effective against the wishes of governments. In another sense the backing which gathered around the Feoffees formed the first nucleus of that party organization which the opposition so badly needed, and which the Providence Island Company was later to furnish. Certainly the suppression proved to be a boomerang. Nicholas Rainton, Lord Mayor of London, was in the dock with the defendants: the other citizens 'commanded rich coffers'.[3] The City companies were not involved in the same way as they were in the Londonderry Plantation, nor were the sums at stake so large: but the psychological effect of the suppression of the Feoffees can be compared with the confiscation of the Londonderry Company's charter, and the imposition of a fine of £70,000 a few years later.[4] The Feoffees were defended by William Lenthall, later Speaker of the Long Parliament, and by Holborne,

[1] Kirby, op. cit., p. 19.

[2] Rushworth, op. cit. ii. 152; *C.S.P.D., 1645–7*, p. 587; Clarke, op. cit., p. 112; Calder, op. cit., p. 763; Davenport, *Letters*, p. 39. See *C.S.P.D., 1634–5*, p. 337, for alleged fraudulent detention of moneys by the former Feoffees' agent.

[3] Fuller, *Church History*, iii. 362. It should perhaps be added that Rainton was not typical of the aldermanic bench: the majority were more sympathetic to government policy than he was. But the effect on public opinion in the City generally would be the same.

[4] The fine was ultimately reduced to £12,000, in 1637 (T. W. Moody, *The Londonderry Plantation, 1609–41*, 1939, pp. 366–7, 385, 413).

soon to win fame as Hampden's counsel in the Ship Money case.[1]
The Puritan and parliamentarian oppositions were fusing.

The weakness of the government's position was demonstrated
by the fact that, although the Exchequer Court stated that it for-
bore to inflict punishment on the individual Feoffees because the
king had reserved further examination of their designs into the
Star Chamber, and a committee including Laud was actually
appointed to consider the matter, no action was taken.[2] The
Exchequer Court had to declare that it thought the buying in of
impropriations 'a pious work'; but the manner in which the
profits were distributed 'would have grown to a great inconvenience, and prejudicial to the government of the church'.[3] A substantial public opinion undoubtedly approved of the scheme.
Attorney-General Noy himself disliked impropriations, although
the fortunes of his family were founded on deanery land.[4] Fuller
tells us that 'both discreet and devout men were (as desirous of the
regulation, so) doleful at the ruin of so pious a project'.[5] Fuller
clearly ranked himself among the 'discreet and devout men'.

That was what the suppression of the design showed: the merely
negative repressive attitude of the government. The old régime
could ruin projects for reform: it could not regulate them. Still
less could it carry out schemes of its own. Laud proposed not
merely to destroy the Feoffees, but to collect money to buy in
impropriations himself; but he succeeded only in the negative
part of his programme.[6] It is indeed very unlikely that he, or any

[1] Kirby, op. cit., p. 17.

[2] *C.S.P.D., 1633–4*, p. 418.

[3] Rushworth, op. cit. ii. 152.

[4] W. Noy, *A Dialogue and Treatise on the Law*, in *Principal Grounds and Maxims . . .
of the Laws of England* (1821 ed.), p. 352; Rowse, *Tudor Cornwall*, p. 331.

[5] Fuller, *Church History*, iii. 372. It is interesting to compare the words of that
other good conformist, William Harrison, about the suppression of an earlier
attempt to train a preaching clergy—the prophesyings. 'Satan', he wrote with delicate
reference to the bench of bishops, '. . . stirred up adversaries . . . who, . . . either by
their own practice, their sinister information, or suggestions made upon surmises
unto others, procured the suppression of these conferences.' (Harrison, op. cit., p.
19.)

[6] Laud, *Works*, iii. 253–5; iv. 175–6. The later use of the Feoffees' assets deserves
investigation. The money confiscated was left for a few years in the Feoffees' hands,
and was used to augment some livings; but only where ministers were nominated by
the king. In January 1639 the Rev. Thomas Turner, a protégé of Laud's and Windebank's son-in-law, and John Juxon, presumably a relative of the Lord Treasurer,
were appointed trustees (Laud, *Works*, iv. 270, 444; vii. 44; and see p. 22 above).
They continued to administer the fund on the same lines. The tithes were still not

other official ecclesiastical figure, could have commanded the rich coffers of the City in the way that the unofficial but influential Feoffees could. Laud had difficulty enough in raising voluntary contributions for rebuilding St. Paul's, a far less controversial project.

Nor is this merely a matter of Laud's personality, or of the business connexions of the Feoffees, important though they were. Deeper issues were at stake. Reform of the church was not a technical question, not a mere matter of ecclesiastical discipline or moral improvement, but a question on which the two sides could agree only that *something* must be done: not what should be done, nor how, still less who should do it. For it was through impropriations that the gentry plundered the church of England and controlled its vicars. The economic development of the century before 1640 had split the gentry into two increasingly differing classes. Therefore any attempt to buy in impropriations raised not only economic problems (how much compensation? how large augmentations?); it also raised political problems. Who was to have the disposal of the vast sums involved? To whom were the augmentations to go? On what conditions?

If Laud and the government controlled the operation, the church in its existing form would be revivified and strengthened. If the purchase and disposal of impropriations was controlled by opponents of the Laudian régime, the church would be reconstructed on very new lines. The gentry, the dominant social group, were too deeply divided on these fundamental political issues for any solution to be arrived at save by force. The old régime was paralysed, and could no more reorganize ecclesiastical finance than it could reorganize state taxation: and ultimately for the same social reasons.

Gardiner, with whose judgments it is always risky to disagree, concluded that 'of all modes of supporting a clergy yet invented, their maintenance by a body of capitalists living for the most part at a distance from the scene of their ministrations is, in all probability, the worst'. But Gardiner no less correctly added that 'there are . . . times when the most irregular manifestations of life

---

restored to the parish from which they originated (*C.S.P.D., 1640*, p. 11). Only in 1640 were some impropriations dissolved, although the crown still retained the right of presentation (ibid., p. 80). See also Kirby, op. cit., pp. 20–22; *C.S.P.D., 1633–4*, pp. 192–3, 287; *1634–5*, p. 337; *1635*, p. 544; *1638–9*, p. 191.

are welcome', and that Laud was 'setting aside the life and energy of individual initiative in favour of the cold hard pressure of official interference'.[1] Laud, in short, could destroy; but he never possessed sufficient force to impose his own solutions. His opponents could create; but they won power to do so only in the process of fighting a civil war. When Parliament imposed its solution, it tried to finance augmentations from impropriations held by its enemies.[2]

So we are left with a final effect of official frustration, and a considerable flutter of public opinion. The preachers in twelve or more cities and towns who lost their augmentations, and their congregations, must have seriously asked themselves what was the way of escape from the apparent impasse: so must many others, not directly affected. Some of the lecturers, we have seen, chose emigration: and Heylyn suggests that silenced lecturers (not merely those maintained by the Feoffees) were influential in persuading their congregations to emigrate too.[3] Many of these émigrés, like Hugh Peter, returned after 1640 to play their part in the revolution. John Davenport, at least, had decided by the time of the suppression of his scheme that congregational autonomy was the only way for religion to escape from the dead hand of the state church. And William Kiffin, the later Baptist leader, who had already been stirred by Foxley's preaching at St. Antholin's, was by Davenport's emigration 'put upon the examination of the reasons' for such conduct.[4] All roads led away from the established church, even those built by the Archbishop.

Reform having failed, the changes desired by the Feoffees and their supporters were brought about by revolutionary means in the Long Parliament. A few weeks after Parliament assembled,

---

[1] Gardiner, *History*, vii. 259.

[2] Cf. an interesting suggestion, reported by Stockdale to Fairfax in May 1641, that the lands of bishops, deans and chapters should be used to compensate impropriators, and all tithes be restored to the church of the parish in which they originated. This, however, he agreed, would only be a satisfactory solution 'if an equal division be contrived of the parsonages, because they differ much in value' (*Fairfax Correspondence*, ed. G. W. Johnson, 1848, ii. 107).

[3] Heylyn, *Cyprianus Anglicus*, p. 367.

[4] Dexter, op. cit., pp. 221–3; Orme, op. cit., p. 13. Davenport noted in his Bible, in gratitude to God for not allowing the Feoffees to be punished as evil-doers, the following resolutions: '(1) To be more industrious in my family; (2) To check my unthankfulness; (3) To awaken myself to more watchfulness for the time to come' (Increase Mather, *Testimony against Sacrilege*, 1706, pp. 22 sq., quoted in Kennett's annotated copy of *The Case of Impropriations*, p. 194).

Scottish commissioners took up residence in the City, and their ministers' sermons drew large crowds to St. Antholin's. The Root and Branch Petition denounced the suppression of 'that godly design', 'sugared with many great gifts by sundry well-affected persons', which the petitioners attributed to the prelates' fear lest the scheme should 'draw the ministers from their dependence upon them'.[1] The same point formed one of the articles of Laud's impeachment, drawn up by a committee of which Samuel Browne, the Feoffee, was a prominent member. The Commons' Committee for Preaching Ministers resumed the Feoffees' work on a vaster scale: the chairman of the Committee was John White, also a former Feoffee. It was merely a minor incident in the work of White's Committee when on 31 December 1640 it was instructed to consider the reversal of the Exchequer decree and the continuance of the work of the Feoffees.[2] So irrelevant had the whole matter become that it was not until March 1648 that anybody remembered to order the deletion of the decree against the Feoffees.[3]

IV

The Feoffees caused a sensation: but theirs was far from being the only semi-public attempt to raise funds for the maintenance of preachers. John Shaw tells us that in 1633 'and formerly' it was 'a custom for the merchants and other tradesmen that lived in London, so many of them as were all born in the same county, to meet at a solemn feast (upon their own charges) together in London, and there to consult what good they might do to their native county by settling some ministers (or some other good work) in that county'. Shaw associated these activities with those of the Feoffees, to which they were closely parallel. The merchants of Devon secured a lectureship for Shaw in that county.[4] London merchants of Lancashire origin contributed every year enough to maintain five or six ministers in their native county in places

---

[1] Gardiner, *Constitutional Documents*, pp. 138–9.

[2] *C.S.P.D., 1640–1*, p. 329; *Commons' Journals*, ii. 61. In 1642 the Feoffees' confiscated funds were diverted to pay for Waller's army (Kirby, op. cit., p. 23).

[3] Gardiner, *History*, vii. 259.

[4] *Life of Master John Shaw*, in *Yorkshire Diaries and Autobiographies in the 17th and 18th centuries* (Surtees Soc., 1875), pp. 126, 129; Matthews, *Calamy Revised*, pp. 434–5. Shaw was chaplain to the fourth Earl of Pembroke.

'where there was neither preaching nor means to maintain it'. Merchants hailing from other counties did likewise. A Londoner who owned an impropriation in the diocese of Carlisle allowed £50 per annum from it for a lecturer there.[1]

Haberdashers seem to have taken an especial interest in this work. Two of the Feoffees for Impropriations, George Harwood and Nicholas Rainton, were Haberdashers.[2] Thomas Aldersey, Haberdasher of London, settled £130 a year on the Company in 1594, drawn from the tithes of Bunbury, Cheshire, and other sources. The Company were to use this money to augment the living of the minister of Bunbury by £66. 13s. 4d. a year: the remainder was to go, in specified amounts, to the curate, the schoolmaster, the usher, and the poor of the same parish.[3] The Haberdashers subsequently claimed that this bequest gave them 'power to place and displace at their pleasure, without any respect of episcopal jurisdiction', Archbishop Neile complained to the king in 1633; and he added, as a natural consequence, 'the place is said to be a good nursery for novelists'. Charles registered the expected disapproval, and minuted the report 'I will not endure that any lay person (much less a corporation) have power to place and displace curates or beneficed priests at their pleasure'.[4]

Another Haberdasher, William Jones, left the Company £600 and a fair house in the City of London, for the maintenance for ever of a godly preacher *to be nominated from time to time by the Company*. He also settled 100 marks and a house on a preacher in Monmouth; and left a further £5,000 to the Haberdashers' Company for the maintenance of a preacher and for poor relief at Newland in Gloucestershire.[5] It is perhaps more than a coincidence that in 1631 Peter Simon, the preacher whom the Haberdashers had appointed to Newland, had to be examined by Bishop Neile for his share in the recent revolt in the Forest of Dean.

[1] William Walker, *A Sermon preached in St. Pauls Church in London, November 28th, 1628*, Epistle Dedicatory to the third Earl of Pembroke. For other examples see Abbot, *Writings and Speeches of Oliver Cromwell*, i. 80; *Reliquiae Baxterianiae*, i. 95–96; D. Mathew, *The Jacobean Age* (1938), p. 294.

[2] Calder, op. cit., p. 761.

[3] J. Stow, *A Survey of London*, enlarged by J. Strype (1720), book v. 191.

[4] Bridgeman, op. cit., pp. 369–70; *C.S.P.D., 1633-4*, p. 444.

[5] Stow, op. cit., book i. 271. For many other examples of gentlemen, merchants, and yeomen endowing preaching ministers, see Kennett's annotated copy of *The Case of Impropriations*, *passim*. His examples are drawn largely from Yorkshire, from evidence supplied by Thoresby.

He was accused of maintaining the equality of all mankind.[1]
When the Merchant Taylors refused £2,000 left them in 1623
to buy impropriations, the Haberdashers undertook the trust.[2]
In 1621 the East India Company was likewise relieving 'many
poor preachers of the gospel yearly with good sums of money.'[3]

In 1630 there were twelve trustees in Norwich and Norfolk,
whose aim was to provide for lecturers. They collected £200 and
sent it up to 'our proto-trustees in London'. The latter were to
pay to 'one Bridges, an absurd and turbulent fellow' £20 per cent.
yearly.[4] Bridges was presumably the William Bridges (or Bridge)
whom the citizens of Colchester next year wanted as their lecturer.
When they asked Laud to admit him, he complained: 'you must
go first to Dr. Gouge and to Dr. Sibbes for nominations, and then
you come to me; I scorn to be so used. I'll never have him to
lecture in my diocese.'[5] Not only was the hierarchy being by-
passed: the opposition had its rival organization. Despite the
'earnest desire' of the aldermen of Norwich for Bridge's lecture
to be restored, this was refused, and he emigrated to the Netherlands. 'Let him go, we are well rid of him', was Charles's comment.[6] But Bridge returned to be one of the five Independent
dissenting brethren in the Westminster Assembly.

Over and above his activity as a Feoffee, Sibbes was 'trusted by
personages of quality with divers sums of money, for pious and
charitable uses', which he employed to make small donations
to ministers.[7] Another well-known Puritan divine, Stephen
Marshall, vicar of Finchingfield, Essex (a parish in which the
Feoffees had had a reversionary interest in an estate), continued
the Feoffees' work. In 1637 it was reported to the Bishop of
London that Marshall 'governeth the consciences of all the rich
Puritans in those parts and in many parts far remote, and is grown
very rich'. Lady Barnardiston, daughter of a Lord Mayor of

[1] *C.S.P.D.*, *1631-3*, p. 36. See above, pp. 61–62. The Haberdashers also owned at
least one impropriation in Suffolk (*V.C.H.*, *Suffolk*, ii. 46).
[2] Calder, op. cit., p. 765. The testator was Lady Weld.
[3] T. Mun, *A Discourse of Trade*, in McCulloch, *Early English Tracts on Commerce*,
p. 35.
[4] *C.S.P.D.*, *1625-49*, p. 400.   [5] H. Smith, op. cit., pp. 44, 23.
[6] Laud, *Works*, v. 340; W. L. Sachse, *Minutes of the Norwich Court of Mayoralty*,
1630-1 (Norfolk Record Soc., 1942), pp. 49–50. I do not know whether William
Bridge (or Bridges) was related to the Francis Bridges who was one of the citizen
Feoffees.
[7] Catlin, op. cit., p. 258. Catlin was one of the recipients.

London and wife of Richard Knightley's cousin, who was himself an active member of the parliamentary opposition, gave £200 to be bestowed by Marshall's direction. £150 of this went to John Dury, whose schemes for protestant reunion had the solid support of Pym and other parliamentary leaders, and £50 to a lecturer in Wales who preached in Welsh, 'of which he saith there is great necessity'.[1] Again we can dimly discern organizational links, since John White of Dorchester seems to have been involved with Marshall in collecting funds after the dissolution of the

Feoffees.[2] Samuel Browne was one of the trustees to whom £700 was left with which to erect a new church in Southwark and pay the minister £60 a year.[3]

In 1608 a Barbary merchant of London left money for a preacher at Ashbourne in Derbyshire. Twenty-three years later £400 was subscribed and handed over to trustees so that a divinity lecture could be added. This fund attracted the attention of Attorney-General Noy.[4] In 1634 the High Commission was investigating a fund at Leicester, which a number of aldermen had used to buy out one vicar and augment the stipend of his successor.[5]

The mercer, Richard Fishbourne, who died in 1625, gave £2,800 to buy impropriations 'in some northern counties where there is least preaching', as well as leaving £330 to six named ministers, £20 apiece to twenty London ministers whose livings were of small value, a further £20 each to twenty unbeneficed ministers, and £25 a year for a sermon at the Mercers' chapel.[6] His purchase of impropriations was celebrated by William Strode:

> Now Henry's sacrilege is found to be
> The ground that sets off Fishbourne's charity,
> Who, from lay owners rescuing church lands,
> Buys out the injury of wrongful hands.[7]

---

[1] *C.S.P.D., 1636–7*, p. 545; H. Smith, op. cit., p. 53. For Knightley, see p. 271 below.   [2] Rose-Troup, *John White*, pp. 47, 294.

[3] Stow, op. cit., book iv. This was Christ Church, Paris Gardens.

[4] T. S. Willan, *Studies in Elizabethan Foreign Trade* (1959), pp. 195–6; *Hist. MSS. Commission, Ninth Report, Appendix*, ii. 394.

[5] *Associated Architectural Societies' Reports and Papers*, xxix. ii. 521–2.

[6] Nathaniel Shute, *Corona Charitatis* . . . : *A Sermon Preacht in Mercers Chappell, May 10 1625, at the solemne Funerals of* . . . *Mr. Richard Fishbourne*, p. 34. Shute urged the Wardens and Committee of the Company, 'when the presentation of these new-born benefices shall be devolved upon you' to appoint, without fear or favour, discreet, learned, and middle-aged ministers (p. 38).

[7] Strode, op. cit., p. 84.

Since Strode, as we have seen, was highly critical of the Feoffees, it is a little ironical that he should have singled out for praise a man who incurred the bishops' wrath by leaving his money to the Mercers' Company in London. For they in their turn set up lecture-ships in various towns, including one at Huntingdon (Fishbourne's town as well as Cromwell's) which was filled, without any refer-ence to the bishop, by a protégé of Ames and Dod whom the ecclesiastical authorities promptly inhibited from preaching.[1] The Mercers also bought impropriated tithes in Northumberland, from which they allowed £80 a year each to lecturers at Berwick and Hexham. At Berwick, 'the prime man of that [Puritan] faction', Robert Fenwick, worked in close consultation with the Company, and the lecturer they appointed was so 'factious' that in 1639 the king himself ordered the Mercers to pay him no more salary, and to appoint a Scottish nominee of his own in the lecturer's place.[2]

Edward Baesh in 1636 left money to buy in impropriations in Hertfordshire, Essex, Leicestershire, and Gloucestershire, at fifteen years' purchase, in default of heirs. But this clause never came into operation. Baesh's second son got so badly into debt during the Interregnum because of his royalism that after the Restoration he had to obtain an act of Parliament authorizing him to sell some of the property.[3] Among other purchasers we may note Baptist Hickes, Lord Campden, another Mercer, whose 'servant' Fishbourne had been. Hickes bought four impropriations to the value of £2,346 and restored them to the church.[4] He was more likely to be in sympathy with the hierarchy than with the Puritans. On the other hand Richard Knightley, who restored two impropriations, came of an old opposition family whose tradition he maintained, and was Hampden's cousin.[5] Hampden himself restored an impropriation worth £120 a year to the church of Kimble Magna.[6] Sir John (later Lord) Scudamore acted in the closest consultation with Laud when he restored impropriations to the value of £50,000 to the church: he had indeed taken a lot

[1] Laud, *Works*, v. 321; vi. 349–51; *C.S.P.D., 1637–8*, p. 426; S. Palmer, op. cit. i. 168. See pp. 59, 261, above.

[2] *C.S.P.D., 1636–7*, pp. 549–50; *1638–9*, p. 303; *1639–40*, pp. 104, 393; *City of Exeter MSS.*, pp. 195–6. See p. 329 below.

[3] Newcourt, op. cit. i. 889.

[4] Stow, op. cit., book ii. 288; Shute, op. cit., pp. 26–27.

[5] J. Stephens, Preface to Spelman's *Larger Treatise Concerning Tythes*, in *English Works*, i. lxiii.

[6] S.P. 16/274/12. I owe this reference to Miss Doreen Slatter.

of convincing, despite his Laudian views on theology.[1] Mrs. Ferrar also worked through the ecclesiastical authorities when she gave back glebe and impropriated tithes to the church of Little Gidding. 'An example for all the gentry of England', the Bishop of Lincoln called it.[2] His ecstasy would suggest that the occurrence was unusual. As Little Gidding was a depopulated parish, the Puritans at least would think that the tithes might with greater advantage have gone elsewhere to maintain a preacher. Richard Whittington, rector of Wheldrake, who died in 1628, 'appropriated all his substance to the redemption of tithes'.[3]

In 1631 Richard Garth, in agreement with the ecclesiastical authorities, reconverted the vicarage of Morden, Surrey, into a rectory by endowing it with the great tithes and 14 acres of glebe. The hierarchy also approved of the proposal which the inhabitants of Sherborne made three years later, for the perpetual settlement of lands upon the vicarage.[4] We may presume co-operation with the hierarchy in the case of Sir Henry Spelman and some at least of the others whom his editor, Jeremiah Stephens, recorded as restoring impropriations. Often, Stephens adds, impropriations were presented to an Oxford or Cambridge college: 'which course, if it had been observed by them who lately were employed in the purchasing of impropriations, they had freed themselves from sinister suspicions, by divesting themselves wholly of any profits reserved to their disposing'.[5] They would not, however, have met the criticism that they were still not restoring the tithes to the parish in which they originated; and there could be more than one view about the desirability of financing colleges out of impropriations.[6] But the Puritan Henry Burton

---

[1] Trevor-Roper, op. cit., pp. 450–3; G[eorge] W[all], *A Sermon at the Lord Archbishop of Canterburys Visitation Metropolitical held at All Saints in Worcester by Dr. Brent his Graces Vicar-General* (1635), quoted in Kennett's annotated copy of *The Case of Impropriations*, pp. 202, 206; also appendix, pp. 30–35. See also pp. 292, 319–20, below. As Ambassador in Paris Scudamore won Laud's praise by refusing to join in communion with the Huguenots. His chapel was 'adorned according to the new device, so that many papists there said they were at the English mass' (R. S. Bosher, *The Making of the Restoration Settlement*, 1951, p. 82; ed. R. N. Worth, *Buller Papers*, 1895, p. 128).   [2] Ed. B. Blackstone, *Ferrar Papers* (1938), p. 69.

[3] J. B. Morrell, *The Biography of the Common Man of the City of York* (1947–8), p. 20.

[4] Lysons, *Environs of London*, i. 363; *C.S.P.D.*, *1634–5*, p. 6.

[5] Spelman, *English Works*, 1. lxii–lxiv; Kennett, annotated copy of *The Case of Impropriations*, appendix, pp. 3–7, 27–29; Fuller, *Worthies*, ii. 22, 486. For evidence of Spelman's influence, see Kennett, op. cit., p. 237.   [6] See above, pp. 150–2.

had recommended bequeathing impropriations to colleges;[1] and Laud busied himself about securing impropriations for St. John's.[2]

V

One advantage of handing impropriations over to a college, or on the other hand of leaving money in trust to a City company, was that this evaded the prohibitions of the Statute of Mortmain and the various statutes of Henry VIII's reign leading up to the Statute of Uses. Of especial importance was 23 Hen. VIII, c. 10, which declared void all feoffments to parish churches made for longer than twenty years, since such feoffments were as great a loss to the king and lords as lands given in mortmain. Coke held that this statute did not apply to the granting of lands to endow a school or a preacher, or for other charitable uses.[3]

This is a complex subject, on which it is difficult for the layman to speak with confidence; but contemporaries certainly thought that to restore impropriations to the church 'now is not lawful in an ordinary way without charge', i.e. without a licence in mortmain. Bancroft wanted legislation to enable lands to be given to parish churches.[4] The Commons' Sub-Committee on Religion in 1625 adopted an article, subsequently rejected, recommending the drafting of a bill to enable any holder of an impropriation 'by deed enrolled to make the same presentative, or to charge it with an annuity for the maintenance of the minister'.[5] A pamphlet of 1641 again called for legislative action: failing that, the king might be able to give the necessary authorization by letters patent.[6]

An example will illustrate the difficulties. In the reign of James I, Robert Chapman bought the impropriate rectory, tithes, and glebe of Crowland, Lincolnshire, and left them to the parish by his will. During the Interregnum the will was challenged and set aside 'as contrary to the Statute of Mortmain'. After the Restoration Chapman's heirs tried to give effect to his intentions; but

---

[1] H. Burton, op. cit., p. 123.

[2] Laud, *Works*, vii. 306, 376, 582–3; cf. p. 434, vi. 519.

[3] Gibson, op. cit., p. 645; cf. Watson, op. cit., pp. 378–9, Lysons, *A View of the Revenues of the Parochial Clergy*, p. 21.

[4] Collier, op. cit. vii. 353.

[5] Gardiner, *1625 Debates*, p. 22.

[6] *A Certificate from Northamptonshire*, pp. 9–10. In Ireland an act was passed to enable impropriations to be restored: see p. 335 below.

long disputes ensued even after they had gone through elaborate legal ceremonies in the attempt to transfer ownership of the tithes, and this even after 17 Car. II, c. 2, which was intended to enable impropriators to restore or devise tithes to the vicarage, the Statute of Mortmain notwithstanding.[1]

[1] Notes in Kennett's annotated copy of *The Case of Impropriations* on unnumbered pages at the beginning of vol. i and at the end of vol. ii. *A Certificate from Northamptonshire* says vaguely 'it hath been reported that it was once voted in Parliament in Queen Elizabeth's time' that it should be lawful for impropriators to restore their tithes to the church if they so desired (loc. cit.). This may be a dim recollection of the recommendations of the Commons' Sub-Committee on Religion in 1625, which the House did not accept (Gardiner, *1625 Debates*, p. 22). The fact that it amounted to a perpetual repeal of the Statute of Mortmain was used as an argument against Queen Anne's Bounty (Ecton, op. cit., p. x).

XII

THE TITHES OF LONDON

Shall men of worldly employments be enabled by their trades
to buy what they need and to command what is requisite, by the
power of the purse, and shall God's ministers, in a case of
extremity, stand to courtesy?

F. ROBARTES, *The Revenue of the Gospel is Tythes* (1613), pp. 113–14

Public hatred of the clergy was not a little increased upon a
jealousy occasioned by the activities of some bishops and others
of the clergy, in searching by law to recover some church
revenues out of the usurpers' clutches. . . . This bred the like
hatred in London (and other incorporations and nests of the
faction) against the City clergy, upon their suit for increase of
tithes in City livings. . . . [London citizens] would rather spend at
law, or give a lecturer of their own choice, twice as much as their
full tithe came to, than pay their dues to the parson. . . . This
seeking by law to recover their due was called (by the covetous
of the world) the covetousness of the clergy.

[Anon.], *Persecutio Undecima* (1648), pp. 10–11

I

The Victoria County History of London, one of the few books to
mention the dispute over the tithes of London under Laud, con-
cludes that the quarrel 'does not seem to have been of very great
interest or importance'.[1] I believe that this view is quite mistaken,
and that London was the scene of a determined attempt, under
Laud's patronage, to make good to ministers the loss of personal
tithes: an attempt whose significance extended far beyond the
walls of the City itself.

As early as the thirteenth century a rent charge was established
in the metropolis in lieu of offerings due to the church. By the
fifteenth century this had been stabilized as a rate of 3s. 6d. in the
pound on house rents. Disagreements remained about personal
tithes. Were they due as well? Two statutes of Henry VIII's

[1] *V.C.H., London*, i. 326.

reign (27 Hen. VIII, c. 21, 37 Hen. VIII, c. 12) declared that personal tithes were included in the rate, which was at the same time reduced. Henceforth inhabitants of London and the liberties were liable to pay 2*s*. 9*d*. in the pound on the rents of their houses: or, if no rent was reserved, according to what their houses had last been let for. If they were and always had been occupied by the owner, they did not pay.[1]

But by the seventeenth century payment at the full rate was avoided by what an ecclesiastical historian regarded as 'general fraud'. Tithe was not paid on entry fines; or rent was deliberately kept low whilst fines were increased; or part of the rent was disguised as an annuity, a pension, interest, a New Year's gift, payment for a well, or for house-fittings. Or there might be two concurrent leases, 'one at a low contemptible rent to gull the incumbent of his dues, the other with a rent four or five times as great to keep down the tenant'.[2] Tithe was evaded on newly built or newly divided houses. In 1607 the common-law judges declared that these evasions were perfectly legal so long as the rent paid was not less than had been paid in Henry VIII's reign.[3]

In all these practices the richer were the most successful. Some aldermen rendered no more than 10*s*. tithe a year, which assumes that they paid £3. 10*s*. in rent: Aldermen Pratt, Gurney, Garnett are named as examples. Yet such persons, as Heylyn dryly remarked, 'do not use to dwell in sheds and cottages'. 'Sir N.R., a rich alderman', who is presumably the Feoffee Nicholas Rainton, was asked to contribute to a minister 'because he was a man of much merit'. He replied, if we can believe a royalist pamphleteer, that 'if the minister were an angel from heaven, he should have of him but 10*s*. per quarter'. 'Some farmer not worth £500 pays more tithe than all the aldermen of London', said Brian Walton. By this means, Laud added, all the offerings of the London clergy were 'shrunk away into nothing but a poor Easter-book'.[4]

---

[1] Selden, *Works*, iii. 1071, 1202; Degge, op. cit., p. 258; Little, op. cit., p. 76.

[2] Heylyn, *Cyprianus Anglicus*, pp. 281–5. Ecclesiastical landlords also preferred taking heavy entry fines from tenants to raising their rents.

[3] Coke, *Second Part of the Institutes*, pp. 659–60.

[4] *Hist. MSS. Commission, Fourth Report, Appendix*, p. 117; Heylyn, loc. cit.; *Persecutio Undecima*, p. 12; B. Walton, *A Treatise concerning the payment of Tythes in London*, in S. Brewster, *Collectanea Ecclesiastica* (1752), pp. 173 sq.; Laud, *Works*, iv. 105; Dale, *The Inhabitants of London in 1638*, pp. vii, 171; W. Maitland, *History of London* (1756), i. 305–6; Collier, op. cit. ix. 343. Walton's treatise is in Lambeth MS. 273.

The Feoffee Richard Stock testified to the abuse no less than the Laudians Walton and Heylyn. Stock died in 1626. In his youth he had declared publicly that 'the meaner sort were overburdened whilst the rich and great ones escaped with more ease', and he repeated the allegation in his old age.[1] It was confirmed by a pamphlet of 1641. 'There is great inequality of paying tithe in London, the rich men, for the most part, paying very little . . . so that the minister's maintenance ariseth, for the most part, from the meanest and poorest people, in which respect that little maintenance he hath falls short many years in a great part, especially in hard times; . . . the richest citizen in London hardly paying so much as a countryman that hath but £20 or £10 land per annum in his occupation.' In remedy the pamphleteer recommended that 'fines may be cast up into the account of the rent, that the rich by paying great fines and small rents do not deceive the minister, as it hath been hitherto'.

Sub-letting caused additional problems. Bancroft in 1610 had urged that tithe on houses should be paid by the landlord, not by the sub-tenant. The pamphlet of 1641 thought that tithes 'should not be assessed according to the old rent, but as they were let by the prime lessor', i.e. lessees' profits should be tapped.[2] Here again the facts would have been very difficult to ascertain unless property-owners could be put on oath.

In consequence of all this the London clergy got a great deal less than 10 per cent. of their parishioners' earnings, though we should not take too literally the graphic phrase of another pamphleteer: 'the barren mountains of Wales afford not so many poor . . . livings together as are to be found within the walls of London'.[3] But it was true that, as the ministers complained, for want of 'independent maintenance' they were 'daily thrust upon dangerous and great inconveniences'.[4]

Brian Walton, rector of St. Martin Orgar's, and post-Restoration Bishop of Chester, is our main source for the clergy's point of view. He himself received £73. 7s. 10d. clear annually from his parish, of which the 'true tithe' (i.e. 7½ per cent., not 10 per cent.) was estimated at £1,600. Pluralism, however, saved him

---

[1] S. Clarke, *A Martyrologie* (1652), p. 146; cf. Stock, op. cit., pp. 77–80, 224.
[2] [Anon.], *Good Works* (1641), pp. 2–4.
[3] *A Letter from Mercurius Civicus to Mercurius Rusticus*, pp. 582–3.
[4] Rushworth, op. cit. ii. 269. See below, pp. 300–1.

from destitution. He had a rectory in Essex which his parishioners alleged was worth £200 a year, and a prebend of St. Paul's. He had also held for a short time the living of St. Giles in the Fields.[1] Walton was accused of having defrauded the parish of St. Martin Orgar's of tenements which on expiry of lease would be worth over £200 per annum. He had set aside a decree in Chancery, it was alleged, by means of his favour in the church courts. He was continually at law with his parishioners over tithes, and himself took the lead in petitioning the king for an increase in London tithes.[2] In view of all this, his record of the reasons for the successful evasion of tithe in the City is suspect, but not without interest.

There were five reasons, he thought. First, post-Reformation mistrust of the clergy. Secondly, socially inferior post-Reformation parsons. His third reason is worth quoting in full:

The disciplinarian faction by their lectures and the tribunitial sermons bringing the parsons, and withal the service of the church, into contempt with the people, drawing both their affections and their purses to themselves, persuading the people they might withdraw the means from unworthy men, and lawfully confer the same upon men more deserving, meaning themselves, for we may observe that at what time that faction began to take root in the City, that then these frauds began, and not before.

His fourth reason was prohibitions issued by the common-law courts, his fifth the fact that the Lord Mayor acted as judge in tithe cases.[3]

This last was a particularly sore point. The statutes of Henry VIII's reign authorized the Lord Mayor of London to try tithe disputes if either party appealed to him. Citizens of London naturally always did appeal to him, since the Lord Mayor was himself an interested party, very apt to understand the tithe-payer's standpoint. Appeal from him lay only to Chancery, and that was costly and tedious. Walton recalled that Lord Chancellor Hatton

---

[1] Walton had been Richard Stock's curate. The parliamentary surveyors of 1650 valued Walton's living at Sandon, Essex, at £115 (H. Smith, op. cit., p. 257).

[2] *The Articles and Charge proved in Parliament against Dr. Walton*, pp. 7–10. Walton was also accused of neither preaching the Sunday afternoon sermons for which he was paid nor allowing his parish to hire a deputy. See also pp. 171, 180 above.

[3] B. Walton, op. cit., pp. 176–8. The accusation against Puritan lecturers is curiously like those made against friars two centuries earlier. Cf. Maitland, op. cit. i. 306.

remitted one case from Chancery to the Arches, disregarding a common-law prohibition. But later chancellors, who had no Bancroft for their chaplain, did not follow the precedent. In 1607 the Court of Common Pleas ruled that London ministers might not sue for tithes in the church courts.[1]

The clergy tried desperately to restore the jurisdiction of the ecclesiastical courts, or at least to compel the Lord Mayor to expedite the hearing of suits, to put witnesses on oath, and to insist on the production of leases in court.[2] But the City was strongly placed to resist any change. By keeping low the payment legally due to the minister, the wealthier citizens could exercise some control over him by granting or withholding voluntary augmentations: or, if he proved intractable, they could subscribe for the maintenance of a more complaisant lecturer. 'In some small parishes', Walton tells us, 'they give £100 per annum to a lecturer (where the tithe is not £50), which £100 is as much increase of tithe as is demanded in the greatest.'[3] But money paid to a lecturer was voluntary and withdrawable; to those who paid it, it seemed very different from the legally binding and legally enforceable increase in tithes which the clergy were demanding.

In 1581 the London clergy stated their case to Convocation. The citizens 'are for their riches stout, and will not pay', they declared. Most of the parsonage houses were in citizens' hands. Ministers and parishioners could not agree together in a single parish: 'the cause thereof', the clergy thought, 'is the private reading in houses, and our public crying out against usury'.[4] Bills aimed at scaling up London tithes were defeated in the Parliaments of 1604, 1614, and 1621. One reason for rejection was no doubt a proposal that commissioners should be appointed to inquire *on oath* into the value of houses. The Commons would have no truck with oaths in tithe cases.[5] In 1618 the clergy seemed to have won a great victory when, after consultations involving the greatest

---

[1] Coke, *Second Part of the Institutes*, pp. 659–60.

[2] Dale, op. cit., p. vii; B. Walton, op. cit., pp. 178–9. The Lord Mayor's jurisdiction appears first to have been challenged in an address from the lower to the upper house of the 1554 Convocation of Canterbury; but after that time the matter often recurred (Cardwell, *Synodalia*, pp. 437, 445).

[3] B. Walton, op. cit., p. 224. Cf. the second epigraph to this chapter.

[4] Collier, op cit. ix. 343–6.

[5] *Hist. MSS. Commission, Fourth Report, Appendix*, p. 117; Walton, op. cit., pp. 180–1; Notestein, Relf, and Simpson, op. cit. ii. 249, v. 314; E. Nicholas, op. cit. i. 204–5.

dignitaries in the government,[1] the Exchequer Court declared that tithes should be paid at the rate of 2s. 9d. in the pound on the *true yearly value* of all property. If this decision could have been made effective, parsons would have got their full share of the increase in the wealth of the capital since Henry VIII's reign. But the decision had to be enforced by legal action in each particular case: and 'there was no contending with the purse of the City' at law. The victory remained on paper only. The City authorities ignored suggestions that a compromise solution should be worked out by mutual agreement.[2]

In 1620 Oxford and Cambridge were brought into the struggle: each university issued a statement denouncing the citizens' practices. Eighteen bishops published a similar statement. In the following year Montagu, in a book attacking Selden, laid down the principle that 'the tenth is due in London as well as in the country: the tenth of increase, as well in merchandise and trading and manual arts, as of cattle, corn, or any other fruits of the earth'.[3] The programme was there: what was lacking was power to carry it out.

II

Laud's advent to the primacy seemed to give the London clergy their opportunity. Laud certainly sympathized with their aspirations. He set himself the task of seeing 'the tithes of London settled, between the clergy and the City'.[4] This project was never ticked off as 'done', as some of the others were; but the Archbishop remained convinced that 'I had been much to blame, having been Bishop of London, should I have had other thoughts'. He defended his intention as having been 'no more than that the City would voluntarily yield to some reasonable addition, when right and need appeared'.[5]

Right and need, however, proved difficult to define to everyone's satisfaction. In May 1634, shortly after Laud had become Archbishop, the City clergy again petitioned the king, since it had 'pleased God to raise up some who, under his Majesty (the great patron of the church) laboured to free the church from that

[1] B. Walton, op. cit., p. 181; Bacon, *Works*, xiii. 291.
[2] Heylyn, *Cyprianus Anglicus*, pp. 284–5.
[3] B. Walton, op. cit., pp. 182–6; Montagu, op. cit., p. 67. Cf. p. 320 below.
[4] Laud, *Works*, iii. 254.
[5] Ibid. iv. 104–5.

Egyptian bondage into which it had been cast by the iniquity of former times'.[1] This petition was referred to the Archbishop and others to consider. Next month a shrewd observer reported that this committee had 'taken such pains . . . as will produce sudden and good effects'. He believed, rather prematurely, that 'the ministers of London are in a fair way for increasing their means'.[2]

In fact it did not turn out to be as easy as that. Attempts were first made to reach agreement by discussions between representatives of the City and of the ministers. The aldermen procrastinated, insisting on separate negotiations in each parish; and complaining that the rates demanded by the clergy would lead to some ministers receiving £1,000–2,000 a year. Why not? they replied. Finally, both parties agreed to accept the king's arbitration—a difficult thing to refuse. But the government was already at loggerheads with the City over Ship Money, the Londonderry Plantation and the incorporation of the suburbs, and Charles was in no hurry to add another grievance by awarding in favour of the clergy. Meanwhile the citizens got an order staying all tithe-suits until the king had made up his mind, which meant that even payment of tithes at the old rate was evaded for some months, until a countermanding order was issued. From June 1635 onwards we find a great increase in tithe disputes in London. 'Not a lawyer in a parish but was commonly the parson's busy enemy.' Voluntary contributions to ministers began to fall off.[3]

Laud then tried a new tactic, the significance of which has not, I think, been properly appreciated. In March 1636 Laud's successor as Bishop of London was appointed Lord Treasurer. The office had been vacant for a year, though Juxon had been mentioned as a possible candidate from the first.[4] Of course there were many other reasons for Juxon's appointment: but it was *inter alia* an attempt to follow up the Exchequer decision of 1618. London was surely not out of Laud's mind when he penned the famous exclamation of joy in his *Diary*, ending 'And now if the church will not hold up themselves under God, I can do no more'.[5]

---

[1] B. Walton, op. cit., pp. 186–7.

[2] The Rev. George Garrard to Wentworth, 20 June 1634, in Knowler, op. cit. i. 265.

[3] B. Walton, op. cit., pp. 193–202; Dale, op. cit., pp. vi–x; Rushworth, op. cit. ii. 269–72; *C.S.P.D., 1634–5*, pp. 48, 161–3; *1637–8*, p. 399; *Persecutio Undecima*, p. 13; *The Curates' Conference*, p. 498.

[4] Knowler, op. cit. i. 388.

[5] Laud, *Works*, iii. 226.

Heylyn is quite explicit about the reasons for Juxon's appointment, and is worth quoting at length:

> The peace and quiet of the church depended much on the conformity
> of London, and London did as much depend in their trade and pay-
> ments upon the love and justice of the Lord Treasurer.

Juxon's appointment, therefore, was

> the more likely way to conform the citizens to the directions of their
> Bishop, and the whole kingdom unto them; no small encouragement
> being thereby given to the London clergy for the improving of their
> tithes. For with what confidence could any of the old cheats adventure
> on a public examination in the Court of Exchequer . . . when a Lord
> Bishop of London sate therein as the principal judge?[1]

Time, however, was running short. The legal battles raged for
three years. The clergy petitioned again in April 1638. The king
met one of their demands by restoring the clergy's right to sue for
tithes in the church courts, pending his award.[2] But the real issue
was evaded by referring it back for negotiation in the parishes.
Agreed assessment of 'equitable' increases proved impossible to
arrive at. Each parish presented its suggestions, normally the
minimum increase they thought their parson could be persuaded
to accept; and the clergy submitted counter-suggestions for larger
increases.

It is difficult to be quite sure about figures. The following
totals are given with reserves. They cover eighty-four parishes
within the walls:

1. Tithes, 1636	2. Tithes, glebe, and casual profits, 1636	3. Tithes, 1638	4. Tithes and other profits, 1638
£6,472. 9s. 9¼d.	£8,222. 2s. 9¼d.	£6,968. 19s. 5d.	£8,520. 12s. 5d.

5. 'Clear revenue', 1638	6. 'True tithe', 1638	7. Tithes demanded by ministers, 1638
£6,855. 14s. 4¼d.	£148,266. 8s. 10d.	£10,605. 0s. 0d.

The figures in columns (1) and (2) are taken from values printed
by Richard Newcourt in 1708.[3] If various odd sums given by
Newcourt for sermons, &c. were added, column (2) would very
nearly equal column (4). But this would be misleading, since

---

[1] Heylyn, *Cyprianus Anglicus*, pp. 284–5, 304.
[2] *C.S.P.D., 1638–9*, pp. 344–5.   [3] Newcourt, op. cit. i. 236–566, *passim*.

although the totals roughly correspond there is considerable variation in the individual parishes. Columns (3), (4), (5), and (6) are from reports drawn up in 1638 by ministers and church-wardens, though in many cases they are signed by the minister only, the churchwardens having refused to certify.[1] The 'clear' revenue is after making all deductions, some of which are no doubt exaggerated. The 'true tithe' or 'moderate rent' is the estimate made in the same document of 10 per cent. with one-quarter abated (i.e. $7\frac{1}{2}$ per cent.) on the true value of house rents. Column (7) gives the actual demands made by the clergy in 1638, after the lay authorities in the City had refused to make any offer.[2]

It will be seen that the revenues actually received averaged roughly £100 a parish, tithes about £80. The 'true tithe' as estimated in 1638 averaged £1,765 a parish. The actual amount of tithe asked by the City clergy worked out at an average of £126. 5s. a parish. That is to say, the increase sought was of the order of 58 per cent., not the 2,106 per cent. which the 'true tithe' would have justified. A rather greater increase was asked for impropriate churches and for churches outside the walls, in order to raise the revenues of these poorer livings to a comparable figure. Not more than three. churches in the whole City would have been worth as much as £500 a year if the clergy's claims had been accepted in full.

III

But the size of the increases hardly mattered in comparison with the principle involved. If the church had won this battle, it would hardly have stopped there. Further increases would probably have been sought in London: some augmentation would certainly have been demanded in other cities. The conflict in the City extended at once to the parishes adjacent to London, whose ministers associated themselves with the claims put in by the London clergy. Already in April 1638 they were complaining of 'incompetent' livings, where some ministers received no tithe at all. Some parishioners, the ministers said, lived on land that formerly owed tithes; but the new residents paid nothing but 2d. or 3d. at Easter. The clergy added that the king's failure to make an award had deprived them of 'all opportunity of improvement'. The ministers

---

[1] Printed in Dale, op. cit., from Lambeth MS. 272.
[2] B. Walton, op. cit., pp. 203–7.

agreed to accept royal arbitration. The inhabitants of some parishes admitted that they paid no tithes on new buildings. But they told very different stories about the economic position of their incumbents; and refused to submit their differences to the king, insisting that all tithe disputes should be left to the law.[1]

We get a brief glimpse of discussions in the parish of St. Giles in the Fields. There the opposition of the parishioners was attributed to the 'peremptory carriage and uttering of untruths' of George Winder, 'calling himself a messenger extraordinary of His Majesty's Chamber'. Winder, otherwise vulnerable, was easily disposed of. And fortunately the Attorney-General, Sir John Bankes, lived in St. Giles in the Fields, so he was instructed by the Council to 'advise with others of the parishioners' how the maintenance of the minister might be raised to £200 from its present £40, 'or at least how a fit yearly addition may be added to the present means, . . . with all speed by such rates as the Attorney shall think most convenient'.[2] If only there had been Privy Councillors in every parish! Yet the opposition of the parishioners even here, led by a royal employee, shows the difficulties which the clergy were up against, and helps us to grasp the importance which attached to the struggle in London itself.

IV

For London was naturally regarded as a test case. The practice of London, Heylyn tells us, was pleaded by other towns 'for vestries, lectures and some other innovations'.[3] And in the matter of tithes many a provincial burgher stood to lose at least as much as the citizens of London if he was called upon to pay 'true tithes'

---

[1] *C.S.P.D., 1637–8*, pp. 400, 410–16, *passim*; Rushworth, op. cit. iii. 718–19; *Surrey Archaeological Soc. Collections*, xxxvii. 106.

[2] Winder was referred to the Lord Chamberlain to dismiss or otherwise deal with. He also, happily, was discovered to have failed to pay a fine imposed two or three years earlier in respect of new buildings which he had erected in the parish. It was referred to Sir Henry Spiller and Lawrence Whitaker, commissioners for buildings, to survey Winder's houses so that the Council could give order for demolishing those which were new. This should discourage government servants from opposing government policy! Whitaker, who was Clerk Extraordinary to the Privy Council as well as a Middlesex J.P., had been 'affronted' by Winder when he joined the parson of the parish in persuading the parishioners to submit to the king. (Rushworth, op. cit. iii. 720–1; *C.S.P.D., 1637–8*, p. 416. I am indebted to Dr. Aylmer for help with Whitaker and Winder.)

[3] Heylyn, *Cyprianus Anglicus*, p. 282.

or anything approaching them. For, notwithstanding clerical bitterness about the inadequacy of their remuneration in London, the bishops in 1604 had thought the system at work in the capital preferable to the 'utter decay' of personal tithes in towns where there were no great tithes; and they urged the passing of an act of Parliament 'that tithes in such places should be paid according to the house rents of the inhabitants, as it is in London'.[1] This demand had formed part of Bancroft's programme of reform in 1610.

Some parishes in the suburbs of London paid 2s. in the pound on rents in lieu of tithes. There was a rent-tithe on houses in Rotherhithe and 'neighbouring parishes'. Thomas Gataker brought a successful Exchequer suit against some of the poorer sort of his parishioners in Rotherhithe, who had got out of the habit of paying owing to the remissness of his predecessor.[2] At Canterbury 2s. 6d. in the pound was paid (2s. 9d. in one parish); at Coventry 2s., and the same at one parish in Dover; at Royston 1s. Rates were paid on houses in Colchester; and there may have been an agreement of some such sort at Bristol.[3]

In Norwich a determined effort was made to establish the London system. As early as 1607 the Council had ordered the civic authorities to extend to all inhabitants a rate of 1s. 8d. in the pound on house rents, hitherto paid only by Dutch and French immigrants; for ministers were so poor, the Council thought, that they were becoming dependent on the people, and their profession brought into contempt. But this order seems to have been evaded, for in 1621 the ministers were still petitioning for its enforcement.[4] Again Laud's ascendancy proved decisive. In 1638, after both parties had agreed to accept royal arbitration, Charles settled a rate of 2s. in the pound on house rents for the maintenance of the parochial clergy. Refusals were to be tried in Chancery or in the Bishop of Norwich's court, and prohibitions were expressly forbidden.[5] (In 1641 the articles of impeachment against Sir John

---

[1] Usher, *Reconstruction*, ii. 332; i. 337–8. A similar suggestion had been made in *The Reformation of the Ecclesiastical Laws* (pp. 128–9), and had been considered by Archbishop Parker before the Convocation of 1563 (Cardwell, *Synodalia*, pp. 495, 510.)

[2] Gataker, op. cit., pp. 47–50. See p. 126 above.

[3] B. Walton, op. cit., p. 228; *C.S.P.D., 1637–8*, p. 167; Little, op. cit., pp. 76–78; Larking, op. cit., p. 58; Newcourt, op. cit. i. 876; H. Smith, op. cit., pp. 318–19.   [4] *C.S.P.D., 1619–23*, pp. 259–60; Rushworth, op. cit. ii. 48–49.

[5] *C.S.P.D., 1637–8*, pp. 167, 177.

Bramston included his denial of prohibitions in cases affecting Norwich tithes.)[1]

The king's award for Norwich, wrote Prideaux, 'having been made a little before the civil wars, the power which Parliament from the first beginning of those unhappy commotions obtained in the Associated Counties . . . quashed it before it was ever thoroughly put in execution'.[2] But it had caused great alarm. A letter reporting rumours of the royal award declared 'it will make us all run into cottages and not affect great houses except we take inmates'.[3] The attempt to coerce the citizens of Norwich into accepting this rate was one of the charges brought against Bishop Wren on his impeachment in 1641, since 'by the laws of this realm no tithes ought to be paid out of the rents of houses'.[4] In almost every case we look into, we find the Long Parliament thus coming to the rescue of property owners, and its intervention made effective by military victory in the civil war.

There were similar attempts in other cities. A project for a tithe-rate for a second Dover parish was discussed in the House of Commons in 1621.[5] In 1629 the clergy of York petitioned for improvement of their livings, and the Council ordered that they should receive an annual augmentation of up to £24 apiece. It authorized the levying of a rate on house rents, after the example of Norwich, for this purpose.[6] In Ipswich the appointment of a royal commission to inquire into the value of small livings and to augment them produced riots in 1636 by demonstrators 'to the number of 100, being armed with long staves, guns, etc.': and 'had the mariners of the town been at home, worse might have been expected'. The Privy Council, nevertheless, after taking legal advice, authorized the bailiffs and chief burgesses to assess and levy rates for the maintenance of the town's ministers. This order was annulled in 1641.[7] Opposition aroused by these attempts may

---

[1] Nalson, op. cit. ii. 365. [2] Prideaux, op. cit., p. 284.
[3] Anthony Mingay to Framlingham Gawdy, *Gawdy MSS.* (Hist. MSS. Commission), p. 164.
[4] Rushworth, op. cit. iv. 354–5; Nalson, op. cit. ii. 398; Wren, *Parentalia*, pp. 22, 112–13.
[5] Notestein, Relf, and Simpson, op. cit. iii. 5; Larking, op. cit., pp. 57–60.
[6] Rushworth, op. cit. ii. 48–49; Kennett, annotated copy of *The Case of Impropriations*, p. 214; E. R. Turner, *The Privy Council, 1603–1784* (1927), p. 172.
[7] *Hist. MSS. Commission, Ninth Report, Appendix*, i. 261; *C.S.P.D., 1635*, p. xxxii; *1636–7*, pp. 529–30; *1637*, pp. 144, 160; *1640*, p. 504; *1640–1*, pp. 409–10. See pp. 328–9 below.

have had something to do with Charles's dilatoriness in issuing his award for London. It was a ticklish subject, and the advice of the government's lawyers was not necessarily the best guide.

The citizens of London were therefore not isolated as they fought their long delaying action against the power of church and state united in Laud and Juxon. And to their rescue came—our brethren of Scotland. The financial crisis caused by the Scottish war made it impossible to fight London as well. Charles and his Council were persuaded 'to an unprofitable compliance with that stubborn City'.[1]

But it had been a near thing. A great deal of money had been spent on litigation, and far more might have had to be so spent had it not been for the Scots. This perhaps throws some light on the sympathy which the City Fathers subsequently showed not only to the Scots but even to their religion—neither very popular elsewhere in England. It certainly helps to explain their determination that bishops should never rule in the state again. (We may recall Alderman Fowke, who was 'not much noted for religion, but a countenancer of good ministers, one who was present at the act for abolishing kingly government' and was 'deeply engaged in bishops' lands'.[2] Of such was City presbyterianism composed.) Laud's support for the City ministers in this battle was made one of the accusations against him at his trial.

We can perhaps get some idea of the anxieties of those times from a propagandist pamphlet written shortly after the Long Parliament met:

Call to mind the 2*s*. and 9*d*., remember with what vehemency and diligence it was prosecuted: God was pleased to blast it notwithstanding. But had it once been settled, and men's purses with their consciences brought under contribution of their prerogative, as they might as legally have doubled or trebled it upon any occasion afterwards, and that not without pretending full arrearages: so we may be certain, this only privilege of theirs would have quite devoured the subjects' whole property and this consequence have thereupon succeeded, that afterwards there would have been little need to trouble parliament with granting subsidies, the clergy, for continuance of their greatness, might likely have been no less willing than it would have been able to supply such trifling sums out of their boundless revenues.[3]

---

[1] Heylyn, *Cyprianus Anglicus*, p. 285; B. Walton, op. cit., p. 207.

[2] J. Stoughton, op. cit. iii. 148.

[3] [Anon.], *Christs Order, and the Disciples practice concerning the Ministers maintenance, and releeving of the Poore* (n.d. ? early sixteen-forties), p. 13.

That exaggerates, naturally: but it exaggerates what had been a real fear. The battle for the tithes of London deserves a subsidiary place beside the battle over Ship Money in the events which helped to prepare for civil war. It made the clergy hated. Any divine, as he walked through the streets of the City in the late sixteen-thirties, was liable to be met with derisive shouts of 'Two shillings and ninepence!'[1] Such was the outcome of Laud's attempt to enhance the prestige and dignity of the clergy.

London's victory was decisive and final. In 1642 the Lord Mayor found his jurisdiction in tithe cases entirely undisputed, 'the ecclesiastical courts being suppressed, which otherwise have cognizance of the causes of tithes of London'.[2] No attempt was ever again made to increase the tithes of the City. After the Great Fire, 22 & 23 Car. II, c. 15, allotted sums ranging from £100 to £200 a year to fifty-one London parishes in lieu of tithes. These amounts were to be raised by rates levied by the lay authorities, and it was specifically stated in the act that the church courts had no jurisdiction in tithe disputes in the City. In 1745 the London ministers were still complaining of poverty.[3]

Nor was London the only gainer. When there was a proposal in 1677 to impose a charge of 1*s*. 6*d*. in the pound upon houses in Norwich, the city's Recorder had no difficulty in getting it defeated in the House of Commons, with the aid of a judicious mention of the dangers of popery. The legal writers agreed that 'No tithes are due to be paid for houses in any city but London'.[4] The propaganda statement of the managers of Wren's impeachment had become the law of the land.

---

[1] *Persecutio Undecima*, p. 11. The story is all the more credible in that it comes from a source favourable to the clergy's pretensions.

[2] [Bruno Ryves], *Angliae Ruina* (1647), p. 147. The statement is wildly partisan, since it was precisely the cognizance of the ecclesiastical courts that Londoners had disputed.

[3] *The Grievances of the Ministers of London* (1745), in Brewster, *Collectanea Ecclesiastica*, pp. 231–93.

[4] Kennett, op. cit., appendix, pp. 46–47; Sheppard, op. cit., pp. 8–9, 18; cf. [T. Pittis], *A Private Conference between A Rich Alderman and A Poor Country Vicar* (1670), pp. 116–23, where a rate on houses in all towns is suggested.

XIII

AUGMENTATIONS

'Twill be great discouragement to scholars, that bishops should
be put down. For now the father can say to his son, and the
tutor to his pupil, 'Study hard, and you shall have *vocem et sedem
in parliamento*'; then it must be, 'Study hard, and you shall have a
hundred a year, if you please your parish.'

SELDEN, *Table Talk*, pp. 27–28

Alderman. I have one argument beyond the care of any bishops,
or any other that I know of, for your [the vicar's] total resignation
to our disposal: and that is, that your income is not established
by law, nor does any bishop at all encourage ministers that are in
market towns, but suffer them to labour without reward.... And
therefore you are more especially obliged to submit to our wills,
because your dependence is wholly upon them.

[T. PITTIS], *A Private Conference, between A Rich Alderman and A
Poor Country Vicar*, p. 20

I

UNTIL the Long Parliament met, no general scheme for
augmenting stipends on a national scale had any serious
chance of being adopted. But in default of a national
reorganization, there were various ways in which livings could
be improved piecemeal. Most of them the hierarchy detested,
because they were likely to lead to dependence of the minister on
his congregation. The better-off parishioners, whilst refusing to
agree to any increase in tithe payments, might by voluntary contributions add to the income of a preacher of whom they approved.
Among many reasons for opposing the abolition of pluralism,
Whitgift argued in 1601 that the want of a competent maintenance
'will be an occasion for the ministers to preach *placentia*, and to
feed the humours of those from whom they are driven to seek
relief'. This, said Dr. James in the Commons the same year,
'is a thing abhorred even of God Himself'.[1] In 1603 a Puritan

---

[1] Collier, op. cit. vii. 261; D'Ewes, *Journals*, p. 640.

pamphlet declared that 'the next [i.e. nearest] way to enlarge
the ministers' maintenance were to place everywhere worthy men
whose painful labours would provoke men's liberality'.[1] Both
sides agreed that this was the easiest method of augmentation.

In market towns the augmentation was often made by the
establishment of lectureships, which might be given either to the
incumbent of the parish or to an outsider, according as their
theological politics appealed to the influential classes in urban
society. Thus in Yarmouth, where the Dean and Chapter of Norwich leased the rectory to a farmer, the corporation supplemented
by an annual grant from the town's revenue the salary which the
farmer paid the minister. After a series of squabbles, in 1610
the farmer recognized the corporation's right to nominate this
minister, and a lecturer as well. But the Dean and Chapter, backed
by the Bishop, challenged this arrangement, and in 1632, with
Laud's influence in the ascendant, their opposition received the
support of the Privy Council. The corporation's lecturer was dismissed. After a discreet interval, the corporation withdrew its
augmentation in 1638. In 1641 it recovered full right to nominate
the minister; in 1644 the purged lecturer returned at an increased
stipend.[2] In Ipswich, which Sir Nathaniel Brent regarded as an
'exceeding factious town', the preacher appointed by the corporation had his salary increased in twelve years from 100 marks
to £100. He was regularly in trouble with the ecclesiastical
authorities, and in 1635 was suspended by the High Commission.[3]

These struggles in the towns often attracted attention and were
recorded. It is less easy to trace what happened in country parishes,
where a great deal could be done by an influential landowner.
I quote two instances in which Sir John Eliot played a part.

In 1625 the living fell vacant in the parish of Cuddenbeck, a
manor which the Eliot family had long leased from the Bishop of

---

[1] Quoted by Usher, *Reconstruction*, i. 300. Usher gives examples on pp. 274–5.
I think Canon Foster exaggerates when he says that Usher was 'misled' by the Puritan
surveys into thinking that Puritan parishes paid their ministers better than others
(*The State of the Church*, p. lxii). There had indeed been an increase in the value of
many benefices between 1535 and 1604; but there is a distinction to be drawn
between that part of the increase to which the minister had a legal right and that for
which he was dependent on the good will of his parishioners (cf. Bacon, *Works*, x.
126).

[2] Browne, *Congregationalism in Norfolk*, pp. 122–32, 136.

[3] Ibid., pp. 139–43; *C.S.P.D., 1635*, p. xxxii. For similar augmentations, by the
corporation of Newcastle-under-Lyme, see Pape, op. cit., pp. 30, 230, 253.

Exeter, and where they often resided. Eliot wrote to Bishop Valentine Cary to say that he and his parishioners were anxious to settle a Mr. Paige 'here amongst us as our minister in the room of Mr. Dix, now placed elsewhere, and willing at our instance to leave this cure to him. The stipend belonging to it is small, and not worthy of a scholar, or able to maintain him without helps, which have heretofore been added by some particulars, and I believe will be still to a man of their affection and choice.'[1]

The significant thing about that letter is its quietness of tone, what it assumes as a matter of course. The Bishop is expected to listen to the views of the lessee of the manor; the retiring incumbent has rights in the living, but can be squared; the wealthy members of the parish, by voluntary agreement, subscribe to augment the stipend of the minister, and so are able to get a learned man; but they will only so subscribe to a minister of their own choice, and they expect the Bishop to yield to this direct pressure and allow them in effect to present to the living. Their expectations were not disappointed. Bishop Cary complied with their request.[2]

The other example comes some five years later, when Eliot was in the Tower. The minister of Bake, St. Germain's, had died. A friend of Sir John's, Glanvile, leased the presentation from the Dean and Chapter of Windsor. Eliot was asked to use his influence to help the parishioners to get an honest man appointed: in particular he was asked to see that Mr. Glanvile 'would not cross our request unto the house of Windsor for the free election of our said minister, which, in respect that that part of his means which must make it competent must issue from the benevolence of the parish, is not, as I conceive, unreasonable'. This is in a letter between friends, and is therefore more plain-spoken. Even so, to talk of free election, free choice, of the minister as reasonable where a voluntary augmentation exists, is to make a very large claim.[3] It means in effect handing over control of the nomination of ministers entirely to the parishes or to the moneyed class; for augmentations were needed in most parishes in the kingdom.

[1] John Forster, *Sir John Eliot* (1865), i. 463.
[2] This was not the first time that favours had passed between Eliot and the Bishop: see *Cowper MSS.* (Hist. MSS. Commission), i. 157, 177 (courtesies in 1624). By 1626 relations were more strained (ibid., p. 251).
[3] J. Forster, op. cit. ii. 630-1. Eliot's intervention was not, in this instance, successful, but that does not affect my point.

Other examples may be given from unendowed vicarages. In 1566 the inhabitants of Haworth, Yorkshire, bought land in trust to pay a stipend to their minister. The deed of agreement provided that if the trustees should at any time be debarred in their choice of a minister, they might apply the income to other purposes.[1] In Market Weighton, in the same county, in 1577–9, the congregation claimed the right to hire a curate for a chapel without the vicar's consent, 'for that the tithes and oblations of the chapelry were not nor are not sufficient to maintain a curate at the chapel without the good will and supply of the inhabitants'. When the vicar challenged this right, the inhabitants ('or half a dozen of the chief of them'), it was alleged, 'made friends to Sir Marmaduke Constable, knight, for the taking up of the matter'. Constable used his influence to bring the vicar to terms. His words would be convincing, since he appears to have been lay prebendary of Market Weighton, and therefore patron of the living, and also a member of the Council in the North. Later, after Constable had disposed of the prebend, the vicar brought an action in the ecclesiastical courts, which decided (in the face of the surviving evidence) for him and against the now unprotected parishioners and their curate.[2]

Such indications as we find of private augmentations, whether by patron, congregation, or legacy, are necessarily casual. We know, for example, that in the reign of Charles I the Earl of Norwich and Lord Scudamore granted considerable augmentations to ministers in impropriate parishes belonging to them.[3] Sir Henry Spelman followed his own advice by using the income from an impropriation solely to augment livings.[4] The Earl of Bedford augmented Isaac Ambrose's income when he held 'a little cure' in Derbyshire in Charles I's reign.[5] Dr. Willet of Ely persuaded an impropriating friend of his to add £10 a year to the vicarage of Tadlow.[6] The vicar of Rochdale received an augmentation from the Byron family; Archbishop Whitgift, who took the valuable impropriated

---

[1] Addy, op. cit., pp. 440–1. In 1655 the salary was £27. 13s. 4d.

[2] Purvis, *Select Tithe Causes*, pp. 123–4.

[3] Manuscript note in Kennett's copy of *The Case of Impropriations*, p. 216; G[eorge] W[all], *A Sermon*, quoted in ibid., pp. 202, 226.

[4] Ed. Sir H. Ellis, *Original Letters of Eminent Literary Men* (Camden Soc., 1843), p. 156; Spelman, *English Works*, i. lxii–lxiv, where other examples are given.

[5] Halley, op. cit. ii. 198.

[6] Peter Smith, op. cit., sig. b 4ᵛ. For legacies, see Morrell, op. cit., pp. 20, 70.

tithes of Rochdale, graciously settled on the vicar and his successors in perpetuity 'the herbage of the churchyard'.[1] Sir Edmond Allen of Hatfield Purnel, who had risen to the rank of baronet on the spoils of the church, equally generously allowed his vicar £25 a year augmentation out of his winnings.[2] It was to such impropriators that Thomas Adams spoke: 'Perhaps you think to make amends for all, for you will increase the stipend of the vicar. When the father hath gotten thousands by the sacrilegious impropriation, the son perhaps may give him a cow's grass, or a matter of 40s. *per annum*.'[3]

We know, too, since his biographer happens to record the fact, that John Carter, vicar of Bramford, Suffolk, had his income raised by his congregation from 20 marks to £20, probably towards the end of the sixteenth century.[4] St. Alkmund's church, Shrewsbury, received a grant from the Shearmen's Gild.[5] At Dorchester, Dorset, in 1584 the burgesses, 'desiring to procure a competent maintenance for a minister, of which they had been for the most part destitute', bought the advowson of a living in a depopulated parish, and used the income partly towards a free school and almshouses, partly to augment their minister's income. In 1625 his augmentation from this source was £10; but there seem to have been other sources. For one disgruntled parishioner was heard to say that the Rev. William Benn had grown so rich on voluntary contributions that he refused to acknowledge the humbler members of his flock: ministers and lawyers had got all the riches of the land, and were too proud to speak to poor men.[6]

This generalization was perhaps a little too simplified. At Chapel-en-le-Frith, for instance, the minister received only £4. 6s. 8d. from the Dean and Chapter of Lichfield. 'There is no other means', said the parliamentary survey of 1650, '. . . except the people's gratuity', which in that year brought the living up to a total of £10. 13s. 4d.[7] The parishes of Shoreham and Otford Kent, impropriations together worth nearly £300 to the Dean and

[1] Halley, op. cit. i. 162.   [2] H. Smith, op. cit., p. 305.

[3] Adams, op. cit., p. 864; cf. Wither, *Emblems* (1635), book ii, Emblem 15.

[4] Clarke, *A Collection of the Lives*, pp. 3–4.

[5] T. C. Mendenhall, *The Shrewsbury Drapers and the Welsh Wool Trade in the 16th and 17th centuries* (1953), p. 83.

[6] F. Rose-Troup, *John White*, pp. 39, 244.

[7] W. B. Bunting, op. cit., p. 59. At St. Benedict's, Cambridge, the fixed stipend was only £3, to which parishioners added their contributions (Birley, *Life of Fuller*, pp. 115–17).

Chapter of Westminster, had only one curate to serve both cures, to whom a stipend of £24 was paid. Here in the sixteen-thirties the parishioners subscribed to the maintenance of a second minister, who received only their voluntary contributions, and £10 per annum from the lessee of the parsonage, Sir Robert Heath. At Whitstable in the same county, an impropriation belonging to the Archbishop of Canterbury, the lessee was Sir Maurice Abbott, brother of Laud's predecessor in the see. Sir Maurice sublet the rectory for £160 a year, but allowed only £10 per annum to the minister, there being no endowed vicarage. His maintenance was only brought up to reasonable proportions by subscriptions from the parishioners. Most of these were 'mean men', who could not sign their names to the petition to Parliament in April 1641 which asked for assistance.[1]

Because Ralph Josselin's *Diary* has survived, we know that in 1640 he was promised £80 a year from the vicarage of Earl's Colne, Essex (£8. 10s. 8d. in the *Valor Ecclesiasticus*). Tithes accounted for half of this sum; 'Mr. Rich. Harlakenden, wood and money, £20; his tenants, in contribution, £2. Mr. Thos. Harlakenden, £3; the town contribution, £15.' The last item had been a special augmentation to persuade Josselin to accept the living. It is notable that all the other contributions came from members of the leading (Puritan) family in the parish, and its dependants. In fact the promises were not fully realized, and Josselin had to rely on 'many private gifts' from the countryside 'to make amends for the town losses'.[2] The parliamentary surveyors in 1650 recorded Earl's Colne as worth only £28; they took no cognizance of the voluntary augmentations. There had earlier been a lectureship at Earl's Colne, financed by voluntary contributions to the extent of £40 per annum. It was held by Thomas Shepherd until Laud outed him in 1631.[3]

Essex happens to be a well-documented as well as a strongly Puritan county. Several other examples could be given from it of voluntary contributions by parishioners going either to a minister, in return for his undertaking a lecture, or to a curate where an absentee minister could not or would not maintain one

---

[1] Larking, op. cit., pp. 125–9, 201–2.

[2] Ed. E. Hockliffe, *The Diary of the Rev. Ralph Josselin, 1616–1683* (Camden Soc., 1908), pp. vii, 10–11, 21. Richard Harlakenden was the impropriator.

[3] H. Smith, op. cit., pp. 309, 30; *A Viewe of the State of the Clargie* put the value of Earl's Colne at £30 (p. 10).

himself.[1] At Leicester the vicar of St. Nicholas received an annuity of £5 'so long as he should continue to preach there or at any other parish church within the borough'. The contributors were in trouble with the High Commission over this in 1634.[2]

The vicar of Taunton held a lectureship endowed by voluntary contributions, and his Bishop's report on it to Laud in October 1637 is illuminating:

> They say that without this lecture the vicar will not be able to subsist, for the parsonage is impropriate, and the ancient endowment of the vicarage is but £20 *per annum*, unto which the impropriator a good while since added out of the parsonage (which is not worth now above 100 marks yearly) for the better maintenance of the vicar, £30 *per annum* more, but with this proviso, that the vicar should be a preacher and resident. But because all this is not a sufficient maintenance for a preaching minister, in a cure so painful, the town of Taunton did agree with their present vicar (as they did with his predecessor) to give him £30 more *per annum*, to make him a competent maintenance, but upon this condition, that he should preach a sermon every Wednesday throughout the year for the same. Now if this lecture cease, the payment will cease also, and the present vicar will be gone, etc.

Nevertheless the Bishop declared his resolution to put down the lecture.[3]

This instructive example brings many threads together. Both the impropriator and the town made their contributions conditional; the vicar and the town clearly used this in an attempt to force the Bishop's hand. And although the Bishop finally asserted the authority of the hierarchy, the effect was only to deprive the parishioners of preaching for which they were prepared to pay, without providing any alternative. The Bishop's interference had a negative, a frustrating effect.

It is only a very small step forward from the cases we have been considering to the provisions made by Francis Combe, Esq., of Hempstead, in his will made and proved in 1641. Here he left £6. 6s. 8d. a year for ever to 'a godly and learned preacher to be chosen by most voices for a Monday lecture in Berkhamsted' and £13. 13s. 4d. 'for a Thursday lecture in Hempstead . . ., likewise

---

[1] E.g. at Bocking, Castle Hedingham, Copford and Birch Magna, Clavering, Elmden (H. Smith, op. cit., pp. 32, 40, 75–76).

[2] J. Simon, 'The Two John Angels', in *Trans. Leics. Archaeological and Hist. Soc.* xxxi. 37, 47.

[3] Kennett's annotated copy of *The Case of Impropriations*, p. 232.

to be chosen'.[1] Here, before the civil war, we have an attempt to endow something very like congregational Independency. Nor was it an isolated example. At the chapel of Birch, Lancashire, the minister's wage of £17. 2s. 7d. was more than doubled in and after 1640 by a subscription of 'the principal gentry'. The subscribers later turned out to be 'of the congregational way', and withdrew their contributions in 1662 when they could no longer have a minister of their own choice.[2]

There were fourteen parishes in London which claimed a right to nominate their own minister.[3] This claim was much easier to enforce when there was a voluntary augmentation. So much was clear to John Davenport when his election to St. Stephen's, Coleman Street, was challenged by the Bishop of London. 'The parish will maintain their right', he told Lady Vere in 1624, 'and . . . the means will be but £11 *per annum* to any other besides myself.' This consideration, and the mediation of powerful friends, overcame the Bishop's objection.[4] On election, the vicar of St. Stephen's had to sign a declaration that he accepted his augmentation of £39 as a gift, and did not claim it as of right. In 1622 it had in fact been refused to Davenport's predecessor, Samuel German, because of the parish's 'dislike of the conversation and negligence in his ministry, charging his parishioners with continual calumnies in pulpit and out'.[5] This complete economic dependence of the vicar of St. Stephen's on his parishioners is interesting when we recollect that it was the most radical parish in London. Davenport was succeeded by John Goodwin, 'the great red dragon of Coleman Street'. The Five Members took refuge in Coleman Street from Charles I's attempt to arrest them in 1642.

Even men who were far from sharing Davenport's general outlook would have agreed that contribution towards maintenance

---

[1] Kennett, op. cit., p. 235. Payment of this legacy continued until 1660, but then seems to have lapsed. A decree in Chancery twenty years later renewed it (with arrears), but significantly 'it was recommended to the bishop of the diocese to nominate and appoint fit persons to expound the catechism [!] in every such church on every such day appointed'. The bishops, White Kennett tells us, entirely disregarding the testator's intentions, 'have usually appointed the respective incumbents, who thereby receive an augmentation to their livings'.

[2] Halley, op. cit. ii. 153–4.

[3] Cambridge University Library MS. Mm 6/61. Cf. pp. 58–59 above.

[4] Calder, *Letters of John Davenport*, p. 19. Davenport's facts were accurate: see Newcourt, op. cit. i. 536–7.

[5] E. Freshfield, *Some Remarks upon the Book of Records and History of the Parish of St. Stephen's, Coleman Street* (1887), p. 6.

gave a right to a say in nomination. In 1638 Sir John Lambe reported to Laud that the only hope of filling St. Mary's, Stamford (£12 per annum), was to find someone whom 'the parish shall like', and to whose maintenance they would contribute.[1] Even when it was a case of the king appointing to a Hertford living (worth £18) vacated by the emigration of a nominee of the Feoffees for Impropriations, Lambe pointed out to Laud that if a discreet man were chosen the parishioners would freely contribute.[2] William Grant, too, the vicar of Isleworth whom Parliament later sequestrated, believed (or said he did) that 'every man in the parish that paid any thing towards a lecturer' should 'have his free voice also in the choice, that so the major part of the whole parish might carry it'. Grant was arguing that a lecturer had been foisted on the parish by a minority of the inhabitants, so we need not take what he says too seriously as evidence of his own convictions. But he clearly thought the argument one which was likely to impress public opinion, which is what matters for the present argument.[3]

II

Economic facts, then, were creating before 1640 a kind of *de facto* voluntaryism in many parishes, an effective selection of ministers by the congregation or by a town corporation. The selection was no doubt often made or influenced by the well-to-do parishioners. It is perhaps to such economic realities that we are to look for the origins of that Independency which spread so rapidly among Oliver Cromwell's class in the sixteen-forties, rather than (or as well as) to the obscure sectarian congregations in the Netherlands and New England.[4] Although he did not look at the economic aspects of the question, Professor Haller also arrived at the conclusion that something like congregational Independency was already in existence before 1640 in some London congregations which virtually elected their ministers, and in every Puritan group which at any time joined together to engage a lecturer.[5] Once

---

[1] *C.S.P.D., 1637-8*, p. 563.

[2] Urwick, *Nonconformity in Herts.*, p. 525. The royal nominee was sequestrated in 1643 as non-resident and non-preaching.   [3] Grant, *Vindication*, p. 15.

[4] This was suggested by E. Troeltsch, *Social Teaching of the Christian Churches* (1931), p. 927. Cf. Neale, *Elizabeth I and her Parliaments, 1559-81*, pp. 298-9.

[5] Haller, *Liberty and Reformation in the Puritan Revolution* (1955), pp. 106-7, 115-19, 128, 209; cf. A. French, *Charles I and the Puritan Upheaval* (1955), pp. 339-40.

the hierarchy was removed, congregational self-government was revealed as already in existence.

It is difficult to exaggerate the significance of this development as a training in democracy. If wealth and social status counted, still the wealthy had to influence opinion in their congregations by discussion and argument: procedures very different from nomination of a minister by bishop or patron. For the parish was the unit of local government as well as of worship. The Leveller William Walwyn described how he and his friends began their political activities by reforming their church, and then went on to capture the whole ward for their candidates.[1] The Leveller Agreement of the People of 1 May 1649 demanded 'free liberty to the parishioners of every particular parish to choose such as themselves shall approve; and upon such terms, and for such reward, as themselves shall be willing to contribute, or shall contract for. Providing none be choosers but such as are capable of electing representatives', i.e. are not servants or wage-labourers, or paupers, or ex-royalists.[2] Complete disestablishment was essential to democracy: each community should run its own affairs. Such was the radical programme.

It has long been recognized that the Independent and sectarian congregations helped to foster democratic ideas after the outbreak of the revolution, and historians have marvelled at the speed with which their activities developed and their influence spread. The suggestion is that the ground had been prepared by the facts recorded in this chapter. Long before 1640 many congregations had been exercising effective control of the purse. Only the power of the hierarchy had prevented this evolving in the direction of congregational self-government. The congregations were far more than debating halls: they were schools of democratic practice as well. And this seems to have been the case some time before 1640.

So if 'the better sort' took the lead, it was not necessarily in conflict with the rank-and-file members of the congregation. The Levellers and sectaries ultimately found themselves in opposition to the Presbyterians and gentlemen Independents. But before the civil war there was little awareness of these potential rifts, and much awareness of the frustrating presence of the hierarchy. One can understand the indignation of parishioners when less com-

---

[1] W. Walwyn, *A Whisper in the Ear of Mr. Thomas Edwards* (1646), p. 4.
[2] D. M. Wolfe, *Leveller Manifestoes of the Puritan Revolution* (1944), p. 408.

pliant bishops than Valentine Cary not only ignored the requests
of those who paid the piper, but actually went out of their way to
impose ministers whose tunes were utterly out of harmony with
those for which congregations called.

For under Laud the climate was changing. In 1615, for instance,
Bishop King had authorized the inhabitants of Wapping to build
themselves a chapel, and made no difficulty when the rector of
Whitechapel agreed that the inhabitants should nominate their
own curate, to whose maintenance they promised to subscribe £20
a year.[1] But in an identical case fourteen years later Laud reacted
very differently. The inhabitants of Hammersmith, supported by
a peer, asked for permission to build a chapel of ease and to propose the name of an able and conformable minister, to whose
maintenance they bound themselves to contribute £28. 13*s*. 4*d*.
per annum. Laud took a very high line. Notorious disturbers of
the church's peace, he said, might be brought in under such a
description; subscription to a new chapel could give no right to
dispose of the bishop's office. Agreeing that 'to leave the nomination to the inhabitants' would 'advance the minister's maintenance',
Laud nevertheless could not accept 'a popular nomination'.

The negotiations between the Earl of Mulgrave and the Bishop
of London proceeded in an agreeably delicate manner. Everybody
has confidence in Laud, said Mulgrave; but who knows how he
will be succeeded? The inhabitants had no desire to bring in a
busy-headed or factious man. Laud might have asked how the
present parishioners would be succeeded: but he confined himself
to refusing to deprive his successors of their rights. The maintenance must be granted in perpetuity, so as to obviate any danger of
economic control by the subscribers.[2] When in 1634 Nathan
Walworth of London built and partially endowed a chapel at
Ringley, the Bishop of Chester granted him the nomination of
the minister for his life only, and very reluctantly.[3] In 1638, when
a new church was consecrated at Covent Garden, the Earl of
Bedford offered to contribute £100 a year and a house for the
minister, if he was allowed to present. The offer was rejected.[4]

[1] Newcourt, op. cit. i. 671.
[2] Laud, *Works*, vii. 24–27, 30–32; *C.S.P.D., 1629–31*, pp. 115–28; Newcourt,
op. cit. i. 610; Lysons, *Environs of London*, ii. 407.
[3] Ed. J. S. Fletcher, *Correspondence of Nathan Walworth and Peter Seddon* (Chetham
Soc., 1880), *passim*.
[4] Garrard to Wentworth, Knowler, op. cit. ii. 168.

Such evidence perhaps helps us to understand how some at least of the seventeenth-century clergy managed to live notwithstanding their exiguous nominal incomes. The general rise in prices brought automatic improvement to some parsons; but for many ministers more significant increases might be due to decisions by congregations to supplement the revenue of a preacher whom they liked, either by establishing a lectureship or by unofficial voluntary donations. Such supplementation would clearly be impossible where the minister was *persona non grata* with the squire or the wealthy members of the congregation.

It was often alleged that parishioners were more willing to make generous voluntary contributions than to pay their tithes. There were many bitter complaints to this effect from the London clergy in their struggle to win a larger share of their parishioners' incomes. There were good reasons for the apparent illogicality. For the minister had a *right* to tithes, which could be enforced legally : he was at mercy where voluntary contributions were concerned. It was therefore to the advantage of the most generous contributor to deny his *obligation* to be generous for ever. And it was often easy for the less generous to persuade one minister to accept a good bargain for himself, by which the rights of his successors were prejudiced.[1]

In a town it might be difficult to avoid complying with the wishes of one's parishioners. Certainly pressure seems to have been exercised in London, where, Heylyn suggests, ministers, 'being but meanly provided for', were forced to undertake some lectures 'in the hope that gaining the good will thereby of the chief of their parishes, they might be gratified by them with entertainments, presents and some other helps to mend their maintenance'. This bad example, he adds, was followed by other towns.[2] The Puritan George Wither agreed with the Laudian Heylyn on the facts of the case. He knew, he tells us, that London had

> All cities in this kingdom over-passed
> In plentifully preaching of God's word;
> And that thou bountifully dost afford
> Large voluntary pensions to that end . . .
> Thou entertainest preachers, but they must
> Speak pleasing things, or else away are thrust.[3]

[1] Montagu, op. cit., pp. 68–69; see p. 279 above.
[2] Heylyn, *Cyprianus Anglicus*, p. 282.
[3] Wither, *Brittans Remembrancer*, pp. 398, 401.

'Most curates in London lived upon citizens' trenchers', said a pamphlet of 1641, adding that the citizens 'have mainly with-drawn their purses' since the London ministers' campaign to augment their revenues.[1]

More than one London minister was alleged by his parishioners to have tried to solve his financial problem without meeting the theological requirements of his congregation. Mr. Swadlyn, curate of St. Botolph's, Aldgate, although himself a preacher, offered to accept a lecturer desired by the parish if he himself received £30 for his goodwill.[2] The money for this lectureship was found by some mysterious 'persons unknown', who may have been the Feoffees for Impropriations.[3] William Grant, vicar of Isleworth, which for forty years had maintained lecturers at the charge of the parish, was accused in 1641 of having taken £10 a year as the price of his agreement to accept a lecturer, and then to have outed him.[4] Grant denied the charge, but Edward Finch, brother of the Lord Keeper, admitted that he took £20 per annum to permit another preacher to lecture in his parish.[5]

Lecturers were often accused of stirring up sedition by their sermons. One pamphlet associated this specifically with their economic dependence. Their 'maintenance being dependent, [they] . . . must preach such doctrine as may foment disloyalty, and instil such principles into their auditors as may first dispose them to, and after engage them in, rebellion when things were ripe, or else they shall want bread to put into their heads'.[6] No less a personage than the Speaker of the Cavalier Parliament, looking backwards, was prepared to generalize about 'cities and corporate towns,

[1] *The Curates' Conference*, p. 498.

[2] *C.S.P.D., 1628–9*, pp. 543, 593. The lecturer in question was Thomas Edwards, probably the later author of *Gangraena*. He was dismissed by Laud in 1629, despite a declaration of conformity and a promise to preach a sermon of obedience to superiors (ibid., *1629–31*, p. 1). The fact that Swadlyn, himself a preacher, was bribed to make room for Edwards suggests differences with his parishioners (ibid., *1636–7*, p. 65). Swadlyn was sequestrated, and tried as a royalist spy during the civil war (Matthews, *Walker Revised*, p. 59).

[3] Kirby, op. cit., p. 12. See p. 260 above.

[4] *The Petition of the Inhabitants of Isleworth*, p. 3; Grant, *The Vindication of the Vicar of Isleworth*, pp. 5–6.

[5] *Petition and Articles . . . against Edward Finch*, p. 9; E. Finch, *An Answer to the Articles . . .*, p. 18. Finch was pronounced unfit to hold any benefice; among his many other offences was recorded the fact that he was a hinderer of preaching (Matthews, op. cit., p. 47). Cf. pp. 170–1 above.

[6] *A Letter from Mercurius Civicus*, pp. 582–3. The point was echoed by Dugdale, op. cit., p. 36.

where are little or no predial tithes'. There, he thought, 'the preachers for mere want are forced to chant such tunes as may best please the rich men in their parishes'.[1]

In country parishes the augmentation might take the form not of a lectureship but of a concealed chaplaincy. 'Some knights and squires', the Bishop of Peterborough complained in 1639, '. . . diet the vicar, where his maintenance is little: and this they say is not to keep a chaplain, which your Majesty's instructions forbid. Yet most of these read or say service in their houses', and not according to the established liturgy.[2] Again it was the financial whip-hand that enabled these gentlemen to pick out and protect ministers with the theological outlook they favoured.

III

We do not know, and it is from the nature of the case impossible to find out, how normal these various kinds of augmentation were. The Long Parliament discovered that if it wished to obtain information on the subject it would have to undertake a national survey. But Prynne assumed in 1628 that an augmentation from the parish purse was one of the four alternative ways in which vicars and curates could make both ends meet.[3] A petition from Cheshire in 1641 complained that in addition to having to pay tithes, men also had to maintain a ministry out of the remaining nine-tenths of their estates, if they would have any ministry at all.[4] Many parishes wanted preaching, or wanted a different kind of preaching from that which they were offered by the nominees of the hierarchy. It seems to have been taken for granted that they would have to pay to get it, but also that they would have a right of choice if they did pay. The economic position of many ministers would lay them open to insidious offers once congregations had

---

[1] *Speech of Sir Edward Turnor, Knight*, to the king, 30 Oct. 1665. Parliament's remedy then was a bill for uniting small churches and chapels in cities and towns corporate.

[2] Laud, *Works*, v. 368.

[3] Prynne, *A Briefe Survey and Censure of Mr. Cozens His Couzening Devotions* (1628), pp. 42–43. The other ways were tutoring, becoming 'trencher-chaplains or school-masters to some country gentlemen, or to betake themselves to some base, illiberal, mechanical or servile work'.

[4] Sir Thomas Aston, *A Remonstrance against Presbytery* (1641), pp. 1–3. Sir Thomas disapproved of this petition, which had been 'spread abroad . . . amongst the common people' but 'concealed from the gentry'.

appreciated the value to themselves of money so charitably spent. The taxpaying classes were accustomed to the principle of making redress of grievances precede supply.

The only kind of augmentation of which bishops and government approved was that proposed by the inhabitants of Sherborne in 1634: by the perpetual settlement of lands upon a vicarage.[1] In 9 Jac. I Sir John Osborn conveyed the impropriation of Hawnes, Bedfordshire, to trustees for the increase of the maintenance of such vicars as he or his heirs should nominate. In 1641 the House of Lords, reversing a decree in Chancery, supported Sir John's son in refusing to pay the augmentation to a vicar who had 'come in by lapse' (i.e. by the patron's failure to get a minister instituted and inducted within the requisite six months after the living fell vacant). The augmentation was to be paid only to the impropriator's nominee.[2] Here again the Long Parliament protected lay property rights, whilst Chancery under Charles I had been looking after the interests of the clergy.

Indeed, from the minister's point of view, the disadvantages of any augmentation which was not unconditionally settled upon the church were clear enough. When the Earl of Warwick sold his estate in the parish of Duston, Northamptonshire, the vicar lost an augmentation of £5 which had previously formed 20 per cent. of his total receipts.[3] The following objections to voluntary contributions were noted by contemporaries. The augmentation, as in the case just quoted, might be withdrawn without warning, for reasons beyond the minister's control; or in consequence of some unreasonable grievance—if a parishioner was dissatisfied with his pew, disliked the parson's theology, &c. In cities and larger towns, said Prideaux, voluntary contributions nourish heresy, schism, sedition, rebellion, 'as we have sufficiently found by woeful experience in the late reign of King Charles I'. A steady competent maintenance would encourage ministers in loyalty to church and crown; its absence made them fear to offend their parishioners, and so concur with them in faction.[4] Comber contrasted the advantages of tithes, by which 'the clergy are freed from that servile dependence on the people which is inconsistent with their duty. For such as live upon contributions and depend upon the

---

[1] *C.S.P.D., 1634–5;* p. 6. See p. 272 above.   [2] Nalson, op. cit. ii. 382.
[3] *A Certificate from Northamptonshire*, pp. 7–8.
[4] Prideaux, op. cit., pp. 356–8.

charity of their parishioners dare hardly tell them the truth, exhort them to their duty, or reprove them for their sins; or, if they do, either their words are despised, or else they disoblige those on whom they and their families depend for bread'.[1]

It was ultimately the nonconformist congregations which most completely substituted the relationship of contract between minister and congregation for that of patronage. The economic facts leading to that conclusion can be paralleled in other spheres. Thus our period saw the emergence of professional writers, who were ceasing to be dependent upon aristocratic patrons and looked to the general public for their living. This new freedom, or this new bondage to the market, had important consequences for literature. New standards were set by audiences drawn from a different class from the aristocratic patrons who preceeded them. The qualities necessary to please the anonymous public, those of Bunyan and Defoe, would almost certainly never have extorted guineas from Lord X or Sir John Y. Ministers dependent upon their congregations, rather than upon a patron or a bishop, would similarly have to find ways of pleasing the many rather than the few. Once religious toleration was established, a really eloquent preacher could draw his own audience. Ministers had to compete for congregations as authors compete to capture the public by writing best sellers.[2] The effects of these developments, on theology as well as on literature, are subtle and difficult to analyse; but they are worth thinking about. Calvinism, for instance, so powerful during our period, rapidly disintegrated after 1640. Part of the explanation of this startling phenomenon may lie in the unwillingness of the wider public to purchase a doctrine which limited salvation to the few. The free trade in ideas which Milton advocated, and which the revolution established, proved fatal to both the contending creeds of 1640, Laudianism and Presbyterianism, as national religions. They had owed their strength, it was now revealed, to the patronage of rival groups within the narrow class of aristocratic patrons: after 1640 free trade replaced monopoly.

---

[1] Comber, op. cit. ii. 198.
[2] Haller, *Liberty and Reformation in the Puritan Revolution*, pp. 146, 203.

IV

If there is any truth in the suggestion that during our period economic control of ministers by congregations, and especially by their richer members, may have been far more widespread and deliberate than the surviving evidence shows, then the revolutionary expedient of granting augmentations to ministers from the impropriate tithes of delinquent royalists (and from other sources) was only regularizing and generalizing a practice that already existed in many parishes: but it was a major reversal in so far as royalists were thus made to subsidize parsons chosen by their victorious enemies.

State-sponsored augmentations ceased at the Restoration; and it was some years before growing profits from agriculture led to a substantial increase in ministers' stipends. It was not till the eighteenth century that Queen Anne's Bounty began to help the poorest clergymen. Even then, although Eachard had made public opinion conscious of the poverty and contempt of the clergy, the level to which all livings were to be raised was set only at £60 a year, and men calculated that it would take up to 500 years to reach even that minimum if progress continued at the rate at which it began.[1] (We may contrast the ideal of £100 a year for every minister dreamed of by the Elizabethan Puritans, and set as a target by the act of 6 June 1649.)

There must, it seems, have been a time-lag of several decades after 1660, during which many Anglican parsons would be extremely poor if their incomes were not supplemented by voluntary contributions, such as nonconformist ministers got from their congregations. The facts indeed are not clear. Charles II's government continued the Laudian policy of putting pressure on bishops, deans, and chapters to augment vicars' stipends in their richer appropriations. Many augmentations were made by Archbishop Juxon in the diocese of Canterbury just after the Restoration, 'in pursuance of the royal directions at that time issued'.[2] But how generally successful was this policy, and on how significant a

[1] Ecton, op. cit., pp. viii–ix.
[2] Ornsby, op. cit. ii. 124; Kennett, op. cit., pp. 250–9; Newcourt, op. cit. i. 811; ii. 224, 568; Lysons, *Environs of London*, ii. 325–6; iv. 317–20; Ducarel, op. cit., p. 71 and *passim*; W. H. Marah, *Memoirs of Archbishop Juxon and his times* (1869), pp. 85–86. Contrast A. Whiteman, 'The Re-establishment of the Church of England, 1660–3', *Trans. Royal Hist. Soc.*, 5th series, v. 128; and see p. 327 below.

scale? 17 Car. II, c. 2, an act for uniting churches in cities, referred specifically to 'mean and stipendiary preachers . . . who, wholly depending upon the good will and liking of their auditors, have been and are hereby under temptation of too much complying and suiting their doctrine and teaching to the humour, rather than the good, of their auditors'.[1]

There is a field for research here. What about vicarages outside towns? Were lay augmentations revived after 1660? On what scale? Some wealthy members of Anglican congregations might prefer to extend their charity to an extruded nonconformist. Would they also augment the stipend of his supplanter in the vicarage? If not, what happened to him? Did the Anglican clergy really return to a diminished heritage? Or were the gentry sufficiently impressed by the need for a national church to make supplementation fairly general? The object of Queen Anne's Bounty, it was stated in 2 & 3 Anne, c. 20, was to prevent stipendiary preachers 'depending for their necessary maintenance upon the good will and liking of their hearers'. That is sufficiently familiar to suggest that many of the factors discussed in this chapter were still operative at the beginning of the eighteenth century. Have considerations of this kind any bearing on the fact that so many Anglican priests preached non-resistance so long as that doctrine was popular with the wealthy, and no longer? And on the rapid disappearance of the Non-jurors after 1688?[2]

---

[1] Collier, op. cit. viii. 449–50.
[2] There are some suggestive hints on this subject in Halley, op. cit. ii. 171–3, 228–31.

XIV

ARCHBISHOP LAUD AND THE LAITY

God cannot be confined, restrained or concluded by any Parliament. Let no man, therefore, ... think that he hath right to these parsonages because the law hath given them to him. The law of man can give him no more than the law of nature and God will permit.

SIR HENRY SPELMAN, 'The Larger Treatise concerning Tythes', in *English Works*, i. 147

The king and the priest, more than any other, are bound to look to the integrity of the church in doctrine and manners. ... For that's by far the best honey in the hive. But ... they must be careful of the church's maintenance too, else the bees shall make honey for others, and have none left for their own necessary sustenance, and then all's lost. For we see it in daily and common use, that the honey is not taken from the bees but they are destroyed first. Now in this great and busy work the king and the priest must not fear to put their hands to the hive, though they be sure to be stung. And stung by the bees whose hive and house they preserve.

LAUD, Dedication to Charles I of *A Relation of the Conference of William Laud ... and Mr. Fisher the Jesuit*, in *Works*, II. xii

I

LAUD saw the problems of the church as a whole. To be politically useful to the government, Laud and Charles would have agreed, the establishment must enjoy a position of dignity and independence: though the Archbishop would not have thought this desirable only for political reasons. Dignity, in Laud's view, necessitated a well-paid clergy, though paid on a graded scale: independence must also be given an economic basis by setting the clergy free from the financial pressure of laymen, whether they were patrons, impropriators, town corporations nominating and paying lecturers without reference to a bishop, members of congregations augmenting stipends, or the Feoffees for Impropriations.

A large part of Laud's difficulty came from the human frailties of members of the hierarchy. They were a little more circumspect than their Elizabethan predecessors, since Stuart governments and parliaments looked less favourably upon the direct plunder of the church; but they did not rise above the standards of their time, and were difficult to supervise.

The gentle Hooker drew up the most devastating indictment of the bishops of his day. They were, if not simoniacal, at least guilty of 'unadvised gifts'; fees and pensions were the only things sought at visitations; 'palpable and gross corruptions' by 'men who seek nothing but their own gain' prevailed in their courts. 'The executors of bishops are sued if their mansion-house be suffered to go to decay; but whom shall their successors sue for the dilapidations which they make of [their] credit?' 'A wretched desire to gain by bad and unseemly means standeth not with a mean man's credit, much less with that reputation which Fathers of the Church should be in.' 'Herod and Archelaus are noted to have sought out purposely the dullest and most ignoble that could be found amongst the people, preferring such to the High Priest's office' in order to discredit it; and Hooker thought that 'there hath been partly some show and just suspicion of like practice of some' in England.[1]

Those measured words, from the most eloquent defender of the hierarchy, tell us a good deal. They suggest at least that we should be ill-advised to dismiss the case against the bishops as mere Puritan propaganda. And we should note that the accusations are mainly of economic offences. Another friend of the hierarchy, Lord Treasurer Middlesex, complained to James I that many of the bishops were no better than Puritans in their economic habits. They neglected hospitality, were grasping and parsimonious, providing lavishly for their wives and children, to the undoing of their successors. He suggested that this was a Puritan plot, infiltration in order to destroy episcopacy from within; but simpler reasons will no doubt present themselves.[2]

Heylyn agrees about the continued depredations of 'several' bishops before Laud's rise to power, speaking of their 'avarice

[1] Hooker, *Works*, iii. 385–91. Cf. pp. 31–32 above.
[2] Goodman *The Court of King James*, i. 314–15. Bishop Bramhall seems to have shared the view that there was no hope of 'better order and revenue' where the bishop was a 'Disciplinarian'. See his letter to Laud in *Hastings MSS*. iv. 69.

. . . in making havoc of their woods to enrich themselves'.[1] Similar accusations were made against the Deans and Chapters of Norwich and Durham in James I's reign.[2] Bishop Bridgman, writing to the Dean and Chapter of Chester in 1623, referred warningly to 'the sacrilegious and ravenous disposition of those who formerly have been members of this church'. Seven years later Bishop Davenant accused the Dean and Chapter of Salisbury of 'greed of filthy lucre', and by implication of dishonesty and bribery.[3]

Bishop Goodman, who reported Cranfield's dictum, himself provides evidence that not only the puritanically-minded offended against the economic proprieties. In 1633 Goodman is said to have paid a cash sum down to secure his translation from Gloucester to Hereford. This was imprudent as well as simoniacal, for Laud, who no doubt shared Heylyn's view that Goodman 'could pretend no other merit than his money', saw to it that he lost his purchase price as well as the Bishopric of Hereford.[4] It would appear that there may have been literal truth in Falkland's gibe that only £1,500 a year kept bishops like Goodman from proclaiming themselves Catholics. In 1653 Goodman, wise too long after the event, admitted that the sufferings of the clergy had arisen in part because too many of them 'did not spend our church means in a church-like manner, but converted them to our own private uses'.[5]

Goodman was perhaps unlucky in his timing. At a slightly earlier date, in 1607, the offering of a bribe to a secretary of state by Bishop Godwin of Llandaff brought no such swift retribution, and did not hinder his subsequent promotion to Hereford, which he held from 1617 to 1633.[6] His reputation there was that nothing fell into his gift 'but what he sold or disposed of, in regard to some son or daughter'. Theophilus Field, who was twice promoted by

---

[1] Heylyn, *Cyprianus Anglicus*, p. 198.

[2] Williams and Cozens-Hardy, op. cit., p. 45; W. Hutchinson, *The History . . . of Durham* (1785–94), ii. 154.

[3] Burne, 'The History of Chester Cathedral in the Reigns of James I and Charles I', loc. cit., p. 13; Robertson, *Sarum Close*, p. 175.

[4] Heylyn, *Cyprianus Anglicus*, p. 248. Mr. Soden attempts to defend Goodman against this charge, which rests on the evidence of Heylyn. This, if unsupported, would indeed be inadequate. Mr. Soden, however, provides no satisfactory explanation of the admitted fact that Goodman fell into deep disgrace with Laud and the king over the Hereford fiasco. Another contemporary account attributes his loss of Hereford to the fact that Goodman asked to be allowed to continue to hold Gloucester as well! (Soden, op. cit., chap. xix).

[5] Goodman, *The Two Great Mysteries*, sig. a 3ᵛ.   [6] White, op. cit., p. 409.

Laud, and also finally made his way to the desirable see of Hereford, had been impeached in 1621 for brocage and bribery, and
was admonished by Archbishop Abbott in respect of the brocage.[1]

Let us consider a single year, 1626. It was rumoured then that
there was a general policy of selling bishoprics, that Buckingham
had disposed of Salisbury for £3,500,[2] that Dean Young of Winchester had offered £15,000 for the Bishopric of Winchester, and
that Dr. White had bought the Bishopric of Carlisle. Some of these
stories may be malicious gossip, though the last two were related
to the virtuous Archbishop of Armagh by respectable characters.[3]
And in this same year we find that ardent promotion-hunter,
Richard Montagu, writing: 'I must grow miserable [i.e. miserly]
not to buy a bishopric', as though meanness and a feeling that
'I have deserved better of the church' were all that stood between
him and simony.[4] It was also in 1626 that Lewis Bayley, a 'Puritan'
bishop, famous as the author of *The Practice of Piety*, had to answer
charges alleging simony, bribery, and extortion, as well as 'incontinency the most palpably proved that ever I heard'.[5] What is
interesting for our purposes is that some thought the alleged offer
of £15,000 for the Bishopric of Winchester was not excessive,
since the incoming bishop could expect to get £10,000 by leases
at his first entrance.

II

Such were some of Laud's colleagues on the episcopal bench.
What he thought of them may be gathered from Instructions
issued by Charles I in 1629, at Laud's instance. Bishops were
ordered to reside in their sees, in houses belonging to the see,
unless their attendance was necessary at court.[6] They were not to

---

[1] Browne Willis, op. cit. i. 525; Gardiner, *History*, iv. 125.

[2] Weldon, op. cit., p. 120.

[3] Parr, op. cit. ii. 373, 377. If Young did offer £15,000, it proved insufficient to
win him the bishopric. We find him in 1630 keeping a wary eye on the leasing policy
of the successful aspirant, the Laudian Neile, who, the Dean thought, was more
interested in his own pocket than the good of the see (*Diary*, pp. 88–90). The story
about White was generally believed: he was alleged to have sold his books in order
to make the purchase.

[4] Ornsby, op. cit. i. 98.

[5] Birch, op. cit. i. 96.

[6] This was a little severe. Laud himself, when Bishop of St. David's, had regularly
resided in London, paying two brief visits to his diocese in five years. He could plead
court office during this period (*Diary, passim*, in *Works*, ii).

waste the woods of their sees. If translated to another bishopric, they should not, after their nomination, make or renew any leases, or cut any timber.[1]

Leases of bishops' and dean and chapter lands had earlier been limited to three lives or twenty-one years.[2] In 1633 Laud persuaded Charles to forbid leases for lives altogether, both to bishops and to deans and chapters, 'for by that means the present bishop [or dean and chapter] puts a great fine into his own purse to enrich himself, his wife, and children, and leaves all his successors, of what desert soever to us and the church, destitute of that growing means which else would come in to help them. By which course, should it continue, scarce any bishop would be able to live and keep house according to his place and calling.' Time and experience have made it apparent that there is a great deal of difference between leases for lives and years, 'especially in church leases, where men are commonly in great years before they come to those places'.[3] In 1634 these instructions were extended to each prebendary individually. Laud also ordered a survey and inventory of all bishops' and dean and chapter lands, so that a record might be kept, and spoliation and concealment at last be checked.[4]

The motive was double; first, economic, to give bishops and deans and chapters a chance of raising fines and racking rents at shorter intervals, and to reduce sale of the future by taking heavy entry fines for the longer period: second, and chiefly, social, 'that the gentry and yeomanry (and some of the nobility also) holding lands of those churches might have a greater respect to the church and churchmen, when they must depend upon them from time to time for renewing of their said estates at the end of every ten or twelve years at the most'. It is a medieval conception of dependence.[5] The Dean and Chapter of Canterbury, in welcoming the 1634 Instructions, claimed to have been denying leases for lives during the preceding ten years, 'despite the importunity some-

---

[1] Cardwell, *Documentary Annals*, ii. 177–9. The prohibition on felling timber was inserted at Abbott's instance, in view of great transgressions not long since in the north (*C.S.P.D.*, *1629–31*, p. 118; cf. *Hist. MSS. Commission, MSS. in Various Collections*, ii. 195).   [2] See pp. 14–15, 30 above.

[3] Cardwell, *Documentary Annals*, ii. 195–6; *C.S.P.D.*, *1634–5*, p. 88. See Laud's defence of this Instruction in *Works*, iv. 192; cf. v. 359–60.

[4] *MSS. of the Dean and Chapter of Wells* (Hist. MSS. Commission), ii. 410; Cardwell, op. cit. ii. 197–9; cf. Laud, *Works*, vi. 389–90, 601–2; vii. 498.

[5] Heylyn, *Cyprianus Anglicus*, pp. 319–20. Cf. Burnet, *History of my Own Time* (1897), i. 21, and p. 38 above.

times of persons of quality'.[1] In 1636 the Dean of Winchester was attacked in his own Chapter for neglecting the inheritance of the church and failing to collect arrears of rent 'out of a desire to gain the love of the gentry'.[2]

A royal letter, directed to the Bishop of Bristol on 28 March 1634, illustrates the policy of checking plunder by bishops. In this Charles expressed his determination 'to see the bishops decently supplied ... according to their place and dignity', without excessive resort to *commendams*, 'which hath bred some scandal'. The Bishop was therefore instructed that the manor of Abbotts Cromwell, on the lease of which only one life remained, was to be held as demesne after that life fell in; or, if leased, to be leased by the bishop only during his own occupation of the see. A copy of this letter was to be presented to each succeeding Bishop of Bristol on consecration or translation, 'till we shall find an opportunity to annex it for ever by an act of Parliament'. Similar instructions were sent to the Bishop of St. David's in 1637 for the perpetual annexation of two rectories *in commendam*.[3] In 1635 Bishop Wren gratified the king but infuriated his successors at Hereford by persuading Charles to annex an impropriate rectory to the see as demesne.[4]

These royal letters of 1634 and 1637 are only two examples of the minute instructions which were issued to enforce the new policy, and of the determined government supervision which followed. Thus the Bishop of Bangor was ordered to make a survey of all the lands of his see.[5] The Dean and Chapter of Peterborough were told on several occasions how a valuable old lease was to be treated when it fell in.[6] The Bishop of Winchester was ordered to conserve timber by refusing in future to bind himself to find wood for repairs to his tenants' houses.[7] The Deans and Chapters of Chester and Salisbury were rebuked for letting for lives, or for more than twenty-one years, after receipt

---

[1] *C.S.P.D.*, *1634–5*, p. 138.   [2] Young, *Diary*, pp. 120–1.

[3] Lambeth MS. 943, f. 329; cf. Laud, *Works*, v. 353, vii. 413–16; *C.S.P.D.*, *1631–3*, p. 573; *1638–9*, p. 205; Wilkins, op. cit. iv. 535–6.

[4] Wren, *Parentalia*, pp. 51, 31.

[5] Laud, *Works*, vi. 389–90.

[6] S. Gunston, *The History of the Church of Peterborough* (1686), pp. 169–72; *C.S.P.D.*, *1634–5*, p. 432.

[7] Ibid., *1635*, p. 237. Nevertheless, as late as 1656, 'the negligence of the Bishop of Winchester' was blamed for laying waste a wood in Somerset (*Quarter Sessions Records for the County of Somerset, 1646–60*, ed. E. H. B. Harbin, Somerset Record Soc., 1912, p. 316).

of the king's prohibition, and were given precise instructions about leasing houses in the cathedral close. The orders to Salisbury, sent in the king's name, added that all mechanics should be displaced from the close; and Laud also urged the Dean and Chapter to keep a careful eye on a cartway through the close. The Dean and Chapter of York were ordered by the king to pull down houses built up against the minster.[1]

The Dean and Chapter of Winchester also had to be reprimanded for making leases for lives, and the royal authority was invoked against them too : Laud discussed with them the annulling of ancient copyhold customs.[2] The Dean and Chapter of Durham were ordered not to renew leases of houses in the cathedral close; others of their tenants who had collected some £80 for joint action against their landlords' attempt to break their leases were rebuked by the Council, their fund was confiscated, and they were threatened with non-renewal of their leases, in addition to suffering imprisonment. For Laud was convinced that the tenants' action was 'a practice against the church', concealing 'some further design'.[3] He had no such suspicions of the tenants of the disgraced Bishop of Lincoln, who were always appealling to the Privy Council against his leases.[4]

The Dean and Chapter of Bristol were bullied into augmenting their church's revenue, when making leases, at the expense of their own pockets; the Dean and Chapter of Carlisle were made to use fines to pay for repairs to the cathedral.[5] In the last two cases the central authorities used the bishop to put pressure on the dean and chapter. Bishop Coke in 1639 reminded the Dean and Chapter of Bristol that they had promised absolute submission to the decisions of Charles I and Laud, but he still had to threaten them

---

[1] Laud, *Works*, vi. 497–8; *Wilts. Notes and Queries*, i. 19–20, 22, 31; *C.S.P.D., 1633–4*, p. 72. If the 'mechanics' were ejected, they had made their way back by 1641.

[2] Stephens and Madge, *Documents relating to the history of the cathedral church of Winchester*, p. 19; *C.S.P.D., 1639–40*, p. 93.

[3] Rushworth, op. cit. iii. 1051–2; Ornsby, op. cit. i. 216; *C.S.P.D., 1640*, p. 503; *Hist. MSS. Commission, Fourth Report, Appendix*, p. 26; Hutchinson, op. cit. ii. 149–66. The tenants' case was that security of tenure had been guaranteed them by the government in 1577, when the old tenant right (which had included obligations to military service on the Border) had been replaced by 21-year leases. The imprisoned tenants were released after a year, when the Short Parliament was about to meet. In December 1640 they petitioned the Long Parliament for justice against Dean Balcanqual (Rushworth, op. cit. iv. 120). [4] Hacket, op. cit. ii. 88.

[5] *C.S.P.D., 1639–40*, pp. 10–11, 149–50; Laud, *Works*, vi. 601–2.

with trouble at visitation before they gave way. 'What would a thousand Puritans say?' he asked of the Dean's attempt to win the Bishop's co-operation by allowing him to pocket £200.[1]

It is fantastic to think that in December 1638 the man who was in effect prime minister of England spent a great deal of his time considering pews in Chester cathedral, and the effects of the death of Mrs. Berners on leases in the close there.[2] Laud certainly wished high priority to be given to such matters; and this fussy paternalism must have had some effect. But a large and incorruptible civil service would have been needed to make the government's policy work properly. The king might surrender his own interest in a lease to the advantage of the Bishop of Landaff.[3] But too often courtiers were able to frustrate attempts to augment episcopal revenues. Thus Lord Arundell of Wardour stopped Bishop Morton of Durham annulling a lease of coal-mines; and the Earl of Pembroke was able to bully the same prelate, 'a timorous person', into agreeing to the alienation of Durham House in the Strand.[4]

Laud, moreover, was faced with evasions by his own higher clergy. Deans pretended that orders to themselves and their chapters did not affect their rights in regard to leases which they could make alone:[5] and deans and chapters had a mutual interest in continuing to keep entry fines (which they shared) high, at the expense of their successors. Even such good Laudians as Neile and Cosin could not quite accept their master's wholesale repudiation of leases for lives.[6] The Dean of Winchester was accused by his own chapter of ignoring the prohibition of leases for lives, and he did not deny it: Laud's interference here with the Dean's leasing policy was comprehensible.[7] Robert Wright, 'the richest Bishop that ever was of Bristol', appears to have disregarded the veto on leases for lives, impoverishing his see to buy himself lands to the value of over £18,000. After his translation to Coventry he also disregarded the prohibition on cutting timber.[8]

[1] *C.S.P.D.*, *1639–40*, pp. 10–11.

[2] Burne, 'The History of Chester Cathedral in the Reigns of James I and Charles I', loc. cit., pp. 21–24; Wilkins, op. cit. iv. 517–22.

[3] *C.S.P.D.*, *1628–9*, pp. 570, 593.

[4] Ibid., *1634–5*, pp. 170–1; Ornsby, op. cit. i. 148.

[5] Cardwell, *Documentary Annals*, ii. 198–9.

[6] Ornsby, op. cit. ii. 240.   [7] Young, *Diary*, pp. 139–41.

[8] D. Lloyd, *Memoires*, p. 600; *C.S.P.D.*, *1637–8*, pp. 315, 351; *1638–9*, p. 205; A. Wood, *Athenae Oxonienses* (1813–20), iv. 800–1; Laud, *Works*, v. 346. There were unseemly squabbles about dilapidations between incoming and outgoing Bishops at

It was later alleged that, just before the Long Parliament met, bishops who foresaw the deluge imitated the pre-dissolution abbots by alienating land by private agreement. In 1659 Dr. Burgess named nineteen manors 'alienated from the Bishopric of Bath and Wells, before ever the late Parliament seized the rest; and are held by laymen, to their own private uses, without scruple or blame'.[1] Other evidence, from other bishoprics, seems to confirm the existence of an unusually high proportion of leases, on favourable terms, dating from 16 & 17 Car. I.[2]

Far too much havoc had been done before Laud secured the primacy for the new measures to produce any very rapid economic or social improvement. Thus at Chichester, Montagu, a bishop at last, complained bitterly of the leasing policy of his immediate predecessors. He had managed to pick holes in some of their leases, but needed powerful support to be able to do the job properly. So he offered favourable leases to Secretary Dorchester and Endymion Porter, and so presumably left problems for his successors.[3] Laud's annual reports from the dioceses are full of observations like this from Bangor in 1638: 'Everything is let for lives by his [the present Bishop's] predecessors, to the very mill that grinds his corn.' From Norwich, to which he had now moved, Montagu also complained of 'impoverishing of that Bishopric by some of his predecessors..., partly by letting of long leases before the statute restrained it', partly by exchanges.[4]

In this report Montagu added a warning that 'whereas it is said commonly, the Bishopric of Norwich, when Scambler's demise expires, will be worth £3,000 *per annum*, it is ignorantly spoken. It will not be one penny better than it is, unless an honest, conscientious man be then Bishop, who will increase the rents to succession, and not take all to himself by fines.' He recommended an order from the king forbidding any Bishop of Norwich henceforth to let any manors or lands without doubling the old rent,

Durham in 1632, at Norwich in 1634 (Hutchinson, op. cit. i. 499. *C.S.P.D. 1634–5*, p. 102).

[1] C. Burgess, *A Case concerning the Buying of Bishops Lands*, quoted in J. T. Rutt, *Parliamentary Diary of Thomas Burton* (1828), iii. 201–3. If Burgess was right, Bishop Pierce had no doubt taken advantage of the royal revocation of the prohibition on leases for lives, made on 16 March 1641.

[2] For examples see Bodington, op. cit., *passim* (at least eleven in Wiltshire); Lysons, *Environs of London*, i. 13 (lease made to a man who subsequently bought the estate from the parliamentary trustees; his family survived the Restoration as lessees), iii. 31, iv. 317.   [3] *C.S.P.D., 1629–31*, pp. 122–4.   [4] Laud, *Works*, v. 359.

'or taking one-third part of the old rent (beside the whole rent in money) according to the statute of provision' (i.e. in kind).[1] The diocese might then be worth something to his successors, but Montagu had no hopes for himself, 'unless I can void Scambler's lease', by which 'the greatest part of the Bishopric of Norwich' had been demised to Elizabeth for Sir Thomas Heneage for eighty years in 1588; 'which I hope to do with his Majesty's assistance'.[2] When all allowances have been made for Montagu's desire to show himself in a favourable light, that letter describes a real and universal problem: a problem which could only be solved if 'honest, conscientious men' were made bishops, and if for a long period they followed a concerted policy with full government support.

III

Laud made a determined attempt to increase the revenues both of bishops and ministers. Among the projects which he noted down were '(ix) To annex for ever some settled *commendams*, and those if it may be, *sine cura*, to all the small bishoprics. (x) To find a way to increase the stipends of poor vicars. . . . (xxii) If I live to see the repair of St. Paul's near an end, to move his Majesty for the like grant from the High Commission for the buying in of impropriations, as I now have it for St. Paul's. And then I hope to buy in two a year at least.'

The first of these projects was subsequently ticked off as 'done' for Bristol, Peterborough, St. Asaph, Chester, and Oxford.[3] These were settlements in perpetuity, and in addition Oxford received a pension of £100. In 1632 John Bancroft was made Bishop of Oxford on condition that he supplied the see with an episcopal palace at his own expense[4]—a transaction which the purist might regard as approaching simony. Other bishops received licences to hold livings *in commendam*. Thus was pluralism enlisted in the

[1] The reference is presumably to 18 Eliz., c. 6. See p. 99 above.

[2] Lambeth MS. 943, f. 622; *V.C.H., Norfolk*, ii. 285. For Scambler, see pp. 19–20 above.

[3] Laud, *Works*, iii. 253–5. For Bristol, and for the perpetual settlement of rectories on Hereford and St. David's, see p. 312 above. The sinister implication of a 'grant from the High Commission' is that this would come from fines there. Cf. Laud, *Works*, vii. 645.

[4] Ed. J. A. W. Bennett and H. R. Trevor-Roper, *The Poems of Richard Corbett* (1955), pp. xxxiv–xxxv.

service of ecclesiastical reform. In his defence at his trial, Laud recognized that '*commendams* taken at large and far distant caused a great dislike and murmur among many men'. He claimed that he had tried to settle temporal leases or sinecure benefices upon the bishoprics in such a way that 'no other man's patronage might receive prejudice by the bishop's *commendam*: which was not the least rock of offence against which *commendams* endangered themselves'.[1] But the offence remained. 'There was some sense for *commendams* at first', Selden thought; 'when there was a living void and never a clerk to serve it, the bishops were to keep it till they found a fit man; but now 'tis a trick for the bishop to keep it for himself.'[2] So in yet another instance governmental economic reform threatened property rights, without satisfactorily solving the church's problems.

The Instructions of 1634 suggest that Laud's reforming purposes were made a mockery of by some of his colleagues on the episcopal bench. It proved necessary to insist that every bishop who had received a perpetual *commendam* should account for it annually to his metropolitan, in order to ensure that he did not pass it on to a kinsman or friend or other person, 'thereby to frustrate our gracious intention to the bishops succeeding to those several sees'.[3] Charles and Laud showed a certain anxiety about *commendams*, but Bishop Coke of Bristol had fewer scruples. When he wrote to his brother, the secretary of state, to secure his help in obtaining a living in Dorset, his main concern was lest a minister should be appointed before the transaction was completed.[4]

IV

A general augmentation of stipends presented even greater problems than provision for bishops. But there was no doubt about the government's intentions. In 1626 Laud was discussing with the king the restoration of impropriations to the church, and 'the manner of effecting it'. Charles was believed to intend to restore royal impropriations in England as he had done in Ireland.[5] One

---

[1] Laud, *Works*, iv. 177; cf. pp. 234–6 above. Note that Laud is careful to express no disapproval of *commendams* himself.

[2] Selden, *Table Talk*, p. 13.

[3] Cardwell, *Documentary Annals*, ii. 180.

[4] *C.S.P.D., 1636–7*, pp. 507–8; *Cowper MSS.* (Hist. MSS. Commission), ii. 77.

[5] Laud, *Works*, iii. 186, 253–5; iv. 176–7. For Ireland, see pp. 334–6 below.

indication of the king's wishes, not in itself entirely reliable, can be found in a report of some remarks made by Clarendon during his second exile at Rouen:

Milord Clarendon disoit ici que la premiere semence des mouvemens d'Angleterre, qui n'ont que trop éclaté sous le régne de Charles I, venoit de ce que ce prince avoit témoigné peu après qu'il fut monté sur le trône de son père, qu'il vouloit retirer les biens ecclésiastiques des mains de la noblesse avec qui Henri VIII, auteur du schisme, les avoit partagez : cela fit croire aux mécontens qu'il avoit de l'inclination pour la religion catholique, et que c'étoit par cet endroit qu'il vouloit commencer à y entrer; du moins, ils furent bien aises qu'on le crût, et ils en firent courir le bruit.[1]

Despite the gossipy nature of the source, it is difficult to think of any reason why Clarendon, or his reporter, should have invented the story, and it seems to me that the facts assembled here render it inherently probable. We may, however, doubt whether the phrase *les biens ecclésiastiques*, which would appear to include all monastic lands, may not be an incorrect recollection of a reference to tithes formerly appropriated to monasteries.

Charles's good intentions had a habit of not being realized. It was not until the safe year 1646 that he bound himself by a solemn vow to restore impropriations : a vow which neither he nor his most religious successor was ever in a position to carry out.[2] But before 1640 'the sacrilege of impropriations' had been one of 'the most frequent subjects even in the most sacred auditories'.[3] The atmosphere was so favourable that even Bishop Goodman of Gloucester is said to have been applying his mind to a project whereby 'impropriations might be recovered to the church, to make it much the richer, and no man a jot the poorer'.[4] It is a pity that, like those who square the circle or discover the philosophers' stone, he does not seem to have left the details to posterity.

[1] De Vigneul-Marville, *Mélanges d'histoire et de littérature* (Rotterdam, 1700–2), i. 152–3. I have not attempted to modernize the French. John Connell, who quoted part of the passage in his *Treatise on the Law of Scotland respecting Tithes* (1815, i. 216), believed that the reference was to Scotland (see below, pp. 332–3); but then how does Henry VIII come in?

[2] In an anonymous *Essay on Charles I* published in 1748 this famous vow appears in a chapter entitled 'The King weak in religious matters and inclined to superstition' (p. 53). A century later it was quoted by the two Tractarian editors of Spelman's *History of Sacrilege* with rather more approval (1853, p. 231).

[3] Falkland's speech of 9 Feb. 1641, in Nalson, op. cit. i. 768.

[4] Lloyd, *Memoires*, p. 601.

Not that detailed schemes were lacking. That inveterate projector, Richard Day, who no doubt owed his interest in matters ecclesiastical to the fact that his father, two uncles, and his maternal grandfather had all been bishops, put forward in 1628 a plan for buying in impropriations by the crown. The money was to be raised by a general collection, and the incumbents would be allowed to receive the full tithes on payment of a yearly rent to the crown. By this means a constant annual revenue of £55,000–£60,000 would be raised. The scheme was actually referred in 1630 to a committee of the Council (including Laud) for consideration. The only tiny drawback was the utter impossibility of raising the huge initial capital sum required.[1]

Abbott had not been much in sympathy with Laud's aspirations to use the secular arm to improve the economic position of the clergy. He reproved Laud for trying to get Buckingham to reduce the burden of subsidies on ministers.[2] So when in July 1628 Charles I ordered the Archbishop of Canterbury to have an inquiry made throughout his province of all rectories, vicarages, and other ecclesiastical promotions upon which any usurpation had been made by the patrons or other pretenders in the preceding forty years, Abbott appears to have taken no action at all. It was over four years later that letters were sent on to the bishops telling them to institute such inquiries.[3]

Despite the goodwill of the king, then, Laud had no hope of establishing a fund for the repurchase of impropriations comparable to that of the Feoffees whom he suppressed. His highest ambition was to buy in two impropriations a year with the proceeds of fines in the High Commission. This he never even started to do; and at the rate of progress he had set himself it would have been nearly 2,000 years before the church was freed from impropriations. 'Tarrying for the magistrate' was likely to be a lengthy business.

But men knew what Laud wanted. As part of the prolonged pressure which he exercised to make Scudamore disgorge his

---

[1] *C.S.P.D., 1628–9*, p. 357; *1629–31*, p. 174; *1625–49*, pp. 358–9, 398. Day had asked that his scheme should be referred to Sir Benjamin Rudyerd. He also had a project for planting timber trees on bishops' lands, at vast profit to himself: see p. 20 above. He was still at it in 1638, when he offered to help the king and his heirs to a yearly sum of money equal to Ship Money (*Cowper MSS.*, Hist. MSS. Commission, ii. 186).

[2] See p. 194 above.   [3] Kennett, op. cit., p. 221.

impropriations, Laud thus expressed his views on the subject: 'Were your case mine, if I could not give my impropriations back, I would beg God's mercy and sell them, that I might be able to give. And when God had taken off my difficulty and made me able, I would as readily give, if not all at once, then gradually.' And he continued, answering Scudamore's objections: 'Your ancestors bought them. True. But it was of him that had no right to sell, and they had as little to buy. . . . If any man think an act of parliament is an absolution from sin against the moral law of God, he is much out of the way.'[1]

That far-reaching principle was laid down in a private letter. But Richard Montagu had already rushed in where Laud trod warily. In a book published in 1621 he declared roundly that 'laymen . . . had [not], nor have, nor can have right unto [impropriations] by any authority under heaven'. 'Restore us our own, to which we have an eternal right.' Montagu was protected from Parliament and promoted by Laud and Charles. As in the case of the tithes of London, he had laid down the programme which Laud was later to try to carry into effect.[2] The same principle was expressed, as clearly, by Sir Henry Spelman, both verbally and in *The Larger Treatise concerning Tythes*, which was circulating in manuscript in the sixteen-thirties though not published (posthumously) until 1646.[3] The salient passage is quoted as epigraph to this chapter.

The constitutional implications of these dicta of Montagu, Laud, and Spelman, and (what is the same thing) their threat to the property of many subjects, need no emphasis. Behind the conflict of courts for jurisdiction over tithes and impropriations stood the conflict of laws: the Law of God, or statute law? The traditional system of appropriation backed up by divine right: or positive laws deriving their authority from a known 'man or body of men'? Here again two entirely different bodies of ideas and sets of values were in conflict: the sovereignty of Parliament was necessary for the security of property.

---

[1] Trevor-Roper, op. cit., pp. 450–3. See above, pp. 271–2.
[2] Montagu, op. cit., pp. 76, 404. See p. 280 above.
[3] Spelman, *English Works*, i. 137–47. Scudamore asked for Spelman's advice as well as Laud's (Ed. Gibson, *Reliquiae Spelmanniae*, 1698, p. 64).

V

But failing a general resumption of impropriations, there were partial steps that could be taken. Before the Reformation, bishops had claimed the right to see that appropriators provided adequate maintenance for their vicars. This was based on the canon lawyers' claim that the cure of souls within a diocese was *de jure communi* in the bishop, and that if the appropriator allowed the cure of souls to be neglected the tithes would return of right to the bishop. He could decide whether an endowment was adequate, and if necessary order it to be increased.[1] This right had been disputed by monasteries, but never abandoned by bishops. What had happened at the Reformation? The bishops' right had certainly lapsed: but had it been extinguished, either by the statutes dissolving the abbeys, or by disuse?

The lower house of Convocation in 1554 had petitioned for the bishops' right to be recognized.[2] The code of ecclesiastical laws drafted in Edward VI's reign, and supported by the Puritans in Elizabeth's, gave bishops this right.[3] The ecclesiastical lawyers claimed that it still existed. The bishops themselves came near to admitting its legal extinction in suggestions which Bancroft made to the House of Lords in 1610 for the betterment of livings. Here he urged, *inter alia*, that bishops should be granted authority in their dioceses to allot augmentations to endowed vicarages where there was no competent living for a sufficient minister.[4] The question was taken up again, abortively, in the Parliament of 1614. But in the draft 'act touching benefices appropriate' it was proposed that *two justices of assize* should be associated with the ordinary in allotting to the vicar such portion of the tithes and glebe as they thought necessary for his maintenance; and it was stipulated that *only preaching ministers* should benefit. The same suggestion was made in 1621.[5] The provisos which I have emphasized made the proposal very different from that sponsored by the hierarchy.

---

[1] Kennett, op. cit., appendix, pp. 1–2; F. Makower, *Constitutional History of the Church of England* (1895), pp. 330–1. 'Common right is the same thing as common law', [Anon.], *The Grounds and Rudiments of Law and Equity* (1741), p. 338.

[2] Cardwell, *Synodalia*, p. 438.

[3] *The Reformation of the Ecclesiastical Laws*, pp. 96–97.

[4] Collier, op. cit. vii. 352–4; cf. pp. 246–7, 251 above.

[5] *Commons' Journals*, i. 456; cf. Notestein, Relf, and Simpson, op. cit. vii. 640, ii. 301.

In 1625 the view of the House of Commons seems to have been that the ordinary's right to increase vicars' maintenance by charging impropriations had been extinguished by 31 Hen. VIII, c. 13. Charles I's answer to their petition on religion merely proposed that impropriators should allow sufficient stipends to preaching ministers, which suggests that the government did not at that stage think that bishops could legally compel augmentation: or at all events did not wish to say so in public.[1] No parliamentary action followed; and the king's hint was taken by only a few individuals. There were isolated local attempts to revive the bishops' authority. Thus in 1624 a vicar petitioned the Bishop of Winchester to obtain an augmentation for him from the impropriator.[2] At Crediton, alienated from the see of Worcester in 1597, an attempt began in 1631 to challenge the impropriation of the rectory by the corporation, on the ground that there was no endowment for a vicar.[3]

But nothing decisive happened until Laud succeeded to the primacy. Laud appears to have been incited to action by his kinsman, Bishop Morton of Lichfield, who was very anxious to augment poor vicarages. Morton took counsel of Lord Keeper Coventry, Noy, and Sir Henry Marten. All these lawyers agreed that the bishop's authority over churches impropriate had neither been taken away nor any way infringed.[4] There is no evidence that Laud was consulted at this stage, but it appears likely from the sequence of events.

For in 1634 a test case was brought, variously described as Thornborough *v.* Hitchcock, or Hitchcock *v.* Thornborough and Hitchcock. John Hitchcock (or Hitchcot or Hiscop), vicar of Preshute, Wiltshire, complained to the church courts that the lessee of the impropriation did not allow him an adequate maintenance. (He received £13. 6s. 8d. and a little close of meadow, 'whereon heretofore stood the vicarage house, now wholly decayed': the lessee's rent was £23 per annum, for a rectory which the parliamentary surveyors were to value at £183. 4s. 0d.) The rector was canon and Master of the Choristers at Salisbury cathedral—an ecclesiastic. The lessee was John Hitchcock of Preshute, gentle-

---

[1] Gardiner, *1625 Debates*, p. 27; Rushworth, op. cit. i. 183.
[2] *Cowper MSS.* (Hist. MSS. Commission), i. 171.
[3] Gwillim, op. cit. ii. 436–67; see p. 17 above.
[4] Kennett, op. cit., pp. 244–8, quoting Barwick's biography of Morton attached to the funeral sermon on him which was published in 1660.

man: the identity of surname suggests that the action may have been collusive. He tried to get a prohibition of the vicar's case, but it was refused by both the King's Bench and the Common Pleas. The church court then decided that the vicar's suit was reasonable, and that the ordinary had the right to compel the impropriator to increase the maintenance, because in all appropriations made before the dissolution of the monasteries that power had been reserved to the ordinary. The Bishop of Salisbury proceeded to lay an augmentation on the lessee.

Here was glory for the bishops. A prohibition had been refused in a case clearly affecting property-rights. And it had been refused because the common-law courts had recognized the ordinary's power to compel an impropriator to augment. This particular judgment concerned a benefice appropriated to an ecclesiastic. At Preshute, moreover, the bishop's right had been reserved by the appropriator in 1323; and fourteen other vicarages within the diocese of Salisbury are listed in the State Papers in respect of which bishops possessed and exercised the right to augment vicars' portions. (In fact the living of Preshute had been increased from £8 to £13. 6s. 8d. in 1560, by an agreement between rector and vicar which was ratified by Bishop Jewell.) But there was nothing now to stop the church courts extending the validity of the judgment, nothing that is in law. What mattered was the refusal of a prohibition, recognition of the bishop's rights.[1] With the common-law judges as tamed as that, impropriators lay potentially at mercy.

Next year Laud acted. He wrote to Williams, Bishop of Lincoln, urging him to make a general visitation of his diocese in order to augment poor vicarages, in accordance with the express wishes of the king. There may well have been similar letters to other bishops.

Williams replied on 15 July 1635, acknowledging Charles I's

---

[1] Register of Bishops Townsend and Davenant, 1620–1640, ff. 13–14 (Salisbury Diocesan Registry); Rolle, op. cit. ii. 337; *C.S.P.D., 1633–4*, p. 511; Gibson, op. cit., pp. 757–8; Stillingfleet, op. cit. i. 290–1; H. Wood, op. cit. i. 457–8; Bodington, op. cit. xli. 113–15; C. Wordsworth and D. H. Robertson, 'Salisbury Choristers', *Wilts. Archaeological and Natural History Magazine*, clxviii. 203–10; *Wilts. Notes and Queries*, i. 74–75. Preshute is a 'lost' village: *Wilts. Archaeological and Natural History Magazine*, cxcii. 296–7. It was also the residence of Sir Francis Seymour, brother of the Marquis of Hertford, 'who showed himself a very noble friend to the business' of augmenting the vicarage (Laud, *Works*, vi. 430). Seymour subsequently voted against Strafford's attainder and was an active royalist.

most gracious intention 'to better the poor vicarages of the kingdom with an augmentation of their compositions, which all diocesans are supposed able to effect *jure communi*, and some of them *jure particulari*, by special pacts and reservations in the compositions themselves'. He asked for guidance, however, on three points : (1) how to answer the legal argument that impropriations were, since 32 Hen. VIII, c. 7, to all intents and purposes lay fees; (2) how to treat ecclesiastical bodies who had leased their impropriations? Was the augmentation to come from the lessor or the lessee? If charged on the lessor, this would sink many colleges, bishoprics, deans and chapters: if on the lessee, would a prohibition not be issued at once? (3) could anything be done for the most miserable class of all, incumbents of vicarages which were not endowed and who had to drive such bargains as they could with the lay rector?[1]

Laud replied by return that he had already thought about these problems. The king intended bishops to proceed by no other way than *jure communi*. In answer to the first question, Laud admitted that legal opinion was divided, but said that the lawyers upon whom he most relied, including Attorney-General Noy, thought that no statute could affect the nature of tithes. He thus clearly intended that bishops should ultimately be able to compel the owners of former monastic impropriations to augment vicars' portions. Yet as a matter of tactics lay fees should be tackled last. It is worth quoting in full his answer to Williams's second question :

> The lessor's rent is small; . . . the lessee goes away with almost all the profit; therefore the course thought on is that the lessors be desired, as leases determine and come within their power by renewing, to make addition to the several vicarages, endowed or not endowed, and charge it upon the lessee. . . . And where the leases are in lives, or great number of years, then the ordinary may proceed, and *de jure communi* lay the augmentation upon the lessee, ratably to his profits above his rent.

Laud then quoted the case of Hitchcock *v*. Thornborough and Hitchcock, in which a prohibition had been twice refused. 'So we have gained two precedents for the strengthening of *jus commune* in the ordinary. And all my counsel are of opinion that this is the best way to go on and gather strength.' But since the impropriation in the test case had belonged to an ecclesiastical body, it

[1] Laud, *Works*, vii. 425–8; cf. v. 327, also Kennett, op. cit., pp. 218–19, and appendix, pp. 38–41; Lambeth MS. 1030, f. 36.

would be safest to begin with such impropriations; 'and then we may go on to the laity after, if the law shall so far favour us in this very Christian cause'. About 'poor stipendiaries' in unendowed vicarages Laud was less confident. 'Methinks, *a paritate rationis*, the diocesan should have as much or more power here to preserve a poor churchman in livelihood, where there is less allowance than any endowment makes.' But prudently recollecting that law and 'reason' were not always identical, even to the most subservient judges, he recommended that Williams should report further on any such case as it arose.[1]

Here was a vast programme for restoring the church to the economic and political position it had enjoyed before the Reformation. It would have involved a frontal attack on private property rights as most lay property-owners conceived them. It would also have involved a frontal attack on the common law, since 'nothing is more peremptorily delivered throughout the books of the common law than the contrary doctrine', namely, that all impropriations are lay fees over which the ordinary has no power.[2] Laud had secured his prohibition in a case affecting an impropriation belonging to an ecclesiastic. As a matter of tactics he was prepared to bide his time; but he clearly would have liked to tackle laymen. He got a directive from the king to take order for the augmentation of the maintenance of vicars and curates where need required.[3] The Archbishop's policy would have meant 'subjecting the inheritance of every lay impropriator in the kingdom to the power of the ordinary, to be taxed at his pleasure', declared an eighteenth-century lawyer.[4]

In the light of these facts, and of Laud's known belief that impropriations were contrary to the law of God, from which no man could be absolved by act of Parliament, the Archbishop's outburst to Sir Arthur Haselrig, that he hoped 'ere long not to leave so much as the name of a lay-fee in England' acquires considerable significance. It was not mere bluster: it was the possibly incautious revelation of a carefully prepared plan of campaign. For Haselrig had long kept his living of Nosely vacant; he had been protesting to Laud against the presentation of a minister to

---

[1] Laud, *Works*, vi. 429–30.

[2] Gibson, op. cit., p. 758. There is something comical in the plaintive and laborious amazement with which the Bishop of London brings himself to recognize that political fact has triumphed over what used to be the legal rights of the church.

[3] *C.S.P.D., 1640–1*, pp. 342–3. [4] Sir Michael Foster, op. cit., p. 101.

this living by Sir John Lambe, and the laying of an augmentation upon the impropriation.[1] A humbler man petitioned the House of Lords in 1641, alleging that the Archbishop had long wrongfully withheld a lay fee from him; but he had not dared hitherto to seek remedy 'as the times have been, and the greatness of the Archbishop considered'.[2] There may well have been many such.

VI

After this it is something of an anti-climax to record what was actually achieved. Vicars in impropriations belonging to the Archbishop of Canterbury, curiously enough, seem to have received no augmentation. Williams increased the stipends of four or five small vicarages in his diocese, and several 'concealed vicarages' were discovered there.[3] But correspondence in the State Papers suggests that Williams was in no hurry. Vicars in that much-visited diocese appealed to Laud.[4] In 1637 the Archbishop sent seven articles of inquiry direct to poorer Lincolnshire vicars, and some of their replies survive. The vicar of Mumby, who received £15 per annum whilst the impropriation was worth £80, thought his vicarage could only be augmented out of the impropriation. So did the vicar of Rockley, who received £13. 3s. 4d. and valued the Duchess of Buckingham's impropriation at £100. The vicar of Farlsthorpe (£20 a year) thought a restoration of tithes in kind the best way of augmenting his vicarage; the vicar of the 'lost' village of Calceby (£13. 6s. 8d.) had no hope except from a repopulation of his parish in consequence of less oppressive rents. Two vicars who received small stipends from impropriations belonging to the Bishop of Lincoln tactfully refrained from indicating how they thought their livings could be improved.[5]

In addition to Preshute, two more livings were augmented in the diocese of Salisbury.[6] Bishop Morton augmented one living in the

---

[1] *C.S.P.D.*, *1641–3*, p. 547; cf. Laud, *Works*, iv. 184, *V.C.H.*, *Leicestershire*, i. 379. It is hardly an accident that it was Williams, who had connexions with the opposition, who was still concerned about the rights of owners of lay fees.

[2] *Hist. MSS. Commission, Fourth Report, Appendix*, p. 87.

[3] Larking, op. cit., pp. 141–239, *passim*; Laud, *Works*, v. 333–4; Lambeth MS. 943, f. 555.

[4] *C.S.P.D.*, *1637*, pp. 241, 392–3; *1640–1*, p. 343.

[5] Ibid., *1637–8*, pp. 167–81; cf. Laud, *Works*, v. 349, 356.

[6] Register of Bishops Townsend and Davenant, ff. 6–7.

diocese of Lichfield, and his successor another. After his translation to Durham, Morton increased one vicarage from £16 to £80
a year, and a chapel from £6 to £30, and had other augmentations
in view. In one at least of these cases the augmentation was added,
at the lessee's expense, when the lease was renewed. But his
efforts were interrupted when the Scots advanced to the rescue of
property-owners in the north.¹

The Dean and Chapter of Winchester augmented vicarages,
also at the lessee's expense, to the dissatisfaction of the Dean, who
feared lest compliance with the Archbishop's policy should ruin
relations with the local gentry.² In 1637 Laud persuaded the
Provost of Queen's College, Oxford, which leased the rectory of
Wimbledon from the Dean and Chapter of Worcester, to raise the
stipends of the curates of Putney and Mortlake to £40 apiece,
and to make them certain.³ Christ Church, New College, and
Magdalen also augmented some vicars' livings at this time.⁴ The
Bishop of Chester refused large fines for the renewal of the lease
of a rectory on which only one life remained. His intention was to
augment the vicarage (which was worth only 20 marks a year)
when the lease fell in, and to reserve an improved rent for his
successors in the see.⁵

But Laud was proceeding simultaneously by other means.
Petitions for augmentation at the expense of impropriators began
to flow in to the Council from vicars and curates. Clergymen also
intensified their efforts to revise *modi* to their advantage, with the
support of the church courts.⁶ The Council received many pleas
for protection against powerful adversaries in tithe suits. Such
petitions were almost always referred to the Archbishop to consider, usually in company with the Lord Keeper and the Bishop of

---

¹ Spelman, *English Works*, I. lxiv; Kennett, annotated copy of *The Case of Impropriations*, pp. 234, 247–8; Walker, op. cit. ii. 18. After the Restoration Bishop
Cosin reduced the augmentation from £64 to £16 (Hutchinson, op. cit. i. 538).

² Young, *Diary*, pp. 121–2, 148.

³ Laud, *Works*, vi. 488; Lysons, *Environs of London*, i. 414, 535. In 1658 Putney and
Mortlake were made separate rectories, endowed with great tithes to the value of
£80 and £70 respectively. But this of course did not survive the Restoration.

⁴ Lysons, *A View of the Revenues of the Parochial Clergy*, p. 74.

⁵ Bridgeman, op. cit., pp. 447–8, 421. Lloyd rather vaguely suggests that Manwaring of St. David's also refused fines in order to augment vicarages (*Memoires*,
p. 275).

⁶ For examples of tithe disputes between vicars and impropriators, see *C.S.P.D.*,
1637, pp. 96, 243; *1637–8*, pp. 189, 200, 396, 602; Newcourt, op. cit. ii. 330, 493,
518–19. Cf. pp. 119, 124–31 above.

London.¹ Reference to Laud was often asked for by petitioners;² or they might address themselves to him direct.³ In such cases, where the impropriator was an ecclesiastic or ecclesiastical corporation, an agreed settlement could be arrived at.⁴ On lay impropriators or lessees, the Council exercised pressure, often through the bishop of the see; and when a settlement had been extorted, ordered it to be registered in the Council Book.⁵ They issued orders to assist parsons in collecting arrears of tithe from mighty parishioners.⁶ They sent letters to the judges in tithe suits, e.g. when the Dean of Worcester appealed for protection against Lord Craven, who 'lies heavy upon the cathedral', and whose purse and power were too formidable.⁷ 'We shall find', said Falkland in February 1641, 'some bishops and their adherents . . . to have encouraged all the clergy to suits, and to have brought all suits to the Council-Table, . . . encouraging them to exact more of both [revenue and reverence] than was due.'⁸

By these means important victories were won. The Bishop of Worcester was able to persuade the town of Warwick to give their vicar £60 a year, besides fees, and to replace an undesirable curate by a conformable man.⁹ The Bishop of Lichfield and Coventry, acting on behalf of the Council, wrested tithes to the value of £80 per annum from laymen in Shrewsbury; they were granted as an augmentation to the vicar of another parish in the city. The impropriators of several churches in the same city agreed, after negotiation and threats of compulsion, to augment the stipends of their vicars or curates to a quarter the annual value of the tithes. The town's claim to nominate ministers was rejected.¹⁰ In Ipswich the civic authorities were allowed to assess rates for the maintenance of the town's ministers, including impropriators in the

---

¹ e.g. *C.S.P.D.*, *1633–4*, pp. 287, 548; *1634–5*, p. 434; *1635–6*, pp. 217, 520–1; *1637*, p. 479; *1637–8*, pp. 318, 405, 412, 461, 476; *1638–9*, pp. 54, 72, 211, 469–70.
² Ibid., *1637*, p. 241; *1637–8*, pp. 362, 606; *1638–9*, p. 383.
³ Ibid., *1637*, pp. 392–3; *1637–8*, p. 468; *1640*, p. 139.
⁴ Ibid., *1634–5*, p. 422; *1635–6*, p. 406; *1637*, p. 95.
⁵ Ibid., *1635*, p. 544; *1637–8*, pp. 205, 411–12; Turner, op. cit. i. 172; Soden, op. cit., p. 263. In Feb. 1636 Chancery ordered an impropriator to pay an augmentation (Usher, *High Commission*, p. 270).
⁶ *C.S.P.D.*, *1639*, p. 131.
⁷ Ibid., *1634–5*, pp. 435–6; cf. pp. 102–3, 313 above.
⁸ Nalson, op. cit. i. 769.   ⁹ *C.S.P.D.*, *1633–4*, p. 243.
¹⁰ Ibid., *1634–5*, p. 377; *1638–9*, pp. 209, 394–5; *1640–1*, pp. 342–3. One of the livings had been in the patronage of the Feoffees for Impropriations. Most of the parties appealed directly to Laud.

assessment. Again the town's right to nominate these ministers was denied.¹ In a long quarrel in Berwick-on-Tweed, the Council at one stage asked Laud to intervene with the Mercers' Company of London, who nominated and paid a lecturer in Berwick, or—even better—to secure an augmentation of the vicarage from the impropriators, the Dean and Chapter of Durham.²

Nor were corporations the only victims. The Bishop of Ely was expected to be able to persuade the Earl of Bedford to augment the living of a minister.³ When a member of the Boteler family fell ward, the king seized the opportunity to cancel leases of the parsonage, glebe, and tithes of a Herefordshire vicarage which was in their patronage.⁴ The Dean and Chapter of Durham, their enemy Peter Smart alleged, 'wrongfully' took a lease from Sir John Fenwick, and refused to renew it except for the unreasonably large fine of £2,000. This was foolish, since that 'worshipful, religious and virtuous knight' was a kinsman of the Earl of Bedford.⁵ In Lancashire Sir Ralph Assheton was compelled to surrender a lease for three lives of the rectory of Whalley, and to resume it for twenty-one years at a rent raised by £60 a year, and with a fine of £1,600. The increased rent was 'to add means to the several curates to the chapels of ease'.⁶ It is less surprising to find Sir Ralph commanding the parliamentarian forces in Lancashire in the civil war than that Sir John Fenwick was a royalist.

In another example from Lancashire we see the process halted half-way. In 1636 the vicar of Leigh petitioned the king, complaining of poverty and diminished revenue. His petition was referred from the Star Chamber to Laud and the Lord Keeper, who asked the Bishop of Chester to make inquiries. He certified that the vicar received £12. 11s. 4d. per annum net, plus a house, whilst the impropriator's revenue was £632 a year. The vicar's appeal for help would seem wholly justified. But it was too late for effective action to be taken; and in 1707, when the Bishop's successor reported again with a view to augmentation from

¹ Ibid., *1636-7*, pp. 529-30. See also p. 286 above.
² Ibid., *1636-7*, pp. 549-50; *1637-8*, pp. 60-61, 216; *1638-9*, pp. 217-18, 303; *City of Exeter MSS.*, pp. 195-6. See p. 271 above.
³ *Cowper MSS.* (Hist. MSS. Commission), i. 468. (Sir John Coke to the Bishop of Ely, 6 Aug. 1632.)
⁴ *C.S.P.D.*, *1638-9*, p. 60. Charles was careful to instruct the Master of the Court of Wards to see that the crown lost nothing by the restoration.
⁵ Ornsby, op. cit. i. 167.
⁶ Bridgeman, op. cit., pp. 381-4; Laud, *Works*, iv. 147-8.

Queen Anne's Bounty, the vicar's income had increased by only £4. 17*s*.[1]

So several things are noteworthy about these schemes of Laud's for augmenting vicars' livings. First, their far-reaching possibilities, both for lay property-owners and for the economic position of the church. Secondly, their infinitesimal results before 1640; which did not render the potentialities any less menacing. Laud's efforts did succeed in creating several bitter personal enemies for his régime. Thirdly, the crucial importance of the common-law courts. If they could be transformed into docile instruments of government policy, as the Ship Money case and Hitchcock *v.* Thornborough and Hitchcock suggested they had been, then there was no legal obstacle to the execution of Laud's schemes.

As early as 1629 Laud had asked 'that some course may be taken that the judges may not send so many prohibitions', and Charles I issued orders to this effect.[2] There were far fewer prohibitions in the sixteen-thirties than in previous decades. When Lord Chief Justice Finch did at length bring himself to issue his first prohibition against the High Commission, he hastened to assure Laud (February 1638) that 'no man ever sat on a bench that was more tender how he invaded the jurisdiction of other courts, especially those of ecclesiastical cognizance; and for the High Commission Court, I know (as I then openly said) that it is a court of a high and eminent nature, and it behoved us to be very wary of granting prohibitions to stop that court'.[3] Prohibitions, Falkland rightly said in 1641, had been hindered 'first by apparent power against the judges, and after by secret agreement with them'. So the Laudians 'made as it were a conquest upon the common law of the land.'[4]

For the decision in Hitchcock *v.* Thornborough and Hitchcock was only one of a series of Laud's legal triumphs. In James I's reign a prohibition had been issued to stop a suit for tithes of a fulling mill, on the ground that tithes were not payable, except by custom, where the gain came only by the labour of men. This was reversed in 11 Charles I, in a similar case, and a prohibition was refused. There were other verdicts which were undoing the work

[1] Worsley, *The History of the Parish Church of St. Mary at Leigh*, pp. 19–22, 46–47. Cf. p. 141 above.
[2] *C.S.P.D., 1637–8*, pp. 229–30.
[3] Rushworth, op. cit. ii. 7–8, 28.
[4] Nalson, op. cit. i. 769.

of Coke.[1] To these we must add the decision in Drake *v.* Hill, facilitating pluralism;[2] the ruling of the judges in 1637 that no patent under the great seal was needed to enable church courts to be held and to inflict penalties: and that 1 Ed. VI, c. 2, which asserted the contrary, was no longer in force. This statute had been repealed by 1 Mary, st. 2, c. 2; but that in its turn was repealed by 1 Jac. I, c. 25. So the judges' opinion had the effect of repealing two acts of Parliament.[3]

All these public pronouncements deserve a small place beside the Ship Money verdict as reasons for the alienation of wide sections of opinion from the government and the church. But events of almost equal importance occurred which received less publicity. In the same month as Finch made his humble apology, Laud got an order from the king forbidding the common-law judges to meddle with the ecclesiastical courts without the Archbishop's approbation. In December 1638 similar instructions were given to the Masters of Requests.[4]

Finally, the dates are significant. In 1635, as the letter to Williams shows, Laud still felt it necessary to tread warily around lay impropriations. He chose to proceed with Sir Ralph Assheton by royal intervention, and then by direct bargaining, in order to avoid the 'clamour' to which he knew a legal process would have given rise.[5] The Ship Money verdict was pronounced in 1638; but already the Covenant was being signed in Scotland, and Laud was convinced that it was 'quite beyond episcopal power' to relieve the many poor vicars in Lincolnshire.[6] Two years later the Scottish army entered England. Yet even as late as May 1640 Laud was discussing the 'injustice offered by the impropriators and their farmers to the more indigent clergy'.[7] We often fail to realize quite how close a thing it was, how desperate it must have seemed to the many men whose pockets were or might be affected, how vital the Scottish alliance was, patriotism or no patriotism; and what a tangle of knots the Covenanting sword cut through at one blow.

[1] Rolle, op. cit. i. 641. See also pp. 82, 88, 124–5 above.
[2] See above, pp. 240–1.
[3] Cardwell, *Documentary Annals*, ii. 212–17; Gardiner, *Documents relating to the proceedings against William Prynne*, p. 88; Rushworth, op. cit. iii. 1344.
[4] Trevor-Roper, op. cit., p. 359; *C.S.P.D., 1637–8*, p. 287; *1638–9*, p. 190, cf. pp. 205–6.　　　　　　　　　　　　[5] Bridgeman, op. cit., p. 385.
[6] Laud, *Works*, v. 356; cf. p. 349.
[7] Nalson, op. cit. i. 365.

VII

The remarks which the King of England from time to time made,
or was believed to have made, about the desirability of taking
church property away from the gentry and restoring it to ecclesiastical purposes, could not be lightly dismissed; for Charles as
King of Scotland tried at the very beginning of his reign to do
exactly that.

In 1625 the Act of Revocation endeavoured to resume all
church property which had been granted to laymen since 1542.
Compensation was offered to the possessors, but not nearly so
much as the nobility would have thought reasonable. Every
attempt was made to get the measure accepted: pressure, cajolery,
corruption, the influence of the king himself. Simultaneously a
commission for surrender of tithes was set up to buy out impropriators: again the compensation was deemed inadequate.

The united opposition of the nobility caused both schemes to be
substantially modified; but considerable changes nevertheless
resulted. The revenues of ministers were augmented, whilst tithe
payments by tenants were reduced. Charles, Fuller thought,
hereby won 'the smiles of those who were most in number, but the
frowns of such who were greatest in power'.[1] The nobles, indeed,
were furious. 'Robbed, as they conceived, of the clientèle and
dependence of the clergy and laity'[2]—so the king himself put it—
they had no guarantee that Charles would not revive the full
revocation scheme if ever he felt strong enough to do so. (We
may compare the attitude of English beneficiaries from the dissolution of the monasteries towards catholicism after Mary's
reign.) Hitherto the Scottish nobility had supported episcopacy,
plundering the church themselves through subservient bishops.
But now Charles was trying to restore economic independence to
the church and to churchmen. At the same time—as in England—
he employed bishops in high state office.

All contemporary observers agree that these measures were
decisive in convincing the Scottish aristocracy of the virtues of
presbyterianism, to which they had hitherto been singularly blind;
and in creating the National Covenant. Since the newly strengthened episcopal hierarchy was being used as the instrument of
English rule, it was easy to rally anti-papal and anti-English

[1] Fuller, *Church History*, iii. 398–9.   [2] Charles I's *Large Declaration* (1639), p. 9.

sentiment around the defence of the Kirk, using the Prayer Book of 1637 as a symbol.[1] Burnet, who was well informed on Scottish matters, sums up: 'Enough was already done to alarm all that were possessed of the church lands, and they, to engage the whole country in their quarrel, took care to infuse it into all people, but chiefly into the preachers, that all was done to make way for popery.'[2]

It seems indeed to have been the behaviour of the Scottish aristocracy on this occasion that convinced many royalist observers that religion was merely a popular rallying cry used by those with economic grievances. Such was Charles's own view, expressed in his *Large Declaration* of 1639, and that of Laud; it was also the view of such representative royalists as Spalding, Suckling, Fuller and Sir James Balfour.[3]

Charles and Laud failed lamentably in Scotland, but there were lessons for the English opposition in their failure. (1) The buying in of impropriations was carried much farther than in England, to the advantage of the clergy, and to the disadvantage of impropriators. (2) A serious attempt had been made to revise the post-Reformation settlement, both in ritual and in economics. This threw a sinister light on Charles's and Laud's known dissatisfaction with that settlement in England. Sir William Brereton visited Scotland in 1635 and inquired carefully into these matters. He noted in his diary that, in Scotland, 'the clergy of late extend their authority and revenues'. They would soon recover former monastic lands equal to one-third of the kingdom. Steps were already being taken to restore titular abbots, with seats in Parliament. This would create a permanent royalist party there, Sir William noted, so strong that it would always be able to sway the whole Parliament. Brereton was commander-in-chief of the parliamentary forces in Cheshire during the civil war.[4]

---

[1] Cf. Fuller: 'Thus was the Scotch nation full of discontents when this book, being brought unto them, bare the blame of their breaking forth into more dangerous designs, as when the cup is brim-full. . . .' (*Church History*, iii. 399.)

[2] Burnet, *History of my Own Time*, i. 34.

[3] *The Large Declaration*, p. 6; *His Majesties Declaration concerning His Proceedings with His Subjects of Scotland* (1640), pp. 39–42; Laud to Bramhall, *Hastings MSS*. iv. 83–84; Laud, *Works*, iii. 388; J. Spalding, *Memorialls of the Trubles in Scotland and in England* (1850–1), *passim*; Sir J. Suckling, *Poems, Plays and other remains* (1892), ii. 95, 105, 215; Fuller, *Church History*, iii. 398–9; Sir James Balfour, *Historical Works* (1824), ii. 200.

[4] Ed. J. C. Hodgson, *North Country Diaries, second series* (Surtees Soc., 1914), p. 28.

(3) The weakness of the government behind its apparent strength had been revealed, its powerlessness before a *united* opposition that was not afraid to resort to arms. As Burnet put it: while Charles 'was going to change the whole constitution of that church and kingdom, he raised no forces to maintain what he was about to do. . . . By this means all people saw the weakness of the government, at the same time that they complained of its rigour.'[1] (4) The alliance between parliamentarians and Scots was founded on a firm unity of economic interest. For the Scottish invasion not only broke the royal attempt to raise revenue from the Hostmen's monopoly at Newcastle, thus delighting every buyer of coal in London; it also disturbed Laud's and Juxon's battle for the tithes of London, Morton's efforts on behalf of poor vicars in Durham, and the attempt to deprive the corporation of Crediton of its impropriation. John Hitchcock of Preshute ceased to pay an augmentation to his namesake the vicar.[2] The Scottish invasion relieved all impropriators and inheritors of monastic lands from grave anxieties about the safety of their property. The Scottish army was welcomed by many Englishmen who had never given a thought to the merits and demerits of the presbyterian discipline.

VIII

Events in Ireland were equally disturbing to occupiers of church property in England. Ireland had for long been the happiest of hunting grounds for land-grabbers. Alienations of church property had been 'many and unconscionable'.[3] Irish protestantism has been described, by an Ulster Protestant, as 'an instrument of spoliation'.[4] All the English abuses—lay impropriators, long leases, simony, pluralism and absenteeism, poverty-stricken vicars

---

[1] Burnet, *History of my Own Time*, i. 40.

[2] Bodington, op. cit. xli. 114–15; Robertson, op. cit., p. 201.

[3] Laud to Bramhall, *Hastings MSS.*, iv. 65. Ireland was even worse than England in this respect, the Archbishop thought.

[4] The Rev. James Godkin, *Land War in Ireland* (1870), quoted by T. A. Jackson, *Ireland Her Own* (1946), p. 254. Petty perhaps penetrated deeper when he wrote: 'The differences in Ireland are said to be between Protestants and Papists; they were as great before the Reformation between English and Irish. But indeed they were then, and now, between the rich and the poor—the contented and discontented' (Ed. Lansdowne *Petty Papers*, 1927, ii. 228).

and curates—were present on an exaggerated scale.¹ Strafford set himself to change this.

In 1634 royal impropriations in Ireland were handed over to the church, only an annual rent being reserved. A statute was passed enabling other laymen to return impropriations to the church. The management of the business was entrusted to Bishop Bramhall, who, in the closest agreement with Laud, employed the same methods to influence impropriators as had been used in Scotland—bribery and threats. He investigated title deeds, employed projectors to 'discover' concealments, called in leases of doubtful legality, compounded with those who were prepared to be reasonable. Of Lord Ranelagh, who surrendered two impropriations and sold five others cheap, Bramhall wrote grimly to Laud 'We thank not his devotion so much as the sun shining.'²

But the sun was not to shine for long, as Laud seems to have been aware. He urged Bramhall to 'make your hay apace'. For 'the church there never knew such a time'. Laud's fear sprang partly from the realization that he could not trust his own side in church and state, since 'an ill-minded bishop and a courtier may conspire together and divide the profits and so undo succession'. But he also had deeper forebodings. 'It cannot last always', he wrote in March 1638; 'and therefore you do marvellous well to take your time.' Do all you can, he urged three months later, 'while the state stands as it does, and to prevent as much future harm as you can, against the time that the face of that state shall not look so favourably upon the church as now it does'.³

Bramhall was said to have got back £30,000 a year for the church ('some say £40,000'), but it was done in open conflict with the Anglo-Irish aristocracy.⁴ 'His zeal for recovery of church revenues was called oppression and rapine', said Jeremy Taylor sadly.⁵ 'There is scarce any gentleman of worth', complained a

---

¹ For evidence, see Knowler, op. cit. i. 151, 187–9; Parr, op. cit. ii. 322–3, 429–31, 448–9, and above, pp. 230–1, 236. But see H. F. Kearney, *Strafford in Ireland, 1633–41* (1959), p. 121.

² Knowler, op. cit. i. 122–3, 171–3, 251–2, 302, 380, 382–6; ii. 42–43, 434; O'Grady, op. cit. i. 538.   ³ *Hastings MSS.* iv. 76–79.

⁴ *Fairfax Correspondence*, ii. 165; Kennett, op. cit., p. 436. Lambeth MS. 943, ff. 535–55, gives figures of improvements of livings and bishoprics in the province of Armagh between 1633 and 1638. Quite substantial sums are involved. Cf. also *C.S.P.D., Ireland, 1633–47*, p. 88, for Bramhall's account of how he doubled rents in his own diocese.

⁵ J. Taylor, *Works*, ii. 73–74.

petition of 1640, whom the bishops 'have not bereaved of some part of his inheritance for daring to oppose their unjust commands.'[1] Strafford was accused at his trial of violating the law and infringing the rights of property in order to increase the revenues of the church. He had decided causes concerning impropriations at the Council Board which should, his accusers thought, have been left to the common law.

So in Ireland, even more clearly than in Scotland, the Laudian economic policy was seen in successful operation. Its victims were predatory new landlords; but men like Oliver Cromwell, because of their common hatred of popery and of Laud, regarded the Earl of Cork as a paragon of protestant virtue as well as of economic efficiency.[2] All else was blurred. So the English opposition saw Laud's Irish policy bringing lands back from lay ownership to the church (though it did little, they thought, to advance a preaching ministry);[3] and it did so by an arbitrary interference with the rights of property, 'by ways without law', in Pym's phrase, and by close subordination of the church to the purposes of the civil government.[4]

IX

So there was ground for alarm, not only among those who feared for their property, but also among those who respected the law and those who loved their religion. The Puritan attack on the lands of bishops and deans and chapters was from one point of view an offensive-defensive against a threatened attack on secularized church property. Behind closed doors some Fellows of Queen's were discussing in December 1638 'whether church lands once given be restorable?'[5] The subject might equally well have been

[1] W. J. S. Simpson, *Archbishop Bramhall* (1927), p. 62.

[2] Abbott, op. cit. ii. 150.

[3] Baillie, op. cit. i. 261. At least one Puritan preacher, the Rev. James Stephenson, obtained an augmentation to his Irish vicarage from the Bishop of Ardagh, whose chaplain he was (S. Palmer, op. cit. ii. 368).

[4] Nalson, op. cit. ii. 34; cf. pp. 57-58. We may perhaps contrast the approach to these matters of Ussher, Archbishop of Armagh, between whom and Drs. Preston and Sibbes there was 'a most entire affection', and who retained the favour of the Presbyterians during the Interregnum. Ussher, his biographer tells us, 'was much endeavouring in Ireland the augmentation of the means of the ministry, for which end he had obtained a patent for impropriations to be passed in his name for their use as they did fall, but it was too much neglected by themselves' (N. Bernard, *The Life and Death of . . . Dr. James Usher*, 1656, p. 83).

[5] Boas, op. cit., p. 96.

lands given *to* the church or lands given *from* the church: the possibility of the resumption of either was in men's minds.

So the alternative was posed—bishops' lands, or impropriations and monastic lands? Not only in England, but all over Europe similar economic causes set similar problems in relation to church property. This helps to explain the passionate and partisan interest that so many Englishmen of the propertied class took in questions of foreign policy. The welfare of 'the churches abroad' was of more than doctrinal interest.

Wherever men looked in the world about them, the signs were ominous. In France, war broke out in 1620 over Louis XIII's attempt to recover secularized lands in Béarn. In Germany, Ferdinand II issued the Edict of Restitution in 1629, and Wallenstein carried it with fire and sword into north Germany. Gustavus Adolphus came to the rescue of protestant property as well as of protestant worship. Charles I's co-operation with Richelieu in the suppression of protestant La Rochelle, his failure to take any effective action to aid the afflicted protestants of the Empire, his pro-Spanish foreign policy—all this assumed a highly sinister aspect if considered in relation to Charles's own actions in Scotland and Ireland, and his express intentions for England. To the heightened Puritan imagination it seemed that, all over Europe, the lamps were going out: the Counter-Reformation was winning back property for the church as well as souls: and Charles I and his government, if not allied to the forces of the Counter-Reformation, at least appeared to have set themselves identical economic and political objectives.[1] This is the real basis for the accusation of popery thrown at Laud. He seemed to be trying to get back behind the Reformation, not only in ceremonial, but also in economics. Laud might refuse a cardinal's hat, but that was irrelevant so long as his social policy appeared to be that of the Counter-Reformation.

[1] Cf. B. H. G. Wormald, *Clarendon* (1951), p. 247. In certain respects the British Counter-Reformation went even farther back than the continental. The Edict of Restitution resumed all lands secularized since 1552: the Scottish Act of Revocation went back to 1542.

CONCLUSION

The lands belonging to bishops, deans and chapters, as also to
universities and colleges, together with the value of appropriate
tithes, are not worth one million per annum, but are [the] motive
that makes differences in religion. For to gain that good position
(which men think due to those who can teach the best way to
heaven) many competitors study to propose something which
they hope will pass for such with the people.

SIR WILLIAM PETTY
Political Observations (*c.* 1671), in *The Petty Papers*, ii. 227–8

I

THE object of this book has been to throw some light on
the connexions between economic life and ideas about
religion and church organization. The seventeenth-century
church was a useful subject to take, because it was itself an economic organization; and so the connexions are easier to trace.
Many readers may think these connexions have sometimes been
over-emphasized, or have been described in terms which are too
crude. I would plead the necessity of compression here; and ask
that at all events the *existence* of the connexions should be recognized, however much more subtly they might have been analysed.

Professor Tawney, in a book which has had the greatest influence on the present generation of historians, dealt with *Religion
and the Rise of Capitalism*. This more pedestrian work has been
concerned with the church and the rise of capitalism. It may be
convenient to summarize its conclusions. Economic developments
upset the arrangements for financing the church which had
been handed down from the Middle Ages; the hierarchy desired
things contrary—to protect its heritage and yet to remain on good
terms with the despoilers of the church. Bishops were dependent
on the government and on the ruling groups of a social structure
which it was the church's traditional duty to defend. But under
Elizabeth some members of the ruling class, and of the government, were themselves plundering the church. Hence the contradictions of the Elizabethan and Jacobean *via media*, the waverings

from the semi-Puritan Grindal to Whitgift and Bancroft, and from Bancroft back to the old-style Calvinist Abbott. But slowly, as men began to see a threat to the existing social order lurking behind the demands of the Puritans, a more positive conservative policy was evolved. Whitgift began to stop the rot. Bancroft tried to reconstruct. James I wished to preserve bishops, king, and nobility, and saw that their fates were connected. Abbott, so unaccountably preferred to Lancelot Andrewes, soon became powerless. With Laud the forces of conservatism found their most determined leader. The international situation was propitious to counter-reformation. Yet Laud failed; under him all the contradictions of the old society were exposed.

The rise of capitalism and the Reformation, those connected phenomena, had simultaneously weakened the church economically and led to new demands being made on its ministers. The church itself was being permeated by the new standards, willy nilly. Bishops came from merchant families; pluralism, which used to be a privilege confined to the ruling class and government servants, became one which—like peerages under the first two Stuarts—was purchasable. Entry to the ministry could also be bought. Yet the new educated laity was beginning to insist on a preaching clergy, to criticize pluralism and non-residence.

The church *could* no longer function as guardian of the social order unless it could win back respect; that is, unless it could attract learned and devoted men in greater numbers. But the incomes of the clergy, especially of the lower clergy, were small if considered in relation to the expanding wealth of the business community. Alternative professional or business careers were opening up. There were no economic rewards for more than a narrow circle of well-connected clerics; and too many of those with sincere religious convictions, joining the critics of the church rather than its defenders, found themselves 'church-outed by the prelates'.

A drastic economic reorganization might have saved the situation; but that was just what the hierarchy could never achieve. The universities and the bishops depended on impropriations no less than the king and the gentry. The economic crisis was not one that affected only ecclesiastical landowners. Many lay landlords, and the king above all, were also in financial difficulties. They had nothing to spare for the church: rather the reverse. Few were prepared to restore impropriations or abandon their beneficial leases. And the ruling class itself had been split by the rise of capitalism. Men with a new social outlook came to the fore in the House of Commons, came to dominate and reinterpret the common law. They were not going to allow the finances of the church to be reorganized, any more than those of the state, unless they controlled the operation. It was their entrenched opposition that caused Bancroft's failure. When Laud tried again twenty years later, with greater vigour and determination, and with more enthusiastic support from the king, it was too late.

Laud's failure demonstrates the fundamental dilemma of the *ancien régime*. He had not got the loyal and consistent backing of his own episcopal colleagues, concerned not only with feathering their own nests but also with retaining traditional good relations with the gentry in their dioceses. The king's support was at the mercy of the fluctuations of court intrigue, of the international situation, of the need to retain tolerable financial relations with the City of London, the centre of English capitalism. Laud's disregard for property rights brought him into conflict with *all* sections of the propertied class. So did his attempt to build up a clerical party, to encourage ministers to show independence of their patrons. Laud put bishops and their friends into key governmental positions, and used the Star Chamber and the Privy Council to enforce clerical claims, to protect bishops from criticism.[1] But not all the Laudians were men of unimpeachable disinterestedness. And, said the ablest of the royalists,

this unseasonable accumulation of so many honours upon them, to which their functions did not entitle them (no bishop having been so much as a Privy Councillor in very many years), exposed them to the universal envy of the whole nobility, many whereof wished them well as to all their ecclesiastical qualifications, but could not endure to see them possessed of those offices and employments, which they looked upon as naturally belonging to them; . . . and some of them, by want of temper or want of breeding, did not behave themselves with that decency in their debates towards the greatest men of the kingdom as in discretion they ought to have done.[2]

Laud's policy was to get back behind the Reformation in everything but the papal supremacy—recovering impropriations,

---

[1] Rushworth, op. cit. iii, appendix, 58, 64–65.
[2] Clarendon, op. cit. i. 117.

restoring tithes, if not to a true 10 per cent. at least to what they had been before the rise in prices; restoring the coercive power of church courts, which now meant the complete subordination of the common-law judges to the government, and the ultimate reversal of all the adjustments of the medieval common law to the needs of capitalist society made in the preceding decades; restoring the privileged social position of priests. Even his methods of reform were in this sense reactionary. The revenues of bishops were to be increased by pluralism and non-residence; and that ran counter to the protestant emphasis on a preaching clergy.

Laud was trying to revive the Middle Ages, not only in ceremonial but also in economics: and not only in ecclesiastical economics. His 'social justice' policy involved some attempt to recover common lands from enclosing landlords, and an interference with the absolute right of every man of property to do what he would with his own. Such a policy meant dealing violently with history. The advance of capitalism had been slow, and its standards had begun to influence men's actions before it changed their conscious thought. The gentry had for many years been encroaching upon the property of the church, the common law upon its jurisdiction; statutes had whittled away its independent power and asserted that of Parliament. To set the clock back a hundred years meant attacking the common law, Parliament, and the City of London, as well as the property interests of those whom Parliament represented. It forced a clarification of ideas on both sides, an intellectual as well as a political crisis.

Where could Laud find support for such a policy? In the church? It was riddled with jealousies between court and country clergy, the court clergy rich at the expense of those in the country, thanks to impropriations, pluralism, and unequal taxation. Among the old ruling class? But they wished to continue to exploit the church, through patronage rights, leases and impropriations, which Laud's policy called in question; and many of them were prepared to listen to suggestions that the lands of bishops and deans and chapters might be confiscated as those of abbeys had been. The political rule of bishops outraged the old nobility. To quote Clarendon again: 'Persons of honour and great quality, of the court and of the country, were every day cited into the High Commission Court, . . . and were there prosecuted; . . . the shame (which they called an insolent triumph upon their

degree and quality, and levelling them with the common people)
was never forgotten.'[1] These 'persons of honour and great quality'
ought no doubt to have seen that Laud was trying to save their
society in the only way possible; but that would have demanded
a greater freedom from the prejudices which their own social
position inculcated, and a capacity for disinterested analysis, higher
even than those possessed by Laud's friend and protégé, Edward
Hyde.

Clarendon in his first exile discussed the view that church
property should be restored because its retention was sacrilege:
and he arrived at conclusions very different from those of the
Laudians. 'He must depart too much from his natural understanding who believes it probable that all that hath been taken
from the church in former ages will be restored to it in this or
those which shall succeed, to the ruin of those many thousand
families which enjoy the alienations, though they do not think it
was with justice and piety aliened.' 'Learned, prudent and conscientious men', he continued, 'upon a serious deliberation and
reflection of the great mercy of God' may piously hope that 'He
will not be rigorously disposed to exact the utmost farthing from
the heirs of the transgressors, who, with the authority of the
government under which they lived, . . . became unwarily owners
of what in truth, in a manner, was taken from God Himself.'[2]
This consoling belief in the Almighty's readiness to appreciate the
difficulties of landlords was a far cry from the high and uncom-
promising ideals which gave Laud's conservatism a certain intellectual appeal. Yet it was only Hyde's moderate and realistic
policy that rallied the old ruling class to form a party for Charles I,
and only after Laud's overthrow.

Should Laud then have looked for support among those who
were profiting by the economic changes? But they (apart from the
handful of government-favoured monopolists) were frustrated by
the church at every turn. Tithes hampered agricultural advance
and (in so far as they could be enforced) burdened industry.
Business men viewed with horror any suggestion of increasing
payments to the church, or of strengthening the jurisdiction of
church courts, which were already sufficiently prejudicial to their

---

[1] Clarendon, op. cit. i. 125.
[2] Clarendon, *Essay of Sacrilege*, in *A Compleat Collection of Tracts* (1747), p. 216.
This essay is wrongly dated 1641. It should probably be 1647.

activities (tithe suits, prosecutions for working on saints' days, for usury, &c., and all the vexations and delays and expense of competing jurisdictions). Among the common people? The evidence of their hostility to parsons and the hierarchy, throughout our period, is too strong to be ignored: though we need not assume that presbyterian ministers would have been any more popular. Yeomen and husbandmen were those on whose economic activities tithes might have the most harmful effect. In the more backward areas there was no doubt plenty of docile acceptance of the church; but such support was in its nature passive, and could not be politically decisive in a society dominated by men of property.

And this is leaving out of account all the most important considerations working against the hierarchy—the strength of Puritanism as a religious faith, as a disciplining and organizing force; the strength of English patriotism, which saw the government inactive in face of a desperate situation for our natural allies on the Continent, and which thought it saw that government in Scotland and Ireland working on parallel lines with the Counter-Reformation: the passion for constitutional liberty that made a martyr of Eliot, which saw the Laudians preaching damnation for those who refused to pay non-parliamentary taxes, saw the clergy voting supplies to the government when the House of Commons refused, saw bishops imposing cruel sentences in Star Chamber and High Commission. It was a partisan of the bishops who described 'the people' as being 'so generally peevish and puritanized' that any personal quarrel with a minister redounded to the discredit of the clergy as an order.[1]

Protestantism, patriotism, parliamentarism, and property all worked together against Laud's attempt to reverse history: and they all found expression in the cry of 'No Popery!', just as the bishops saw republicanism and democracy in the opponents of hierarchy and a persecuting state church.

The composite opposition slowly welded itself and produced its own programmes for reorganization. These too contained contradictions—between impropriators and those who opposed impropriations, between patrons of livings and those who opposed lay patronage, between plunderers and Puritans wishing to use bishops' lands to finance preaching and education; between those

[1] *Persecutio Undecima*, p. 13.

who supported a national church and those who wanted congregational autonomy. But men became fully conscious of these divisions only after the hierarchy had been overthrown.

The old régime might have been slowly modified if the common-law courts had been allowed to use prohibitions against the church courts, and so to establish the supremacy of their law as interpreted by Coke. But Bancroft checked prohibitions, and Laud reduced the common-law judges to docility. The opposition tried to reform through Parliament—and was frustrated by the bishops' votes in the Lords. It tried piecemeal reform through the Feoffees for Impropriations—and was frustrated again by the alliance of hierarchy and government. Laud himself could not reorganize, but he could stop others doing it. By making reform impossible, he precipitated revolution. As soon as Laud's imposing edifice was shaken by the external force of the Scottish armies, its internal weakness made it collapse like a house of cards.

The disintegration of the Laudian régime was like the thawing of thickly packed ice on a river. The surface, which frost had forced into jagged and unnatural shapes, breaks up and disappears: there is a period of turbulence and confusion, but water that is not artificially held in seeks its own level, and in the end a smooth and evenly flowing surface reappears. Once the constricting crust was removed, what remained was the dominance of the propertied classes over the church. Impropriations and lay patronage had established a *cujus regio ejus religio* system in the church, through which the gentry controlled it. As the advance of capitalism intensified divisions within the landed class, these were reflected in the clergy whom patrons presented, and the creation of a nucleus of Puritan ministers itself facilitated the spread of Puritan ideas and the outlook of the composite opposition. The hierarchy, by intermittently purging Puritans, and by refusing them promotion, had forced the opposition gentry and bourgeoisie into devious means for assisting ministers whilst maintaining control over their appointment—by augmentations, by establishing lectureships in corporations. A pamphlet of 1649 gave three things as having been 'the bane of monarchy'. They were weekly lectures, corporations and trained bands[1]—the religious, economic, and military organizations of the opposition.

The destruction of the hierarchy revealed divisions about the

---

[1] [Anon.], *Lex Talionis* (1649), p. 9.

way in which the church should henceforth be controlled. Some advocated an all-embracing national church, run by Parliament and lay elders (who would be men of property) instead of by bishops. The 'Presbyterians' hysterically opposed toleration, not least because they feared the political and social heresies of lower-class sectaries. Others were more confident in the ability of wealth to prevail in a system of free competition, and were prepared to accept congregational Independency as the price of alliance with the sectaries, the most determined enemies of the old régime and of the monopoly privileges of projectors, peers, or priests. But in either a Presbyterian or an Independent national church the men of substance would have preserved their supremacy: it could have been shaken only by the abolition of tithes. The restoration of king, lords, and bishops in 1660 reunited the gentry but did not restore the old ruling class to its pre-1640 dominance. The supremacy of squire over parson which followed was untroubled either by the dreams of a Laudian central government or by the aspirations of democratic sectaries.[1]

To some of my readers the scales may seem to have been over-weighted, the case against Laud to have been over-stated. He was, after all, a virtuous, conscientious, and industrious man, who tried hard to realize not ignoble ideals. But the case against Laud is not that his ideals were bad, but that they were irrelevant. They were at least a century out of date, and *could not* be realized. I tried to argue this in the chapters on tithes and fees, both of which were appropriate as the main method of financing the clergy in one state of society, and not in another. There are clearly two conceptions of right in conflict when one side says, 'It is just that the priest should receive his traditional 10 per cent. of the produce of the community —no more and no less'; and the other side says, 'It is just that the minister should receive that amount which has been contracted for—whether by the congregation directly or by the representatives of the community in parliament'. The first statement contains assumptions about the relations of the priest to the community; the second makes assumptions about representative

---

[1] To discuss the differences between Presbyterians, Independents, and sectaries exclusively in social terms, as here, is as unhistorically one-sided as to discuss them in exclusively religious terms; and is very insulting to the genuine religious convictions of most of the members of the congregations. But, as throughout this book, I am abstracting one aspect for analysis, and I assume that readers do not need continual reminders of all that is omitted.

government. But considered as abstract propositions neither is manifestly more false than the other. Their validity can only be tested in relation to the historical circumstances.

But when we have considered in detail the application of the first conception of justice in the City of London in the sixteen-thirties, we can see what would have been the consequences of the only logic by which Laud's actions could be justified. What he was trying to do was so revolutionary in its reactionariness as to be either impossible, or possible in the long run only by methods of violence which it would be difficult to defend. One can therefore condemn Laud without accepting the standards of his opponents as any more eternally valid than Laud's own, which had served very well in the Middle Ages. We cannot consider individual morality without taking into account its implications for the whole of society.

II

This book deals only with the economic effects of the rise of capitalism on the church. In every sphere examined there appears to be a similar conflict between the church-state relationship which had come down from the Middle Ages and the new conceptions which were slowly and painfully forming in men's minds. It was because of changes in the economic life of society that tithes and the traditional fees ceased to be a satisfactory method of financing the church. This caused bitter wrangles and tithe-suits; but it also led men to think deeply about the justification of tithes, about the duties of ministers, about the rights of congregations. The outcome was a challenge to the whole idea of a state church, the evolution of voluntaryist ideas of a contractual relation between minister and congregation. These new ideas themselves were one example of a whole group of contractualist theories which came into prominence in many spheres of human activity and thought during our period.

From their own angle the common lawyers were putting a quite new emphasis on contract, and this worked to the disadvantage of ministers trying to collect tithes. Thomas Hobbes, who held Puritans and common lawyers and clergy in equal disesteem, was likewise working out a political philosophy in which the state and the rights of its members were all founded on contract. It seems difficult to avoid the conclusion that there is a common factor in these converging tendencies in thought: and the common factor can only be found in the changing economic life of the country, in the rise of capitalism.

Conceptions of divine right were appropriate to the authoritarian Middle Ages, where custom was its own justification, and where the element of force in the exploitation of serfs by lords and in the relation of vassals to overlords was never well concealed. But in capitalist society the fundamental relations—between workers and employers, between members of companies—are contractual. Open force is not normally visible. In all spheres of life the sixteenth and seventeenth centuries saw the replacement of divine right by contractual theories, of arbitrary authority by reason. Kings ceased to rule by divine right and came to owe their thrones to contracts of one kind or another with their people, contracts which were equally applicable to the government of a republic. Marriage ceased to be a sacrament and became a civil contract. 'The sacraments', wrote Calvin, 'are a kind of mutual contract, by which the Lord conveys his mercy to us, and by it eternal life, while we in our turn promise him obedience.'[1] So the highest mysteries of the medieval church were made comprehensible to the bourgeoisie. Clergymen ceased to collect tithes by divine right, and reluctantly accepted them as a legal due. In many sectarian churches there were covenants between the members, and specific contracts with the minister. The defenders of toleration regularly compared a congregation with a trading company.[2] The school of Perkins, Ames, and Preston, to which the Feoffees Sibbes, Gouge, and Davenport belonged, worked out a whole subtle scheme of salvation, the Covenant Theology, which is based on a contractual relation between man and God, with mutual obligations to which either party can be held.[3]

Historians have been slow to recognize the underlying unity of these ideas from such different spheres, and of the battles in which those ideas were weapons. We have tended to divide up 'religious aspects', 'constitutional aspects', and 'economic aspects'. Such departmentalism is a natural consequence of the increasing

[1] J. Calvin, *The Institutes of the Christian Religion*, translated by H. Beveridge (1949), ii. 477.

[2] e.g. Roger Williams, *The Bloody Tenent of Persecution* (1848), p. 46; John Goodwin, *Theomachia* (1644), p. 31, in Haller, *Tracts on Liberty in the Puritan Revolution*, iii.

[3] See Perry Miller, *The New England Mind: the 17th century* (1939), book iv, *passim*.

specialization of functions in the intellectual sphere which has developed parallel with the division of labour that capitalist production has made possible. There have been few polymaths since the seventeenth century. The departmentalism goes back perhaps to that division between science and religion which Bacon and his successors found essential if they were to be able to discuss science free from the persecution, or at least the disapprobation, of clerics. But now it is a hindrance rather than a help.

Men in the seventeenth century were conscious of society as a unity, although they expressed that unity in religious terms. All citizens were members of the national church: the church *was* society. Only a handful of radicals conceived of a church which was not co-extensive with society. All rights were divine because thought had for centuries been the monopoly of clerics and so all ideas tended to be religious ideas, even those which challenged the clerical monopoly and its system of thought. But the evolution of specialized sciences of politics and economics (Hobbes, Petty) necessitated cutting those subjects free from religion, as Bacon had cut natural science loose. Thought had to be departmentalized if it was to advance.

Today we take the departmentalization for granted, and the danger is that we may project it backwards into history as a division in society itself, rather than a convenient device for the study of society. But society is one and the individual personality is one. The way a man thinks about politics cannot be separated from his religious or philosophical beliefs, his relations with his wife and family, the way he earns his living. The connexions between different groups of ideas are subtle and difficult to analyse, but they exist: they exist because of the unity of the individual and of the society in which he lives. It is to the structure of society that we must look for the keys to interpretation. Otherwise we shall distort and do violence to the history we are studying.

III

One danger of ending the story in 1640 is that I may seem to have over-proved my case. The Church of England, after all, was restored in 1660, and has survived: has this book not exaggerated the problems by which the hierarchy was faced in the years before 1640?

There are two answers to this accusation, each of which have been suggested from time to time in the course of the argument. In the first place, what was restored in 1660 was not, to quote Usher's notorious phrase, 'the church as Bancroft left it'.[1] After the Restoration there was no High Commission, and no other prerogative courts to enforce the will of the government and the bishops when this conflicted with the views of Parliament and common-law courts. Nor indeed were bishops associated with the government in the same close way that they had been before 1640. Sheldon was the last bishop to hold government office, if we except the diplomat John Robinson in Anne's reign, who happened to be Bishop of Bristol as well as Lord Privy Seal. But he did not use his state office to pursue an episcopal policy.

Separate taxation of the clergy by Convocation was abandoned after the Restoration. Without the High Commission to back them up, church courts declined, and the sentence of excommunication proved increasingly ineffectual, except when imposed on the very poorest members of society. The existence of rival sects, first semi-legally, then with full legal status, made it impossible for the established church or its courts to hold the same place in the national life as they had done when the church's monopoly position was upheld with all the authority of the state. After 1660 presentments for nonconformity came to engross the attention of church-wardens, to the exclusion of other matters: so the establishment of toleration after 1689 brought the effective activity of church courts to an end.[2] Divine right languished, of bishops as of kings: and never recovered after 1688. In 1660 the Laudians had recaptured some of the key positions in the church, but this only exposed their inability to wield their old power.[3] They could not shape the policy of the church; and they had no disciples. There were no more attempts to increase tithe payments, to recover secularized church property, or to enforce a clerical social programme.

Secondly, and this is another aspect of the first point, the world into which the church was restored in 1660 had changed too. The

---

[1] 'The Restoration restored neither the old monarchy nor the old parliament, neither the old courts nor the old law, but the church as Bancroft left it' (Usher, *Reconstruction*, ii. 266). Except as concerns the church Usher's statement is unexceptionable.

[2] K. Major, 'The Lincoln Diocesan Records', in *Trans. Royal Hist. Soc.*, 4th series, xxxii. 59, 63; Whiteman, ibid., 5th series, v. 128–31.

[3] Bosher, op. cit., *passim*.

House of Commons, and the class which it represented, had triumphed at every point that had been disputed with Charles I. The sovereignty of Parliament was established, including a *de facto* sovereignty over the church. The canons of 1640 were never recognized as legally binding because they had not been accepted by Parliament. The common-law courts established their supremacy over every other jurisdiction in the realm, including the church courts; and in the common-law courts the word of Coke was now law on all disputed points. There could have been no more complete defeat for the Laudian aspirations than that.

Not only had the mighty central government gone, which had sheltered the hierarchy and which the hierarchy to a considerable extent controlled. Feudal tenures had gone too, with all that they had meant of dependence and subordination. A king and an Archbishop of Canterbury had been executed after a trial conducted in the name of the Parliament of England: a unique event in each case. Their successors did not forget that they had a joint in their necks. Monopolies had gone, monopolies of opinion-forming as well as of material production. The social groups which controlled the government, especially after 1688, were those for whom public credit, trade, and the colonies were more important than the ceremonies of the church or the wealth and dignity of clerics.

On the other hand, it is true that in ecclesiastical matters as in everything else the English Revolution got stuck half-way. The Puritan Revolution was defeated. So was the Leveller and Quaker campaign to get rid of hireling priests and establish congregational democracy. 1660 was a patched-up compromise between conservative parliamentarians and defeated royalists; and the restoration of the church was part of the patching up. 'The question is not whether bishops or no, but whether discipline or none', said Baxter in 1660.[1] The church was restored in the attempt to bring back discipline for the lower orders. The City vestries which had been thrown open in 1640–1 were closed again in 1660. So patched-up solutions had to be found for outstanding problems.

Some of the economic problems of the church were solved *ambulando*, by the agricultural prosperity of the 150 years which followed the abolition of feudal tenures, free trade in corn, and

---

[1] R. Baxter, *A Sermon of Repentance*, preached before the House of Commons on 30 Apr. 1660, p. 43.

the end of restraints on enclosures. Queen Anne's Bounty was to solve others. But many received no solution at all. This century and a half was the age of the dependence of the parson on the squire, a dependence which was fundamentally an economic dependence, although it was also in part an economic alliance. Of this position of inferiority for ministers neither Laud nor Milton would have approved. The fact that the problems of the church were not solved as the idealists of either wing wished does not disprove the existence of those problems. It merely proves that the men of conviction, Laudians no less than radicals, were defeated. The age of the latitude men and occasional conformity would have shocked Laud no less than it would have shocked Milton. The Earl of Warwick and John Selden, or even the Earl of Clarendon, might have found it more tolerable.

But a proper answer to the accusation that the case has been over-proved could be given only after analysing in detail the effect of the changes of the Interregnum upon the church, and after studying in equal detail the economic position of the church and its parsons in the decades after 1660. If any of the over-simplified first statements in this book provoke others to under-take such studies and provide truer answers they may even have served a useful purpose.

What I believe stands is that in the decades before 1640 there was a whole complex of causes, apart from the narrowly doctrinal, which might make men hostile to the ruling hierarchy in the Church of England. And among them the economic problems selected for examination in this book seem to deserve more prominence than is usually given to them in accounts of the causes of the English Revolution. We need not accept the passage from Petty quoted at the head of this chapter as *the* explanation of 'differences in religion'; but it is surely *an* explanation.

I also believe that a proper understanding of the place of the church in the life of the seventeenth century, including its signifi-cance as an economic institution, may help to free historians from two complementary misconceptions. The first is contained in the phrase 'the Puritan Revolution', which implies that the decisive force in the years between 1640 and 1660 was religion, *tout court*. The second, the more modern heresy, is the view that the rise (or alternatively, the decline) of the gentry sufficiently explains the motive forces of the English Revolution, and that the ideas and aspirations of a Cromwell or a Milton are to be seen as no more than epiphenomena of economic decline (or rise).

I think that the interaction of economics and ideas is far more complex and far more difficult to analyse than that. But it can be analysed; if we look at society in all its complexity we can see connecting links between the high ideals which led a Vane or a Harrison to martyrdom, and the baser motives of the land speculators; between the principled refusal to pay tithes for which the Quakers suffered so cruelly, and the simpler concern for their own pockets of Hertfordshire husbandmen and London citizens. And if we look into our own hearts we may suspect that, though these motives can be separated for the purposes of analysis, in historical fact they frequently existed within the same muddled human being. Like Bunyan, we may see dirt in our own tears, and filthiness in the bottom of our prayers.[1]

This leads to the further conclusion that in the last analysis any rigid antithesis between a bourgeois revolution and a Puritan revolution is superficial. For Puritanism, though it embraces nobler ideals than the triumph of capitalism, is unthinkable without a bourgeoisie; and the English Revolution could not have succeeded even to the limited extent it did without the power of Puritanism to awaken and organize and discipline large masses of people who knew what they fought for and loved what they knew. Yet the Puritan and democratic revolution was defeated: it was the bourgeois revolution that succeeded. Only after that catastrophe did Puritanism, evolved in criticism of the institutions and standards of an unequal society, sink into acquiescent acceptance of the new inequality; and the exploitation of man by man continued to be justified in the name of a Saviour in whom there had been neither bond nor free.

[1] J. Bunyan, *The Holy War*, in *Works* (1860), iii. 301.

INDEX

Peers and bishops are indexed under their surnames

A a

PRINTED IN GREAT BRITAIN
AT THE UNIVERSITY PRESS, OXFORD
BY VIVIAN RIDLER
PRINTER TO THE UNIVERSITY